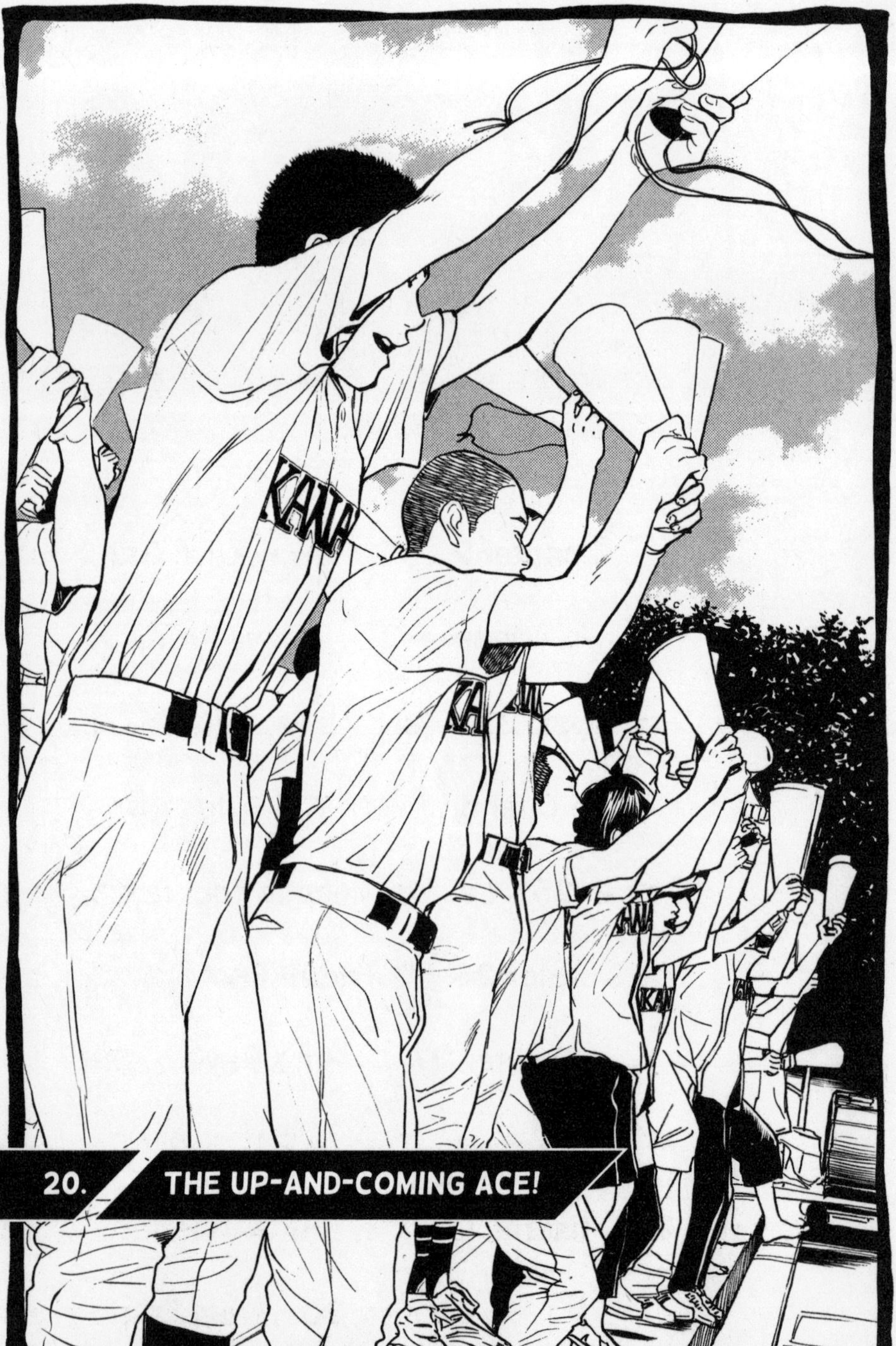

20. THE UP-AND-COMING ACE!

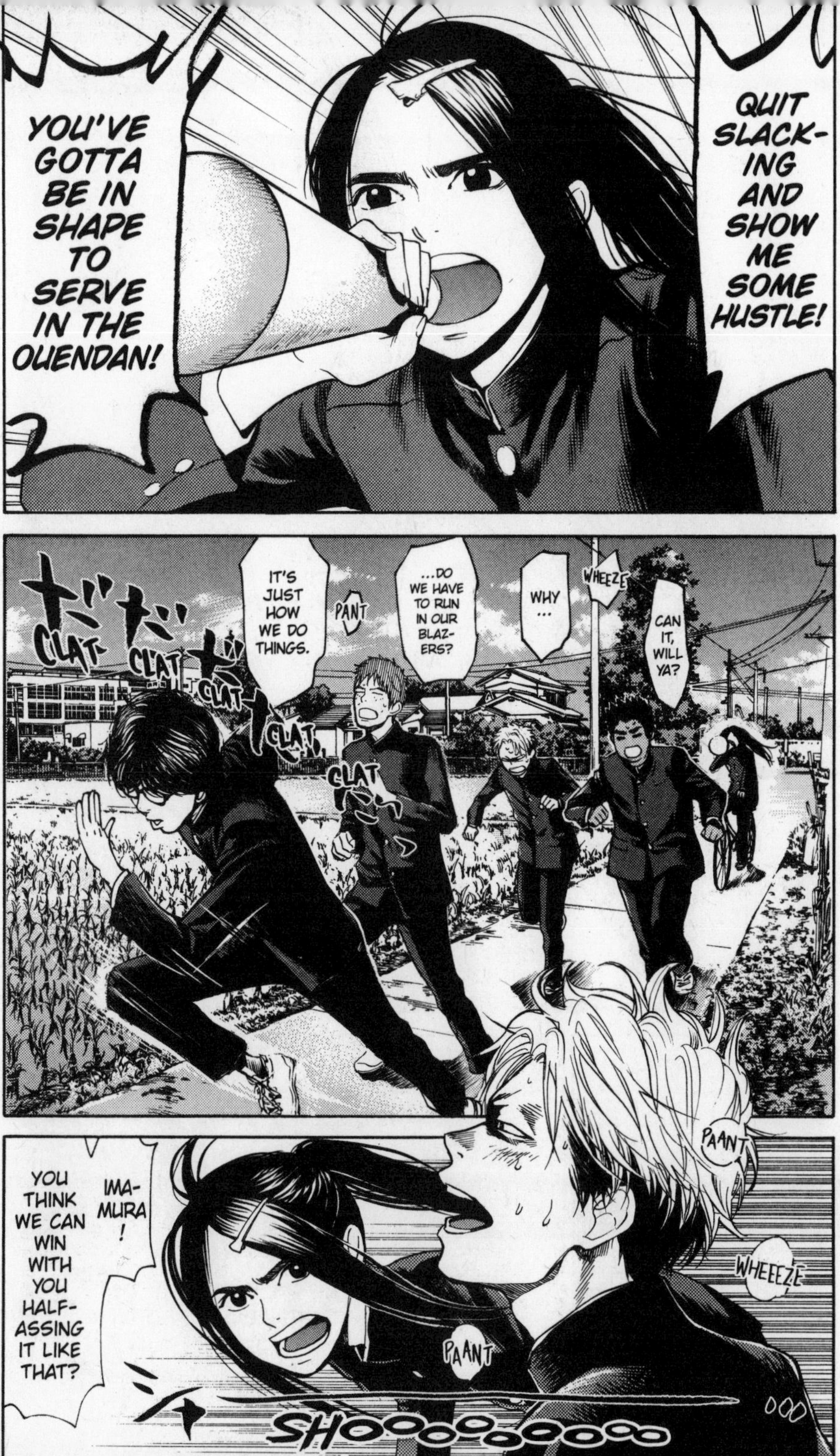
QUIT SLACKING AND SHOW ME SOME HUSTLE!
YOU'VE GOTTA BE IN SHAPE TO SERVE IN THE OUENDAN!
CAN IT, WILL YA?
WHEEZE
WHY ...
...DO WE HAVE TO RUN IN OUR BLAZERS?
PANT
IT'S JUST HOW WE DO THINGS.
CLAT
CLAT
CLAT
CLAT
CLAT
PAANT
WHEEEZE
IMAMURA!
YOU THINK WE CAN WIN WITH YOU HALF-ASSING IT LIKE THAT?
PAANT
OOO
SHOOOOOOOOOO

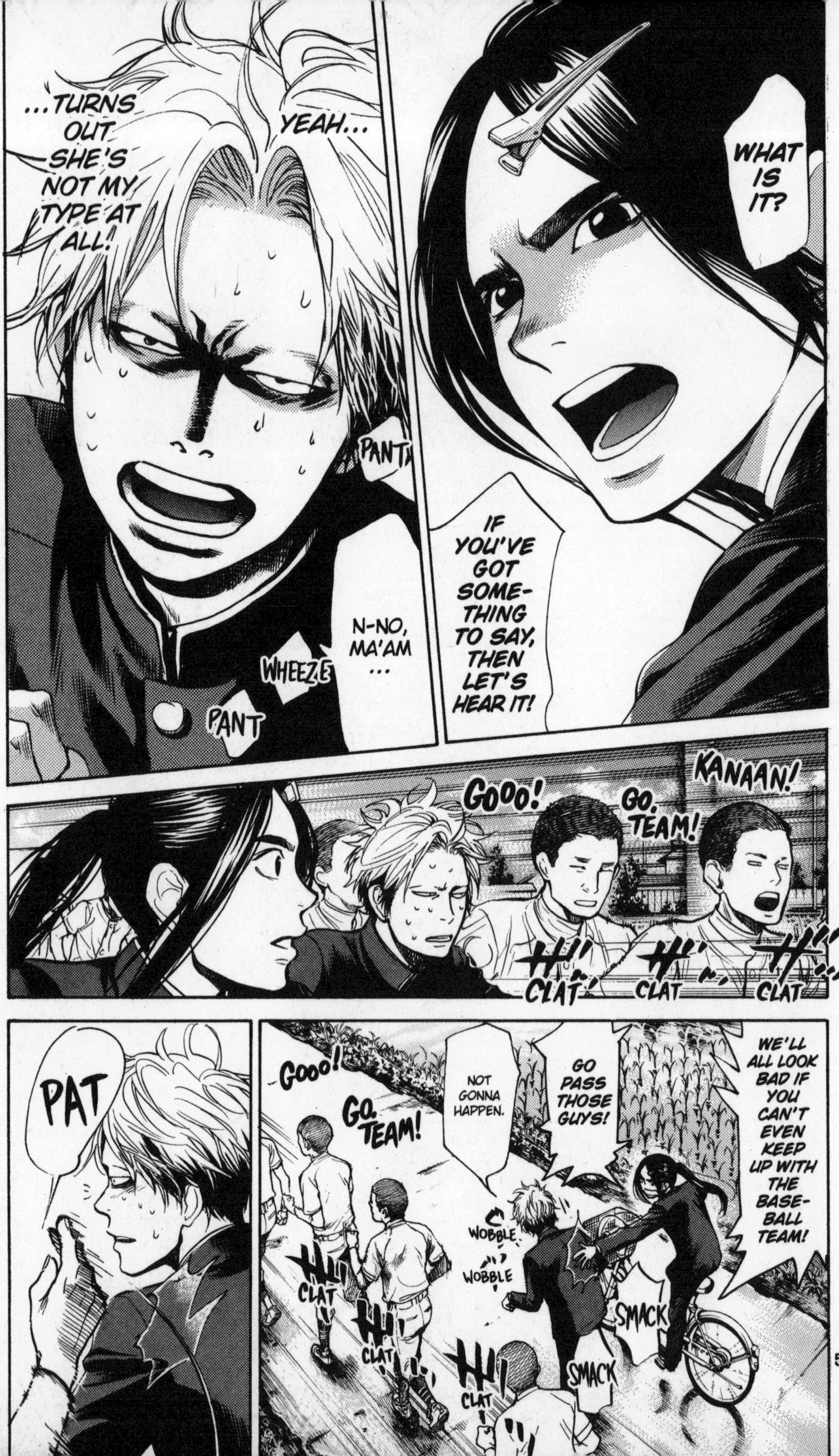
WHAT IS IT?
IF YOU'VE GOT SOMETHING TO SAY, THEN LET'S HEAR IT!
YEAH...
...TURNS OUT SHE'S NOT MY TYPE AT ALL!
PANT
N-NO, MA'AM ...
WHEEZE
PANT
KANAAN!
GO. TEAM!
GOOO!
CLAT
CLAT
CLAT
WE'LL ALL LOOK BAD IF YOU CAN'T EVEN KEEP UP WITH THE BASE-BALL TEAM!
GO PASS THOSE GUYS!
NOT GONNA HAPPEN.
GOOO!
GO. TEAM!
WOBBLE
WOBBLE
SMACK
SMACK
CLAT
CLAT
CLAT
PAT

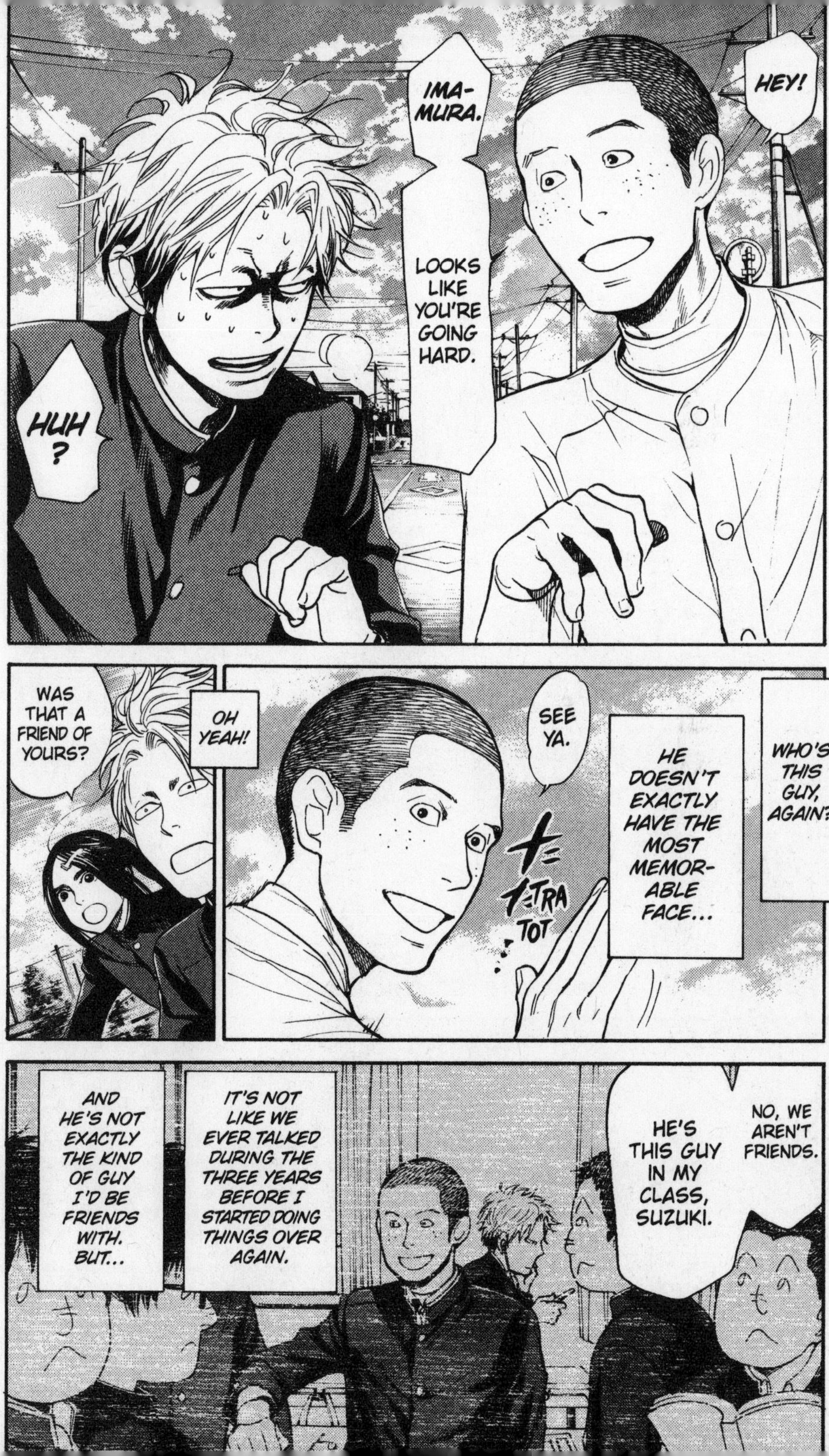
HEY!
IMA-MURA.
LOOKS LIKE YOU'RE GOING HARD.
HUH?
WHO'S THIS GUY, AGAIN?
HE DOESN'T EXACTLY HAVE THE MOST MEMOR-ABLE FACE...
SEE YA.
TRA TOT
OH YEAH!
WAS THAT A FRIEND OF YOURS?
NO, WE AREN'T FRIENDS.
HE'S THIS GUY IN MY CLASS, SUZUKI.
IT'S NOT LIKE WE EVER TALKED DURING THE THREE YEARS BEFORE I STARTED DOING THINGS OVER AGAIN.
AND HE'S NOT EXACTLY THE KIND OF GUY I'D BE FRIENDS WITH. BUT...

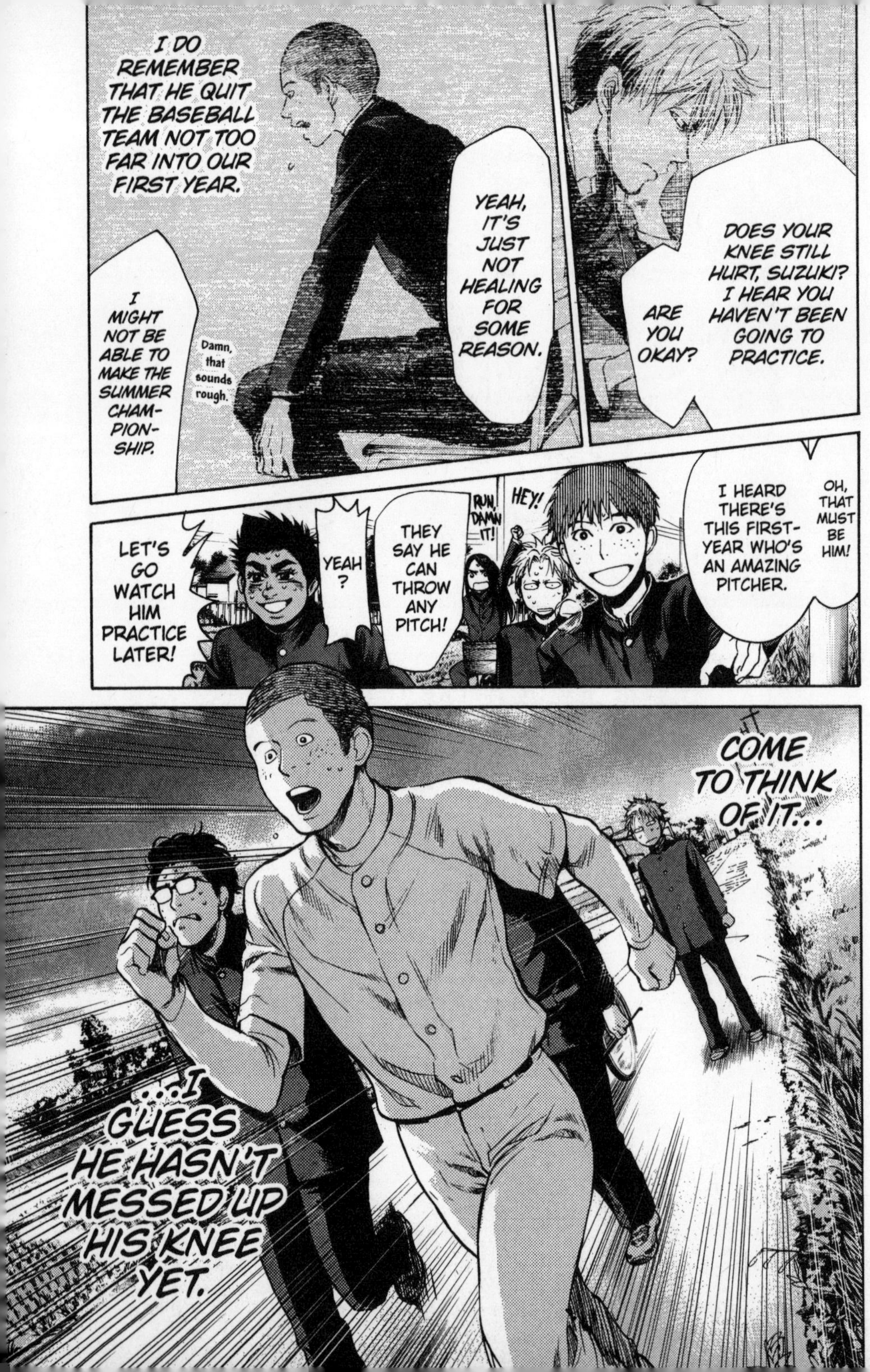
DOES YOUR KNEE STILL HURT, SUZUKI? I HEAR YOU HAVEN'T BEEN GOING TO PRACTICE.
ARE YOU OKAY?
I DO REMEMBER THAT HE QUIT THE BASEBALL TEAM NOT TOO FAR INTO OUR FIRST YEAR.
YEAH, IT'S JUST NOT HEALING FOR SOME REASON.
I MIGHT NOT BE ABLE TO MAKE THE SUMMER CHAMPIONSHIP.
Damn, that sounds rough.
OH, THAT MUST BE HIM!
I HEARD THERE'S THIS FIRST-YEAR WHO'S AN AMAZING PITCHER.
HEY!
RUN, DAMN IT!
THEY SAY HE CAN THROW ANY PITCH!
YEAH?
LET'S GO WATCH HIM PRACTICE LATER!
COME TO THINK OF IT...
...I GUESS HE HASN'T MESSED UP HIS KNEE YET.

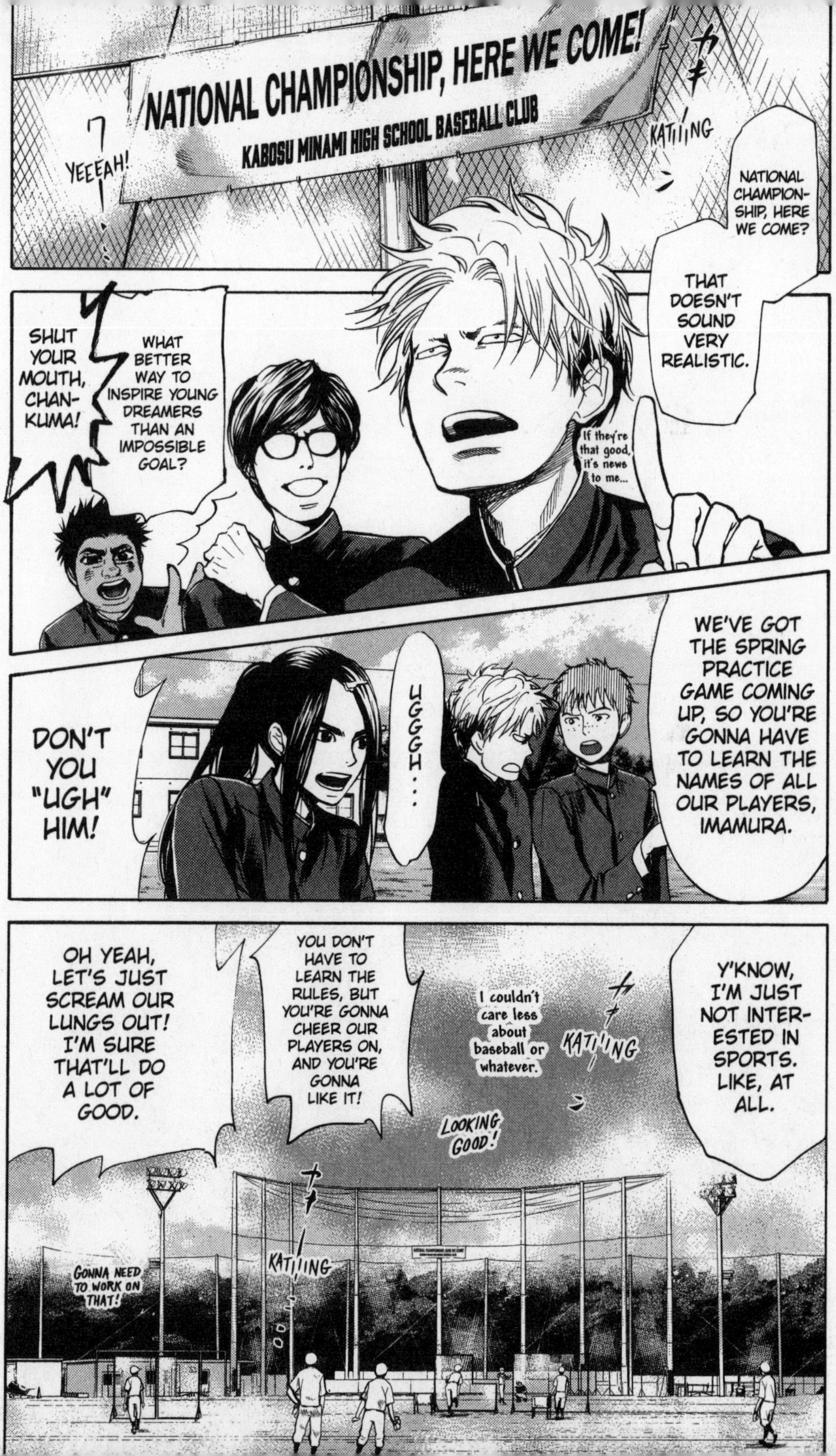

NATIONAL CHAMPIONSHIP, HERE WE COME!
KABOSU MINAMI HIGH SCHOOL BASEBALL CLUB
KATIIING
YEEEAH!
NATIONAL CHAMPIONSHIP, HERE WE COME?
THAT DOESN'T SOUND VERY REALISTIC.
If they're that good, it's news to me...
WHAT BETTER WAY TO INSPIRE YOUNG DREAMERS THAN AN IMPOSSIBLE GOAL?
SHUT YOUR MOUTH, CHAN-KUMA!
WE'VE GOT THE SPRING PRACTICE GAME COMING UP, SO YOU'RE GONNA HAVE TO LEARN THE NAMES OF ALL OUR PLAYERS, IMAMURA.
UGGGH...
DON'T YOU "UGH" HIM!
Y'KNOW, I'M JUST NOT INTER-ESTED IN SPORTS. LIKE, AT ALL.
KATIIING
I couldn't care less about baseball or whatever.
YOU DON'T HAVE TO LEARN THE RULES, BUT YOU'RE GONNA CHEER OUR PLAYERS ON, AND YOU'RE GONNA LIKE IT!
OH YEAH, LET'S JUST SCREAM OUR LUNGS OUT! I'M SURE THAT'LL DO A LOT OF GOOD.
LOOKING GOOD!
KATIIING
GONNA NEED TO WORK ON THAT!

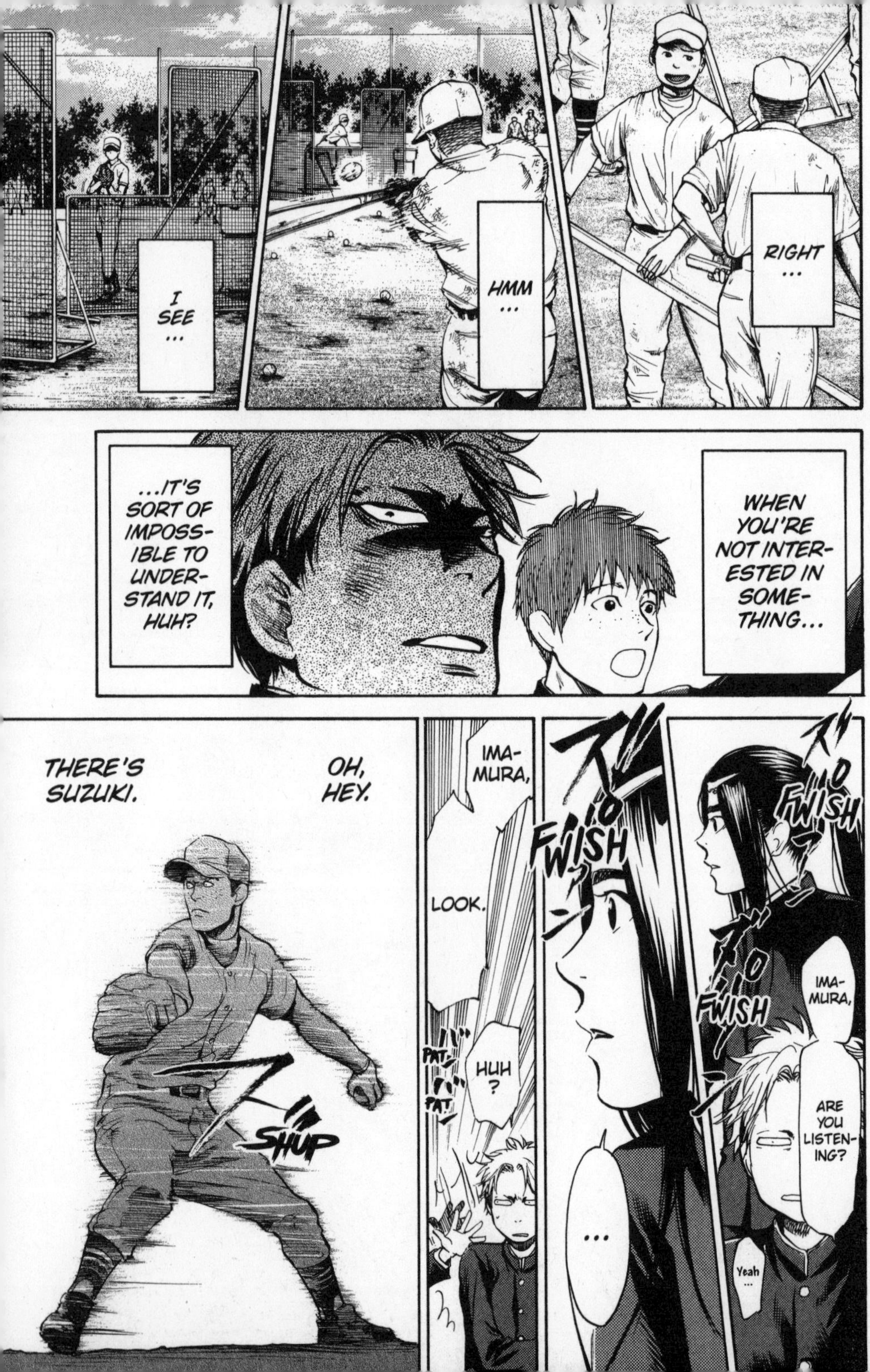
RIGHT ...
HMM ...
I SEE ...
WHEN YOU'RE NOT INTERESTED IN SOMETHING...
...IT'S SORT OF IMPOSSIBLE TO UNDERSTAND IT, HUH?
FWISH
IMA-MURA,
FWISH
ARE YOU LISTENING?
Yeah ...
FWISH
...
IMA-MURA,
LOOK.
HUH?
PAT PAT
OH, HEY.
THERE'S SUZUKI.
SHUP

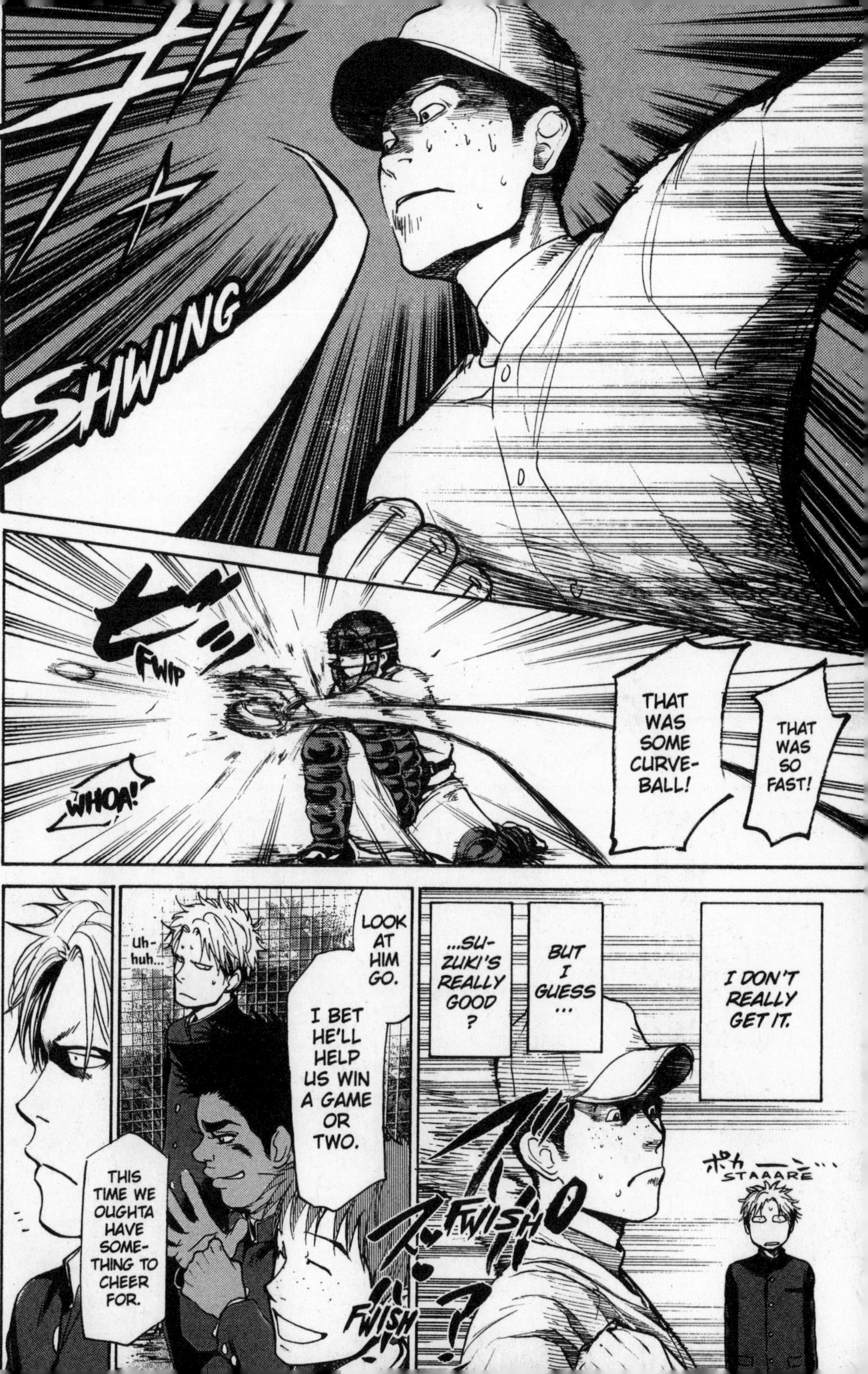
SHWING
THAT WAS SO FAST!
THAT WAS SOME CURVE-BALL!
FWIP
WHOA!
I DON'T REALLY GET IT.
BUT I GUESS...
...SU-ZUKI'S REALLY GOOD?
STAAARE
FWISH
FWISH
LOOK AT HIM GO.
I BET HE'LL HELP US WIN A GAME OR TWO.
Uh-huh...
THIS TIME WE OUGHTA HAVE SOME-THING TO CHEER FOR.

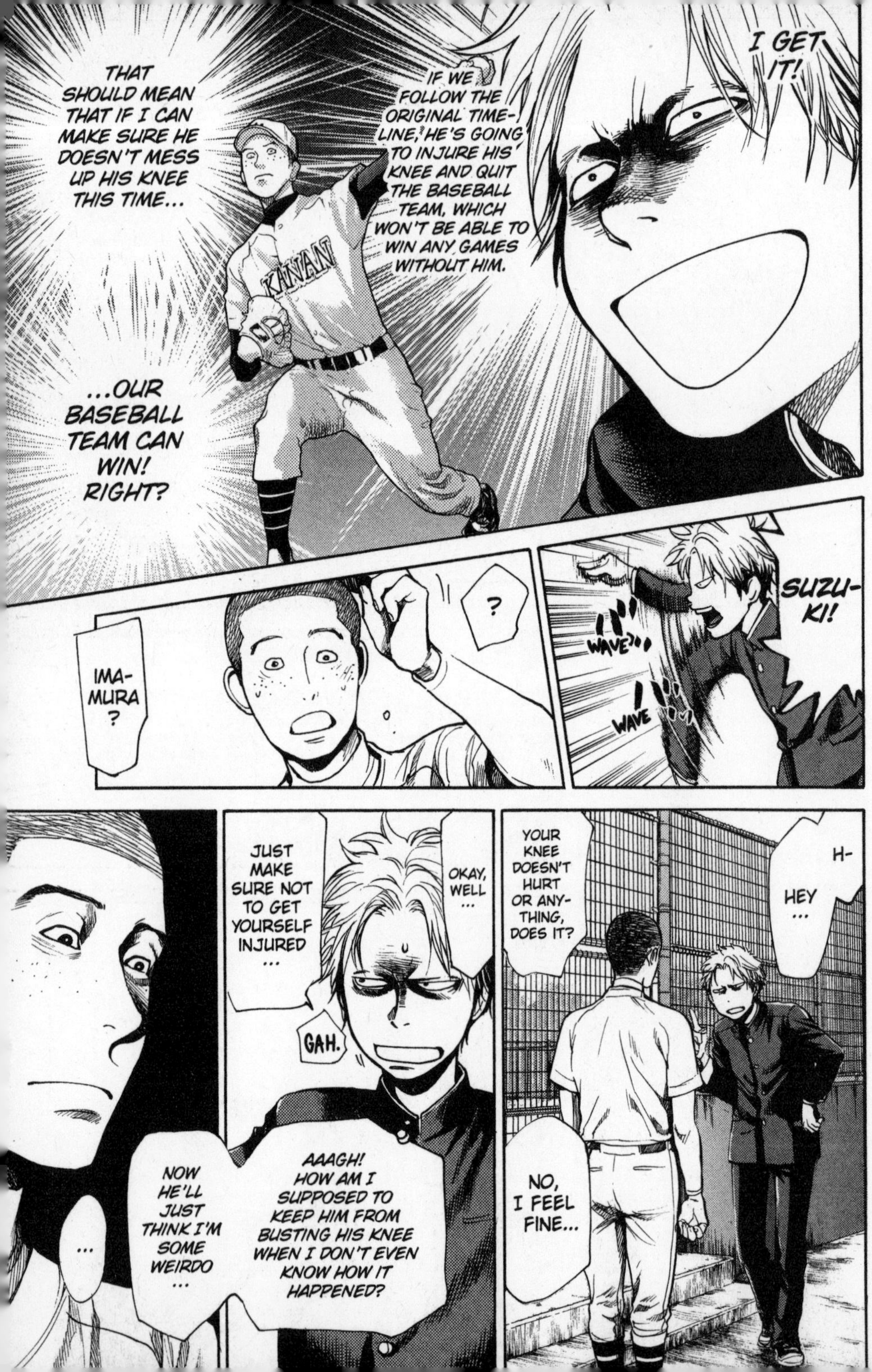
I GET IT!
IF WE FOLLOW THE ORIGINAL TIME-LINE, HE'S GOING TO INJURE HIS KNEE AND QUIT THE BASEBALL TEAM, WHICH WON'T BE ABLE TO WIN ANY GAMES WITHOUT HIM.
THAT SHOULD MEAN THAT IF I CAN MAKE SURE HE DOESN'T MESS UP HIS KNEE THIS TIME...
KAINAN
...OUR BASEBALL TEAM CAN WIN! RIGHT?
SUZU-KI!
WAVE
WAVE
?
IMA-MURA?
H-HEY...
YOUR KNEE DOESN'T HURT OR ANY-THING, DOES IT?
NO, I FEEL FINE...
OKAY, WELL...
JUST MAKE SURE NOT TO GET YOURSELF INJURED...
GAH.
AAAGH! HOW AM I SUPPOSED TO KEEP HIM FROM BUSTING HIS KNEE WHEN I DON'T EVEN KNOW HOW IT HAPPENED?
NOW HE'LL JUST THINK I'M SOME WEIRDO...
...

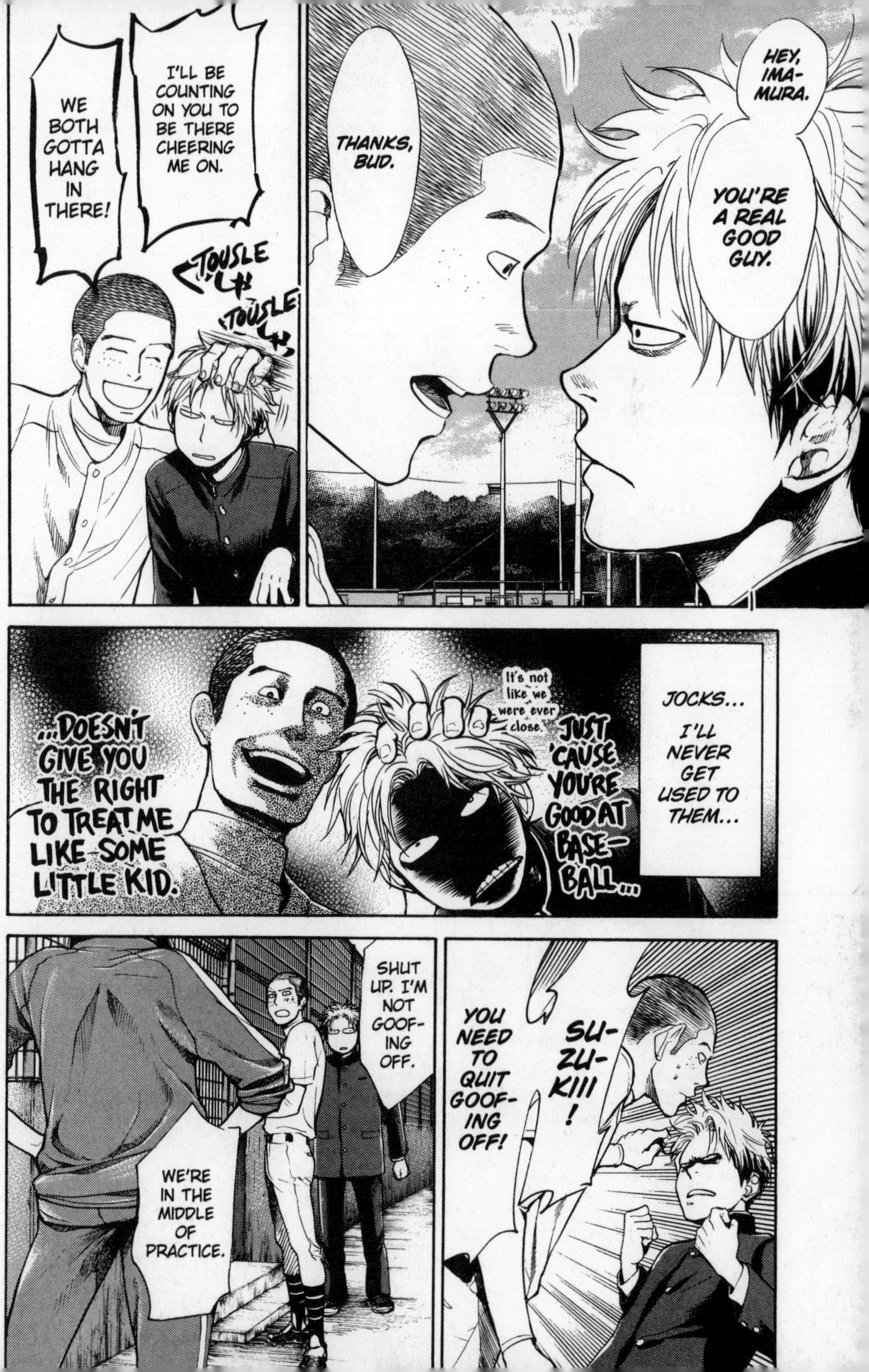
HEY, IMA-MURA.
YOU'RE A REAL GOOD GUY.
THANKS, BUD.
I'LL BE COUNTING ON YOU TO BE THERE CHEERING ME ON.
WE BOTH GOTTA HANG IN THERE!
TOUSLE
TOUSLE
JOCKS...
I'LL NEVER GET USED TO THEM...
JUST 'CAUSE YOU'RE GOOD AT BASE-BALL...
It's not like we were ever close.
...DOESN'T GIVE YOU THE RIGHT TO TREAT ME LIKE SOME LITTLE KID.
SU-ZU-KIII!
YOU NEED TO QUIT GOOF-ING OFF!
SHUT UP. I'M NOT GOOF-ING OFF.
WE'RE IN THE MIDDLE OF PRACTICE.

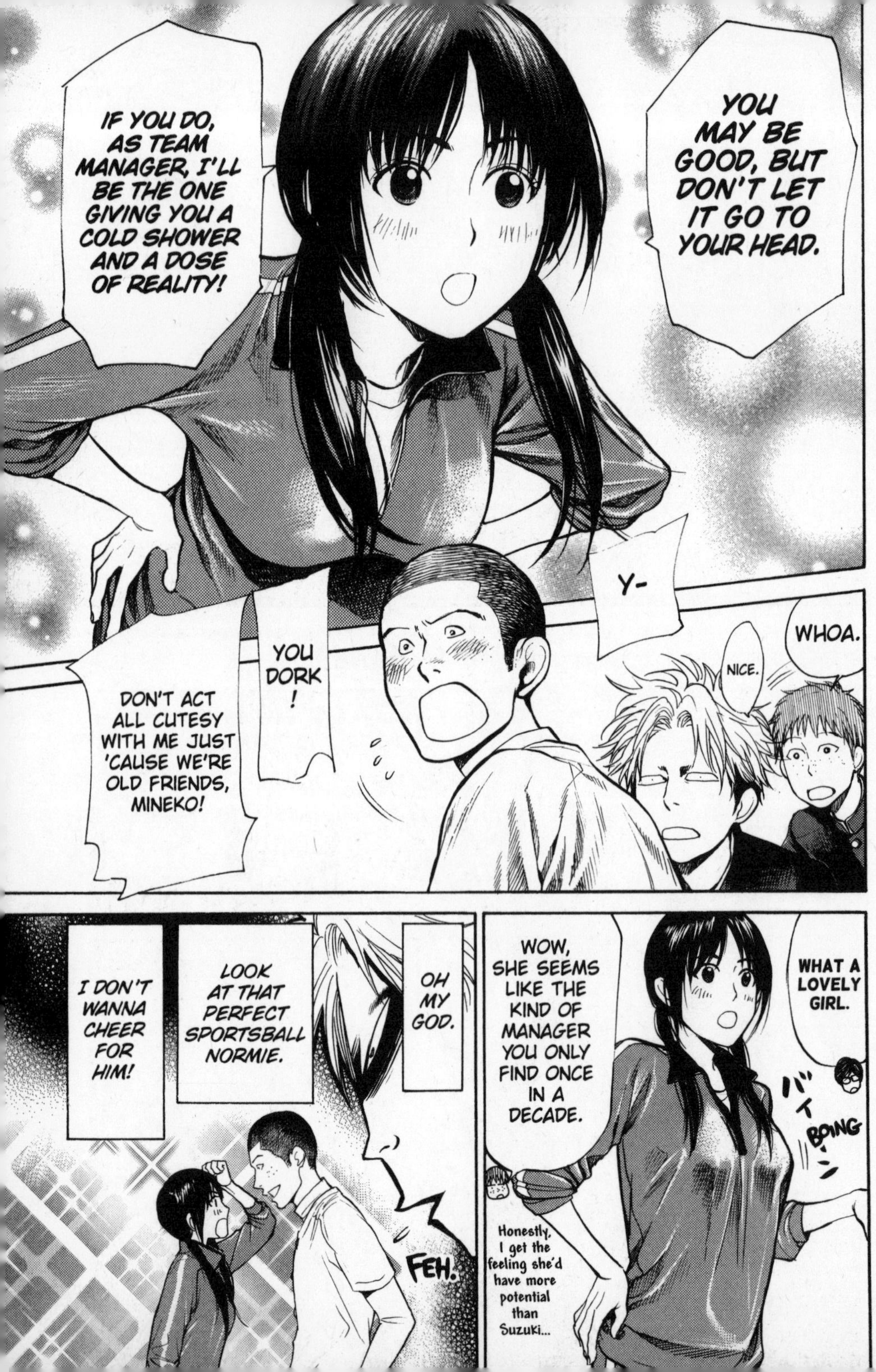
YOU MAY BE GOOD, BUT DON'T LET IT GO TO YOUR HEAD.
IF YOU DO, AS TEAM MANAGER, I'LL BE THE ONE GIVING YOU A COLD SHOWER AND A DOSE OF REALITY!
WHOA.
NICE.
Y-
YOU DORK!
DON'T ACT ALL CUTESY WITH ME JUST 'CAUSE WE'RE OLD FRIENDS, MINEKO!
WHAT A LOVELY GIRL.
WOW, SHE SEEMS LIKE THE KIND OF MANAGER YOU ONLY FIND ONCE IN A DECADE.
バイ
BOING
Honestly, I get the feeling she'd have more potential than Suzuki...
OH MY GOD.
LOOK AT THAT PERFECT SPORTSBALL NORMIE.
I DON'T WANNA CHEER FOR HIM!
FEH.

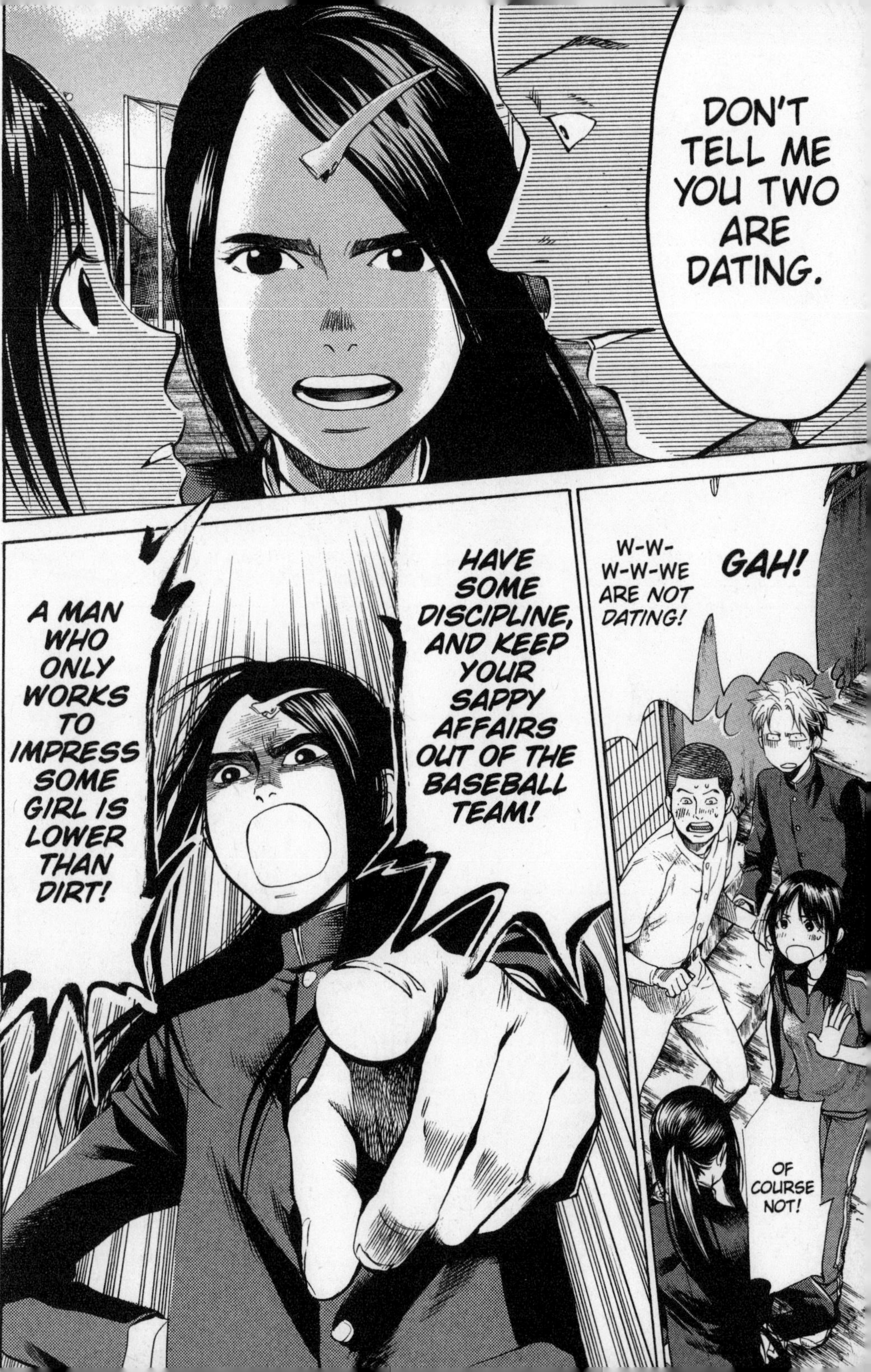
DON'T TELL ME YOU TWO ARE DATING.
GAH!
W-W-W-W-WE ARE NOT DATING!
OF COURSE NOT!
HAVE SOME DISCIPLINE, AND KEEP YOUR SAPPY AFFAIRS OUT OF THE BASEBALL TEAM!
A MAN WHO ONLY WORKS TO IMPRESS SOME GIRL IS LOWER THAN DIRT!

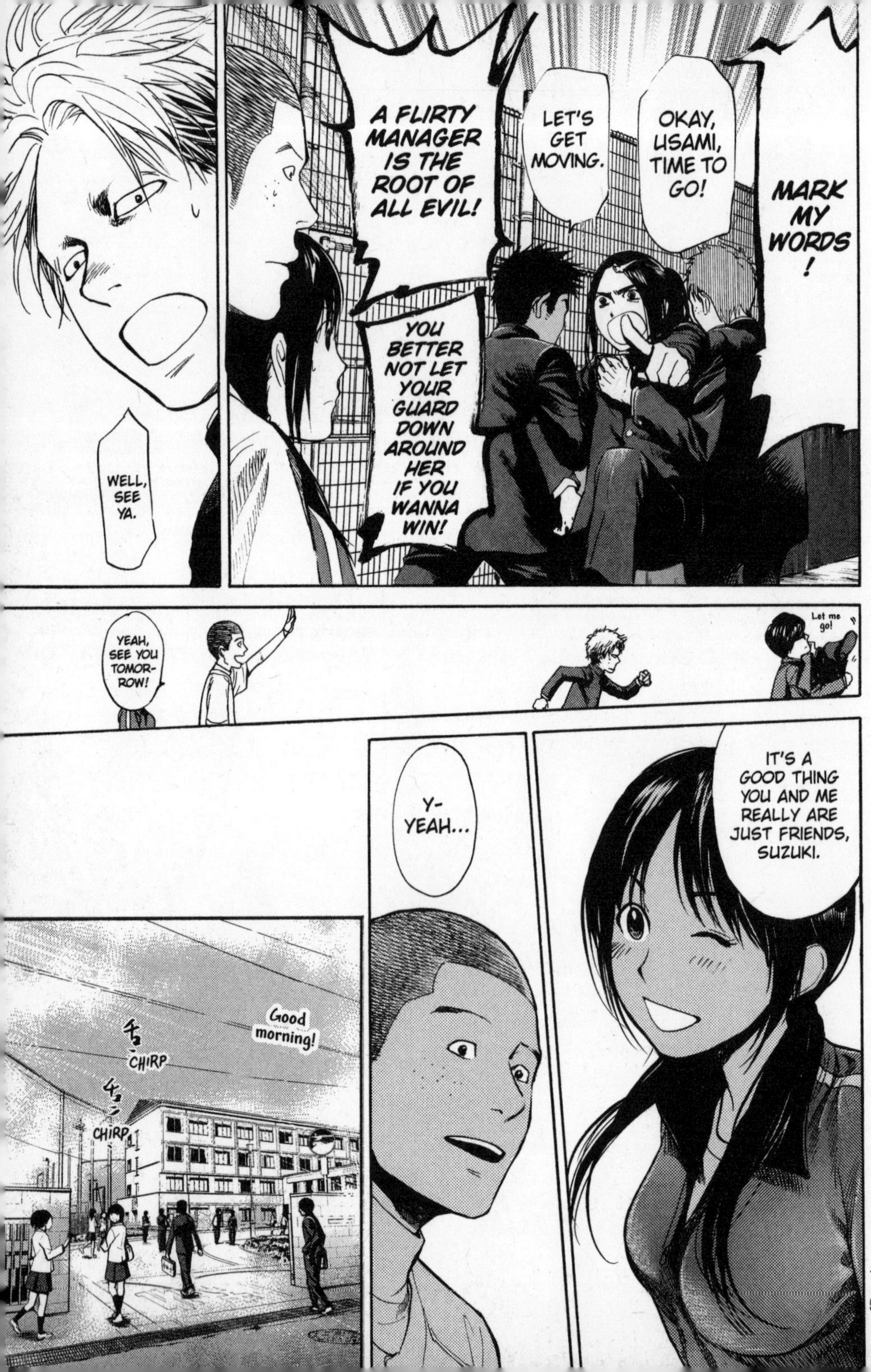
OKAY, USAMI, TIME TO GO!
MARK MY WORDS!
LET'S GET MOVING.
A FLIRTY MANAGER IS THE ROOT OF ALL EVIL!
YOU BETTER NOT LET YOUR GUARD DOWN AROUND HER IF YOU WANNA WIN!
WELL, SEE YA.
Let me go!
YEAH, SEE YOU TOMOR-ROW!
IT'S A GOOD THING YOU AND ME REALLY ARE JUST FRIENDS, SUZUKI.
Y-YEAH...
Good morning!
CHIRP
CHIRP

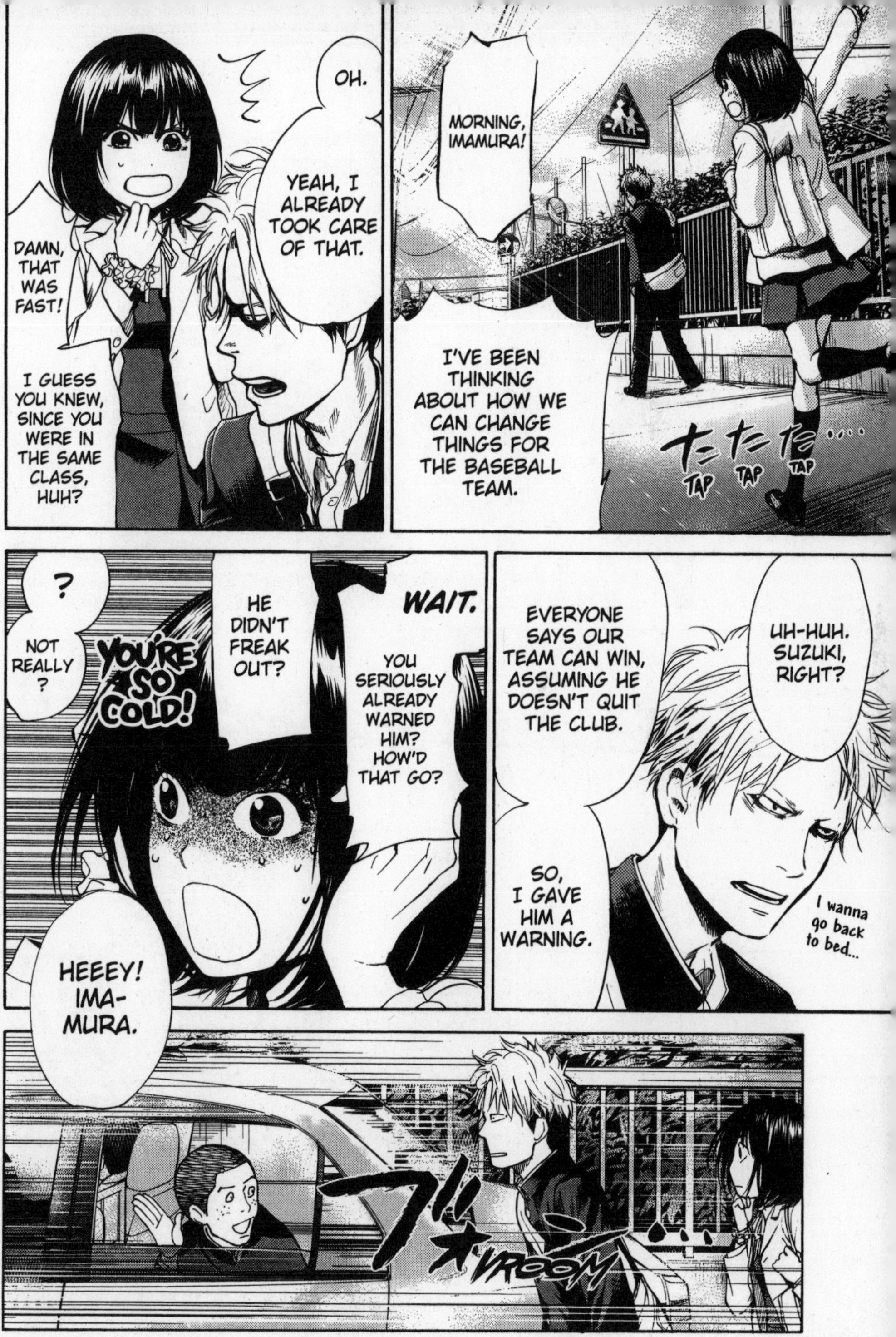
MORNING, IMAMURA!
I'VE BEEN THINKING ABOUT HOW WE CAN CHANGE THINGS FOR THE BASEBALL TEAM.
TAP TAP TAP
OH.
YEAH, I ALREADY TOOK CARE OF THAT.
DAMN, THAT WAS FAST!
I GUESS YOU KNEW, SINCE YOU WERE IN THE SAME CLASS, HUH?
UH-HUH. SUZUKI, RIGHT?
EVERYONE SAYS OUR TEAM CAN WIN, ASSUMING HE DOESN'T QUIT THE CLUB.
SO, I GAVE HIM A WARNING.
I wanna go back to bed...
WAIT.
YOU SERIOUSLY ALREADY WARNED HIM? HOW'D THAT GO?
HE DIDN'T FREAK OUT?
?
NOT REALLY?
YOU'RE SO COLD!
HEEEY! IMA-MURA.
VROOM
...

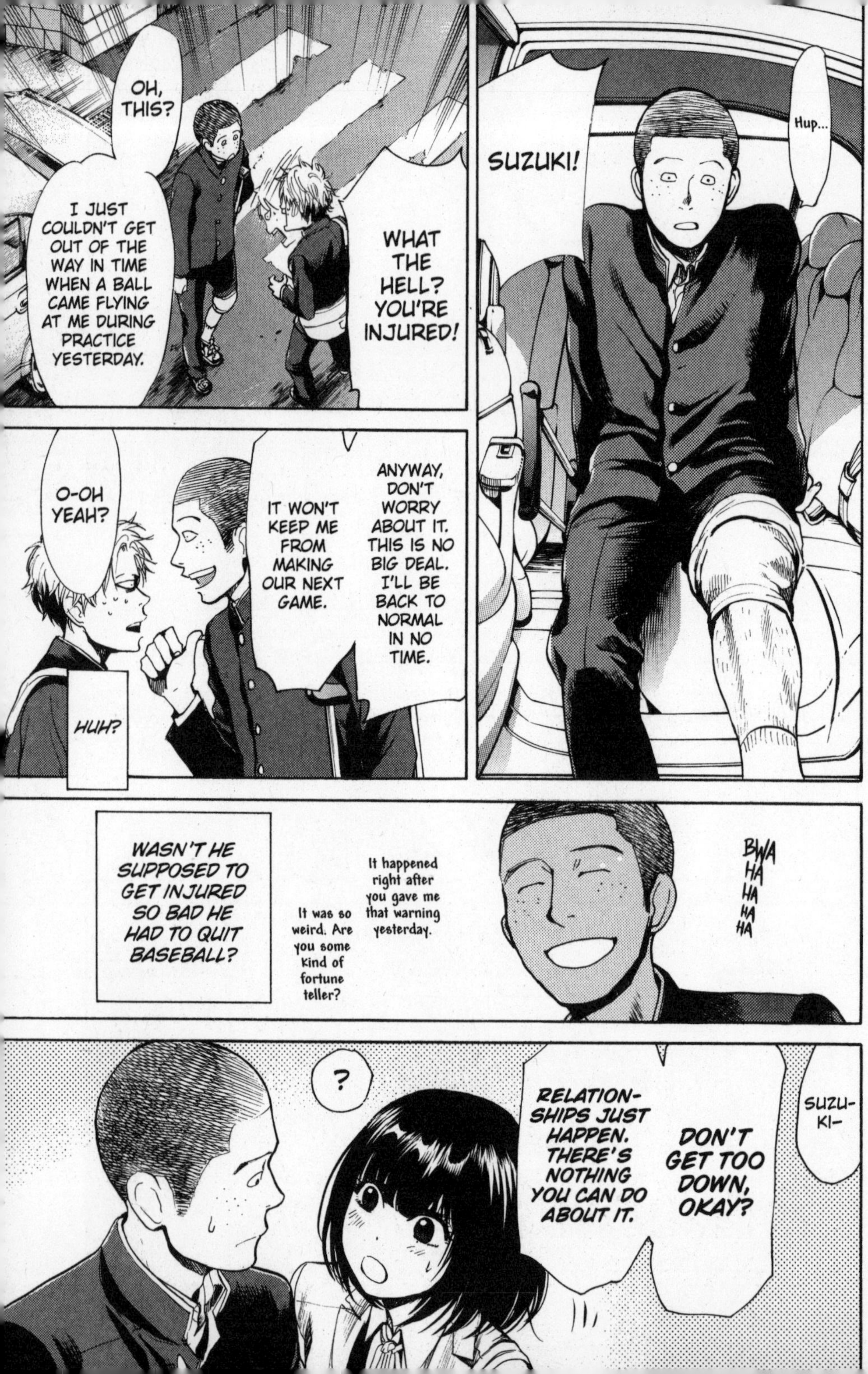
Hup...
SUZUKI!
WHAT THE HELL? YOU'RE INJURED!
OH, THIS?
I JUST COULDN'T GET OUT OF THE WAY IN TIME WHEN A BALL CAME FLYING AT ME DURING PRACTICE YESTERDAY.
ANYWAY, DON'T WORRY ABOUT IT. THIS IS NO BIG DEAL. I'LL BE BACK TO NORMAL IN NO TIME.
IT WON'T KEEP ME FROM MAKING OUR NEXT GAME.
O-OH YEAH?
HUH?
BWA HA HA HA HA
It happened right after you gave me that warning yesterday.
It was so weird. Are you some kind of fortune teller?
WASN'T HE SUPPOSED TO GET INJURED SO BAD HE HAD TO QUIT BASEBALL?
SUZU-KI-
DON'T GET TOO DOWN, OKAY?
RELATION-SHIPS JUST HAPPEN. THERE'S NOTHING YOU CAN DO ABOUT IT.
?

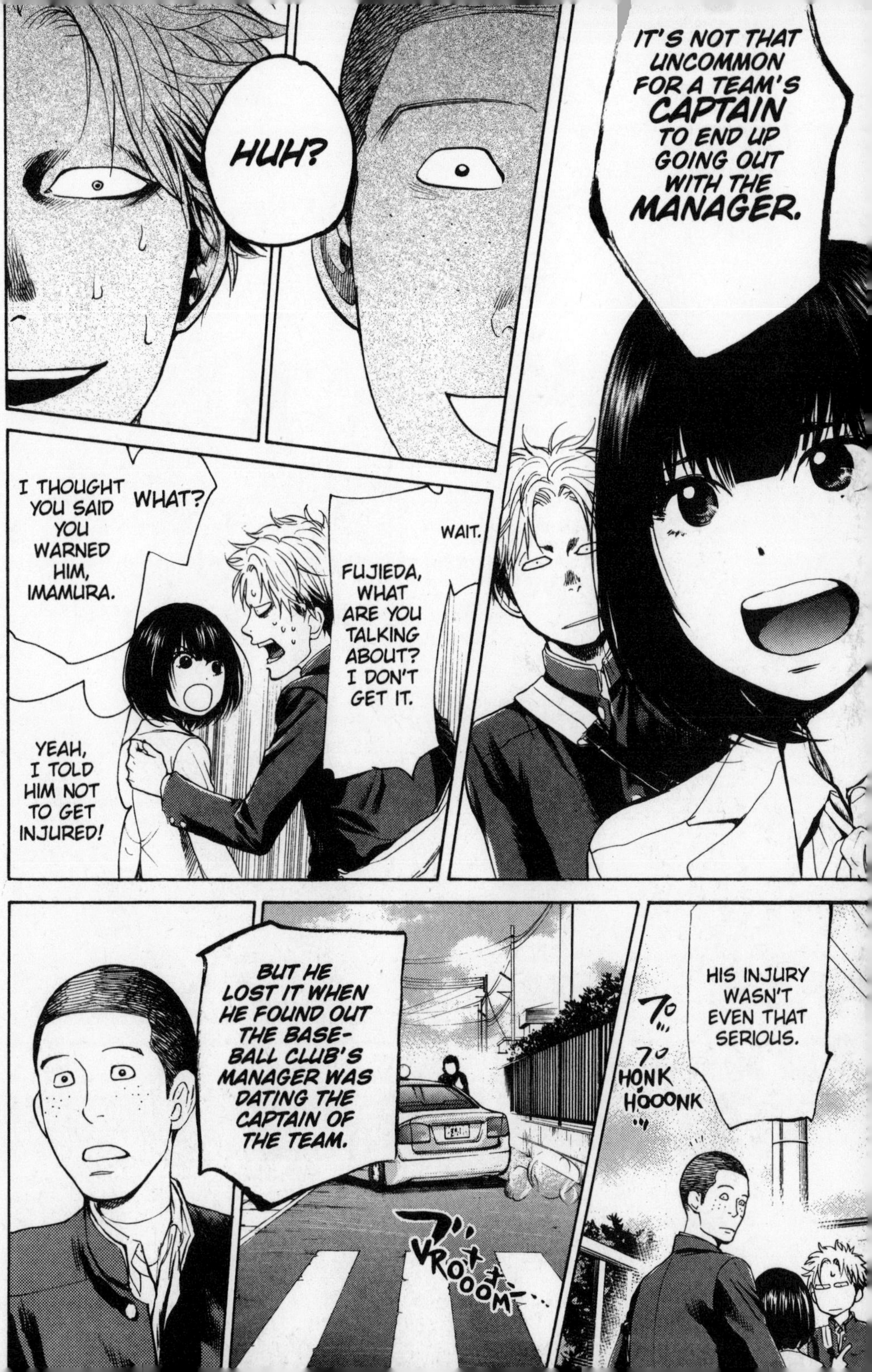

IT'S NOT THAT UNCOMMON FOR A TEAM'S CAPTAIN TO END UP GOING OUT WITH THE MANAGER.
HUH?
WAIT.
FUJIEDA, WHAT ARE YOU TALKING ABOUT? I DON'T GET IT.
WHAT?
I THOUGHT YOU SAID YOU WARNED HIM, IMAMURA.
YEAH, I TOLD HIM NOT TO GET INJURED!
HIS INJURY WASN'T EVEN THAT SERIOUS.
HONK
HOOONK
VROOOM
BUT HE LOST IT WHEN HE FOUND OUT THE BASE-BALL CLUB'S MANAGER WAS DATING THE CAPTAIN OF THE TEAM.

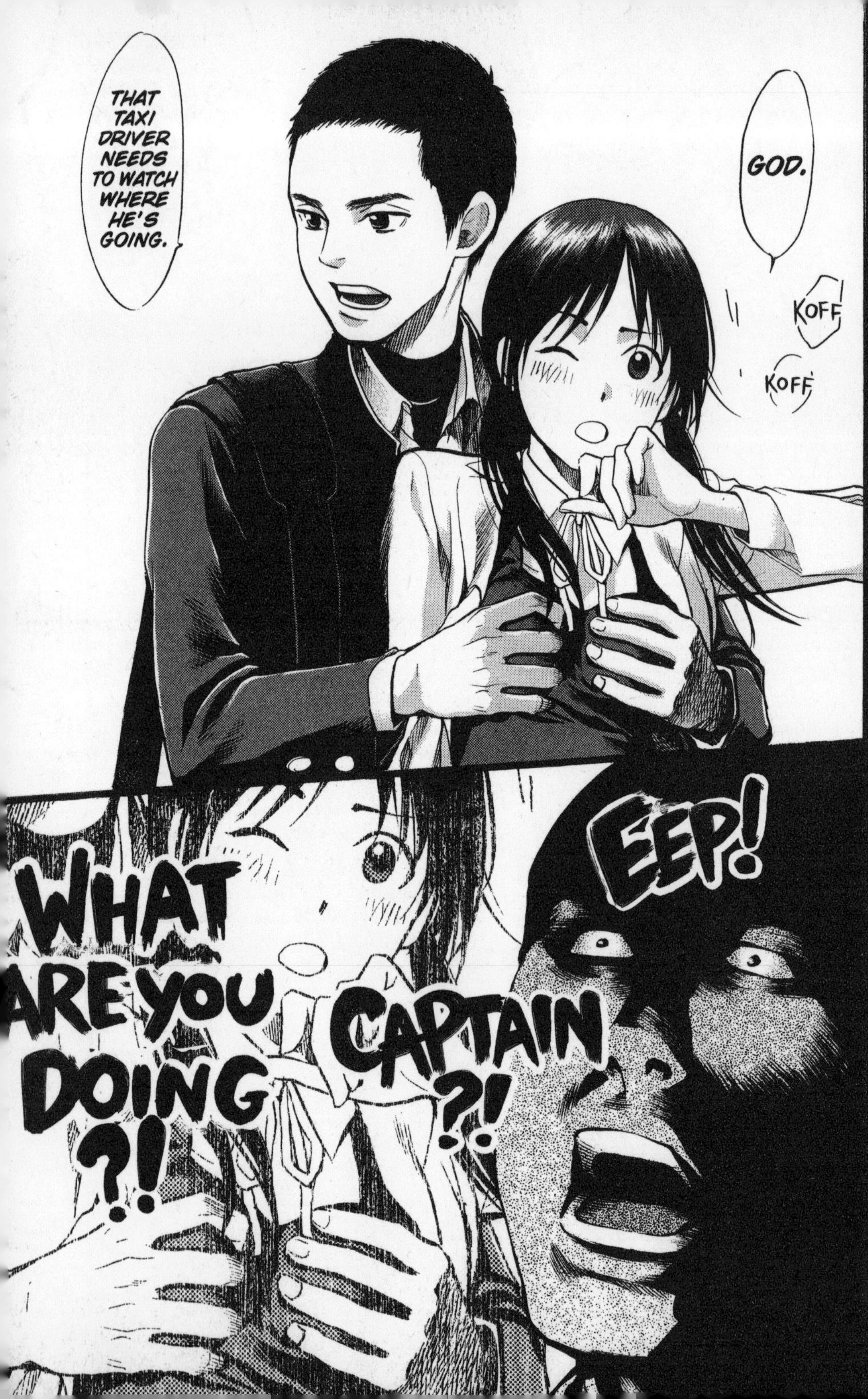
GOD.
KOFF
KOFF
THAT TAXI DRIVER NEEDS TO WATCH WHERE HE'S GOING.
EEP!
WHAT ARE YOU DOING ?!
CAPTAIN ?!

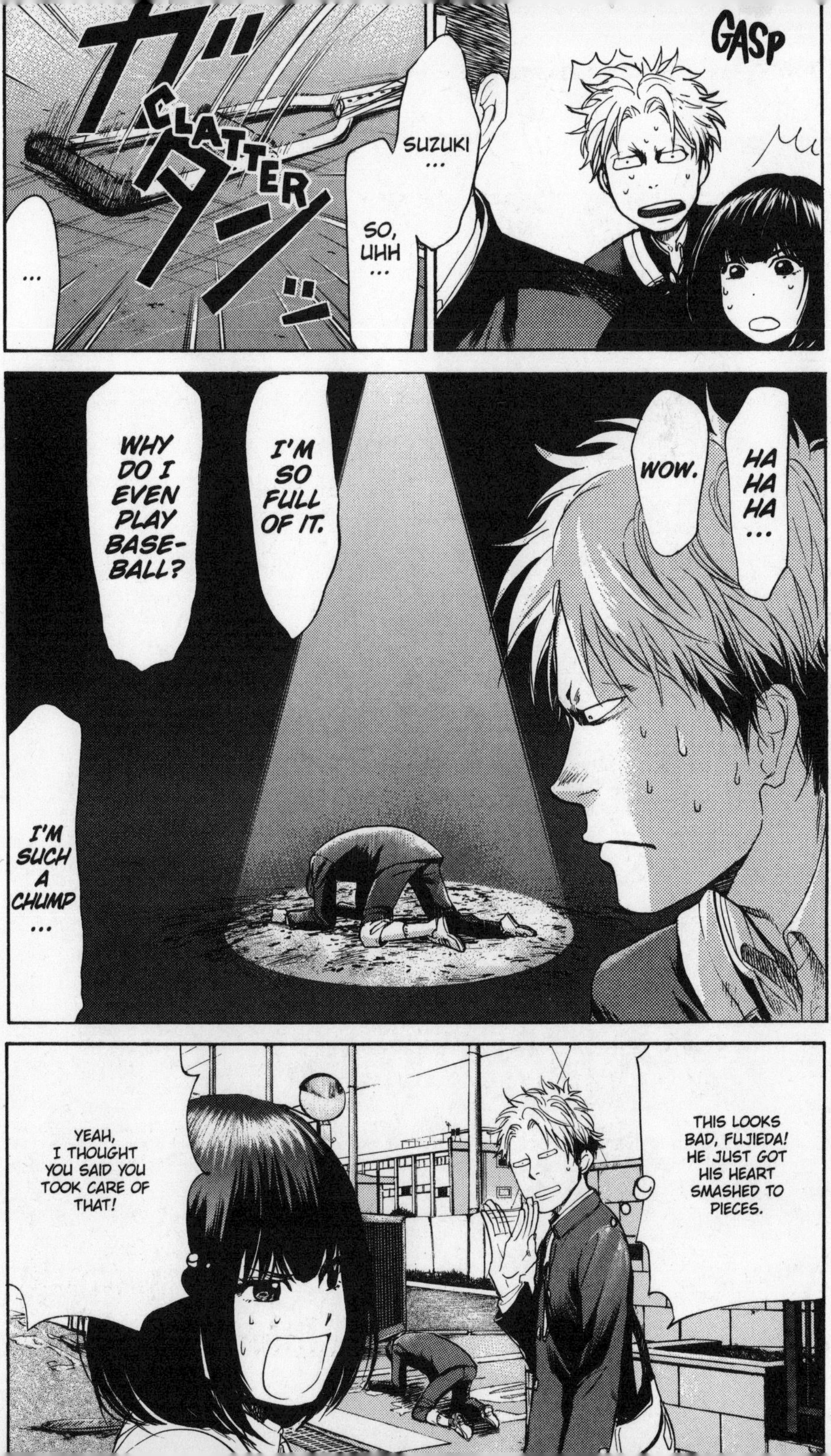
GASP
SUZUKI ...
SO, UHH ...
CLATTER
...
HA HA HA ...
WOW.
I'M SO FULL OF IT.
WHY DO I EVEN PLAY BASE-BALL?
I'M SUCH A CHUMP ...
THIS LOOKS BAD, FUJIEDA! HE JUST GOT HIS HEART SMASHED TO PIECES.
YEAH, I THOUGHT YOU SAID YOU TOOK CARE OF THAT!

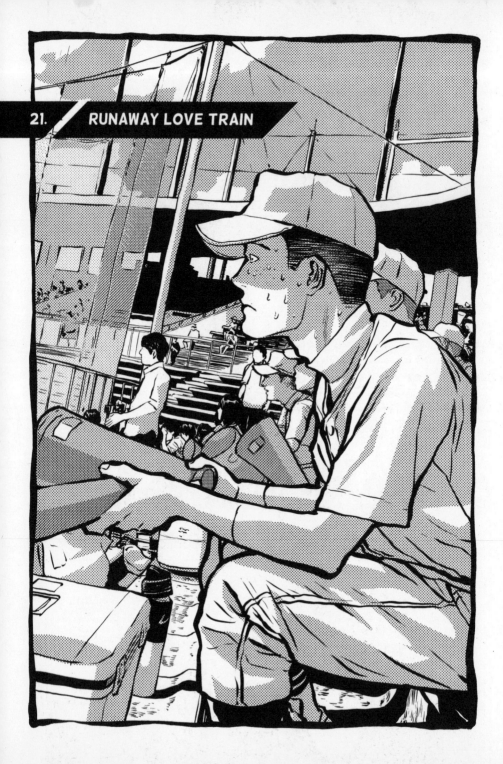

21. RUNAWAY LOVE TRAIN

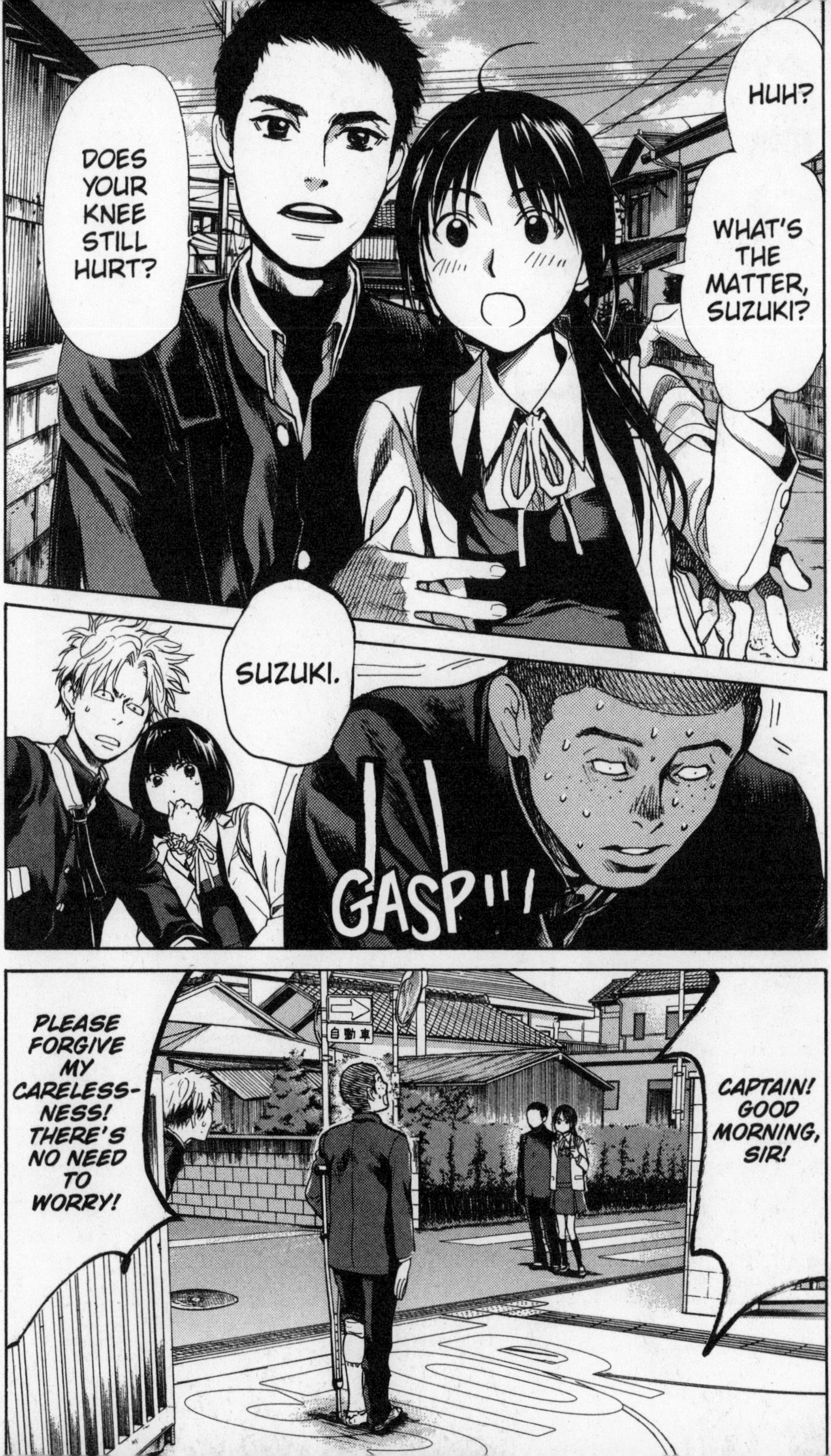
HUH?
WHAT'S THE MATTER, SUZUKI?
DOES YOUR KNEE STILL HURT?
SUZUKI.
GASP!!
CAPTAIN! GOOD MORNING, SIR!
PLEASE FORGIVE MY CARELESS-NESS! THERE'S NO NEED TO WORRY!
自動車

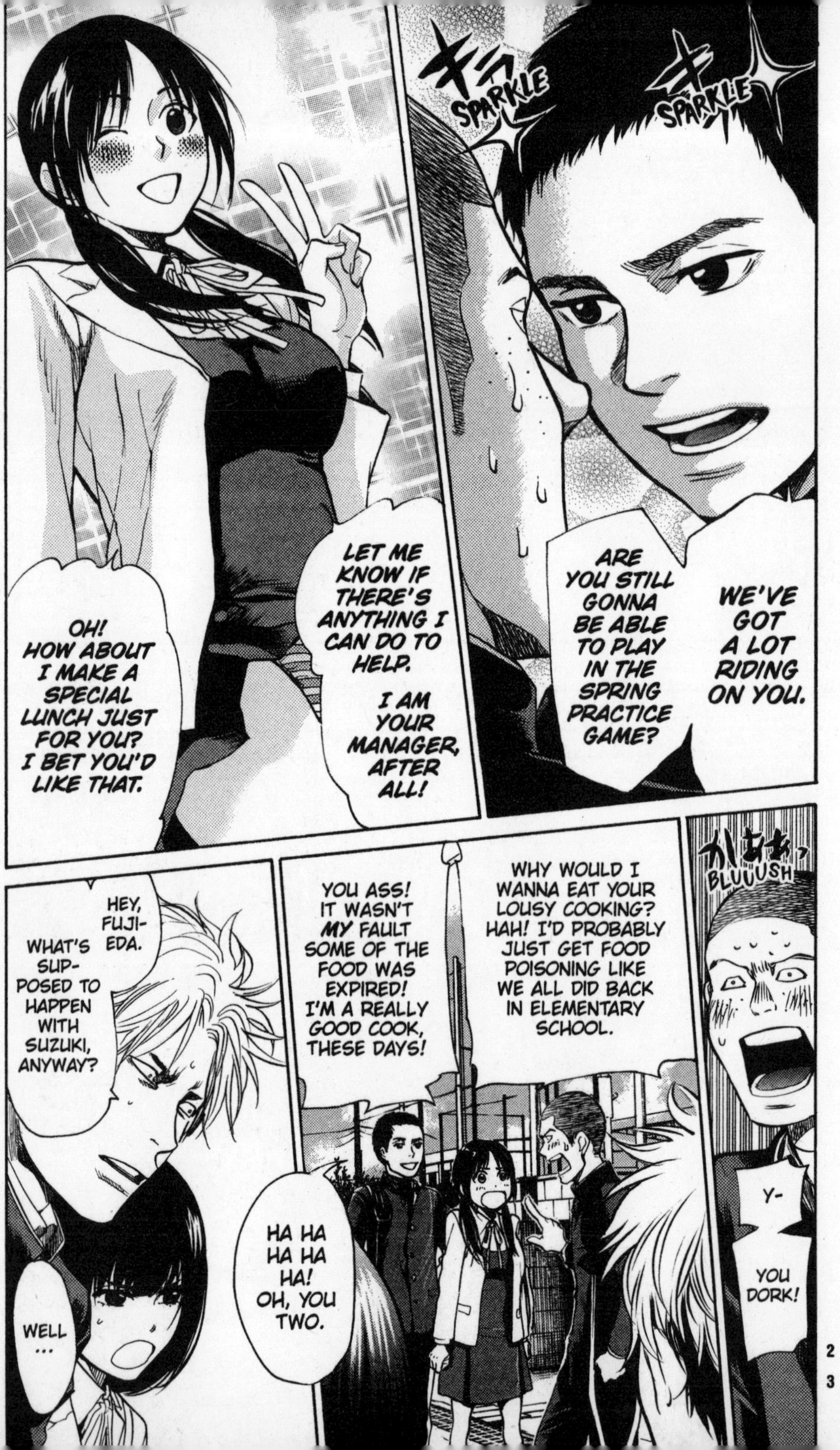
SPARKLE
SPARKLE
WE'VE GOT A LOT RIDING ON YOU.
ARE YOU STILL GONNA BE ABLE TO PLAY IN THE SPRING PRACTICE GAME?
LET ME KNOW IF THERE'S ANYTHING I CAN DO TO HELP.
I AM YOUR MANAGER, AFTER ALL!
OH! HOW ABOUT I MAKE A SPECIAL LUNCH JUST FOR YOU? I BET YOU'D LIKE THAT.
BLUUUSH
Y-
YOU DORK!
WHY WOULD I WANNA EAT YOUR LOUSY COOKING? HAH! I'D PROBABLY JUST GET FOOD POISONING LIKE WE ALL DID BACK IN ELEMENTARY SCHOOL.
YOU ASS! IT WASN'T *MY* FAULT SOME OF THE FOOD WAS EXPIRED! I'M A REALLY GOOD COOK, THESE DAYS!
HA HA HA HA HA! OH, YOU TWO.
HEY, FUJI-EDA.
WHAT'S SUP-POSED TO HAPPEN WITH SUZUKI, ANYWAY?
WELL ...

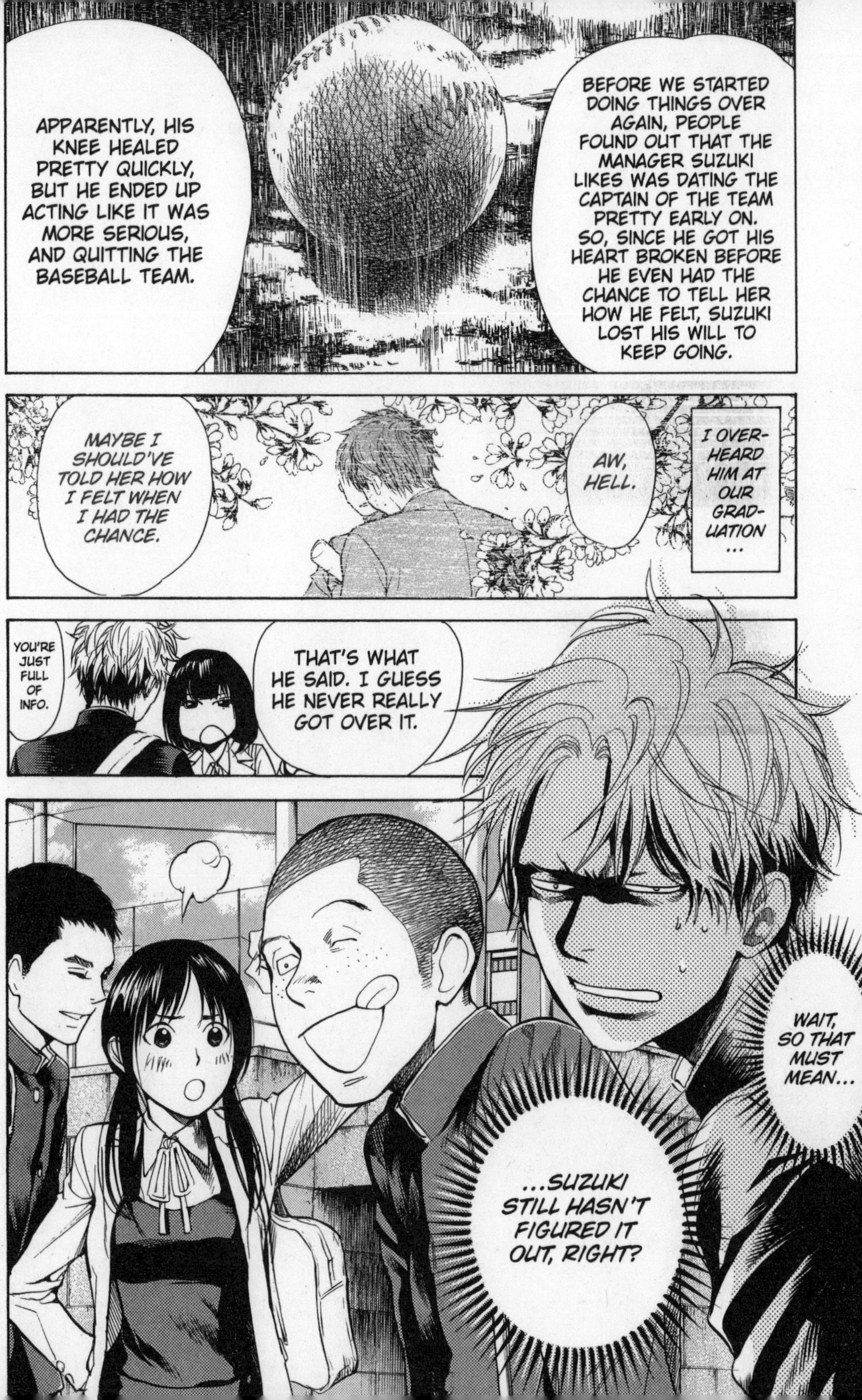
BEFORE WE STARTED DOING THINGS OVER AGAIN, PEOPLE FOUND OUT THAT THE MANAGER SUZUKI LIKES WAS DATING THE CAPTAIN OF THE TEAM PRETTY EARLY ON. SO, SINCE HE GOT HIS HEART BROKEN BEFORE HE EVEN HAD THE CHANCE TO TELL HER HOW HE FELT, SUZUKI LOST HIS WILL TO KEEP GOING.
APPARENTLY, HIS KNEE HEALED PRETTY QUICKLY, BUT HE ENDED UP ACTING LIKE IT WAS MORE SERIOUS, AND QUITTING THE BASEBALL TEAM.
I OVER-HEARD HIM AT OUR GRAD-UATION...
AW, HELL.
MAYBE I SHOULD'VE TOLD HER HOW I FELT WHEN I HAD THE CHANCE.
THAT'S WHAT HE SAID. I GUESS HE NEVER REALLY GOT OVER IT.
YOU'RE JUST FULL OF INFO.
WAIT, SO THAT MUST MEAN...
...SUZUKI STILL HASN'T FIGURED IT OUT, RIGHT?

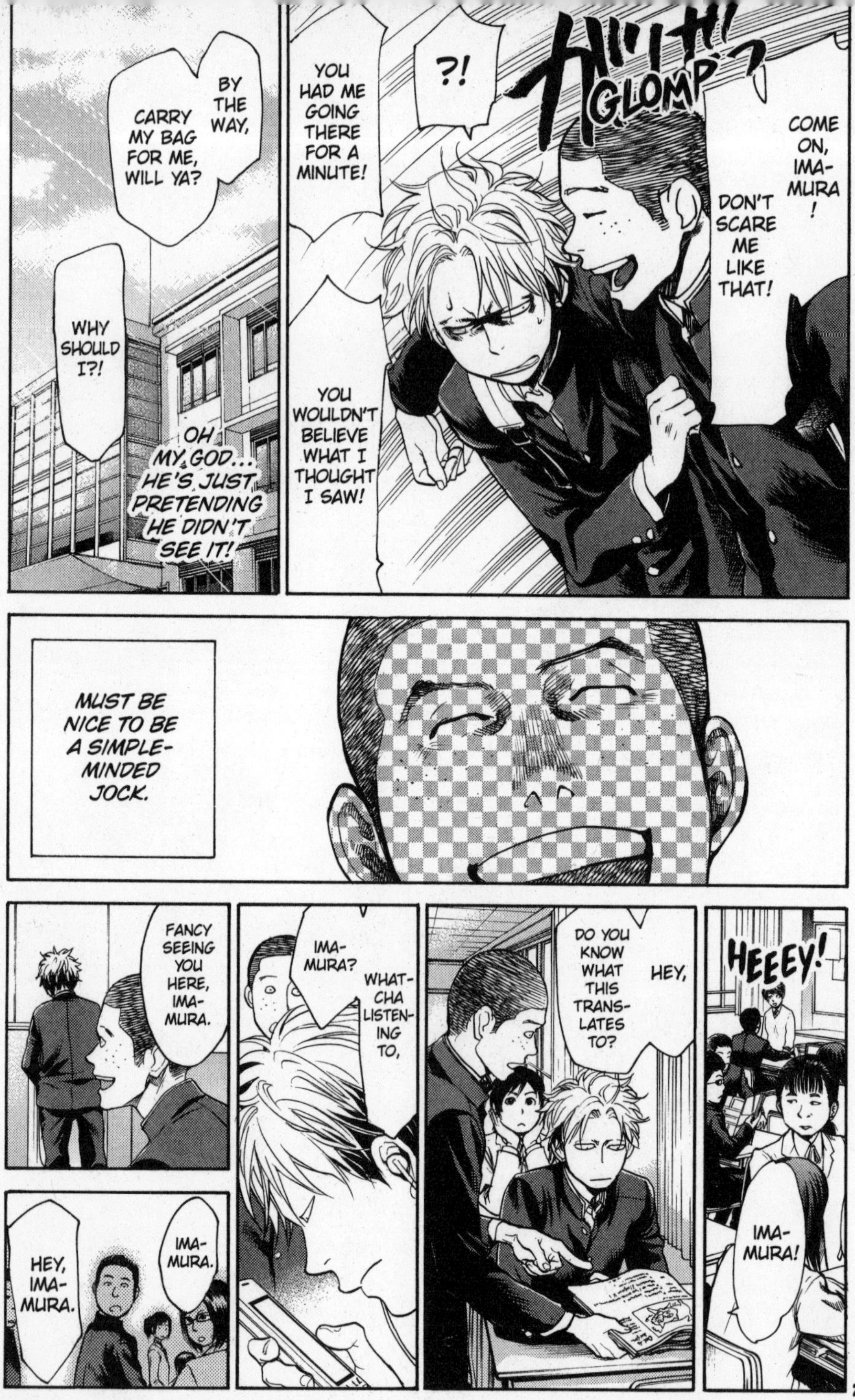
COME ON, IMA-MURA!
DON'T SCARE ME LIKE THAT!
GLOMP
?!
YOU HAD ME GOING THERE FOR A MINUTE!
YOU WOULDN'T BELIEVE WHAT I THOUGHT I SAW!
BY THE WAY,
CARRY MY BAG FOR ME, WILL YA?
WHY SHOULD I?!
OH MY GOD... HE'S JUST PRETENDING HE DIDN'T SEE IT!
MUST BE NICE TO BE A SIMPLE-MINDED JOCK.
HEEEY!
IMA-MURA!
HEY,
DO YOU KNOW WHAT THIS TRANS-LATES TO?
WHAT-CHA LISTEN-ING TO,
IMA-MURA?
FANCY SEEING YOU HERE, IMA-MURA.
IMA-MURA.
HEY, IMA-MURA.

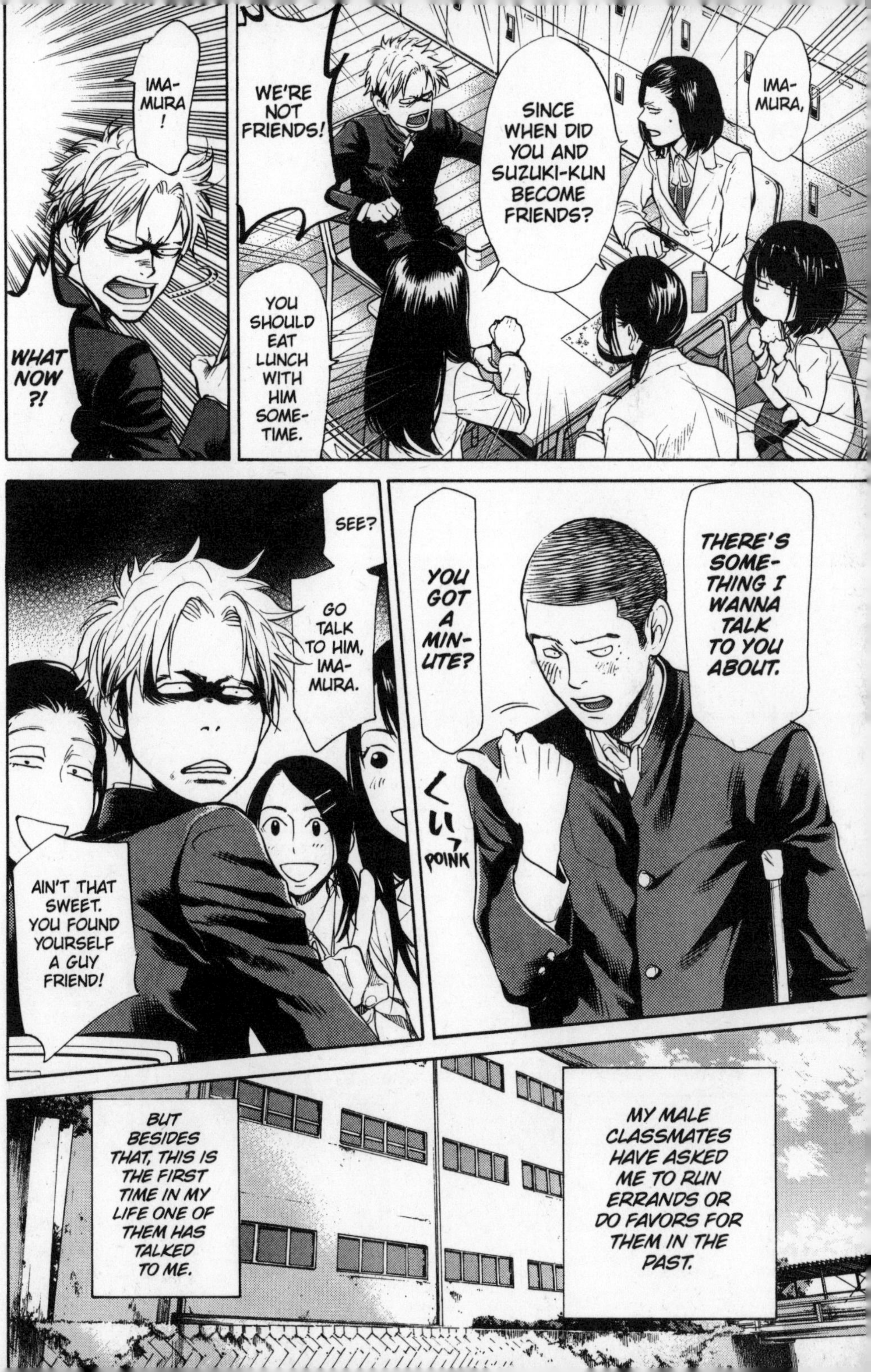
IMA-MURA,
SINCE WHEN DID YOU AND SUZUKI-KUN BECOME FRIENDS?
WE'RE NOT FRIENDS!
YOU SHOULD EAT LUNCH WITH HIM SOME-TIME.
IMA-MURA!
WHAT NOW?!
THERE'S SOME-THING I WANNA TALK TO YOU ABOUT.
YOU GOT A MIN-UTE?
くいっ
POINK
SEE?
GO TALK TO HIM, IMA-MURA.
AIN'T THAT SWEET. YOU FOUND YOURSELF A GUY FRIEND!
MY MALE CLASSMATES HAVE ASKED ME TO RUN ERRANDS OR DO FAVORS FOR THEM IN THE PAST.
BUT BESIDES THAT, THIS IS THE FIRST TIME IN MY LIFE ONE OF THEM HAS TALKED TO ME.

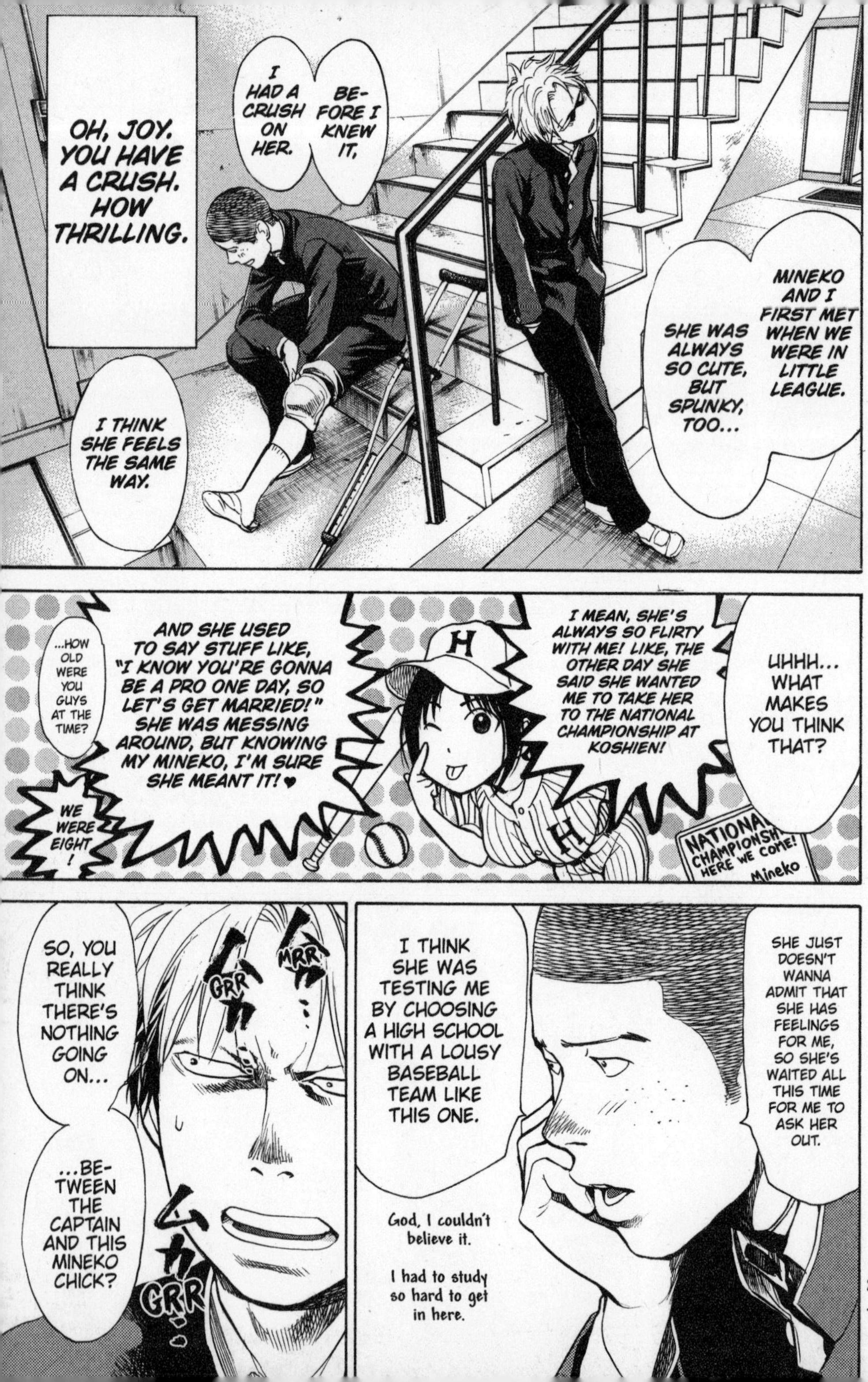
MINEKO AND I FIRST MET WHEN WE WERE IN LITTLE LEAGUE.
SHE WAS ALWAYS SO CUTE, BUT SPUNKY, TOO...
BE-FORE I KNEW IT,
I HAD A CRUSH ON HER.
OH, JOY. YOU HAVE A CRUSH. HOW THRILLING.
I THINK SHE FEELS THE SAME WAY.
UHHH... WHAT MAKES YOU THINK THAT?
I MEAN, SHE'S ALWAYS SO FLIRTY WITH ME! LIKE, THE OTHER DAY SHE SAID SHE WANTED ME TO TAKE HER TO THE NATIONAL CHAMPIONSHIP AT KOSHIEN!
NATIONA CHAMPIONSH HERE WE COME! Mineko
AND SHE USED TO SAY STUFF LIKE, "I KNOW YOU'RE GONNA BE A PRO ONE DAY, SO LET'S GET MARRIED!" SHE WAS MESSING AROUND, BUT KNOWING MY MINEKO, I'M SURE SHE MEANT IT! ♥
...HOW OLD WERE YOU GUYS AT THE TIME?
WE WERE EIGHT!
SHE JUST DOESN'T WANNA ADMIT THAT SHE HAS FEELINGS FOR ME, SO SHE'S WAITED ALL THIS TIME FOR ME TO ASK HER OUT.
I THINK SHE WAS TESTING ME BY CHOOSING A HIGH SCHOOL WITH A LOUSY BASEBALL TEAM LIKE THIS ONE.
God, I couldn't believe it.
I had to study so hard to get in here.
MRR
GRR
SO, YOU REALLY THINK THERE'S NOTHING GOING ON...
...BE-TWEEN THE CAPTAIN AND THIS MINEKO CHICK?
GRR

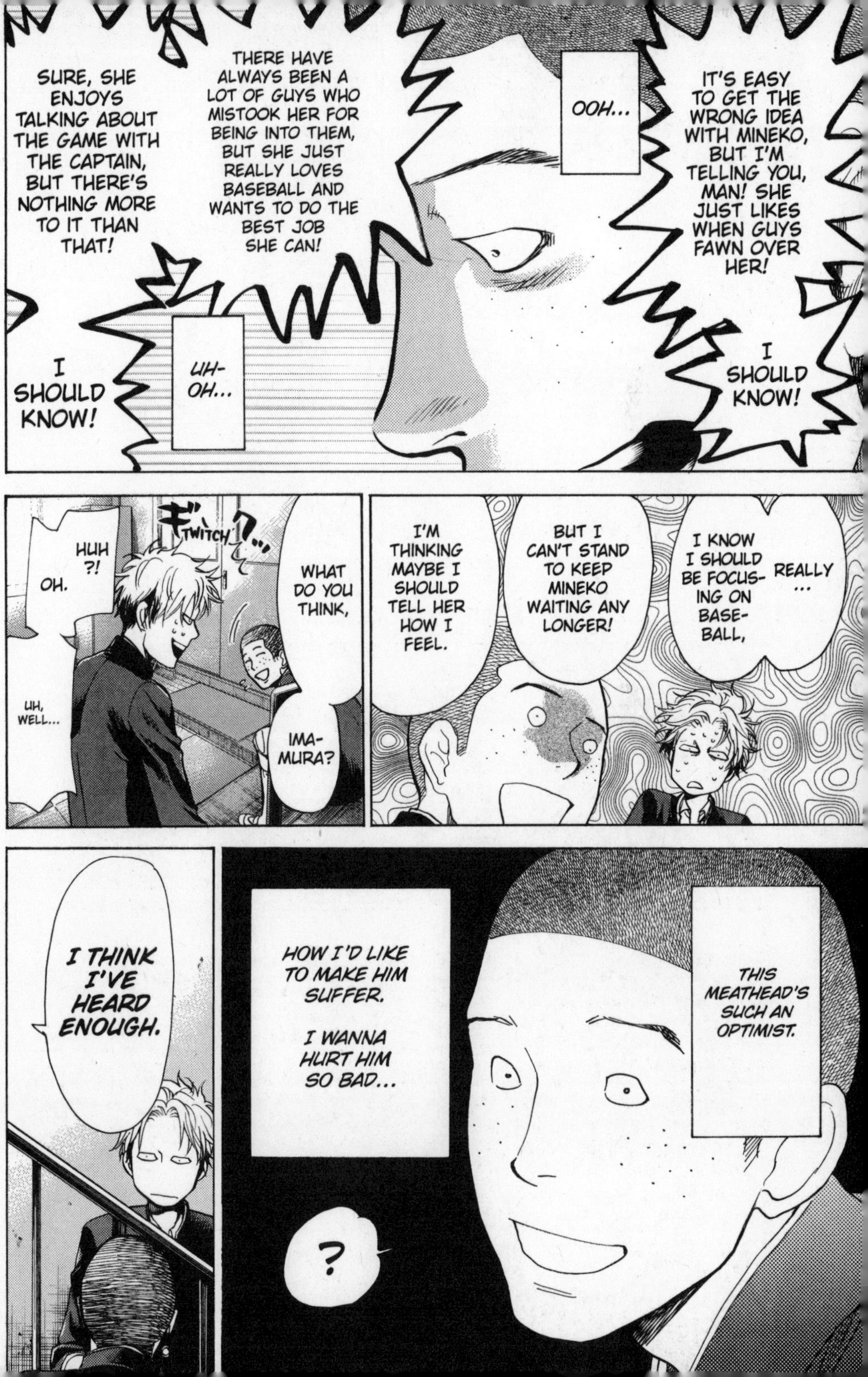
IT'S EASY TO GET THE WRONG IDEA WITH MINEKO, BUT I'M TELLING YOU, MAN! SHE JUST LIKES WHEN GUYS FAWN OVER HER!
I SHOULD KNOW!
OOH...
THERE HAVE ALWAYS BEEN A LOT OF GUYS WHO MISTOOK HER FOR BEING INTO THEM, BUT SHE JUST REALLY LOVES BASEBALL AND WANTS TO DO THE BEST JOB SHE CAN!
SURE, SHE ENJOYS TALKING ABOUT THE GAME WITH THE CAPTAIN, BUT THERE'S NOTHING MORE TO IT THAN THAT!
UH-OH...
I SHOULD KNOW!
REALLY...
I KNOW I SHOULD BE FOCUSING ON BASEBALL,
BUT I CAN'T STAND TO KEEP MINEKO WAITING ANY LONGER!
I'M THINKING MAYBE I SHOULD TELL HER HOW I FEEL.
WHAT DO YOU THINK,
IMAMURA?
TWITCH
HUH?!
OH.
UH, WELL...
THIS MEATHEAD'S SUCH AN OPTIMIST.
HOW I'D LIKE TO MAKE HIM SUFFER.
I WANNA HURT HIM SO BAD...
?
I THINK I'VE HEARD ENOUGH.

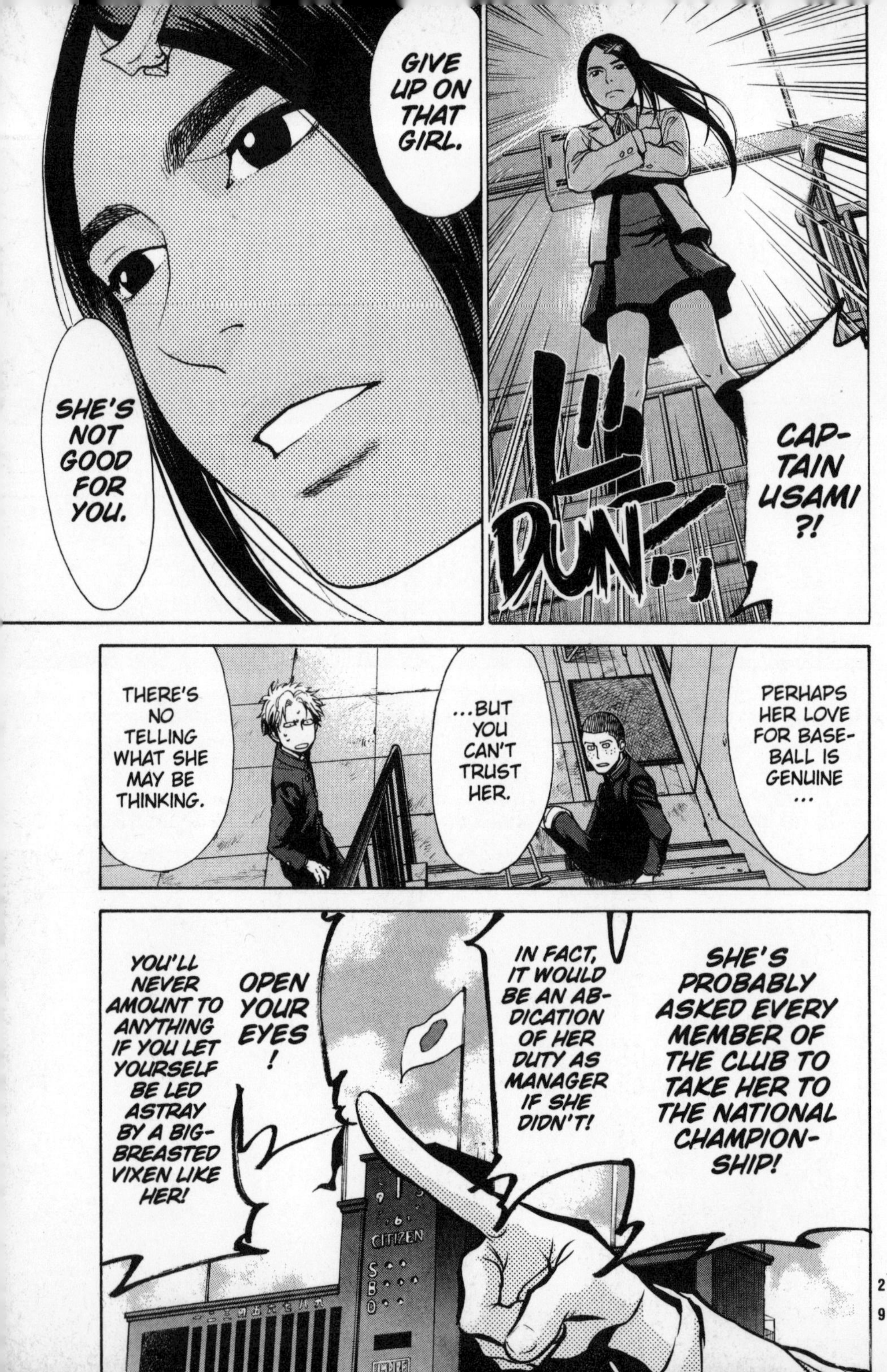
CAP-TAIN USAMI?!
DUN
GIVE UP ON THAT GIRL.
SHE'S NOT GOOD FOR YOU.
PERHAPS HER LOVE FOR BASE-BALL IS GENUINE...
...BUT YOU CAN'T TRUST HER.
THERE'S NO TELLING WHAT SHE MAY BE THINKING.
SHE'S PROBABLY ASKED EVERY MEMBER OF THE CLUB TO TAKE HER TO THE NATIONAL CHAMPION-SHIP!
IN FACT, IT WOULD BE AN AB-DICATION OF HER DUTY AS MANAGER IF SHE DIDN'T!
OPEN YOUR EYES!
YOU'LL NEVER AMOUNT TO ANYTHING IF YOU LET YOURSELF BE LED ASTRAY BY A BIG-BREASTED VIXEN LIKE HER!
CITIZEN

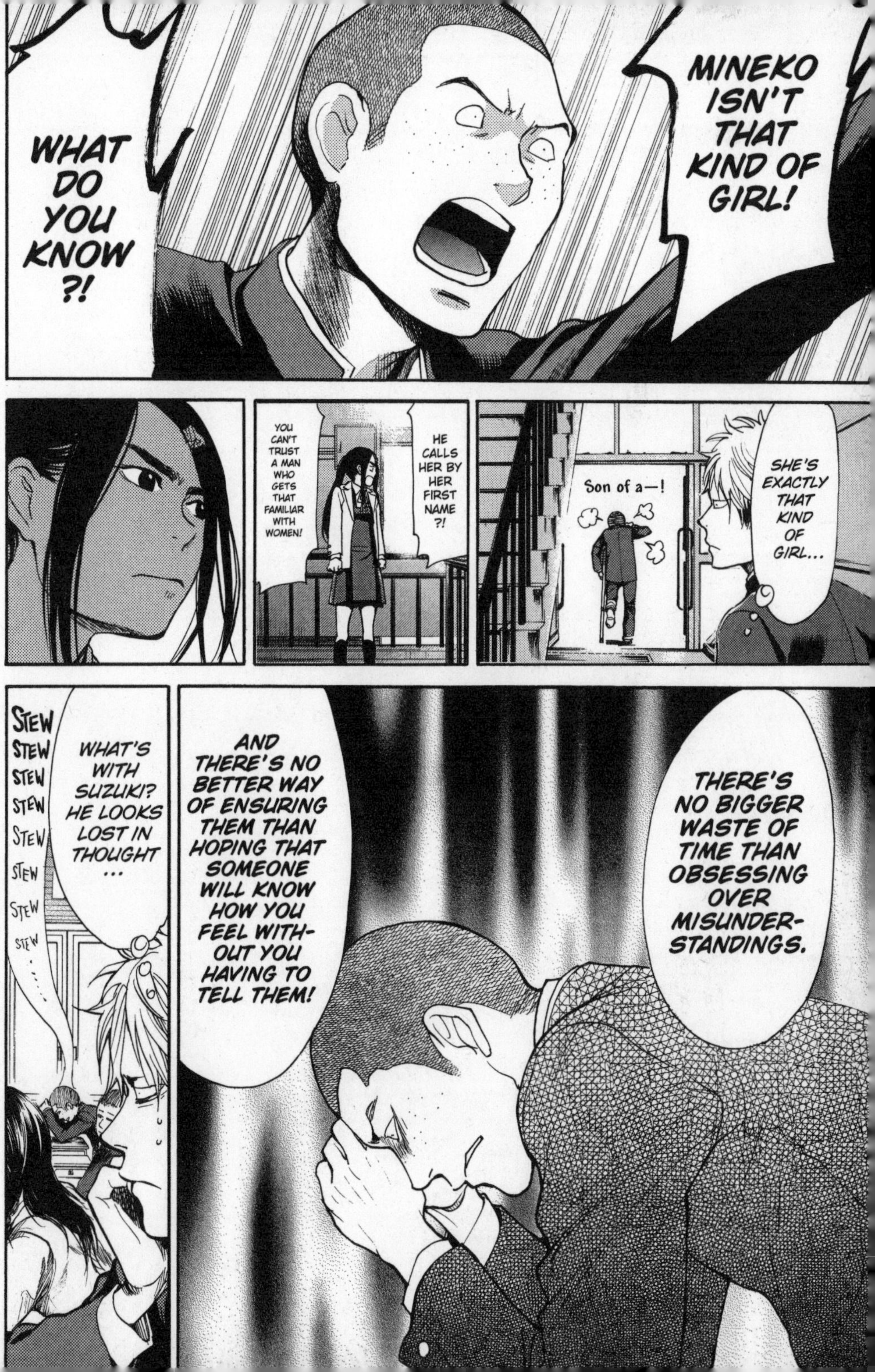
MINEKO ISN'T THAT KIND OF GIRL!
WHAT DO YOU KNOW?!
SHE'S EXACTLY THAT KIND OF GIRL...
Son of a—!
HE CALLS HER BY HER FIRST NAME?!
YOU CAN'T TRUST A MAN WHO GETS THAT FAMILIAR WITH WOMEN!
THERE'S NO BIGGER WASTE OF TIME THAN OBSESSING OVER MISUNDER-STANDINGS.
AND THERE'S NO BETTER WAY OF ENSURING THEM THAN HOPING THAT SOMEONE WILL KNOW HOW YOU FEEL WITH-OUT YOU HAVING TO TELL THEM!
WHAT'S WITH SUZUKI? HE LOOKS LOST IN THOUGHT...
STEW STEW STEW STEW STEW STEW STEW STEW

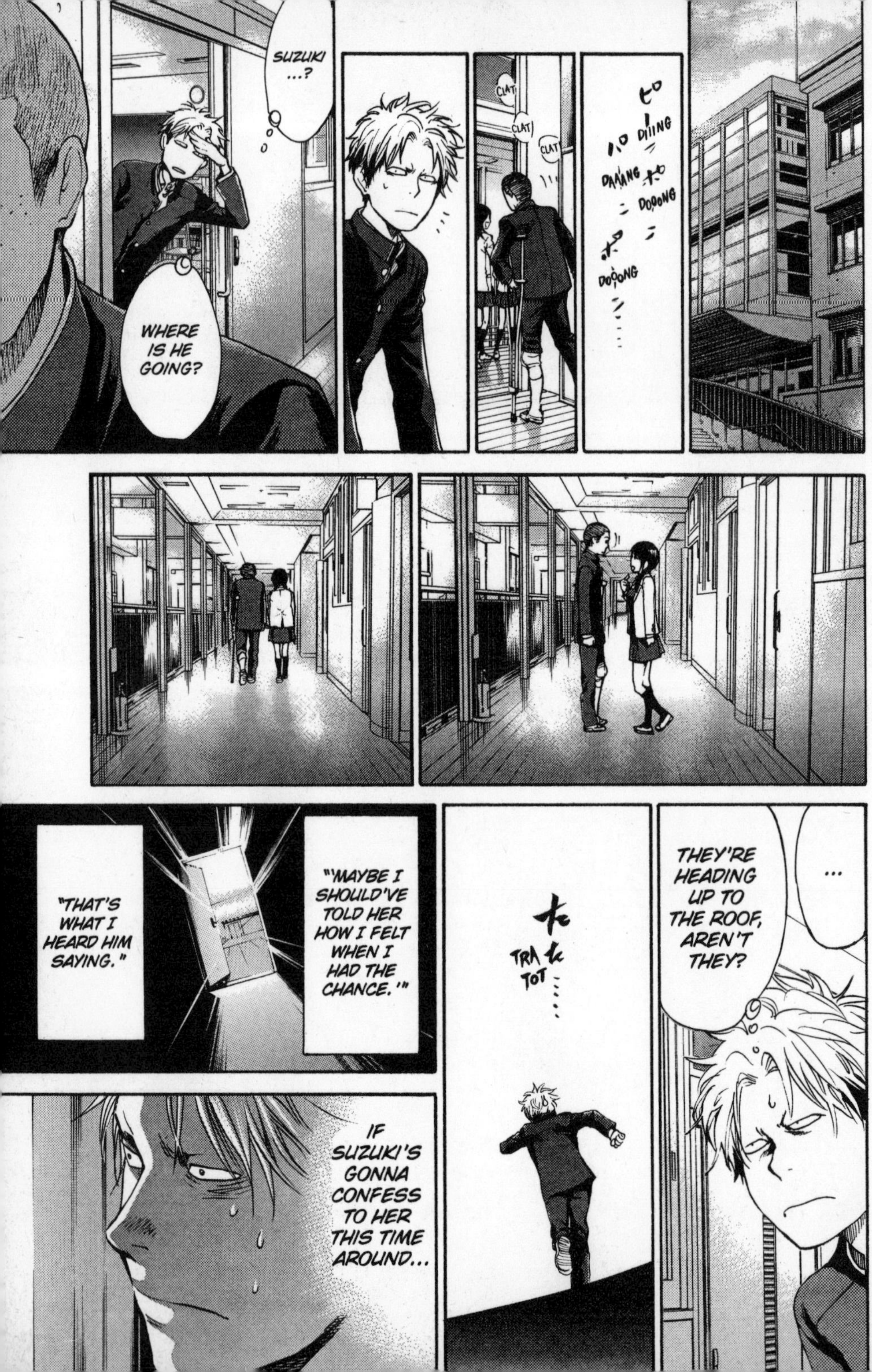

DIIING
DAAANG
DOOONG
DOOONG
CLAT
CLAT
CLAT
SUZUKI ...?
WHERE IS HE GOING?
...
THEY'RE HEADING UP TO THE ROOF, AREN'T THEY?
TRA TOT
"MAYBE I SHOULD'VE TOLD HER HOW I FELT WHEN I HAD THE CHANCE.'"
"THAT'S WHAT I HEARD HIM SAYING."
IF SUZUKI'S GONNA CONFESS TO HER THIS TIME AROUND...

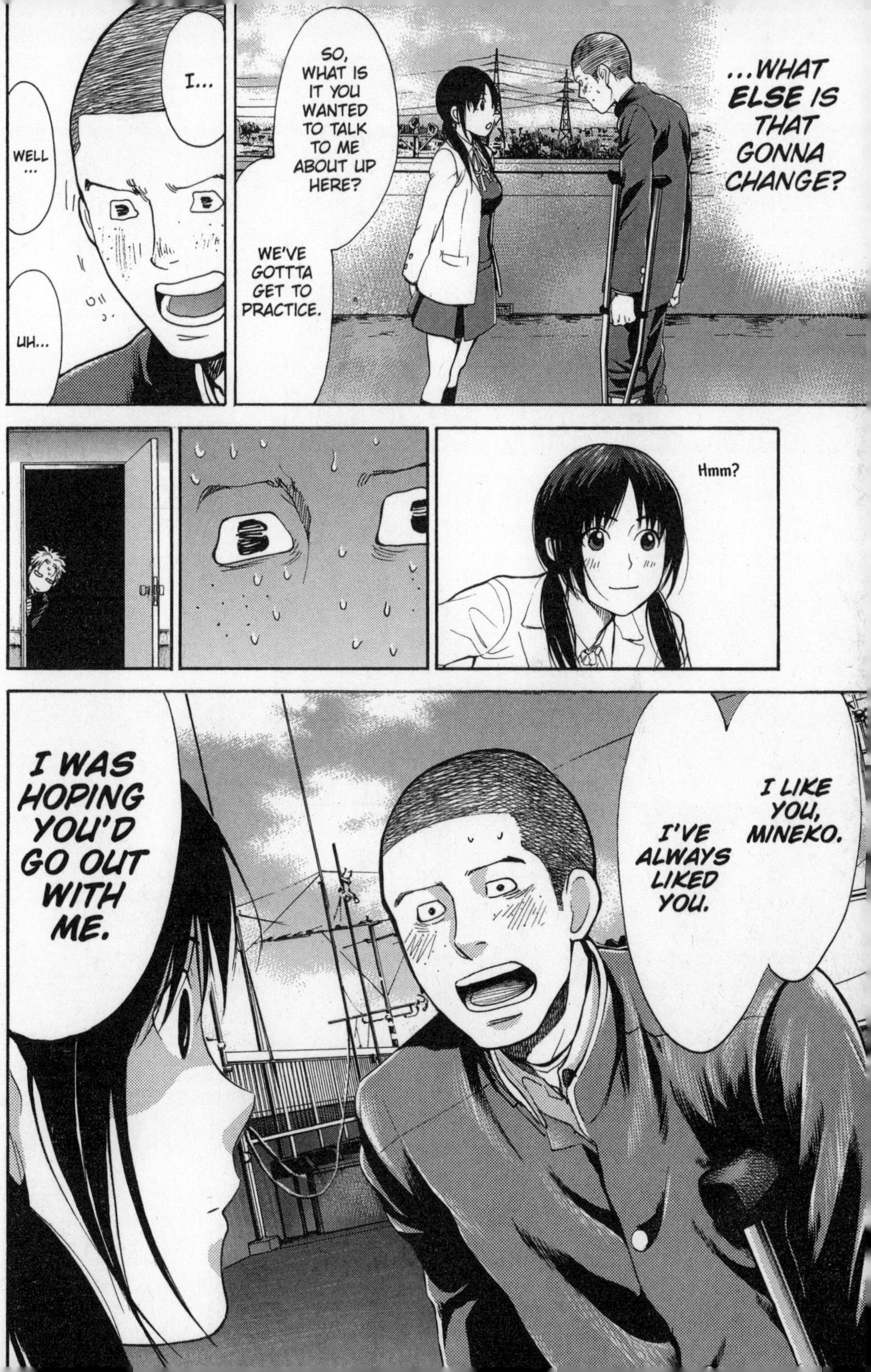
...WHAT ELSE IS THAT GONNA CHANGE?
SO, WHAT IS IT YOU WANTED TO TALK TO ME ABOUT UP HERE?
WE'VE GOTTTA GET TO PRACTICE.
I...
WELL...
UH...
Hmm?
I LIKE YOU, MINEKO.
I'VE ALWAYS LIKED YOU.
I WAS HOPING YOU'D GO OUT WITH ME.

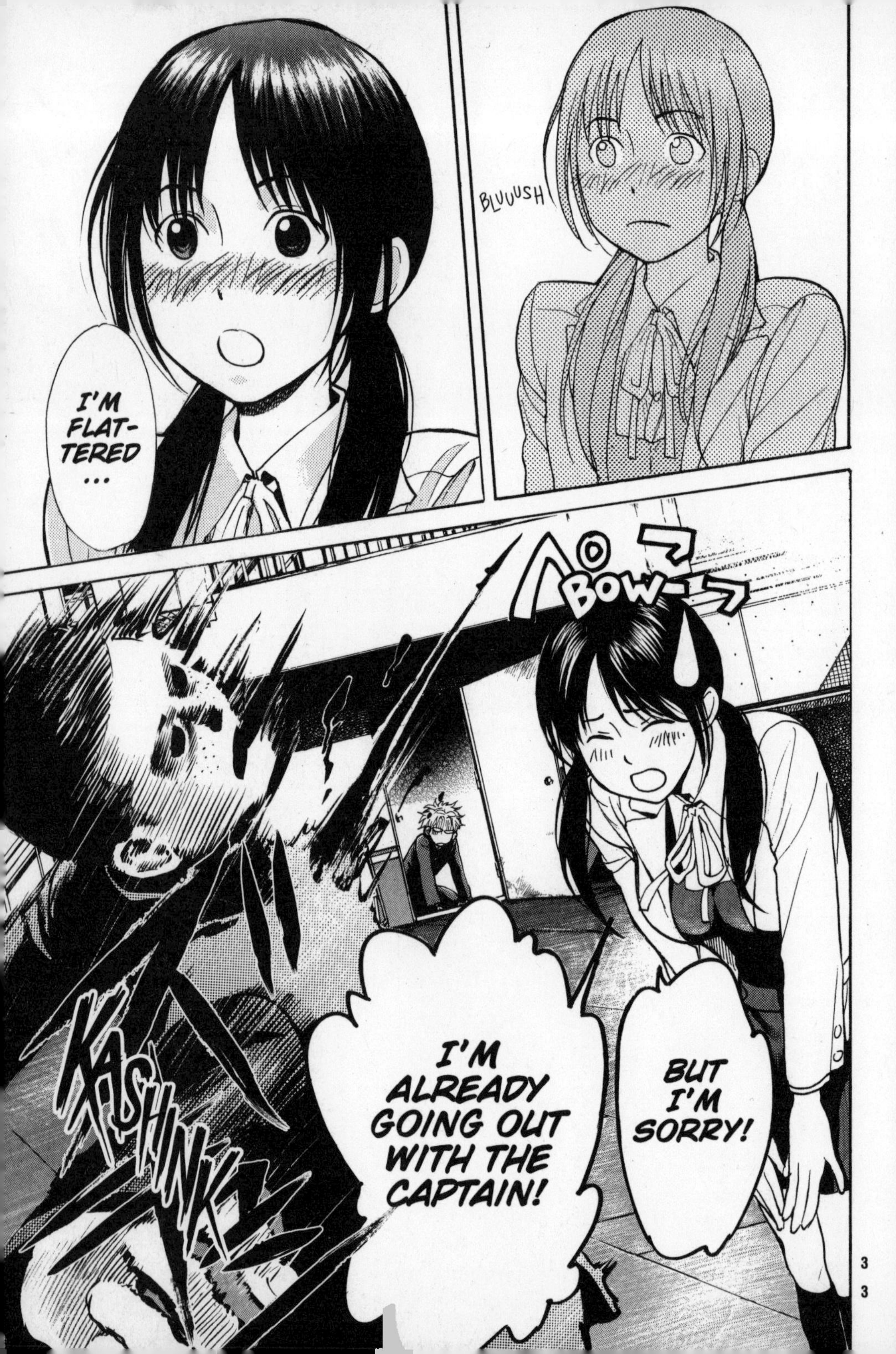
BLUUUSH
I'M FLAT-TERED ...
BOW
BUT I'M SORRY!
I'M ALREADY GOING OUT WITH THE CAPTAIN!
KASHINK

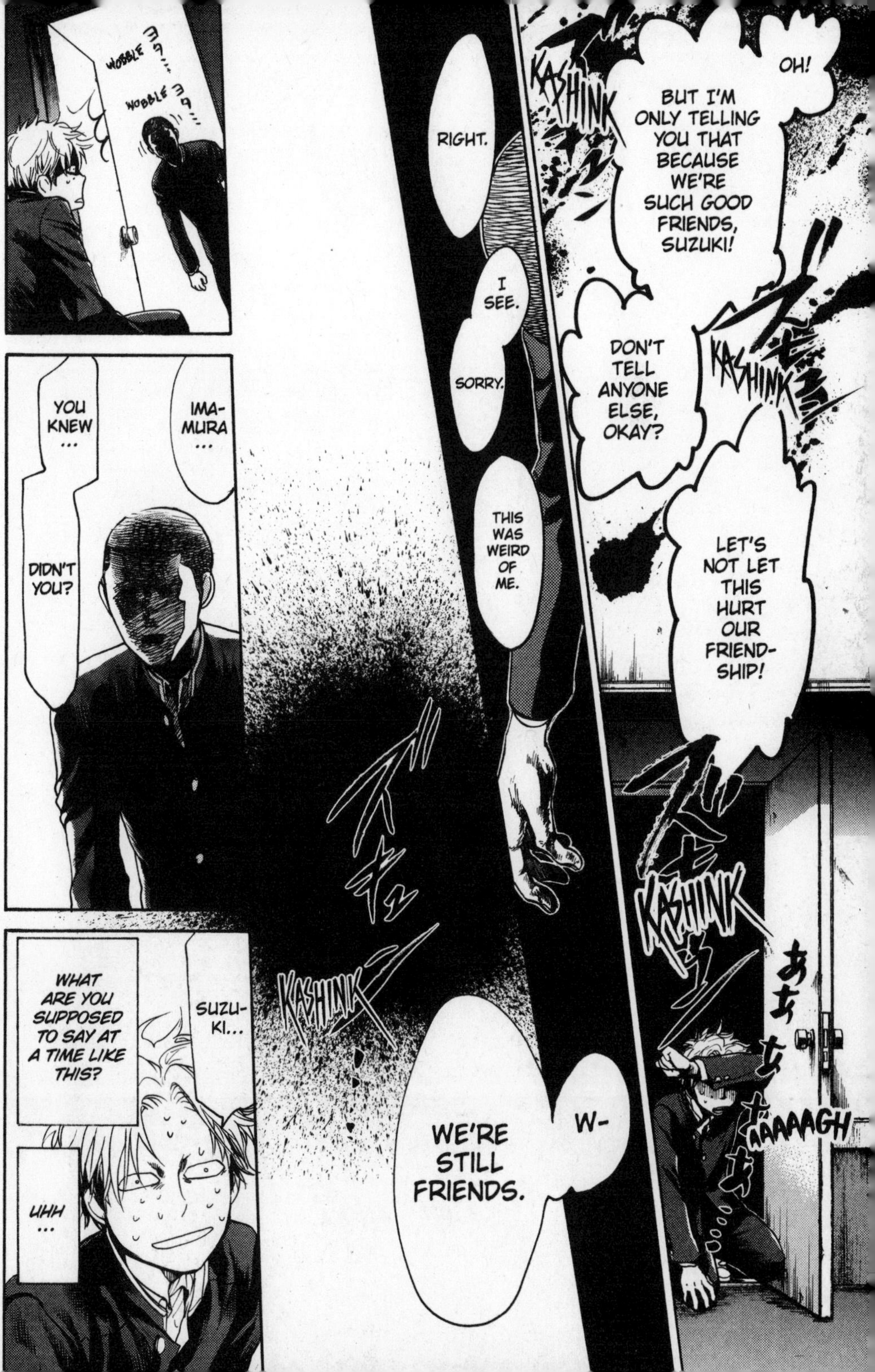
OH!
BUT I'M ONLY TELLING YOU THAT BECAUSE WE'RE SUCH GOOD FRIENDS, SUZUKI!
KASHINK
DON'T TELL ANYONE ELSE, OKAY?
KASHINK
LET'S NOT LET THIS HURT OUR FRIENDSHIP!
KASHINK
AAAAAGH
RIGHT.
I SEE.
SORRY.
THIS WAS WEIRD OF ME.
KASHINK
W-
WE'RE STILL FRIENDS.
WOBBLE
WOBBLE
IMA-MURA...
YOU KNEW... DIDN'T YOU?
SUZU-KI...
WHAT ARE YOU SUPPOSED TO SAY AT A TIME LIKE THIS?
UHH...

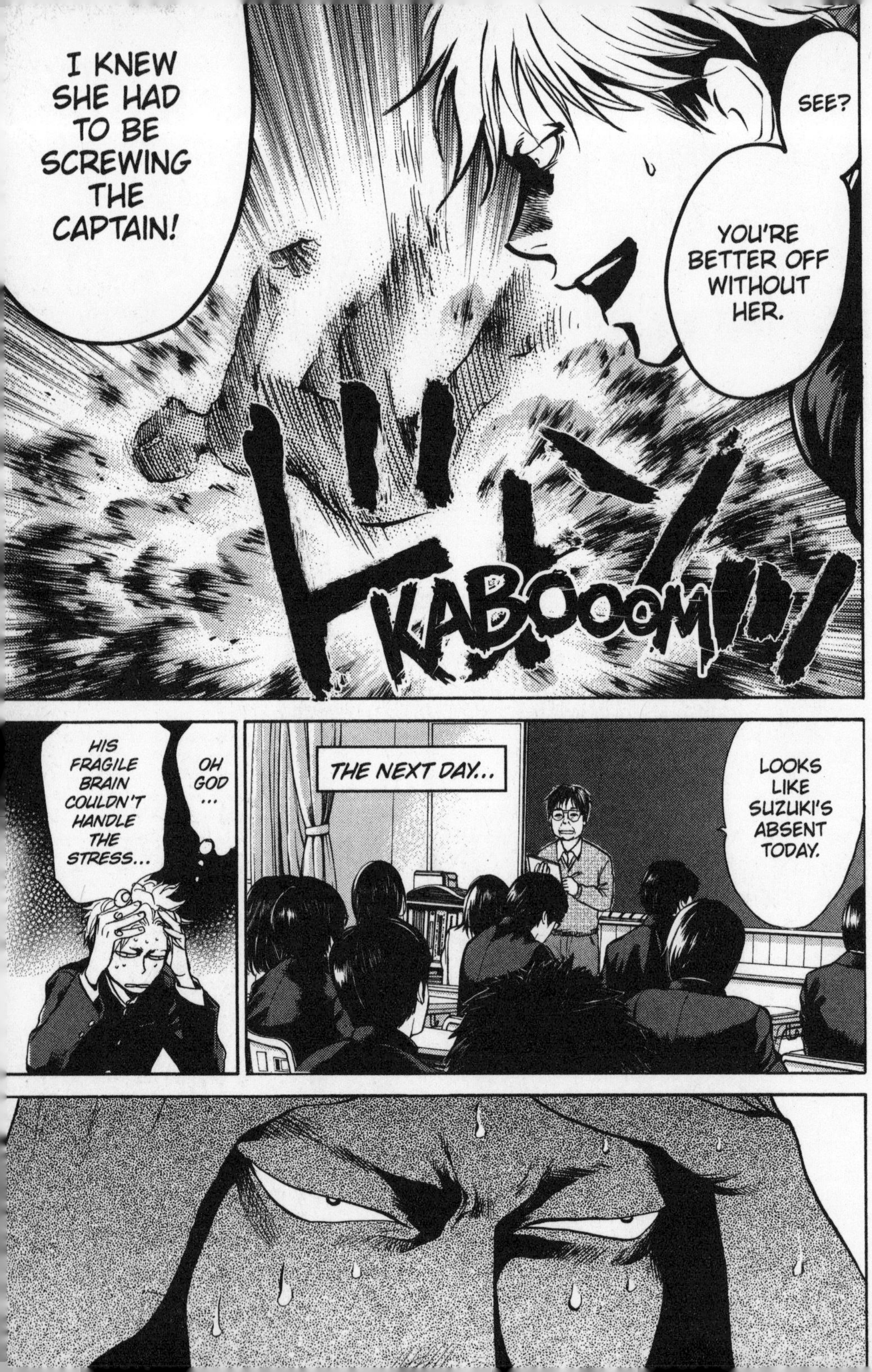
SEE?
YOU'RE BETTER OFF WITHOUT HER.
I KNEW SHE HAD TO BE SCREWING THE CAPTAIN!
KABOOOM!!
THE NEXT DAY...
LOOKS LIKE SUZUKI'S ABSENT TODAY.
OH GOD ...
HIS FRAGILE BRAIN COULDN'T HANDLE THE STRESS...

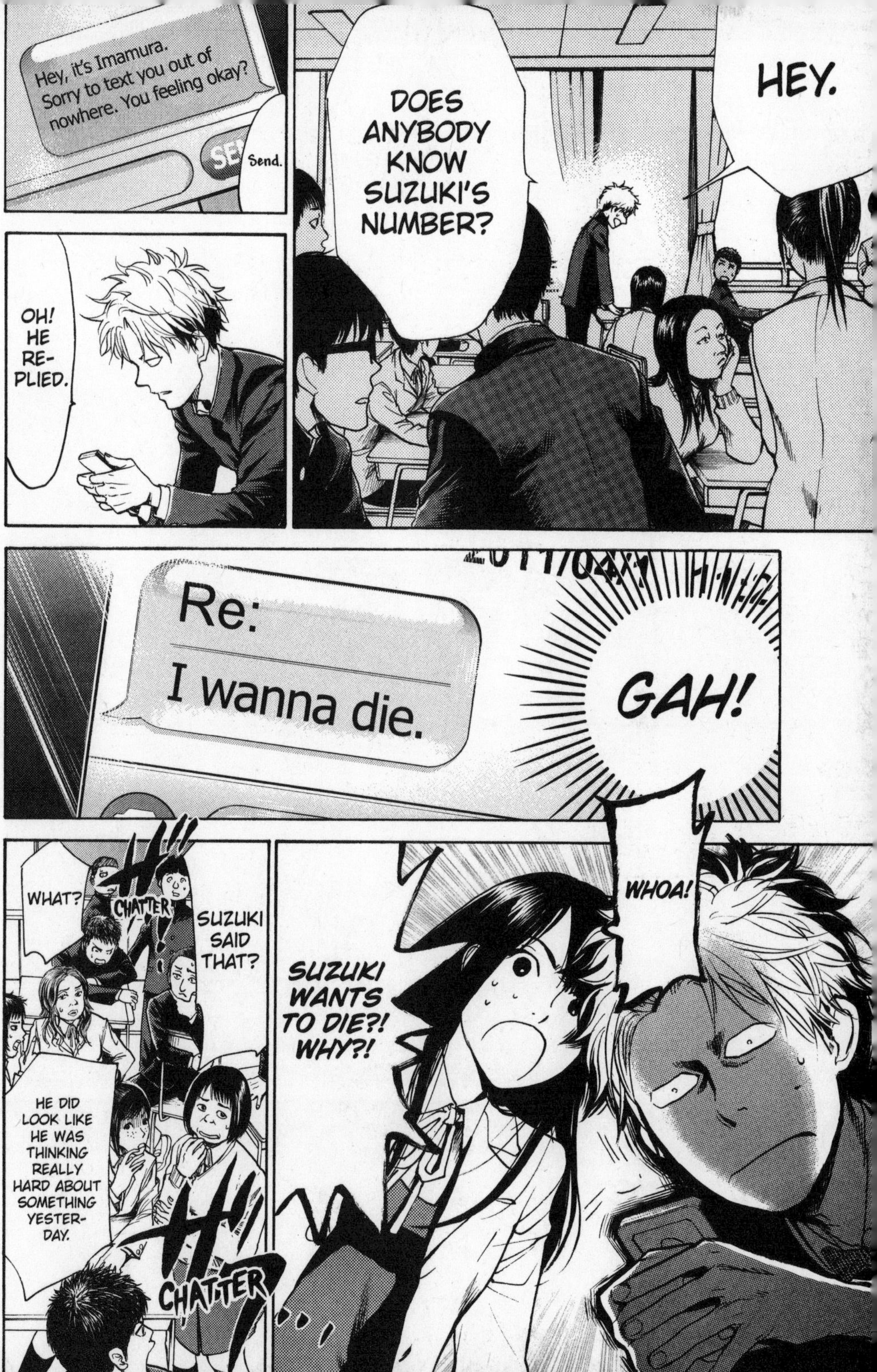
HEY.
DOES ANYBODY KNOW SUZUKI'S NUMBER?
Hey, it's Imamura. Sorry to text you out of nowhere. You feeling okay?
Send.
OH! HE RE-PLIED.
Re:
I wanna die.
GAH!
WHOA!
SUZUKI WANTS TO DIE?! WHY?!
SUZUKI SAID THAT?
CHATTER
WHAT?
HE DID LOOK LIKE HE WAS THINKING REALLY HARD ABOUT SOMETHING YESTER-DAY.
CHATTER

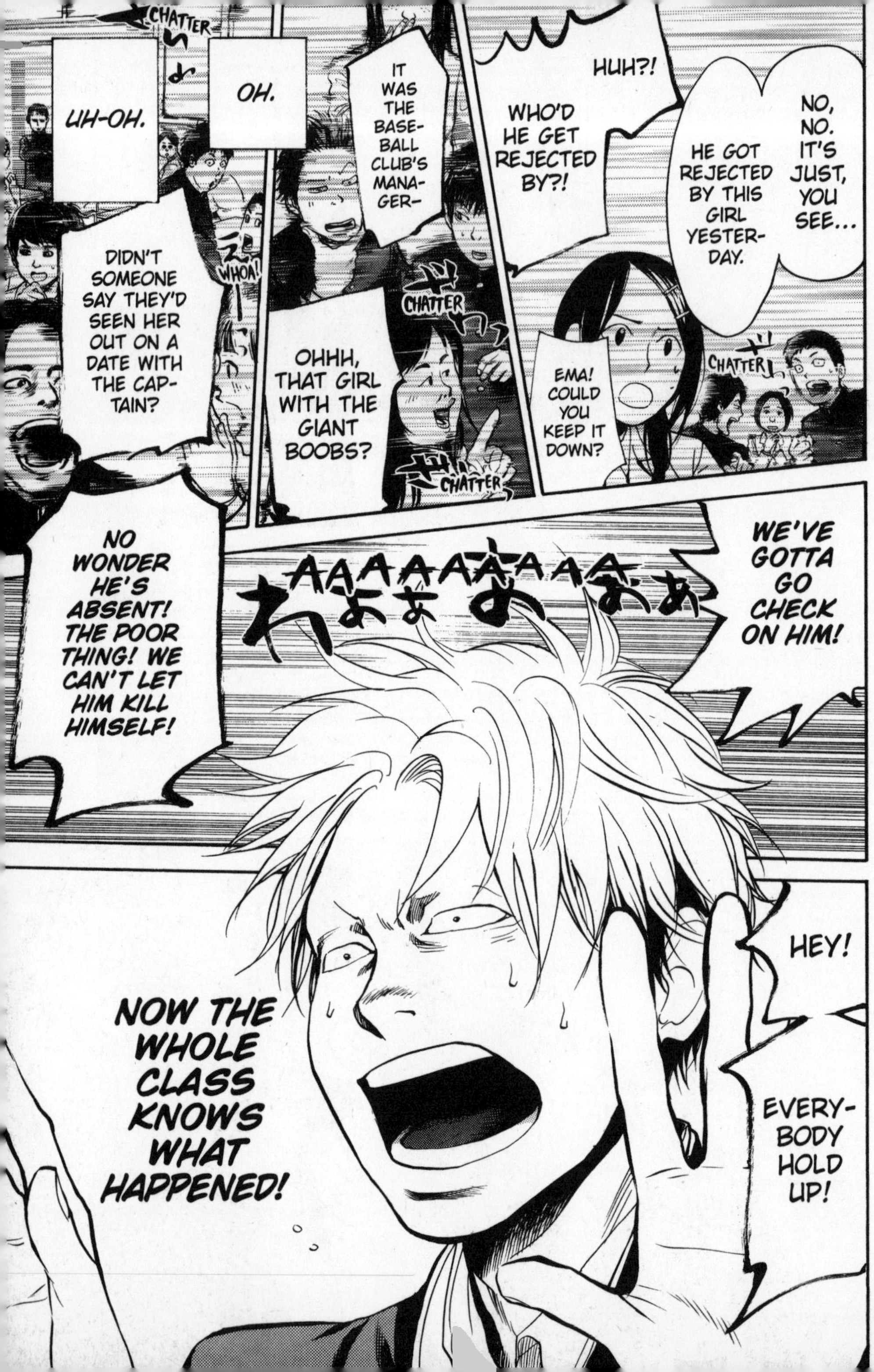

NO, NO. IT'S JUST, YOU SEE...
HUH?!
HE GOT REJECTED BY THIS GIRL YESTERDAY.
WHO'D HE GET REJECTED BY?!
CHATTER
EMA! COULD YOU KEEP IT DOWN?
IT WAS THE BASEBALL CLUB'S MANAGER-
CHATTER
WHOA!
OHHH, THAT GIRL WITH THE GIANT BOOBS?
CHATTER
CHATTER
OH.
UH-OH.
DIDN'T SOMEONE SAY THEY'D SEEN HER OUT ON A DATE WITH THE CAPTAIN?
WE'VE GOTTA GO CHECK ON HIM!
AAAAAAAAA
NO WONDER HE'S ABSENT! THE POOR THING! WE CAN'T LET HIM KILL HIMSELF!
HEY!
EVERYBODY HOLD UP!
NOW THE WHOLE CLASS KNOWS WHAT HAPPENED!

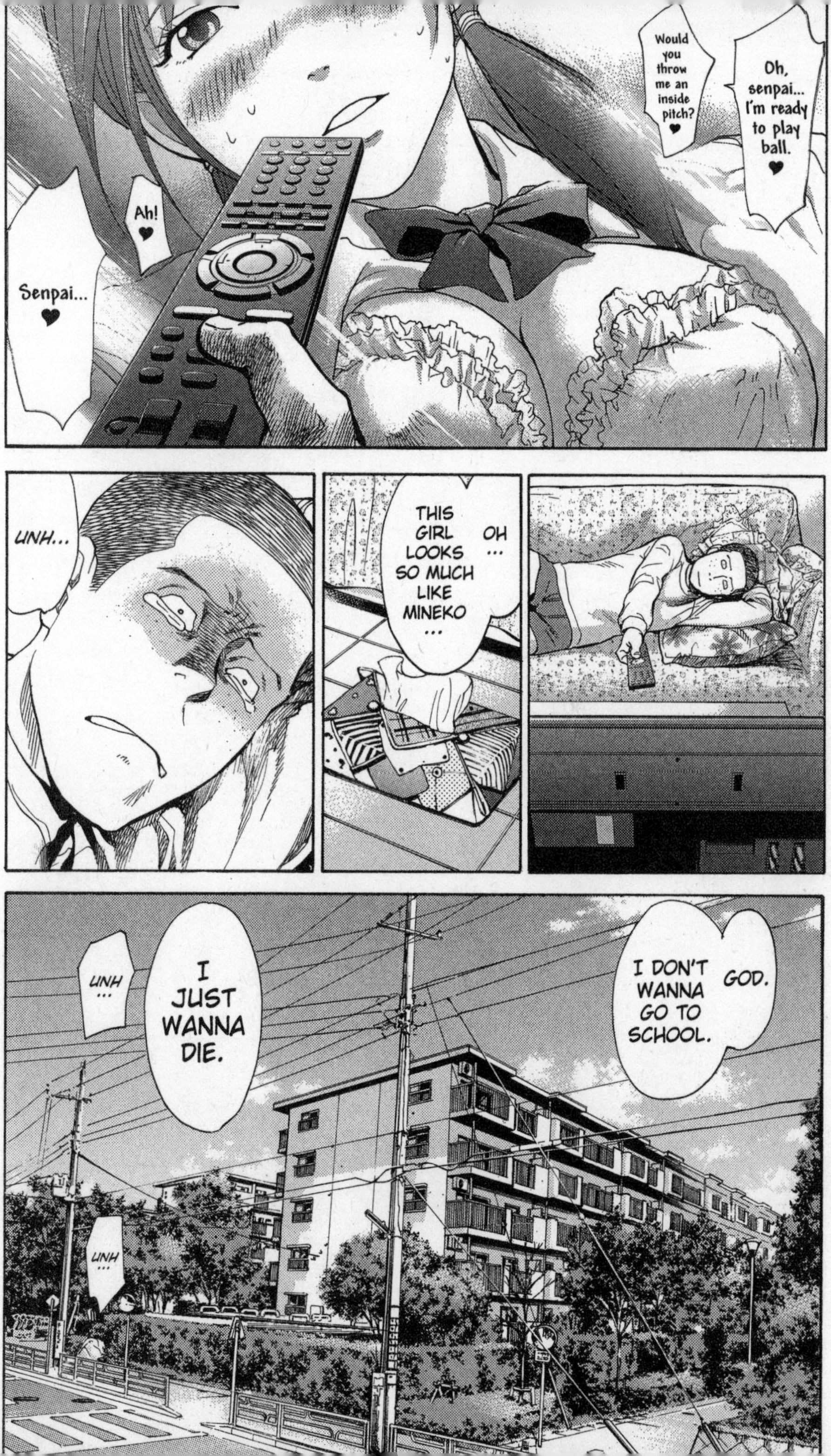
Oh, senpai... I'm ready to play ball. ♥
Would you throw me an inside pitch? ♥
Ah! ♥
Senpai... ♥
OH ...
THIS GIRL LOOKS SO MUCH LIKE MINEKO ...
UNH...
GOD.
I DON'T WANNA GO TO SCHOOL.
I JUST WANNA DIE.
UNH ...
UNH

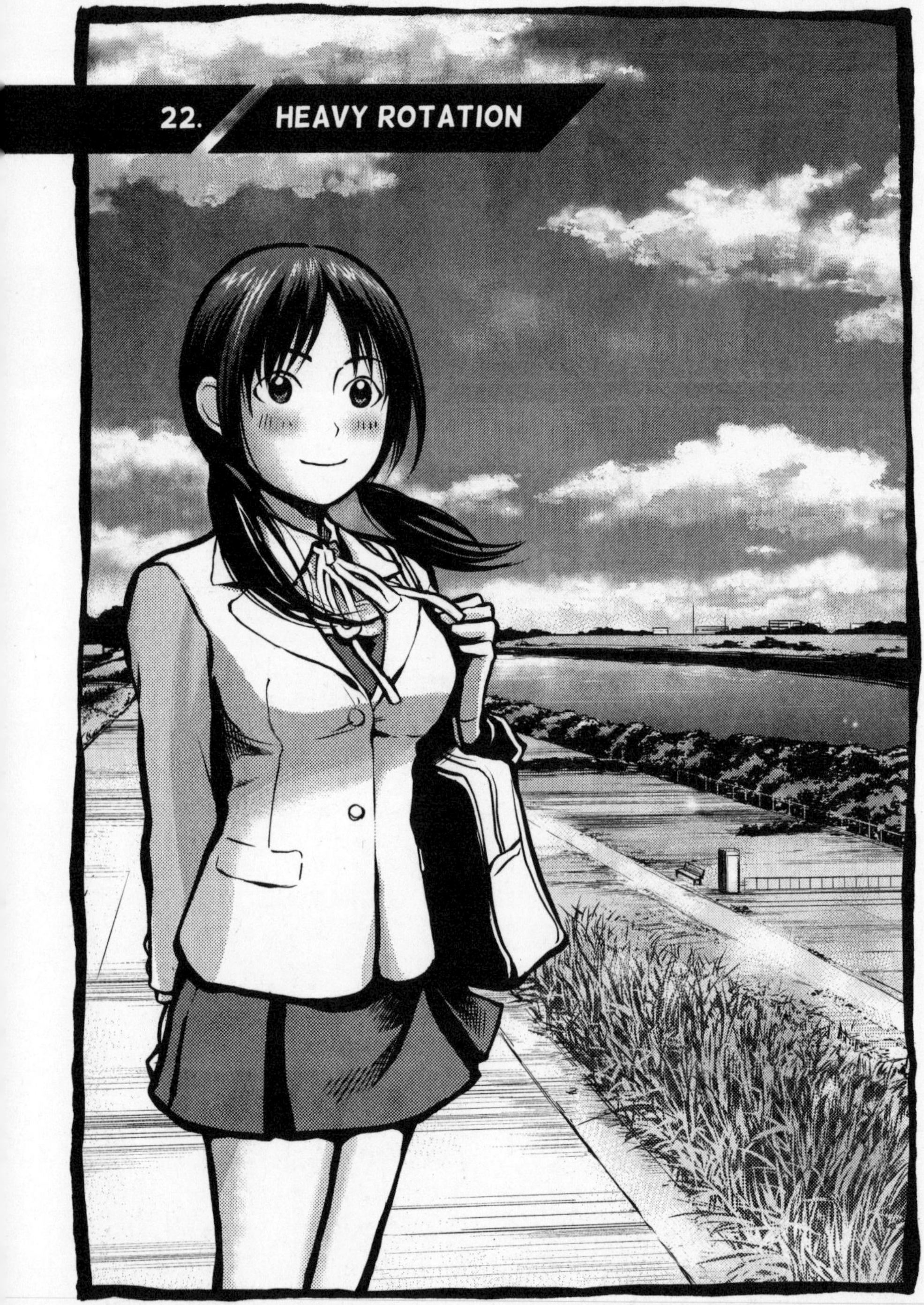
22.
HEAVY ROTATION

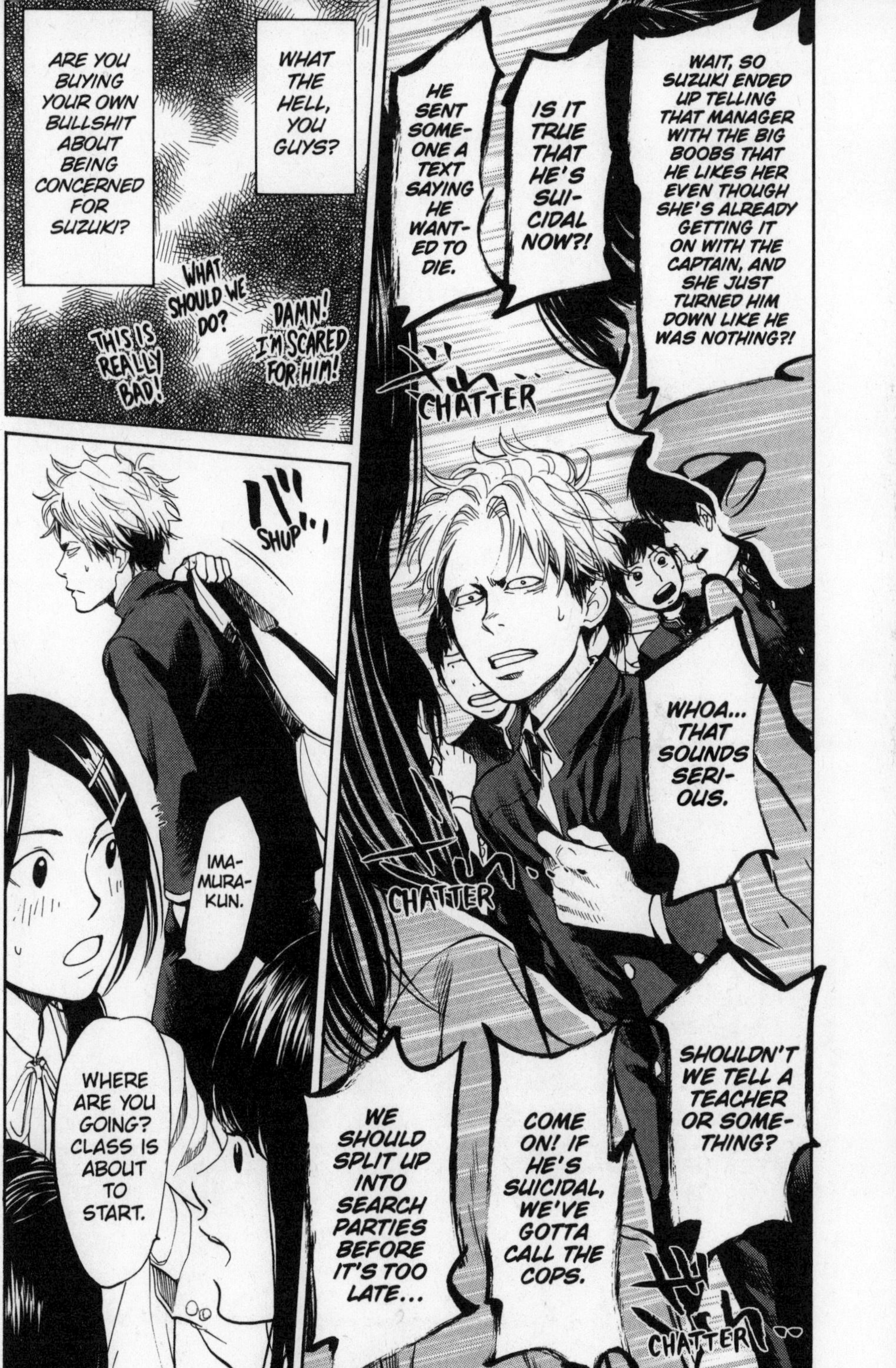
WAIT, SO SUZUKI ENDED UP TELLING THAT MANAGER WITH THE BIG BOOBS THAT HE LIKES HER EVEN THOUGH SHE'S ALREADY GETTING IT ON WITH THE CAPTAIN, AND SHE JUST TURNED HIM DOWN LIKE HE WAS NOTHING?!
IS IT TRUE THAT HE'S SUICIDAL NOW?!
HE SENT SOMEONE A TEXT SAYING HE WANTED TO DIE.
CHATTER
WHOA... THAT SOUNDS SERIOUS.
CHATTER
SHOULDN'T WE TELL A TEACHER OR SOMETHING?
COME ON! IF HE'S SUICIDAL, WE'VE GOTTA CALL THE COPS.
WE SHOULD SPLIT UP INTO SEARCH PARTIES BEFORE IT'S TOO LATE...
CHATTER
WHAT THE HELL, YOU GUYS?
ARE YOU BUYING YOUR OWN BULLSHIT ABOUT BEING CONCERNED FOR SUZUKI?
DAMN! I'M SCARED FOR HIM!
WHAT SHOULD WE DO?
THIS IS REALLY BAD!
SHUP
IMAMURA-KUN.
WHERE ARE YOU GOING? CLASS IS ABOUT TO START.

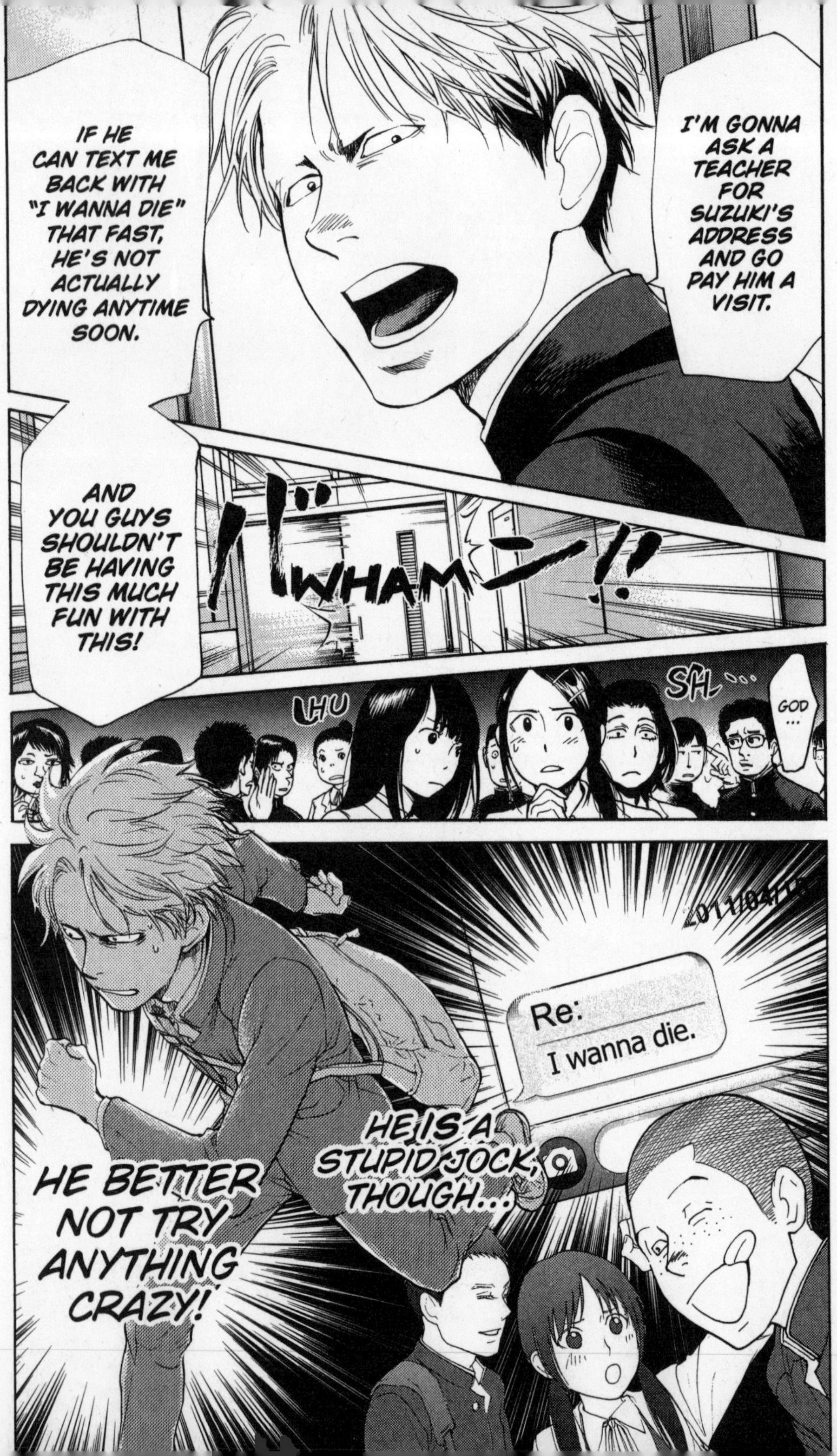
I'M GONNA ASK A TEACHER FOR SUZUKI'S ADDRESS AND GO PAY HIM A VISIT.
IF HE CAN TEXT ME BACK WITH "I WANNA DIE" THAT FAST, HE'S NOT ACTUALLY DYING ANYTIME SOON.
WHAM!!
AND YOU GUYS SHOULDN'T BE HAVING THIS MUCH FUN WITH THIS!
SH...
GOD...
Re:
I wanna die.
HE IS A STUPID JOCK, THOUGH...
HE BETTER NOT TRY ANYTHING CRAZY!

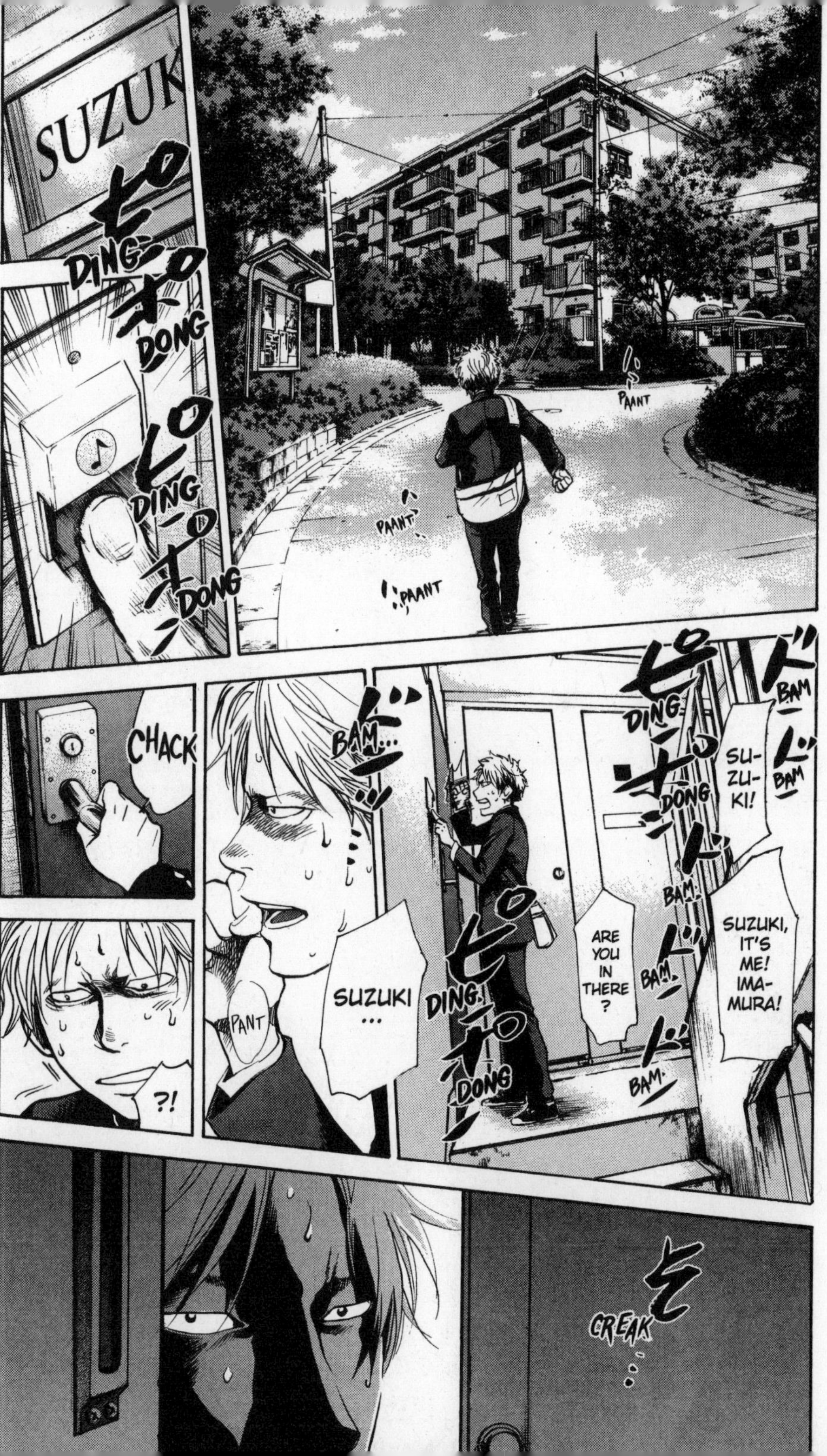
PAANT
PAANT
PAANT
SUZUK
DING DONG
DING DONG
BAM BAM
DING DONG
SU-ZU-KI!
SUZUKI, IT'S ME! IMA-MURA!
BAM BAM
ARE YOU IN THERE?
BAM
DING DONG
BAM...
SUZUKI ...
PANT
CHACK
?!
CREAK

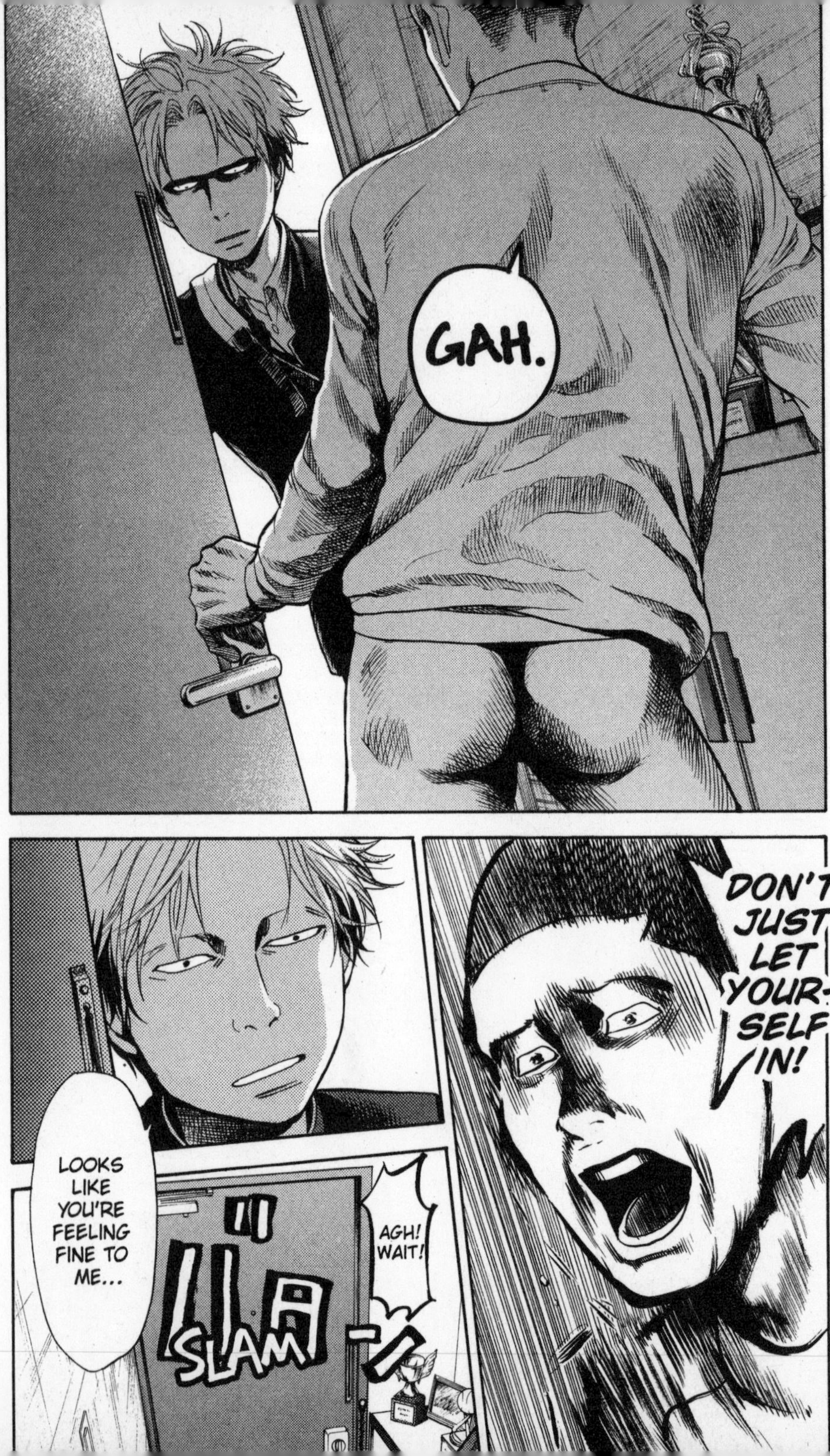
GAH.
DON'T JUST LET YOUR-SELF IN!
LOOKS LIKE YOU'RE FEELING FINE TO ME...
AGH! WAIT!
SLAM

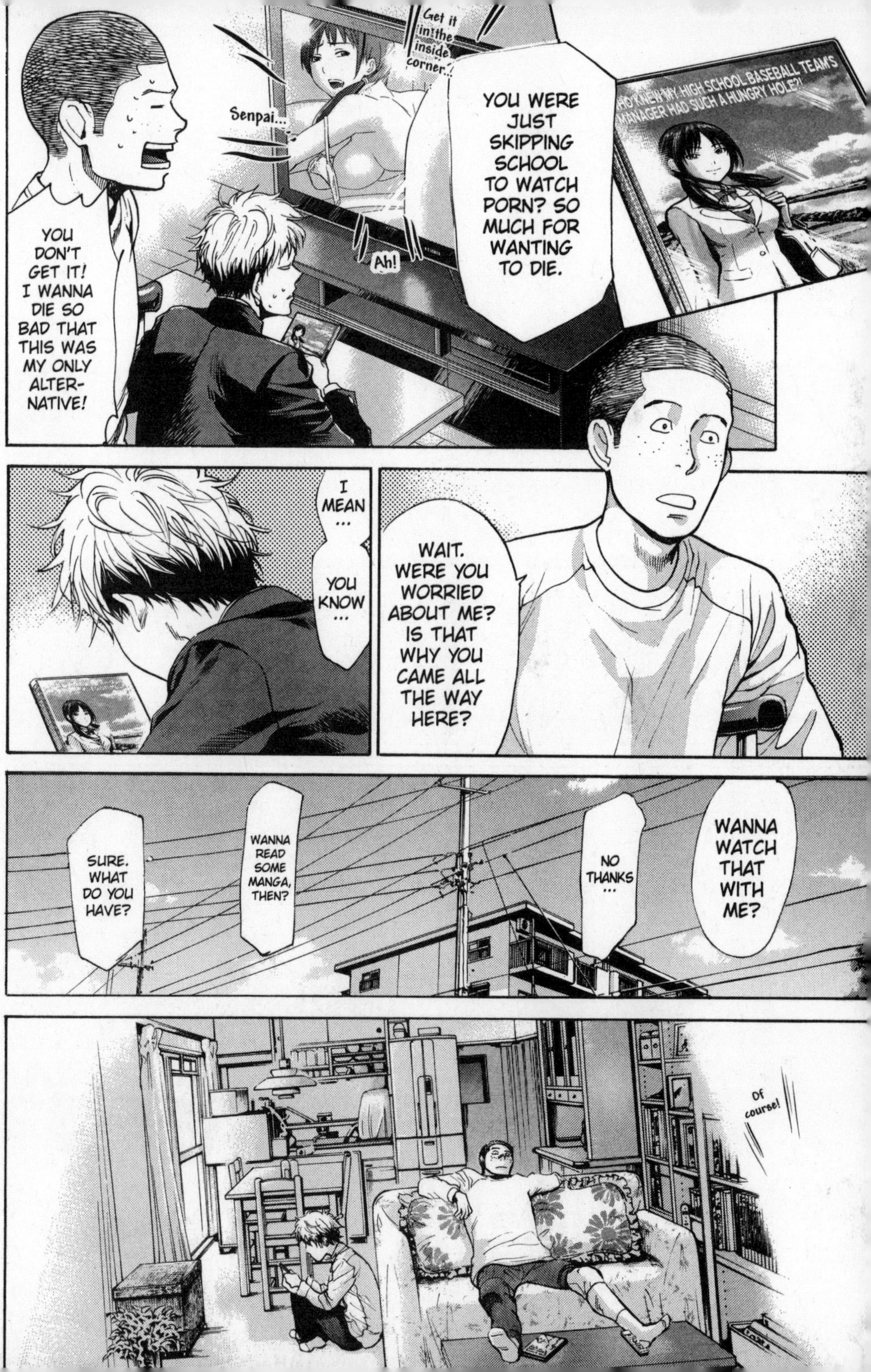
WHO KNEW MY HIGH SCHOOL BASEBALL TEAM'S MANAGER HAD SUCH A HUNGRY HOLE?!
YOU WERE JUST SKIPPING SCHOOL TO WATCH PORN? SO MUCH FOR WANTING TO DIE.
Get it in the inside corner..!
Senpai...
Ah!
YOU DON'T GET IT! I WANNA DIE SO BAD THAT THIS WAS MY ONLY ALTER-NATIVE!
WAIT. WERE YOU WORRIED ABOUT ME? IS THAT WHY YOU CAME ALL THE WAY HERE?
I MEAN ...
YOU KNOW ...
WANNA WATCH THAT WITH ME?
NO THANKS ...
WANNA READ SOME MANGA, THEN?
SURE. WHAT DO YOU HAVE?
Of course!

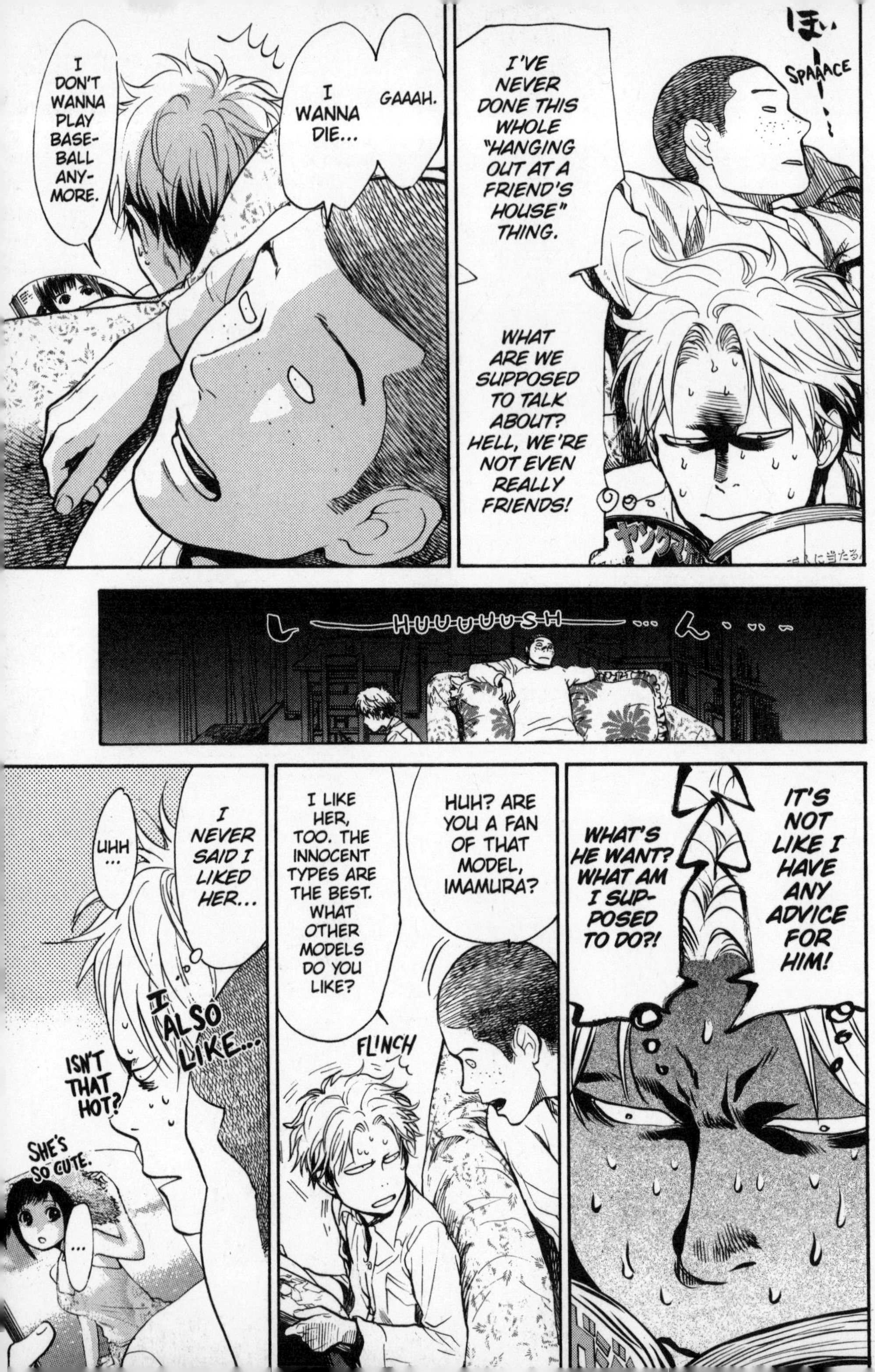
SPAAACE
I'VE NEVER DONE THIS WHOLE "HANGING OUT AT A FRIEND'S HOUSE" THING.
WHAT ARE WE SUPPOSED TO TALK ABOUT? HELL, WE'RE NOT EVEN REALLY FRIENDS!
GAAAH.
I WANNA DIE...
I DON'T WANNA PLAY BASEBALL ANYMORE.
HUUUUUUSH
IT'S NOT LIKE I HAVE ANY ADVICE FOR HIM!
WHAT'S HE WANT? WHAT AM I SUPPOSED TO DO?!
HUH? ARE YOU A FAN OF THAT MODEL, IMAMURA?
I LIKE HER, TOO. THE INNOCENT TYPES ARE THE BEST. WHAT OTHER MODELS DO YOU LIKE?
FLINCH
I NEVER SAID I LIKED HER...
UHH ...
I ALSO LIKE...
ISN'T THAT HOT?
SHE'S SO CUTE.
...

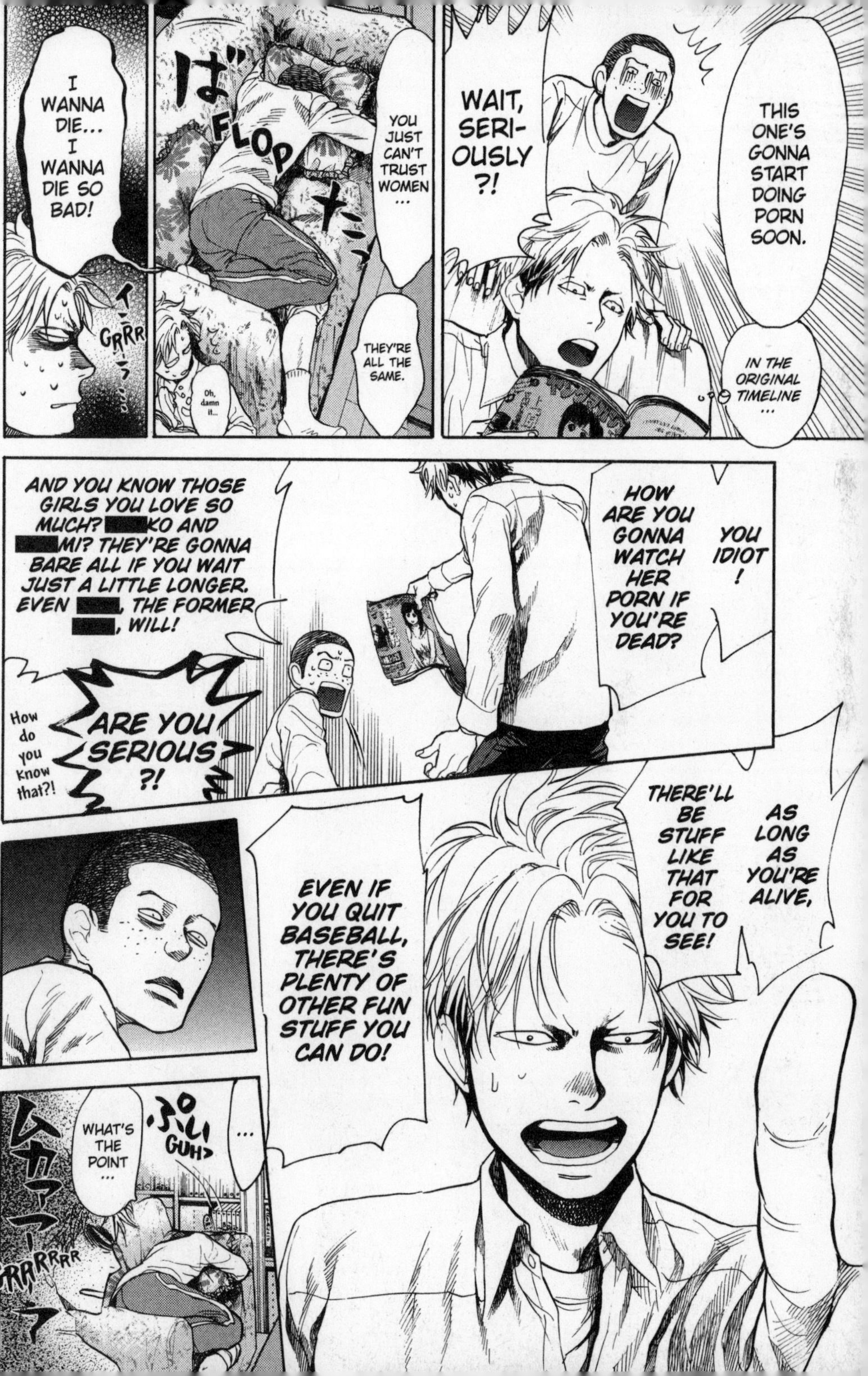
THIS ONE'S GONNA START DOING PORN SOON.
IN THE ORIGINAL TIMELINE ...
WAIT, SERIOUSLY?!
FLOP
YOU JUST CAN'T TRUST WOMEN ...
THEY'RE ALL THE SAME.
Oh, damn it...
I WANNA DIE... I WANNA DIE SO BAD!
GRRR
YOU IDIOT!
HOW ARE YOU GONNA WATCH HER PORN IF YOU'RE DEAD?
AND YOU KNOW THOSE GIRLS YOU LOVE SO MUCH? [redacted]KO AND [redacted]MI? THEY'RE GONNA BARE ALL IF YOU WAIT JUST A LITTLE LONGER. EVEN [redacted], THE FORMER [redacted], WILL!
ARE YOU SERIOUS?!
How do you know that?!
AS LONG AS YOU'RE ALIVE,
THERE'LL BE STUFF LIKE THAT FOR YOU TO SEE!
EVEN IF YOU QUIT BASEBALL, THERE'S PLENTY OF OTHER FUN STUFF YOU CAN DO!
...
GUH
WHAT'S THE POINT ...
GRRRRRR

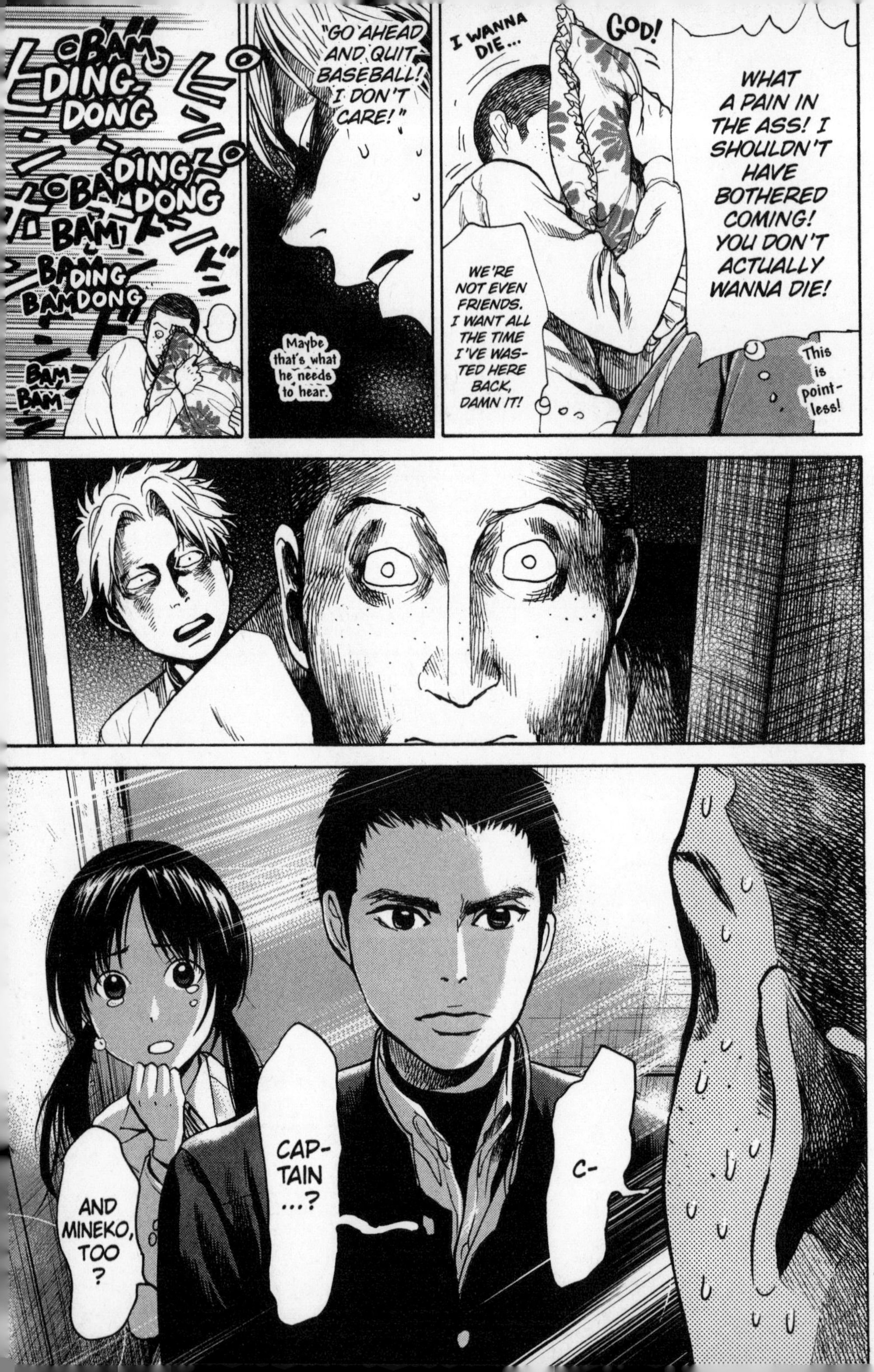
WHAT A PAIN IN THE ASS! I SHOULDN'T HAVE BOTHERED COMING! YOU DON'T ACTUALLY WANNA DIE!
GOD!
I WANNA DIE...
This is pointless!
WE'RE NOT EVEN FRIENDS. I WANT ALL THE TIME I'VE WASTED HERE BACK, DAMN IT!
"GO AHEAD AND QUIT BASEBALL! I DON'T CARE!"
Maybe that's what he needs to hear.
BAM DING DONG
DING DONG
BAM
BAM
BAM DING BAM DONG
BAM BAM
C-
CAPTAIN ...?
AND MINEKO, TOO ?

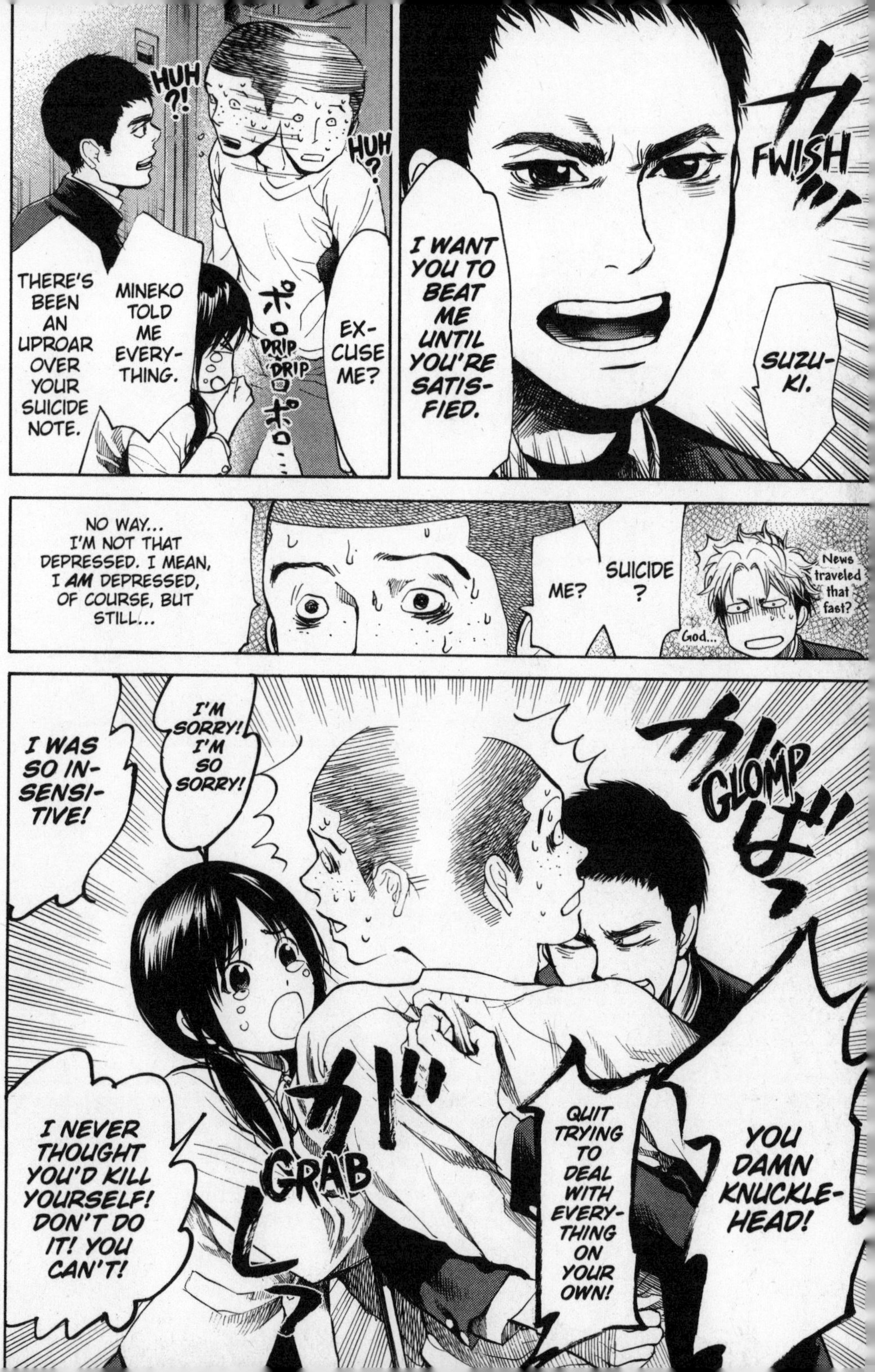
FWISH
SUZUKI.
I WANT YOU TO BEAT ME UNTIL YOU'RE SATISFIED.
HUH?!
HUH?
DRIP DRIP
EXCUSE ME?
MINEKO TOLD ME EVERYTHING.
THERE'S BEEN AN UPROAR OVER YOUR SUICIDE NOTE.
News traveled that fast?
God...
SUICIDE?
ME?
NO WAY... I'M NOT THAT DEPRESSED. I MEAN, I AM DEPRESSED, OF COURSE, BUT STILL...
GLOMP
YOU DAMN KNUCKLEHEAD!
QUIT TRYING TO DEAL WITH EVERYTHING ON YOUR OWN!
I'M SORRY! I'M SO SORRY!
I WAS SO INSENSITIVE!
GRAB
I NEVER THOUGHT YOU'D KILL YOURSELF! DON'T DO IT! YOU CAN'T!

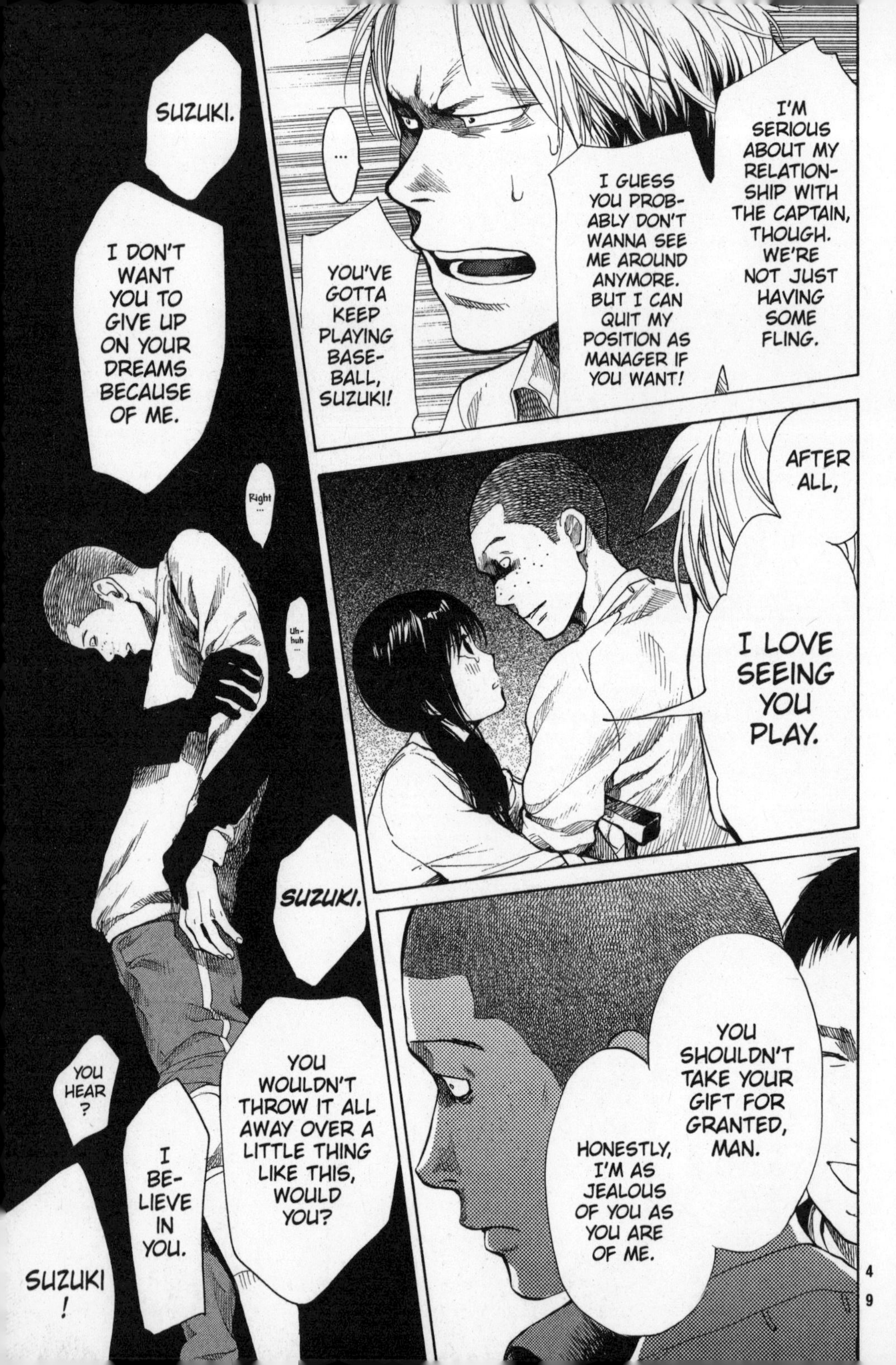
I'M SERIOUS ABOUT MY RELATIONSHIP WITH THE CAPTAIN, THOUGH. WE'RE NOT JUST HAVING SOME FLING.
I GUESS YOU PROBABLY DON'T WANNA SEE ME AROUND ANYMORE. BUT I CAN QUIT MY POSITION AS MANAGER IF YOU WANT!
YOU'VE GOTTA KEEP PLAYING BASEBALL, SUZUKI!
...
AFTER ALL,
I LOVE SEEING YOU PLAY.
YOU SHOULDN'T TAKE YOUR GIFT FOR GRANTED, MAN.
HONESTLY, I'M AS JEALOUS OF YOU AS YOU ARE OF ME.
SUZUKI.
I DON'T WANT YOU TO GIVE UP ON YOUR DREAMS BECAUSE OF ME.
Right...
Uh-huh...
SUZUKI.
YOU WOULDN'T THROW IT ALL AWAY OVER A LITTLE THING LIKE THIS, WOULD YOU?
I BELIEVE IN YOU.
YOU HEAR?
SUZUKI!

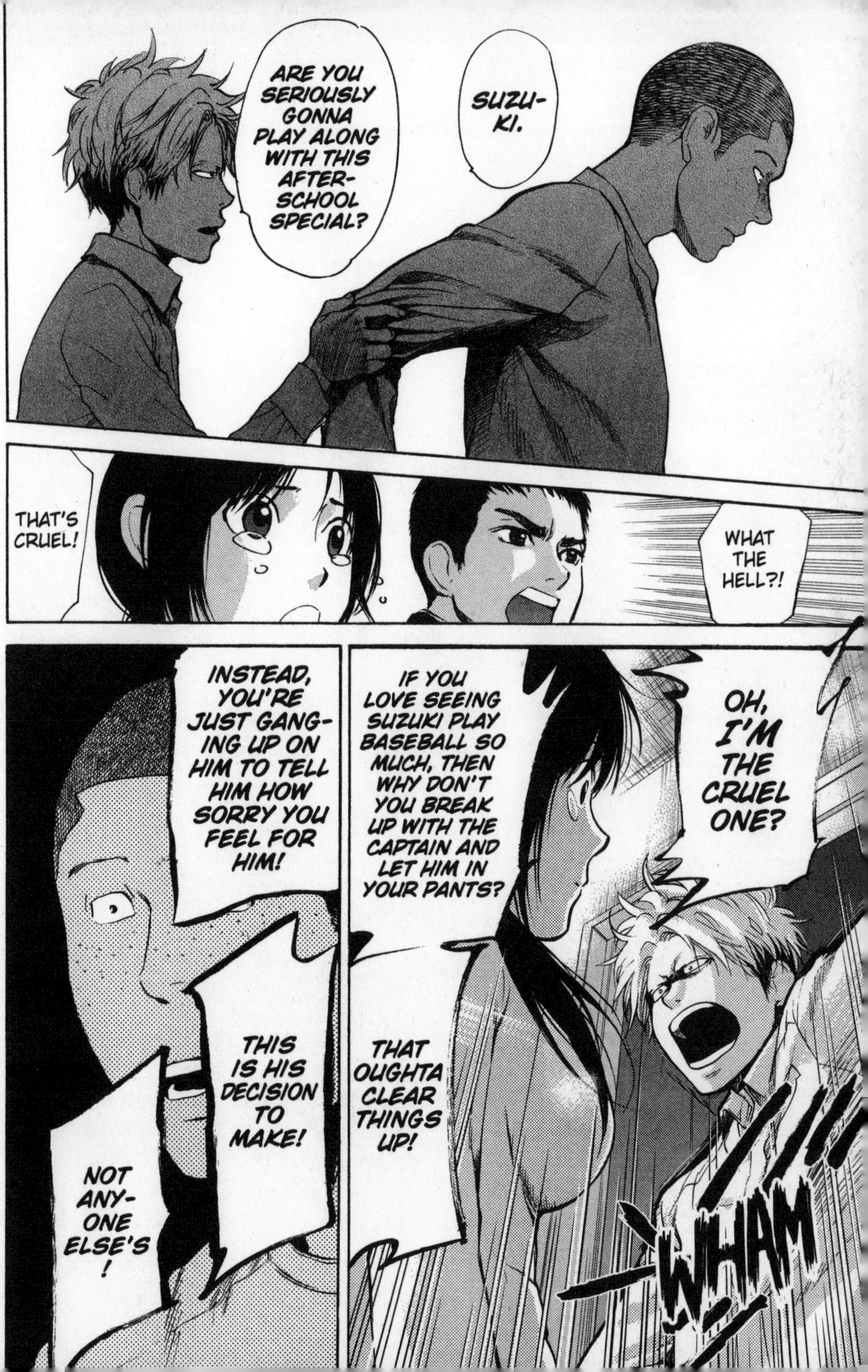
SUZU-KI.
ARE YOU SERIOUSLY GONNA PLAY ALONG WITH THIS AFTER-SCHOOL SPECIAL?
WHAT THE HELL?!
THAT'S CRUEL!
OH, I'M THE CRUEL ONE?
IF YOU LOVE SEEING SUZUKI PLAY BASEBALL SO MUCH, THEN WHY DON'T YOU BREAK UP WITH THE CAPTAIN AND LET HIM IN YOUR PANTS?
THAT OUGHTA CLEAR THINGS UP!
WHAM
INSTEAD, YOU'RE JUST GANG-ING UP ON HIM TO TELL HIM HOW SORRY YOU FEEL FOR HIM!
THIS IS HIS DECISION TO MAKE!
NOT ANY-ONE ELSE'S!

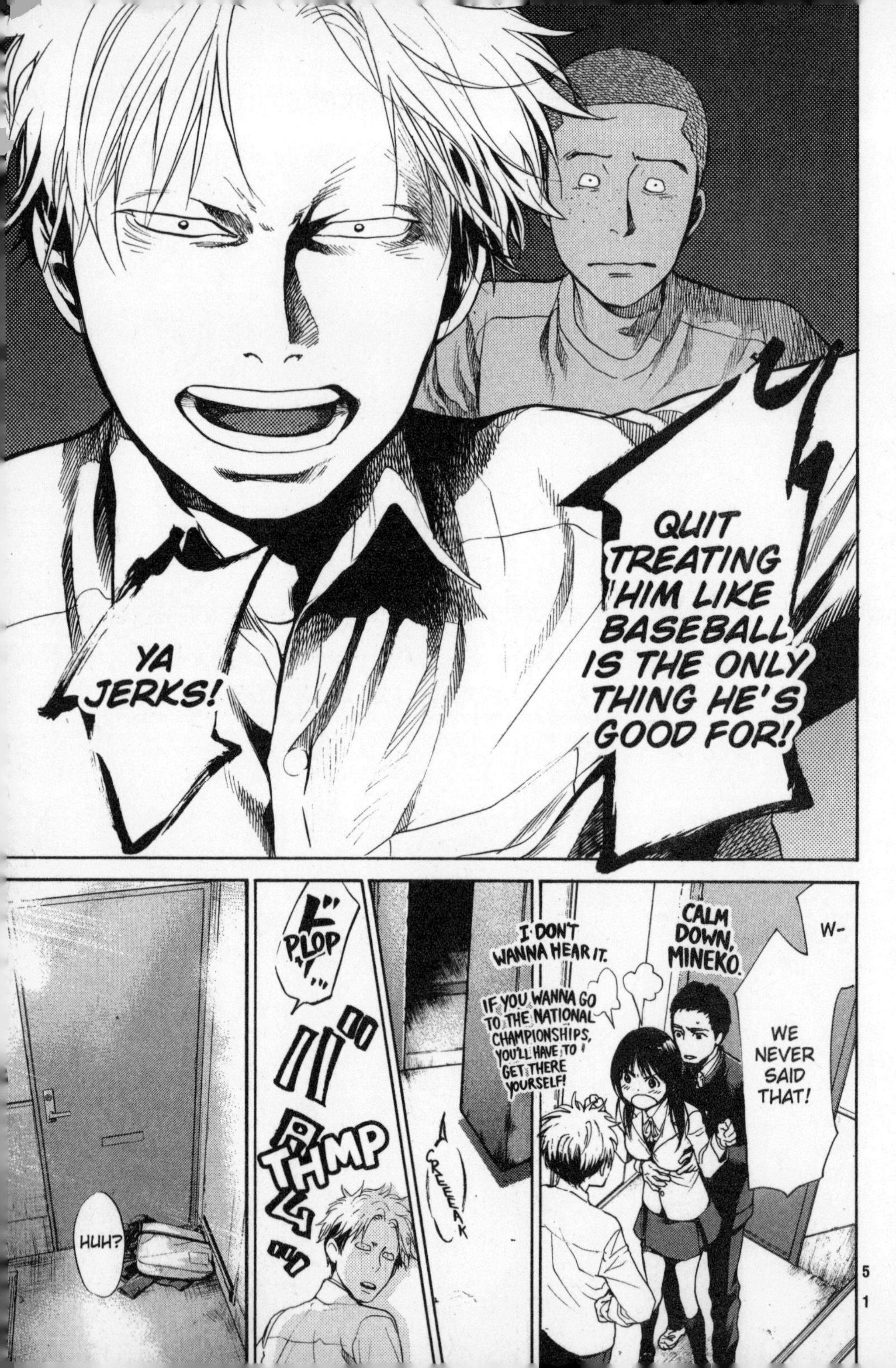
QUIT TREATING HIM LIKE BASEBALL IS THE ONLY THING HE'S GOOD FOR!
YA JERKS!
W-
WE NEVER SAID THAT!
CALM DOWN, MINEKO.
I DON'T WANNA HEAR IT.
IF YOU WANNA GO TO THE NATIONAL CHAMPIONSHIPS, YOU'LL HAVE TO GET THERE YOURSELF!
CREEEAK
PLOP
THMP
HUH?

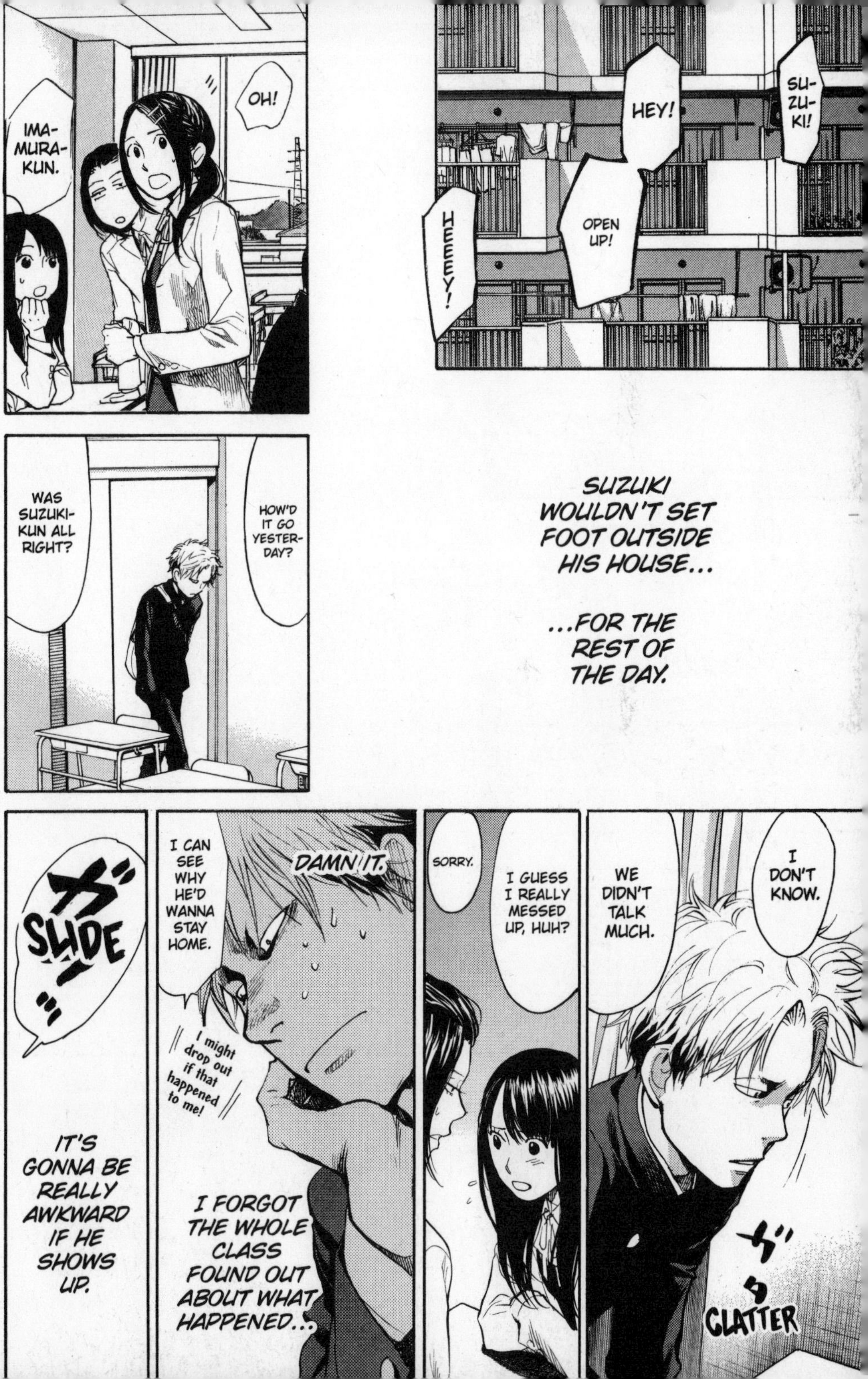
SU-ZU-KI!
HEY!
OPEN UP!
HEEEEY!
OH!
IMA-MURA-KUN.
SUZUKI WOULDN'T SET FOOT OUTSIDE HIS HOUSE...
...FOR THE REST OF THE DAY.
HOW'D IT GO YESTER-DAY?
WAS SUZUKI-KUN ALL RIGHT?
I DON'T KNOW.
CLATTER
WE DIDN'T TALK MUCH.
I GUESS I REALLY MESSED UP, HUH?
SORRY.
DAMN IT.
I CAN SEE WHY HE'D WANNA STAY HOME.
I might drop out if that happened to me!
I FORGOT THE WHOLE CLASS FOUND OUT ABOUT WHAT HAPPENED...
SLIDE
IT'S GONNA BE REALLY AWKWARD IF HE SHOWS UP.

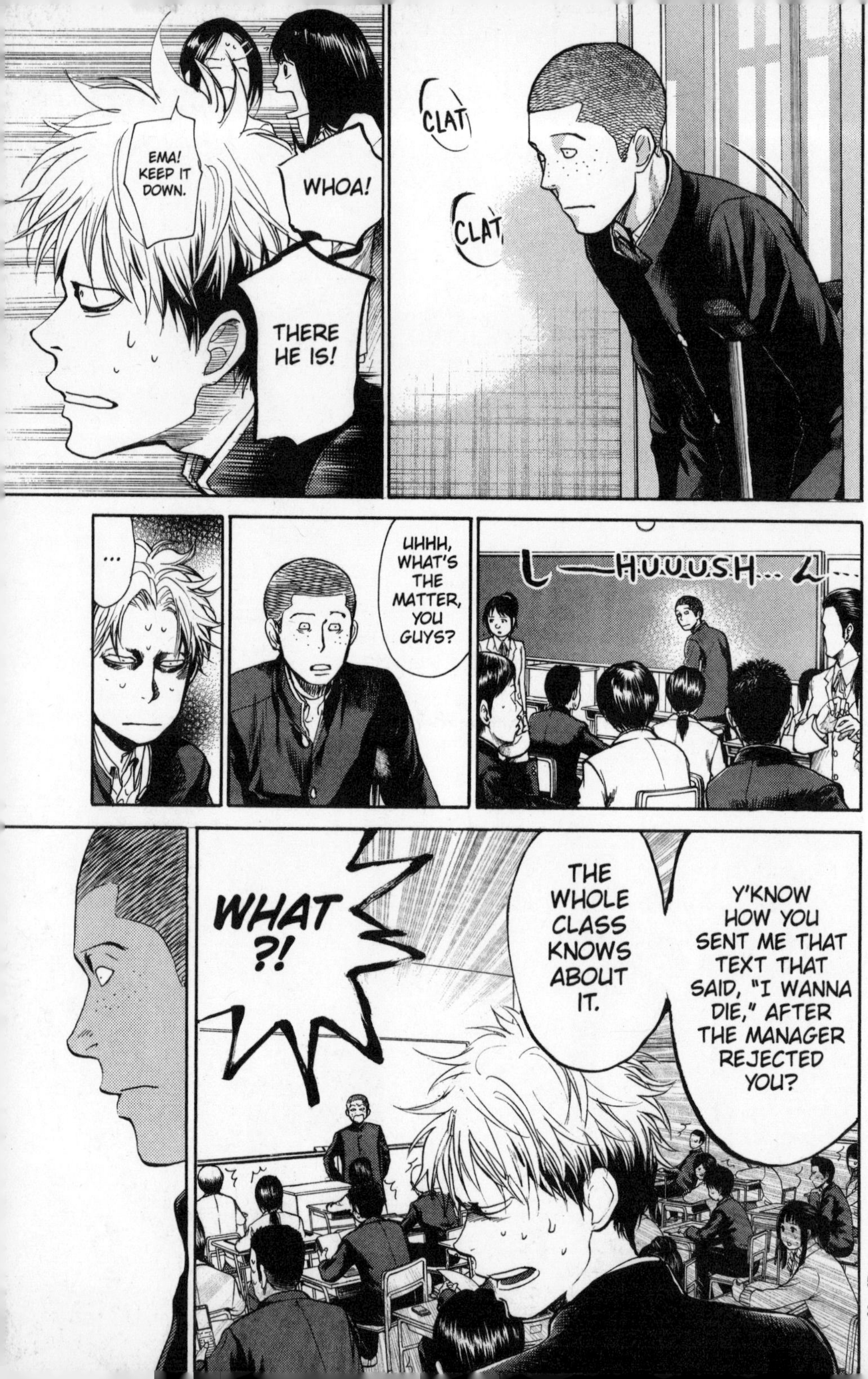
CLAT
CLAT
WHOA!
THERE HE IS!
EMA! KEEP IT DOWN.
HUUUSH...
UHHH, WHAT'S THE MATTER, YOU GUYS?
...
Y'KNOW HOW YOU SENT ME THAT TEXT THAT SAID, "I WANNA DIE," AFTER THE MANAGER REJECTED YOU?
THE WHOLE CLASS KNOWS ABOUT IT.
WHAT ?!

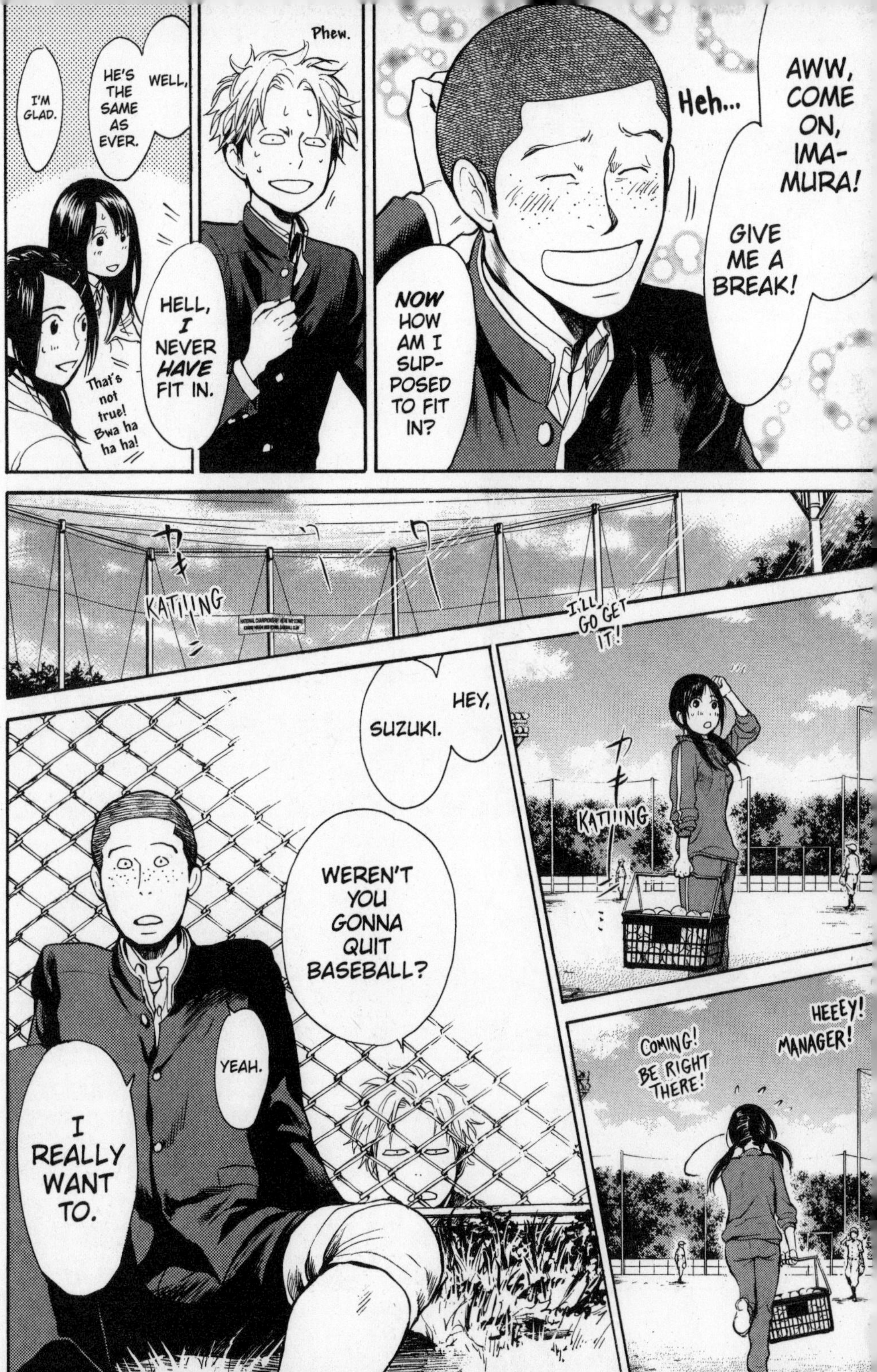

AWW, COME ON, IMA-MURA!
GIVE ME A BREAK!
Heh...
NOW HOW AM I SUP-POSED TO FIT IN?
Phew.
HELL, I NEVER HAVE FIT IN.
WELL, HE'S THE SAME AS EVER.
I'M GLAD.
That's not true! Bwa ha ha ha!
KATIIING
I'LL GO GET IT!
KATIIING
HEEEY! MANAGER!
COMING! BE RIGHT THERE!
HEY, SUZUKI.
WEREN'T YOU GONNA QUIT BASEBALL?
YEAH.
I REALLY WANT TO.

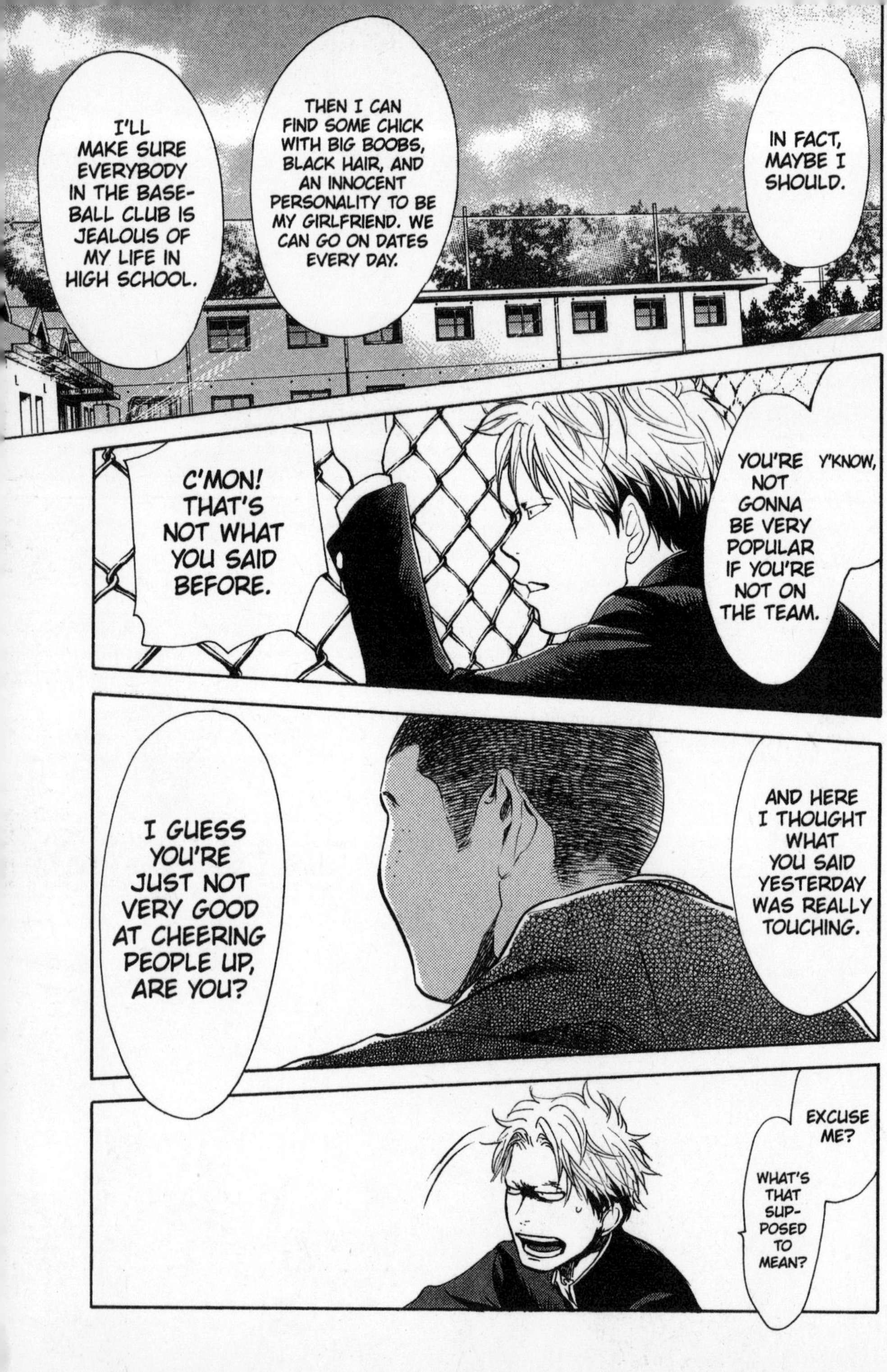
IN FACT, MAYBE I SHOULD.
THEN I CAN FIND SOME CHICK WITH BIG BOOBS, BLACK HAIR, AND AN INNOCENT PERSONALITY TO BE MY GIRLFRIEND. WE CAN GO ON DATES EVERY DAY.
I'LL MAKE SURE EVERYBODY IN THE BASE-BALL CLUB IS JEALOUS OF MY LIFE IN HIGH SCHOOL.
Y'KNOW, YOU'RE NOT GONNA BE VERY POPULAR IF YOU'RE NOT ON THE TEAM.
C'MON! THAT'S NOT WHAT YOU SAID BEFORE.
AND HERE I THOUGHT WHAT YOU SAID YESTERDAY WAS REALLY TOUCHING.
I GUESS YOU'RE JUST NOT VERY GOOD AT CHEERING PEOPLE UP, ARE YOU?
EXCUSE ME?
WHAT'S THAT SUP-POSED TO MEAN?

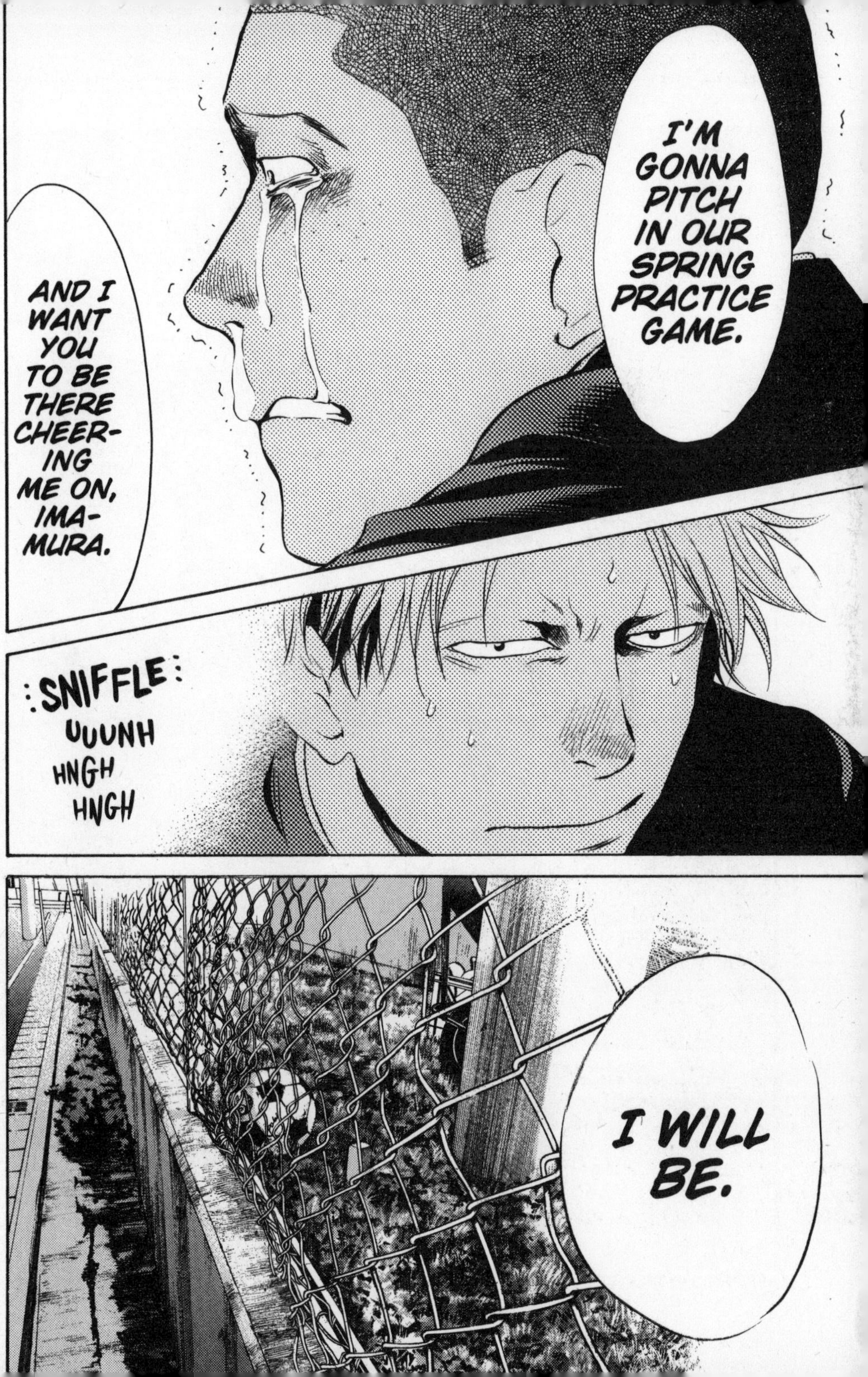
I'M GONNA PITCH IN OUR SPRING PRACTICE GAME.
AND I WANT YOU TO BE THERE CHEERING ME ON, IMAMURA.
SNIFFLE
UUUNH HNGH HNGH
I WILL BE.

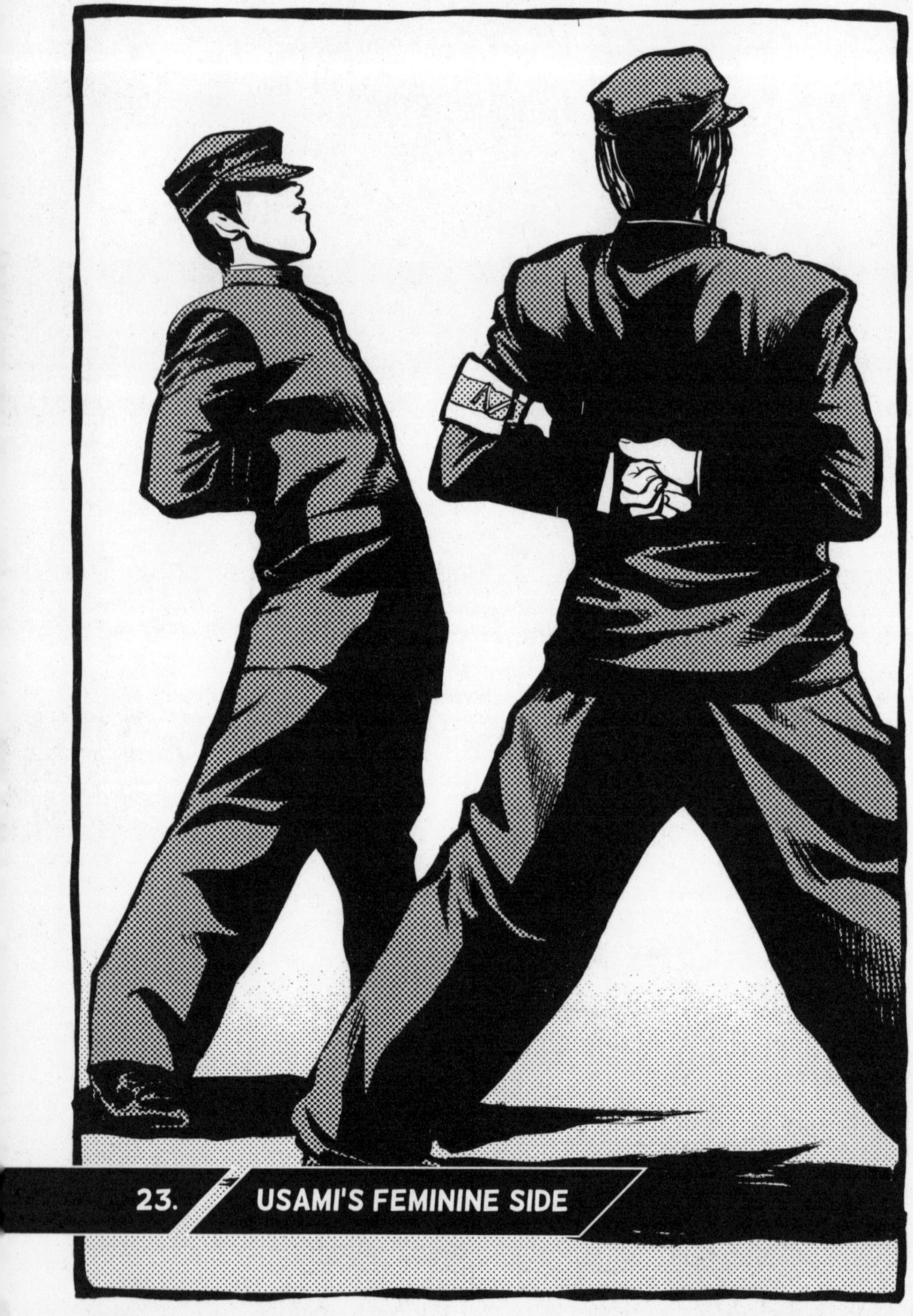

23. USAMI'S FEMININE SIDE

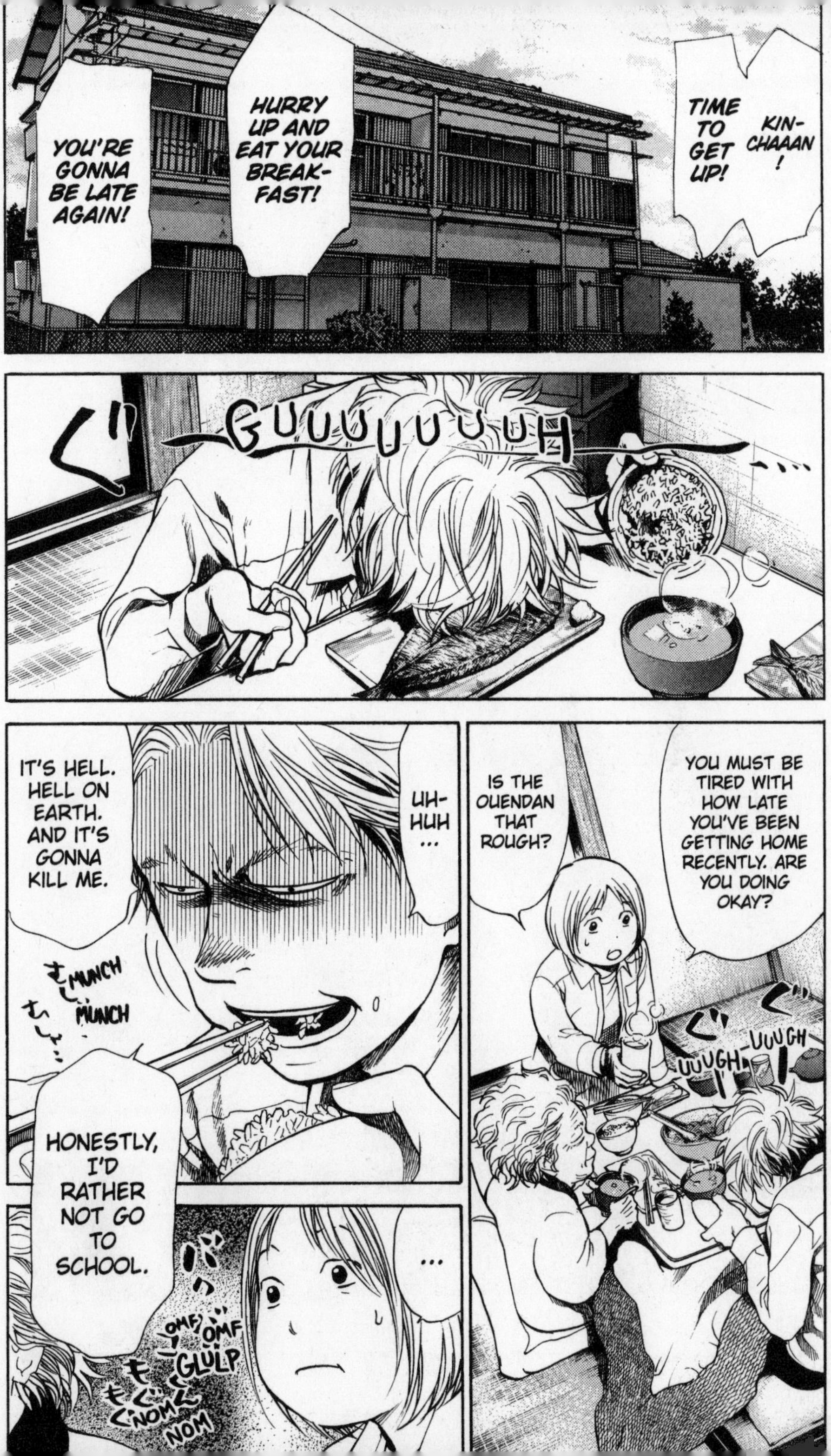
KIN-CHAAAN!
TIME TO GET UP!
HURRY UP AND EAT YOUR BREAK-FAST!
YOU'RE GONNA BE LATE AGAIN!
GUUUUUUUH
YOU MUST BE TIRED WITH HOW LATE YOU'VE BEEN GETTING HOME RECENTLY. ARE YOU DOING OKAY?
IS THE OUENDAN THAT ROUGH?
UUUGH
UUUGH
UH-HUH...
IT'S HELL. HELL ON EARTH. AND IT'S GONNA KILL ME.
MUNCH
MUNCH
HONESTLY, I'D RATHER NOT GO TO SCHOOL.
...
OMF OMF
GULP
NOM NOM

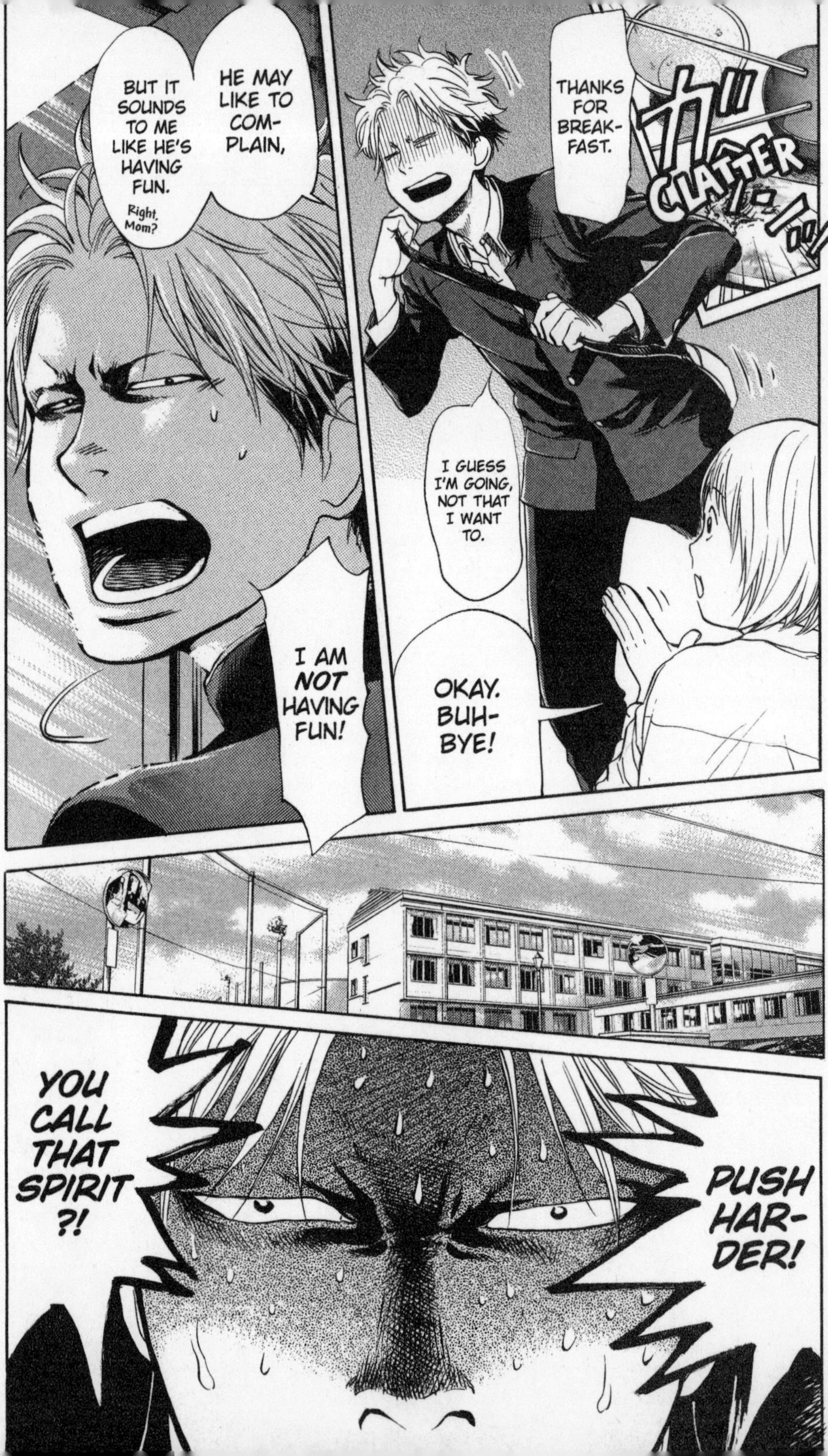
THANKS FOR BREAK-FAST.
カ゛
CLATTER
I GUESS I'M GOING, NOT THAT I WANT TO.
OKAY. BUH-BYE!
HE MAY LIKE TO COM-PLAIN,
BUT IT SOUNDS TO ME LIKE HE'S HAVING FUN.
Right, Mom?
I AM *NOT* HAVING FUN!
PUSH HAR-DER!
YOU CALL THAT SPIRIT ?!

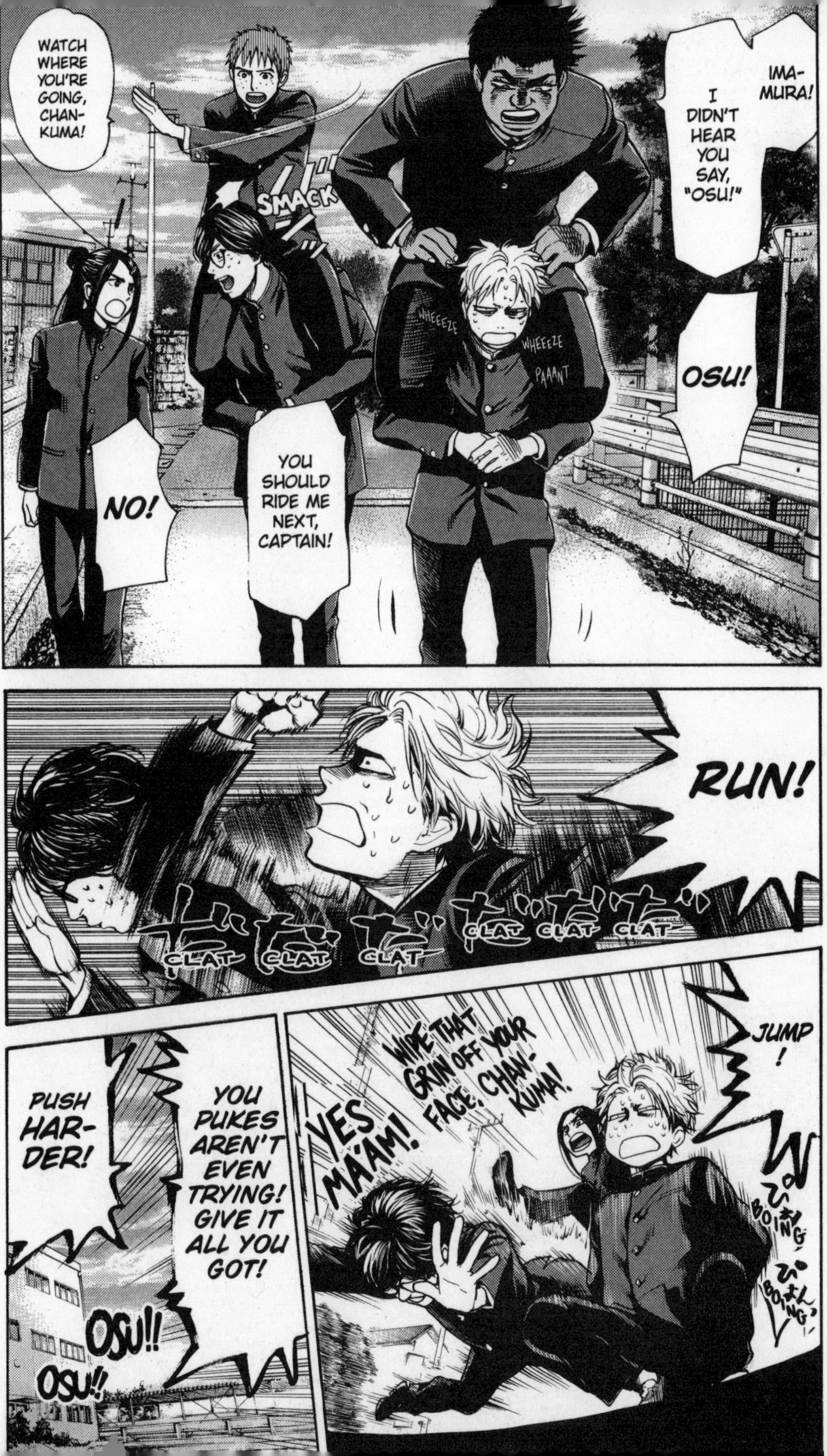
IMA-MURA! I DIDN'T HEAR YOU SAY, "OSU!"
WATCH WHERE YOU'RE GOING, CHAN-KUMA!
SMACK
OSU!
WHEEEZE WHEEEZE PAAANT
YOU SHOULD RIDE ME NEXT, CAPTAIN!
NO!
RUN!
CLAT CLAT CLAT CLAT CLAT CLAT
JUMP!
WIPE THAT GRIN OFF YOUR FACE, CHAN-KUMA!
YES MA'AM!
BOING BOING
PUSH HAR-DER!
YOU PUKES AREN'T EVEN TRYING! GIVE IT ALL YOU GOT!
OSU!!
OSU!!

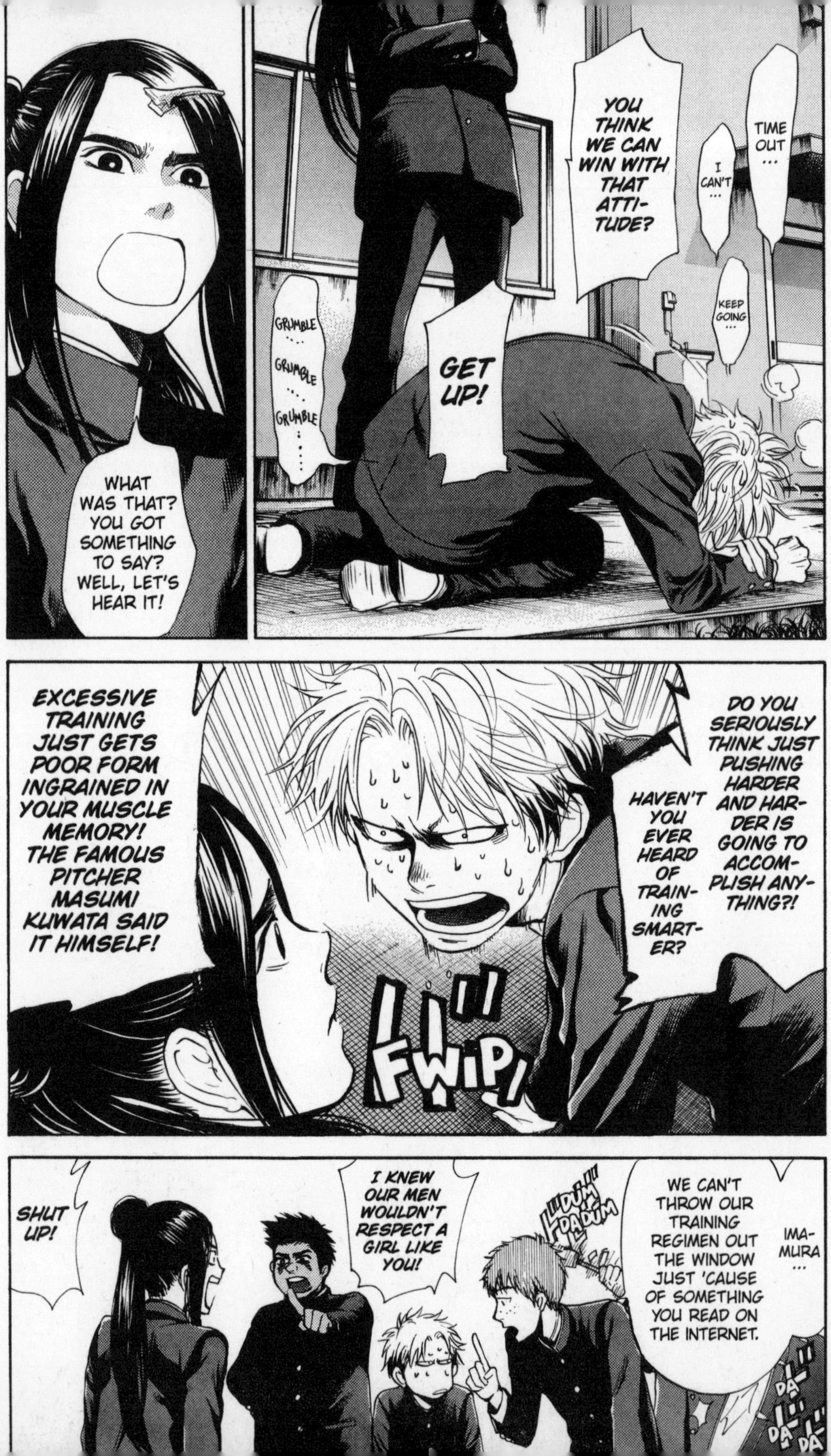

TIME OUT...
I CAN'T...
YOU THINK WE CAN WIN WITH THAT ATTITUDE?
KEEP GOING...
GET UP!
GRUMBLE... GRUMBLE... GRUMBLE...
WHAT WAS THAT? YOU GOT SOMETHING TO SAY? WELL, LET'S HEAR IT!
DO YOU SERIOUSLY THINK JUST PUSHING HARDER AND HARDER IS GOING TO ACCOMPLISH ANYTHING?!
HAVEN'T YOU EVER HEARD OF TRAINING SMARTER?
FWIP!
EXCESSIVE TRAINING JUST GETS POOR FORM INGRAINED IN YOUR MUSCLE MEMORY! THE FAMOUS PITCHER MASUMI KUWATA SAID IT HIMSELF!
DA DA DA
IMAMURA...
WE CAN'T THROW OUR TRAINING REGIMEN OUT THE WINDOW JUST 'CAUSE OF SOMETHING YOU READ ON THE INTERNET.
DUM DA DUM
I KNEW OUR MEN WOULDN'T RESPECT A GIRL LIKE YOU!
SHUT UP!

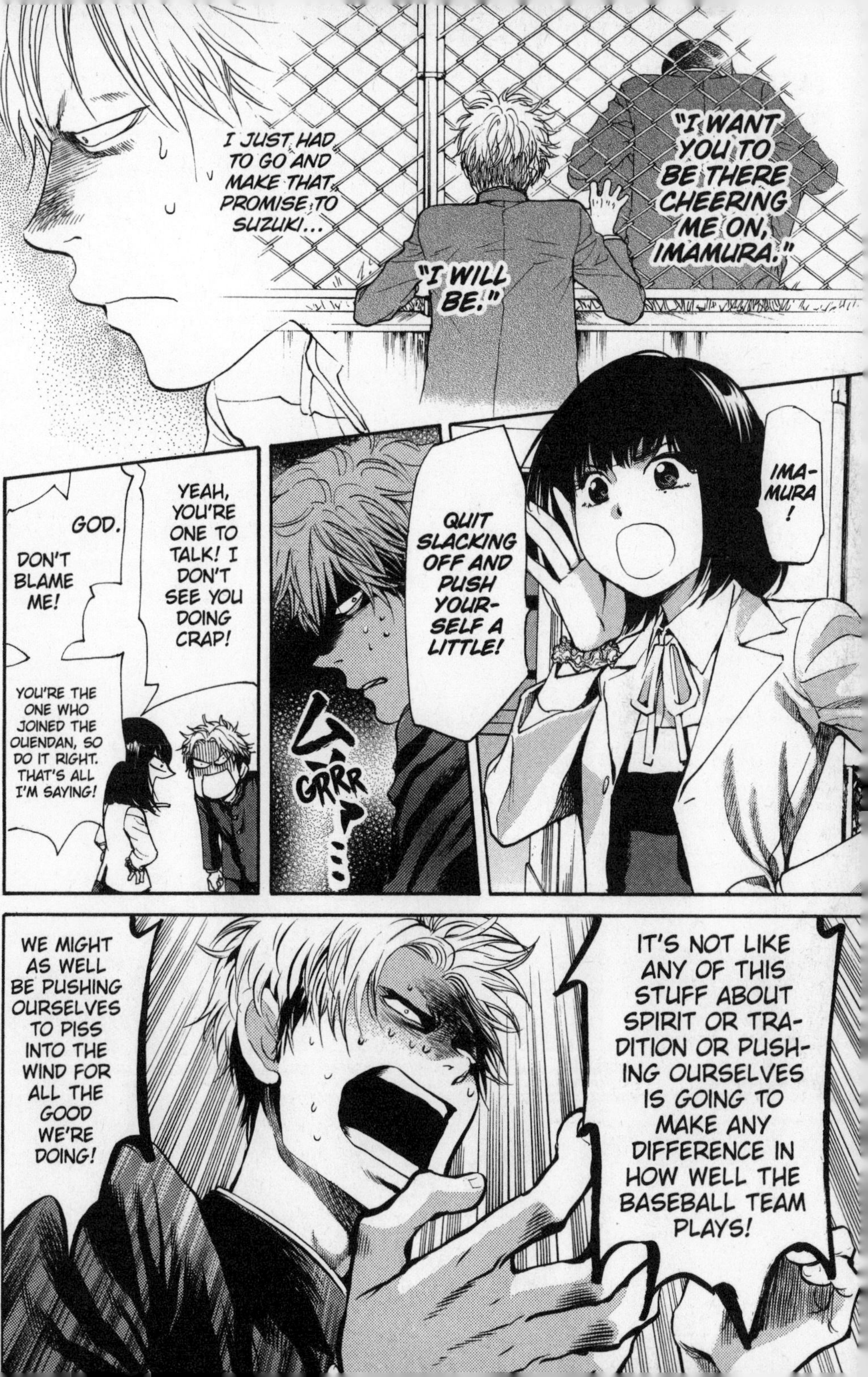
"I WANT YOU TO BE THERE CHEERING ME ON, IMAMURA."
"I WILL BE."
I JUST HAD TO GO AND MAKE THAT PROMISE TO SUZUKI...
IMA-MURA!
QUIT SLACKING OFF AND PUSH YOUR-SELF A LITTLE!
GRRR
YEAH, YOU'RE ONE TO TALK! I DON'T SEE YOU DOING CRAP!
GOD.
DON'T BLAME ME!
YOU'RE THE ONE WHO JOINED THE OUENDAN, SO DO IT RIGHT. THAT'S ALL I'M SAYING!
IT'S NOT LIKE ANY OF THIS STUFF ABOUT SPIRIT OR TRA-DITION OR PUSH-ING OURSELVES IS GOING TO MAKE ANY DIFFERENCE IN HOW WELL THE BASEBALL TEAM PLAYS!
WE MIGHT AS WELL BE PUSHING OURSELVES TO PISS INTO THE WIND FOR ALL THE GOOD WE'RE DOING!

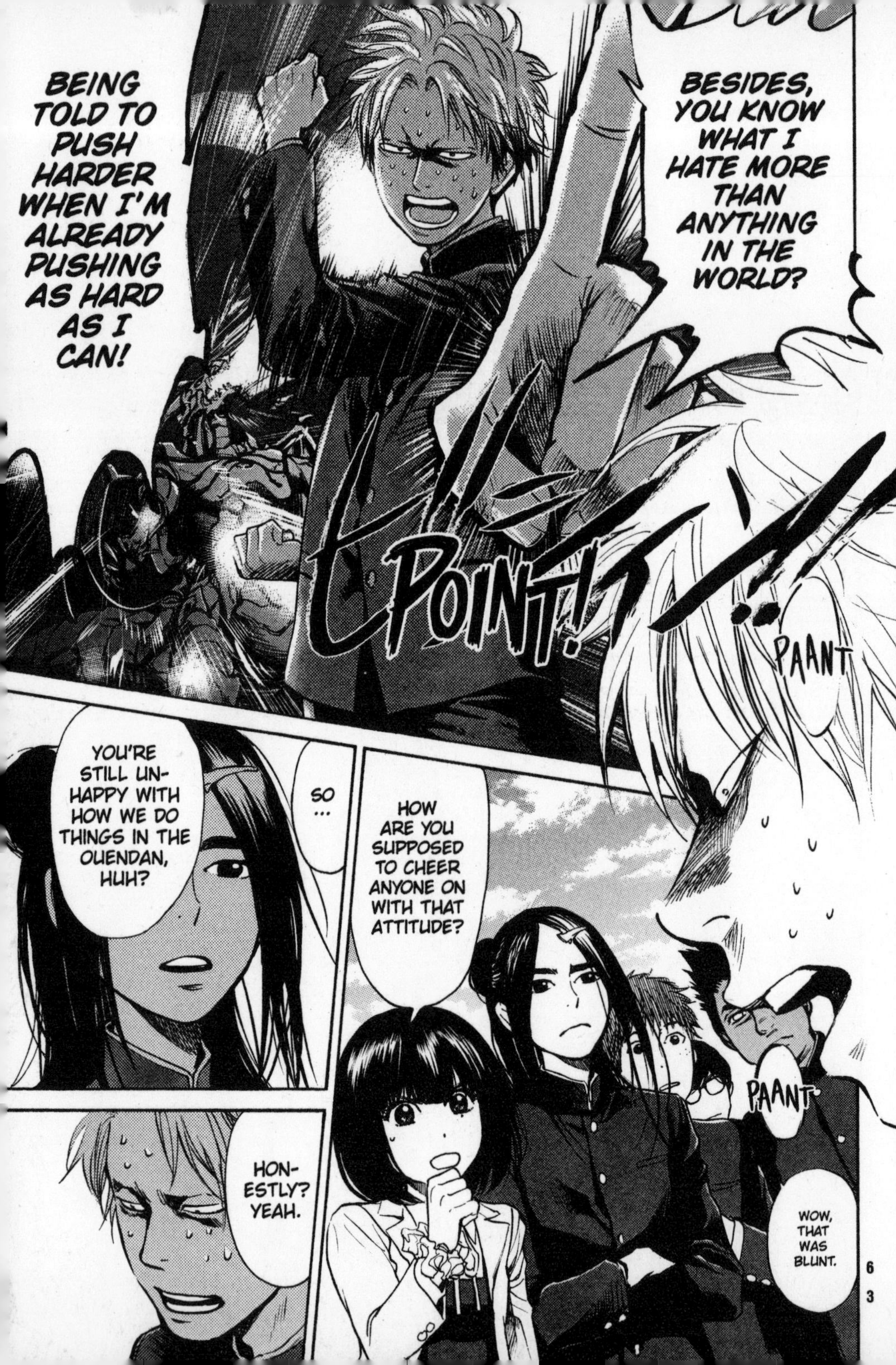
BESIDES, YOU KNOW WHAT I HATE MORE THAN ANYTHING IN THE WORLD?
BEING TOLD TO PUSH HARDER WHEN I'M ALREADY PUSHING AS HARD AS I CAN!
POINT!!
PAANT
SO ...
HOW ARE YOU SUPPOSED TO CHEER ANYONE ON WITH THAT ATTITUDE?
PAANT
WOW, THAT WAS BLUNT.
YOU'RE STILL UN-HAPPY WITH HOW WE DO THINGS IN THE OUENDAN, HUH?
HON-ESTLY? YEAH.

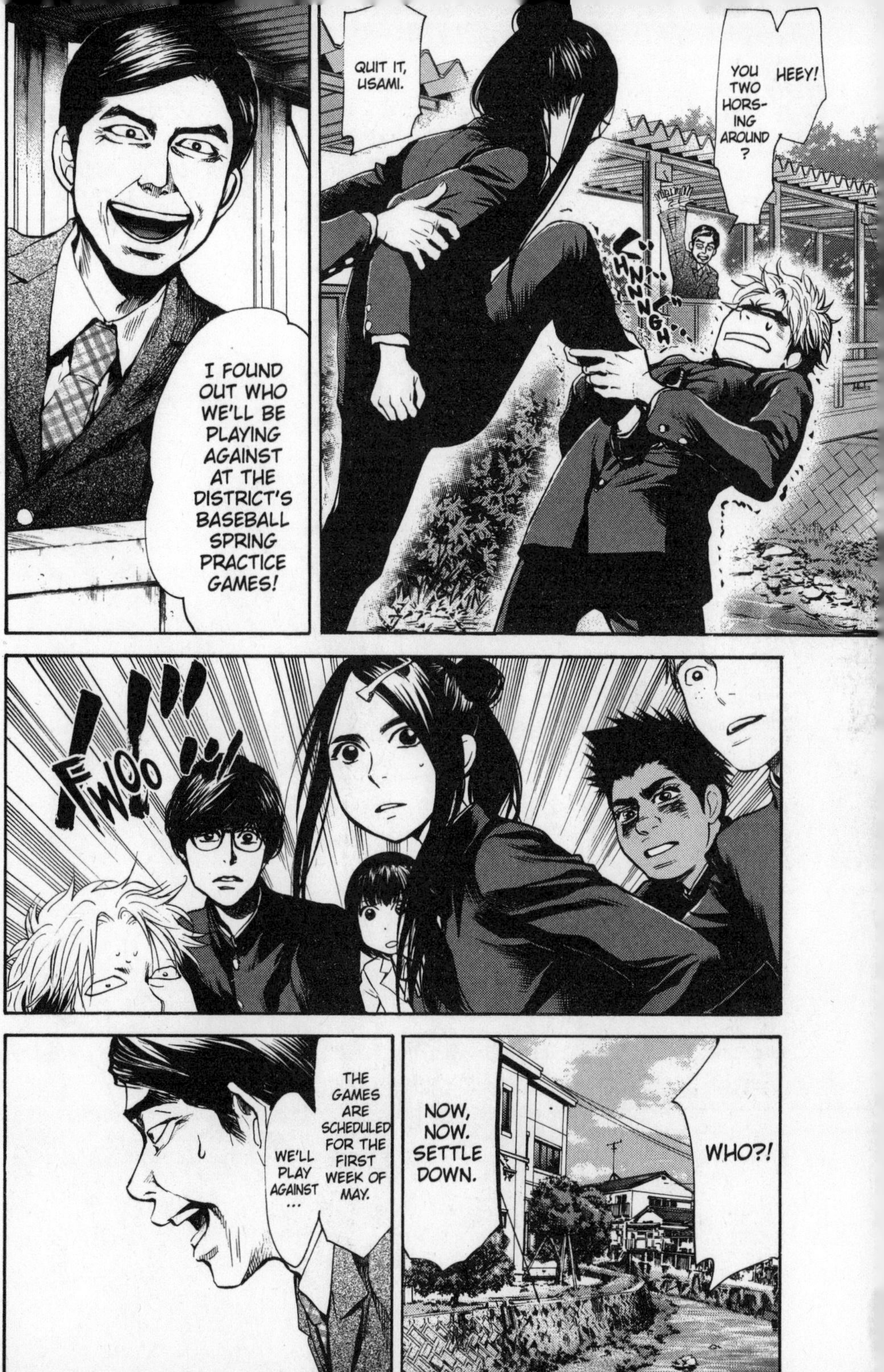
HEEY!
YOU TWO HORSING AROUND?
QUIT IT, USAMI.
HNNNGH...
I FOUND OUT WHO WE'LL BE PLAYING AGAINST AT THE DISTRICT'S BASEBALL SPRING PRACTICE GAMES!
FWOO!!!
WHO?!
NOW, NOW. SETTLE DOWN.
THE GAMES ARE SCHEDULED FOR THE FIRST WEEK OF MAY.
WE'LL PLAY AGAINST...

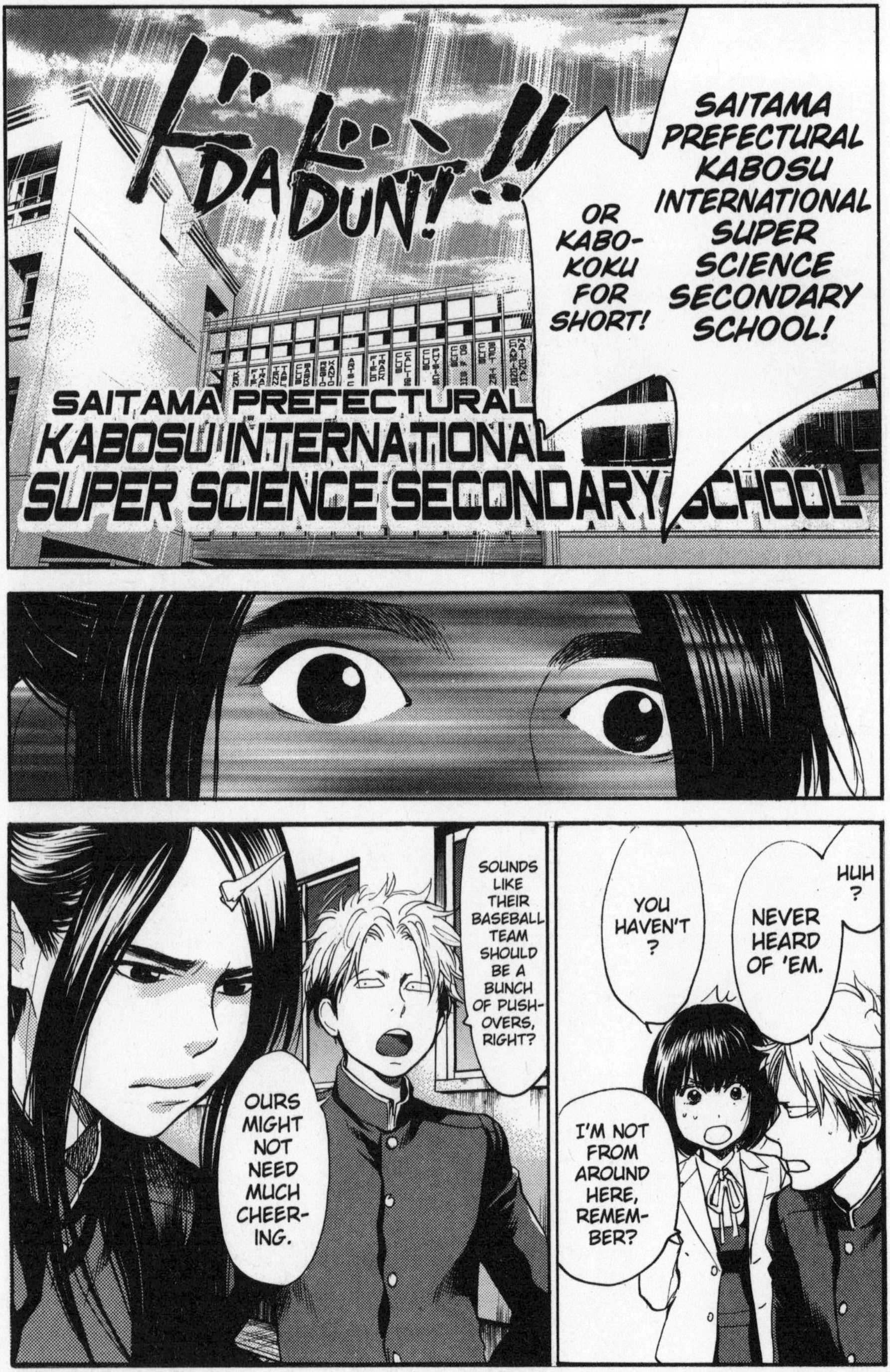
DA DUN!!
SAITAMA PREFECTURAL KABOSU INTERNATIONAL SUPER SCIENCE SECONDARY SCHOOL!
OR KABO-KOKU FOR SHORT!
SAITAMA PREFECTURAL KABOSU INTERNATIONAL SUPER SCIENCE SECONDARY SCHOOL
HUH?
NEVER HEARD OF 'EM.
YOU HAVEN'T?
I'M NOT FROM AROUND HERE, REMEMBER?
SOUNDS LIKE THEIR BASEBALL TEAM SHOULD BE A BUNCH OF PUSH-OVERS, RIGHT?
OURS MIGHT NOT NEED MUCH CHEER-ING.

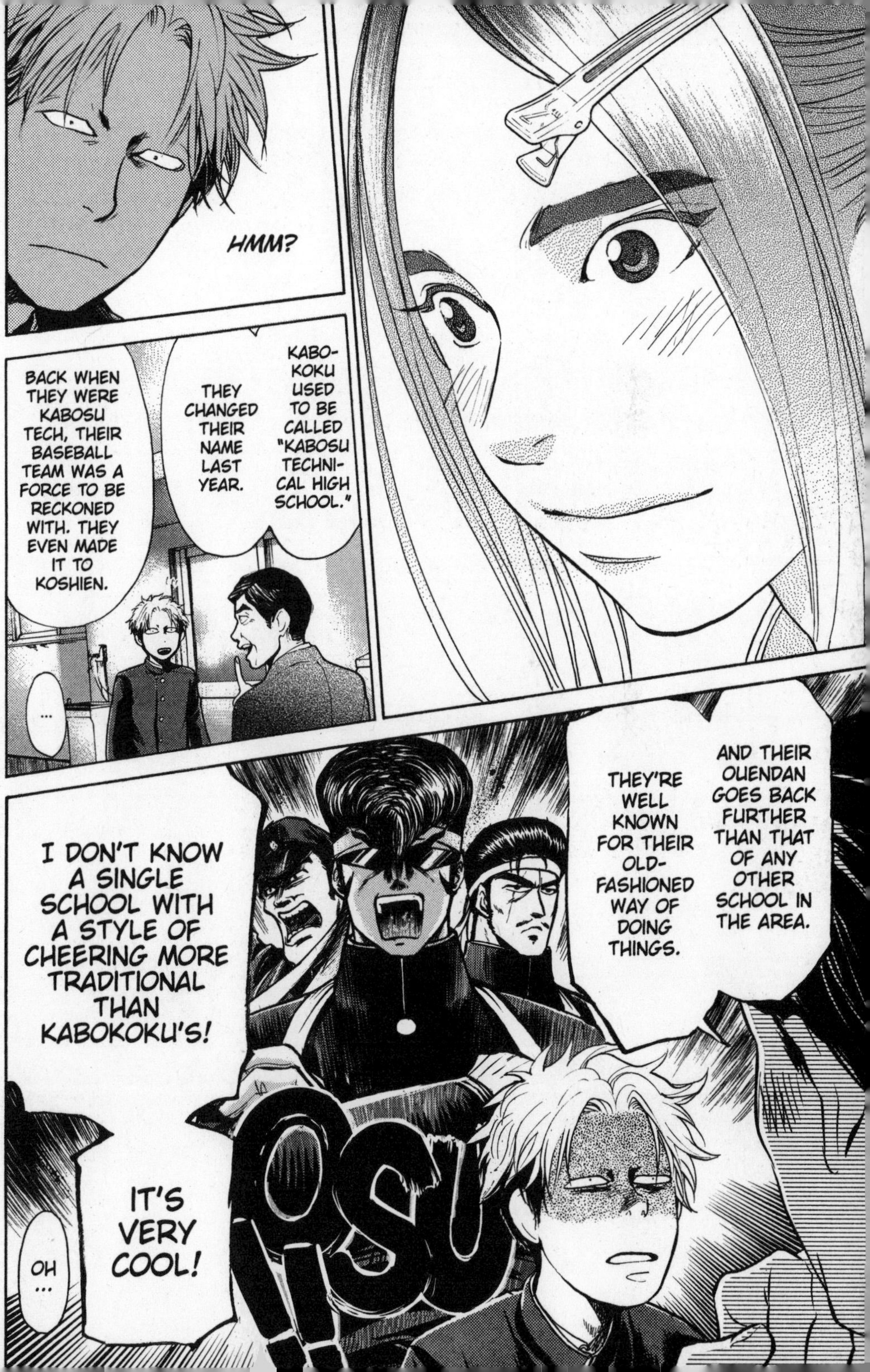
HMM?
KABO-KOKU USED TO BE CALLED "KABOSU TECHNICAL HIGH SCHOOL."
THEY CHANGED THEIR NAME LAST YEAR.
BACK WHEN THEY WERE KABOSU TECH, THEIR BASEBALL TEAM WAS A FORCE TO BE RECKONED WITH. THEY EVEN MADE IT TO KOSHIEN.
...
AND THEIR OUENDAN GOES BACK FURTHER THAN THAT OF ANY OTHER SCHOOL IN THE AREA.
THEY'RE WELL KNOWN FOR THEIR OLD-FASHIONED WAY OF DOING THINGS.
I DON'T KNOW A SINGLE SCHOOL WITH A STYLE OF CHEERING MORE TRADITIONAL THAN KABOKOKU'S!
OSU
IT'S VERY COOL!
OH ...

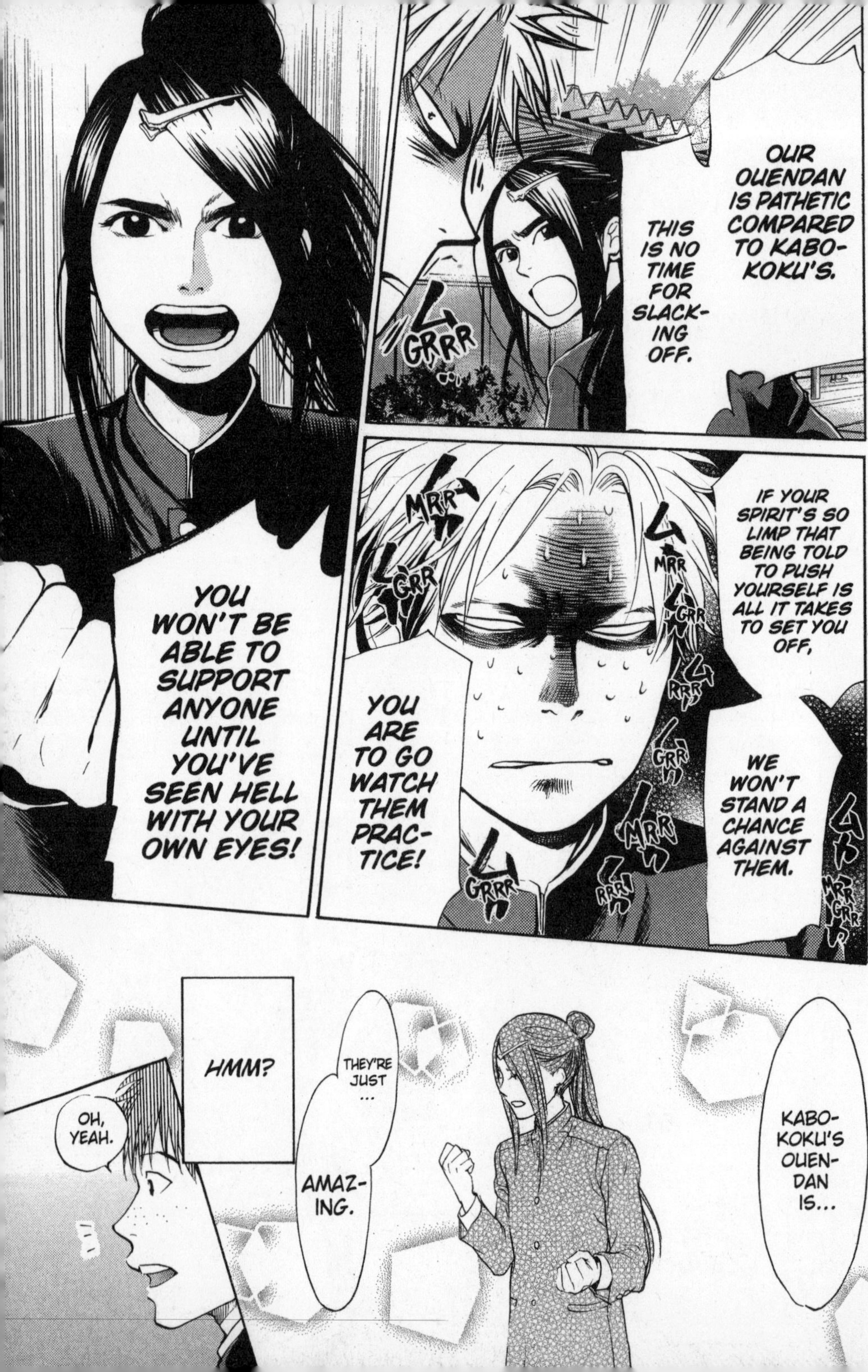
OUR OUENDAN IS PATHETIC COMPARED TO KABO-KOKU'S.
THIS IS NO TIME FOR SLACKING OFF.
GRRR
IF YOUR SPIRIT'S SO LIMP THAT BEING TOLD TO PUSH YOURSELF IS ALL IT TAKES TO SET YOU OFF,
WE WON'T STAND A CHANCE AGAINST THEM.
MRRR GRRR
MRRR
GRR
MRRR
YOU ARE TO GO WATCH THEM PRACTICE!
GRRR
YOU WON'T BE ABLE TO SUPPORT ANYONE UNTIL YOU'VE SEEN HELL WITH YOUR OWN EYES!
KABO-KOKU'S OUEN-DAN IS...
THEY'RE JUST ...
AMAZ-ING.
HMM?
OH, YEAH.

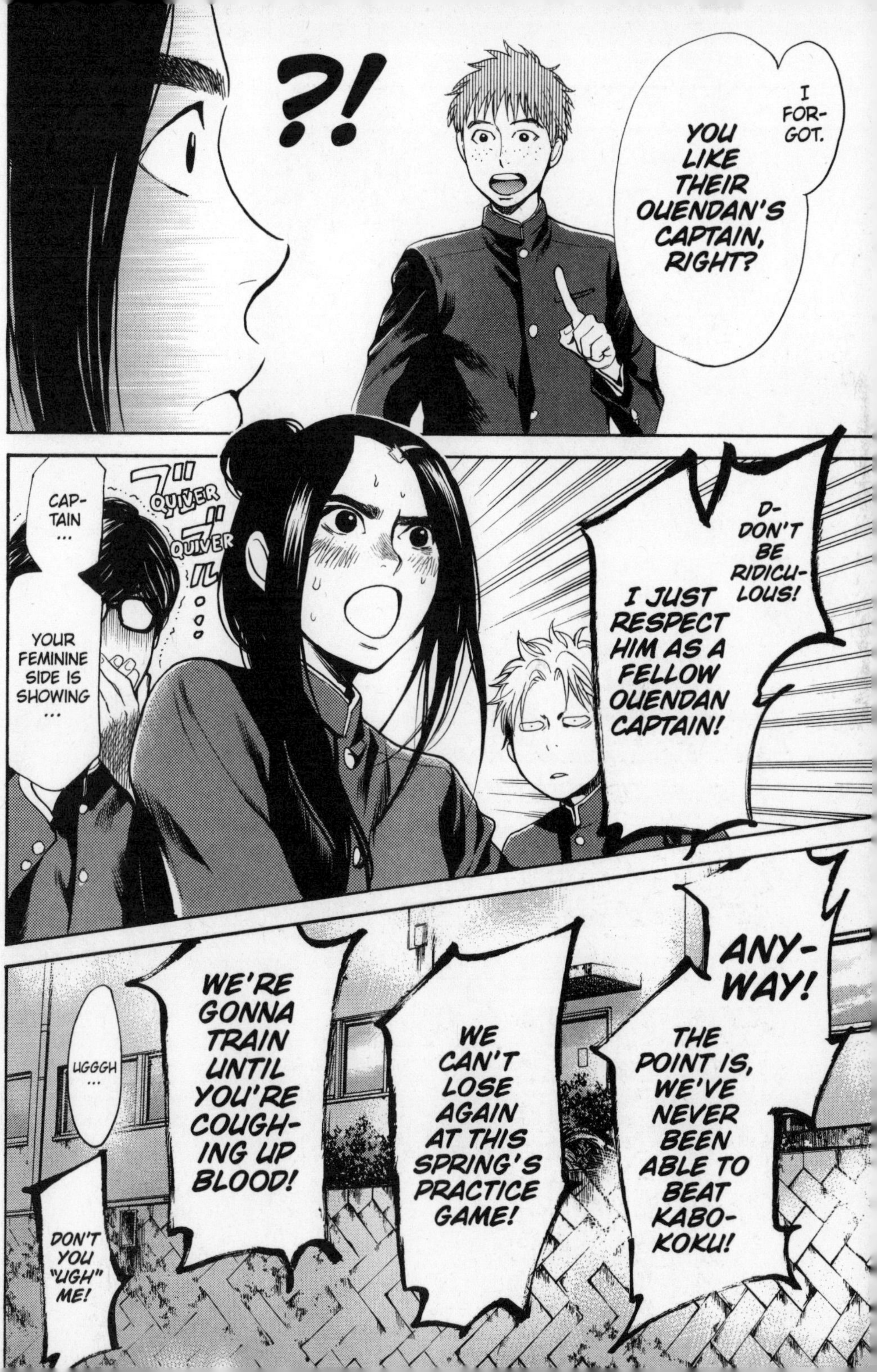

I FOR-GOT. YOU LIKE THEIR OUENDAN'S CAPTAIN, RIGHT?
?!
D-DON'T BE RIDICU-LOUS! I JUST RESPECT HIM AS A FELLOW OUENDAN CAPTAIN!
QUIVER QUIVER
CAP-TAIN ...
YOUR FEMININE SIDE IS SHOWING ...
ANY-WAY! THE POINT IS, WE'VE NEVER BEEN ABLE TO BEAT KABO-KOKU!
WE CAN'T LOSE AGAIN AT THIS SPRING'S PRACTICE GAME!
WE'RE GONNA TRAIN UNTIL YOU'RE COUGH-ING UP BLOOD!
UGGGH ...
DON'T YOU "UGH" ME!

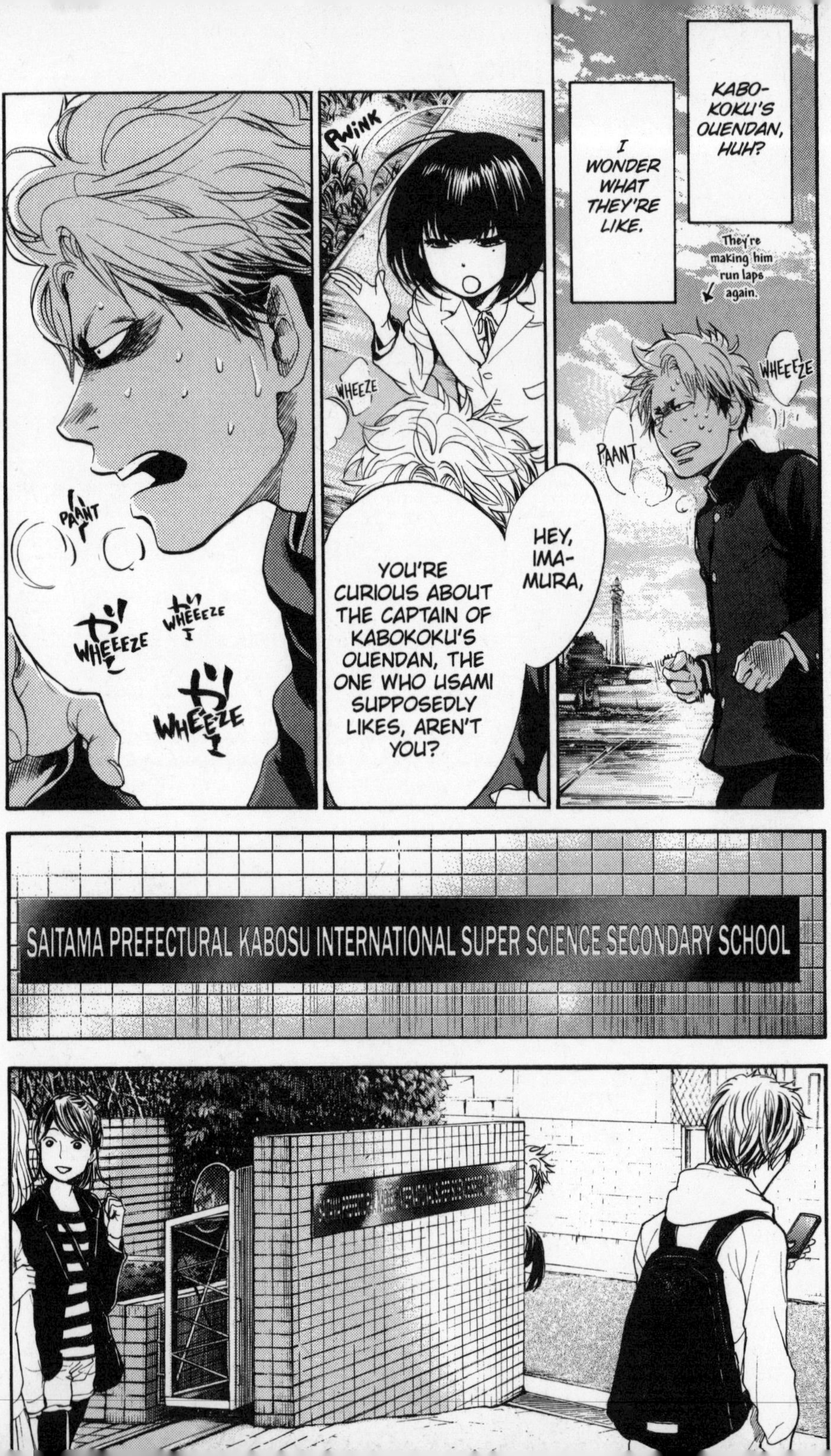
KABO-KOKU'S OUENDAN, HUH?
I WONDER WHAT THEY'RE LIKE.
They're making him run laps again.
WHEEEZE
PAANT
PWINK
HEY, IMA-MURA,
YOU'RE CURIOUS ABOUT THE CAPTAIN OF KABOKOKU'S OUENDAN, THE ONE WHO USAMI SUPPOSEDLY LIKES, AREN'T YOU?
WHEEZE
PAANT
WHEEEZE
WHEEEZE
WHEEEZE
SAITAMA PREFECTURAL KABOSU INTERNATIONAL SUPER SCIENCE SECONDARY SCHOOL

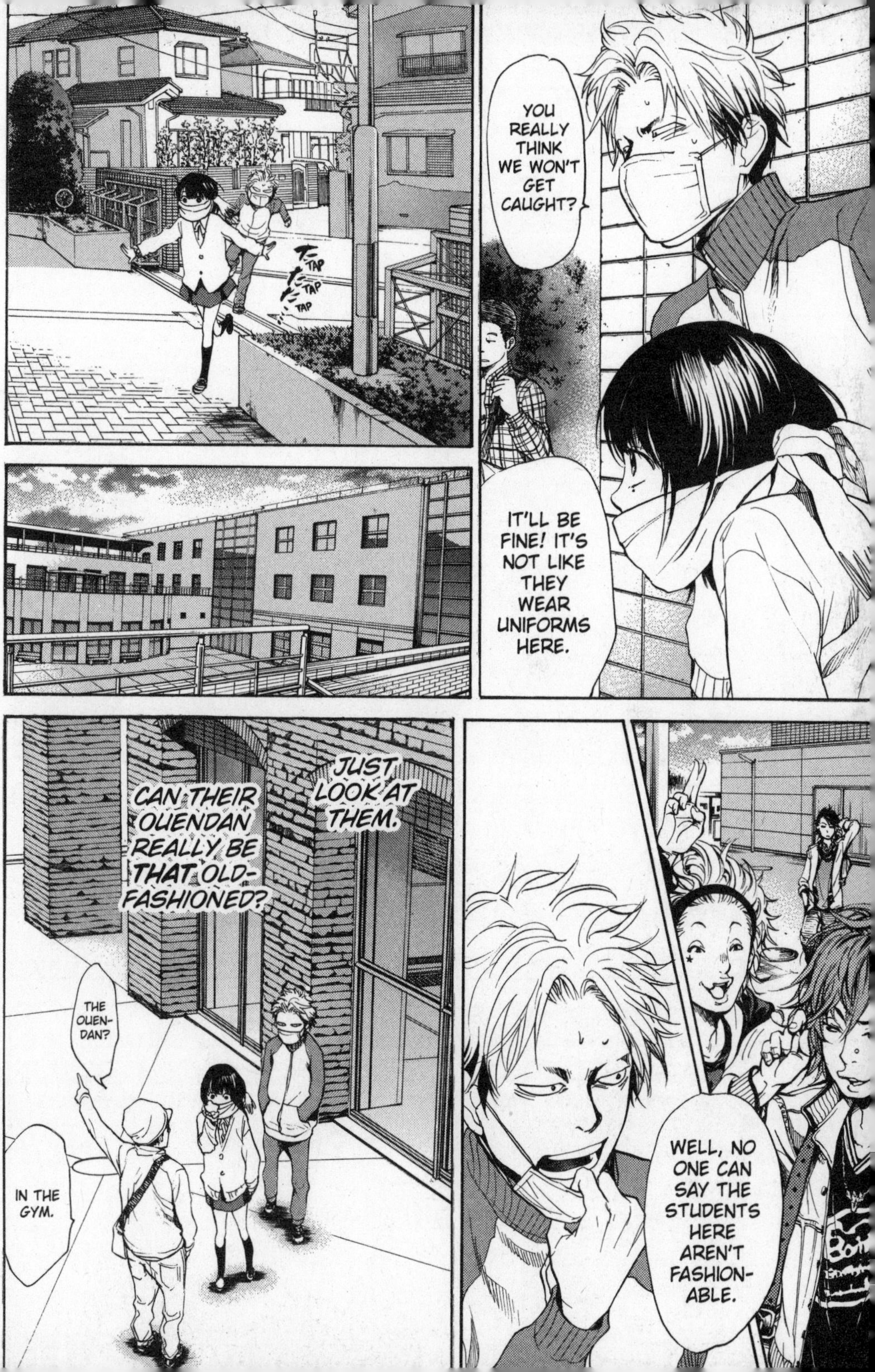
YOU REALLY THINK WE WON'T GET CAUGHT?
IT'LL BE FINE! IT'S NOT LIKE THEY WEAR UNIFORMS HERE.
TAP
TAP
TAP
WELL, NO ONE CAN SAY THE STUDENTS HERE AREN'T FASHIONABLE.
JUST LOOK AT THEM.
CAN THEIR OUENDAN REALLY BE THAT OLD-FASHIONED?
THE OUENDAN?
IN THE GYM.

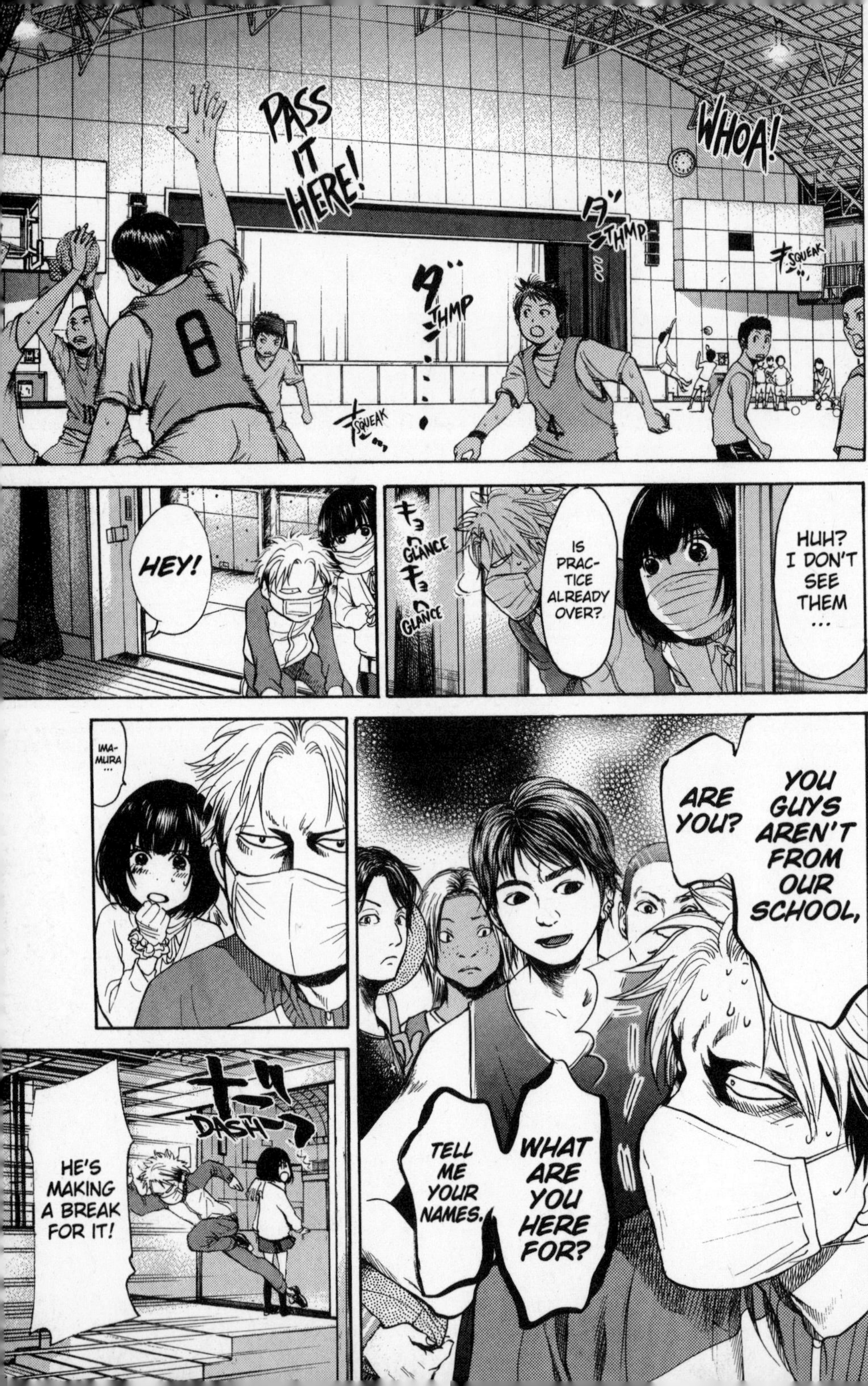

WHOA!
PASS IT HERE!
THMP
SQUEAK
THMP
SQUEAK
HUH? I DON'T SEE THEM ...
IS PRAC-TICE ALREADY OVER?
GLANCE GLANCE
HEY!
YOU GUYS AREN'T FROM OUR SCHOOL,
ARE YOU?
WHAT ARE YOU HERE FOR?
TELL ME YOUR NAMES.
IMA-MURA ...
DASH
HE'S MAKING A BREAK FOR IT!

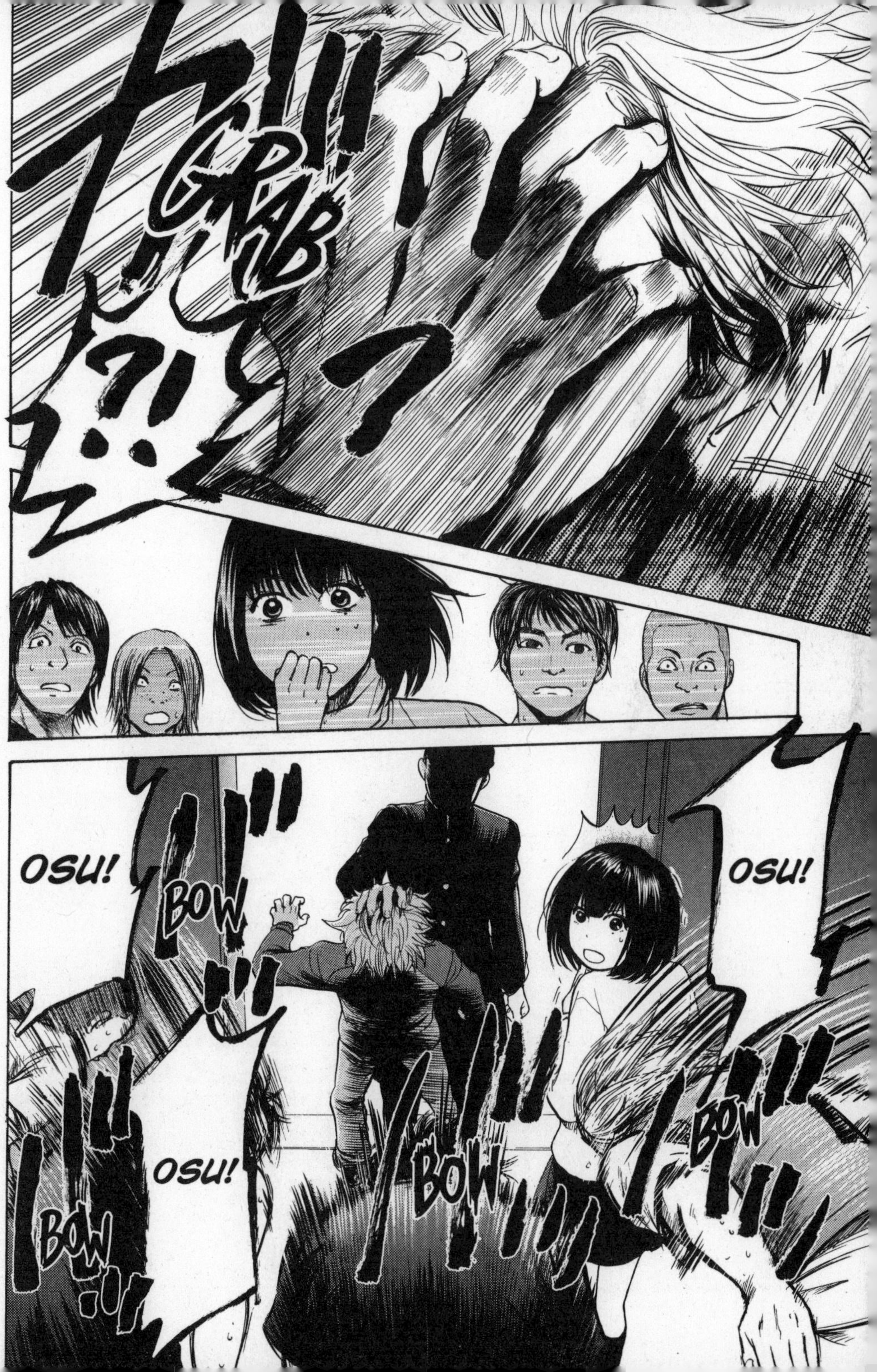
GRAB
?!
OSU!
BOW
BOW
OSU!
BOW
OSU!
BOW

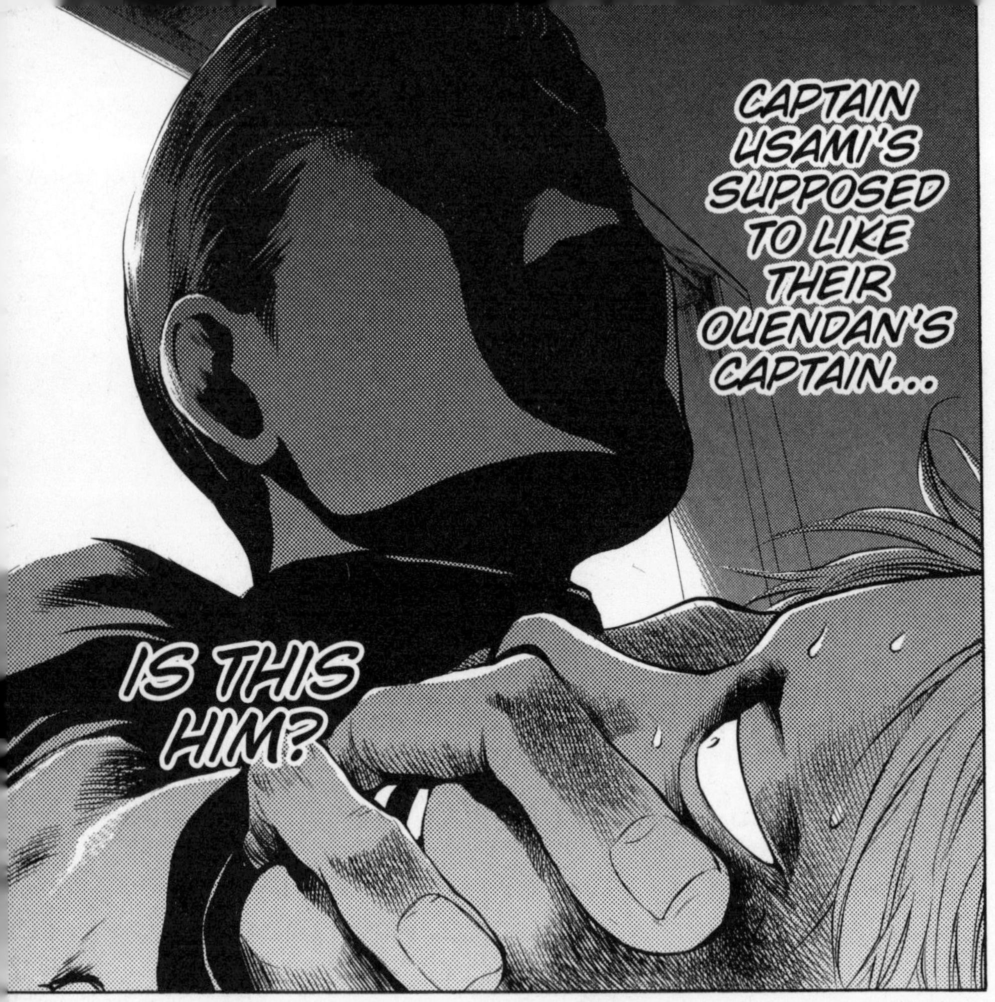
CAPTAIN USAMI'S SUPPOSED TO LIKE THEIR OUENDAN'S CAPTAIN...
IS THIS HIM?

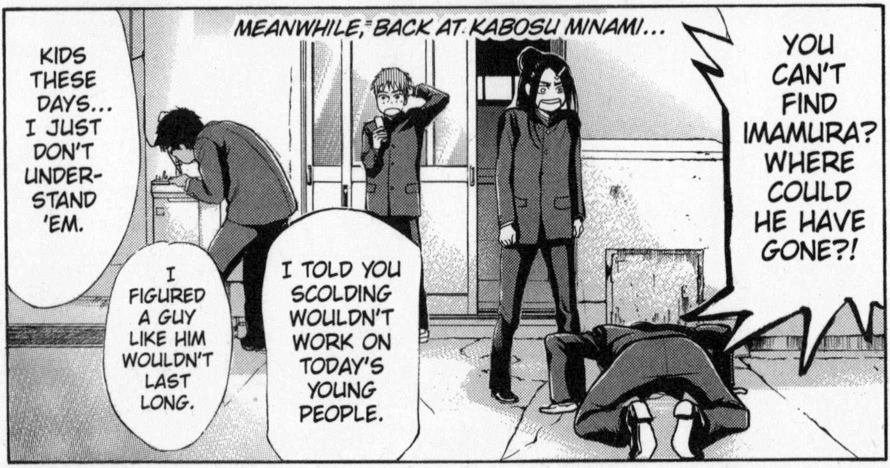
MEANWHILE, BACK AT KABOSU MINAMI...
YOU CAN'T FIND IMAMURA? WHERE COULD HE HAVE GONE?!
KIDS THESE DAYS... I JUST DON'T UNDER-STAND 'EM.
I TOLD YOU SCOLDING WOULDN'T WORK ON TODAY'S YOUNG PEOPLE.
I FIGURED A GUY LIKE HIM WOULDN'T LAST LONG.

Again!!

アゲイン!!

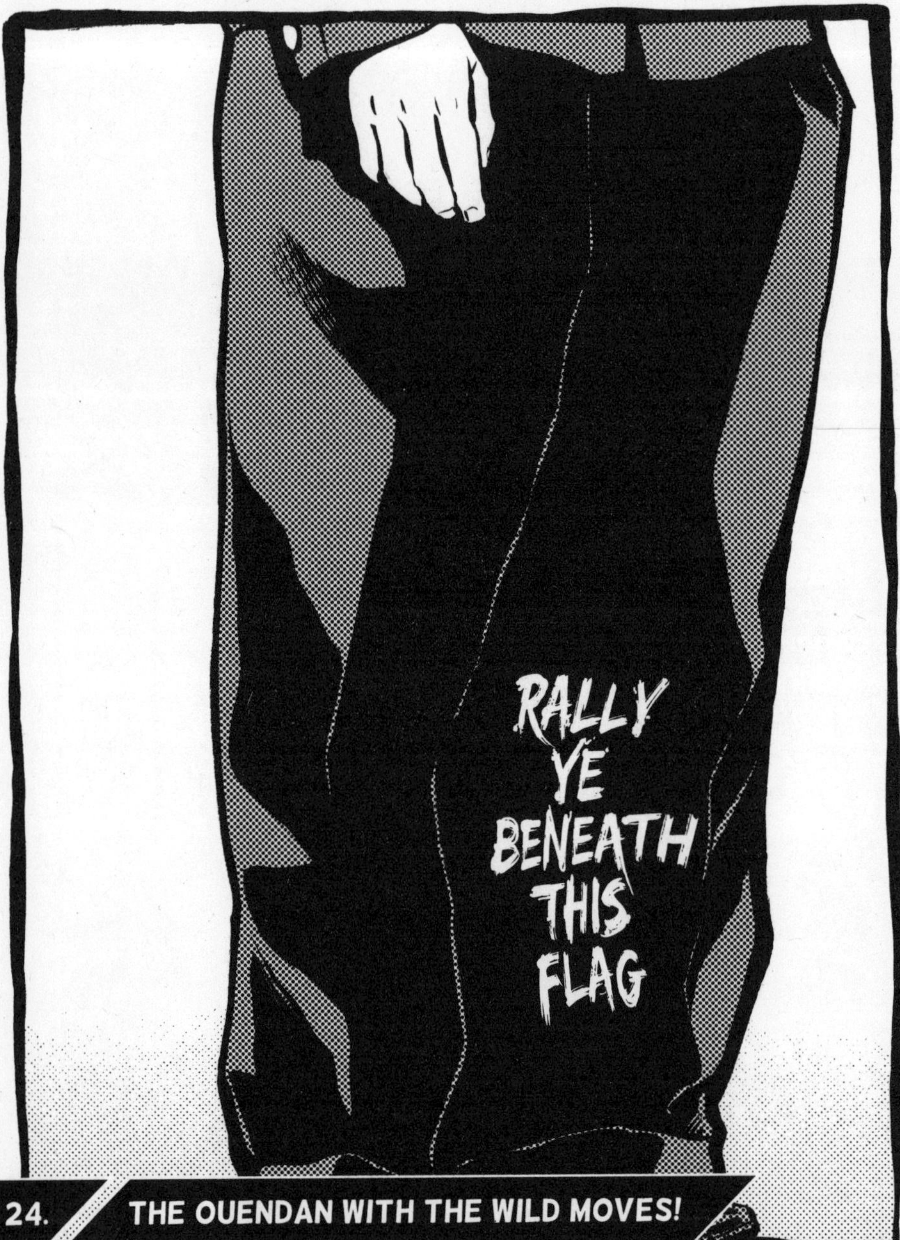
RALLY YE BENEATH THIS FLAG

24. THE OUENDAN WITH THE WILD MOVES!

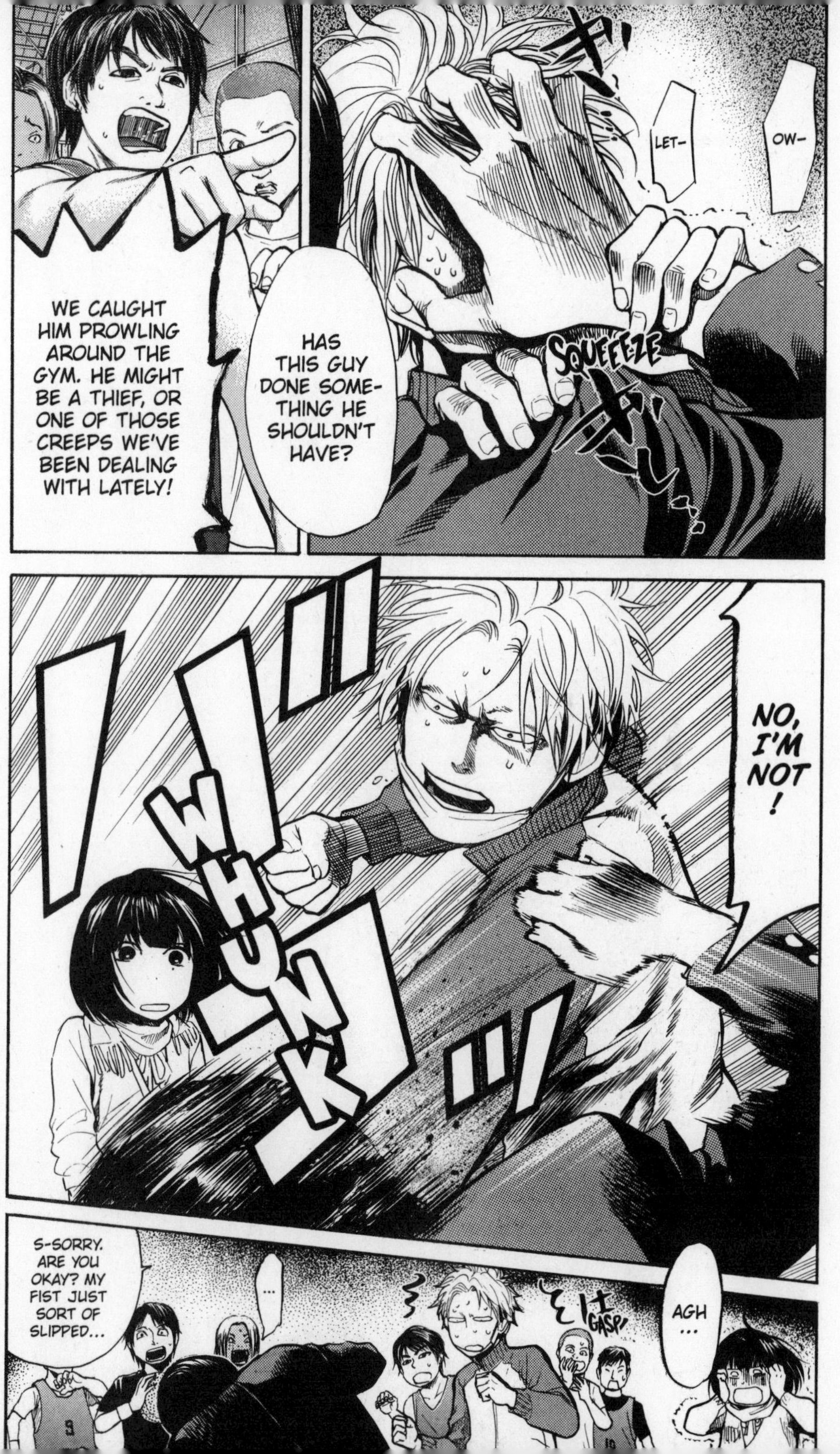
OW–
LET–
SQUEEEZE
HAS THIS GUY DONE SOMETHING HE SHOULDN'T HAVE?
WE CAUGHT HIM PROWLING AROUND THE GYM. HE MIGHT BE A THIEF, OR ONE OF THOSE CREEPS WE'VE BEEN DEALING WITH LATELY!
NO, I'M NOT!
WHUNK
AGH...
GASP!
...
S-SORRY. ARE YOU OKAY? MY FIST JUST SORT OF SLIPPED...

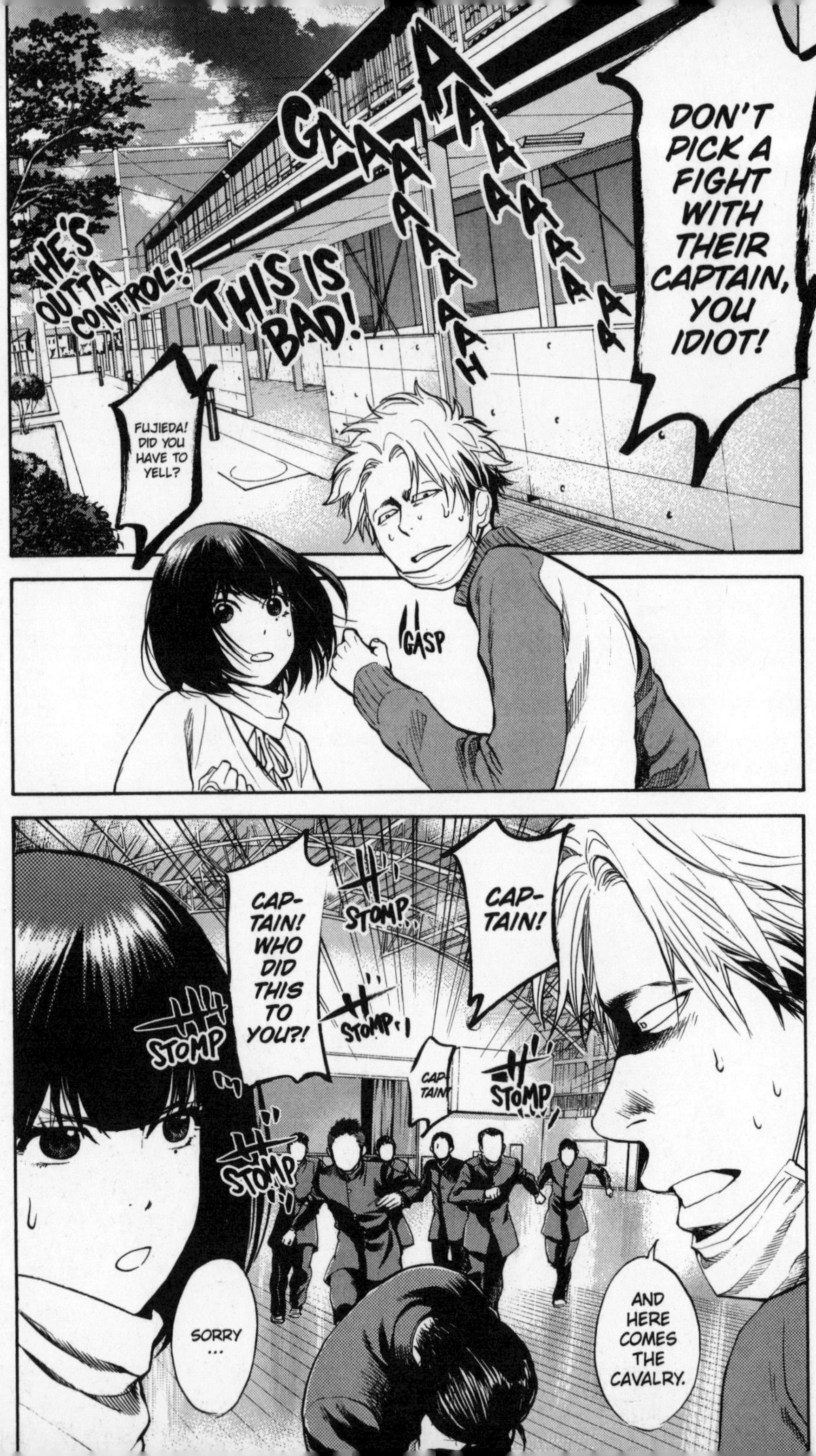
DON'T PICK A FIGHT WITH THEIR CAPTAIN, YOU IDIOT!
GAAAAAAAAAAAAAAAAAAH
THIS IS BAD!
HE'S OUTTA CONTROL!
FUJIEDA! DID YOU HAVE TO YELL?
GASP
CAP-TAIN!
STOMP
CAP-TAIN! WHO DID THIS TO YOU?!
STOMP
CAPTAIN
STOMP
STOMP
STOMP
AND HERE COMES THE CAVALRY.
SORRY...

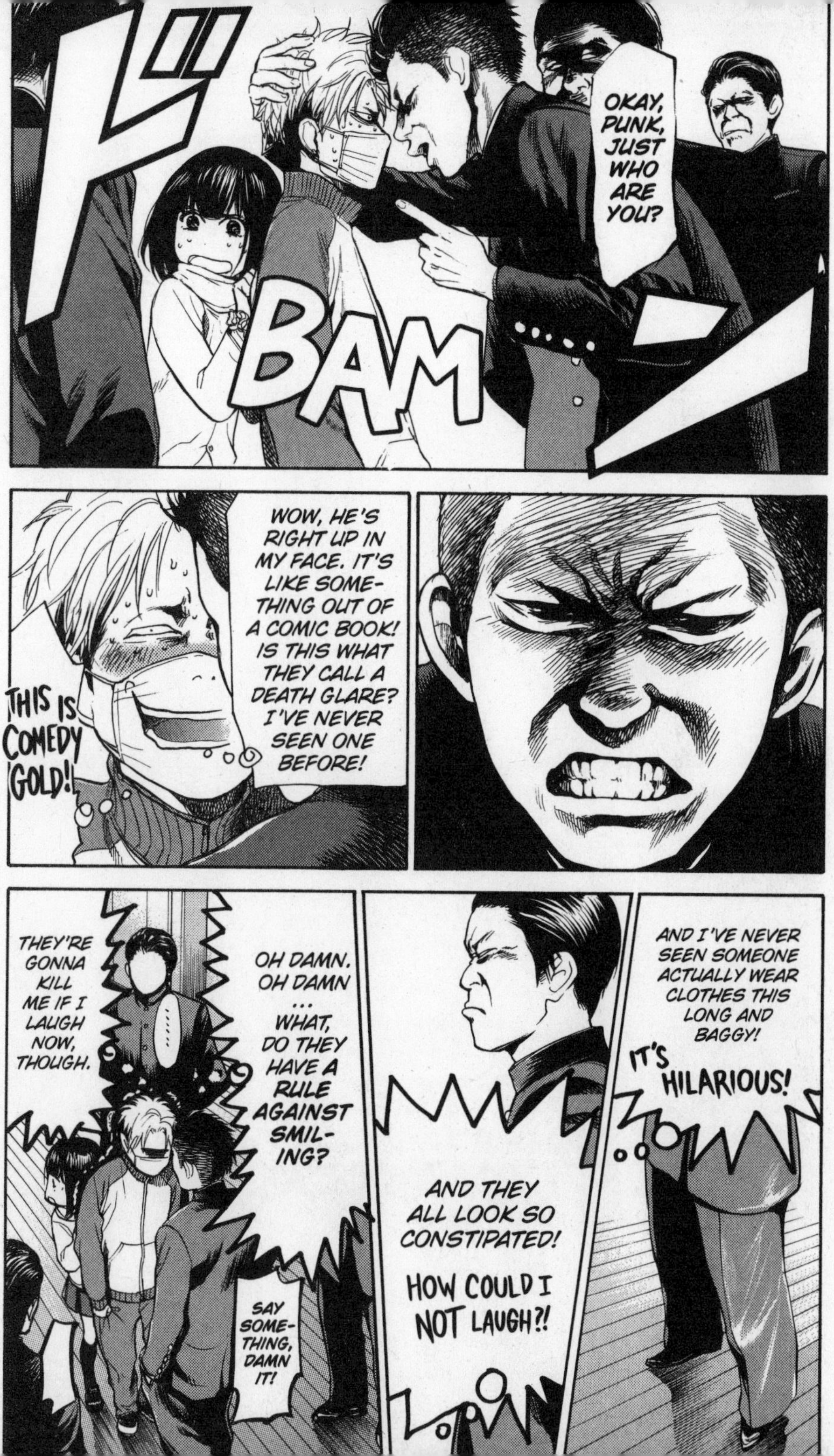
OKAY, PUNK, JUST WHO ARE YOU?
BAM
WOW, HE'S RIGHT UP IN MY FACE. IT'S LIKE SOMETHING OUT OF A COMIC BOOK! IS THIS WHAT THEY CALL A DEATH GLARE? I'VE NEVER SEEN ONE BEFORE!
THIS IS COMEDY GOLD!
AND I'VE NEVER SEEN SOMEONE ACTUALLY WEAR CLOTHES THIS LONG AND BAGGY!
IT'S HILARIOUS!
AND THEY ALL LOOK SO CONSTIPATED!
HOW COULD I NOT LAUGH?!
OH DAMN. OH DAMN ... WHAT, DO THEY HAVE A RULE AGAINST SMILING?
THEY'RE GONNA KILL ME IF I LAUGH NOW, THOUGH.
SAY SOMETHING, DAMN IT!

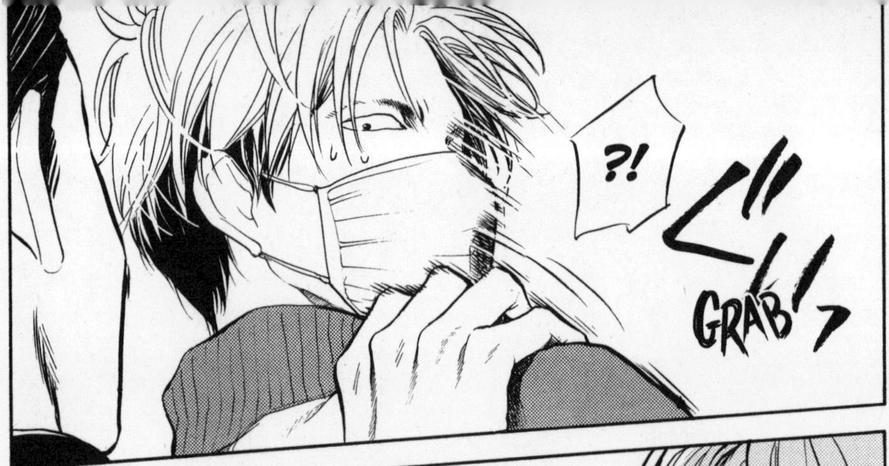
?!
GRAB
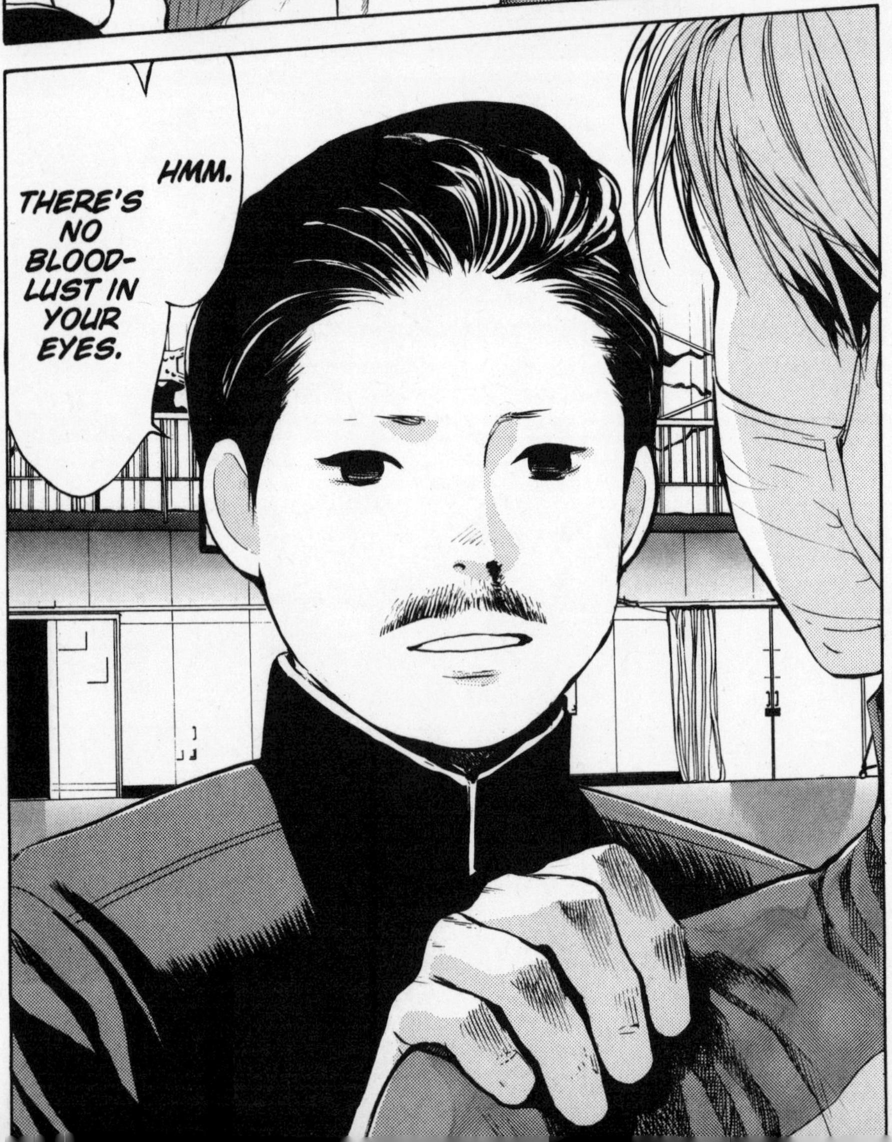
HMM. THERE'S NO BLOOD-LUST IN YOUR EYES.

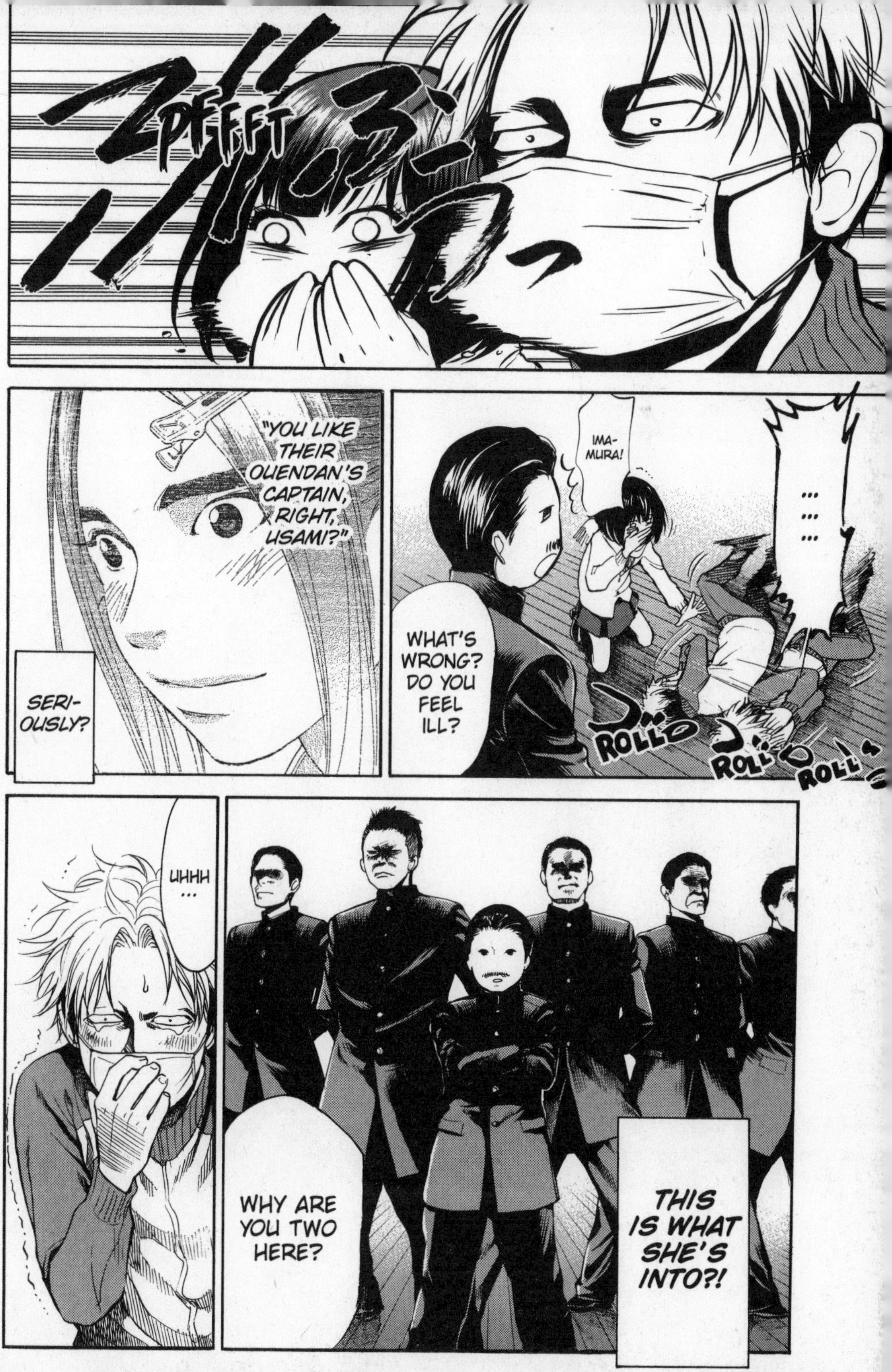
PFFFT
...
...
...
IMA-
MURA!
WHAT'S WRONG? DO YOU FEEL ILL?
ROLL
ROLL
ROLL
"YOU LIKE THEIR OUENDAN'S CAPTAIN, RIGHT, USAMI?"
SERI-
OUSLY?
THIS IS WHAT SHE'S INTO?!
WHY ARE YOU TWO HERE?
UHHH
...

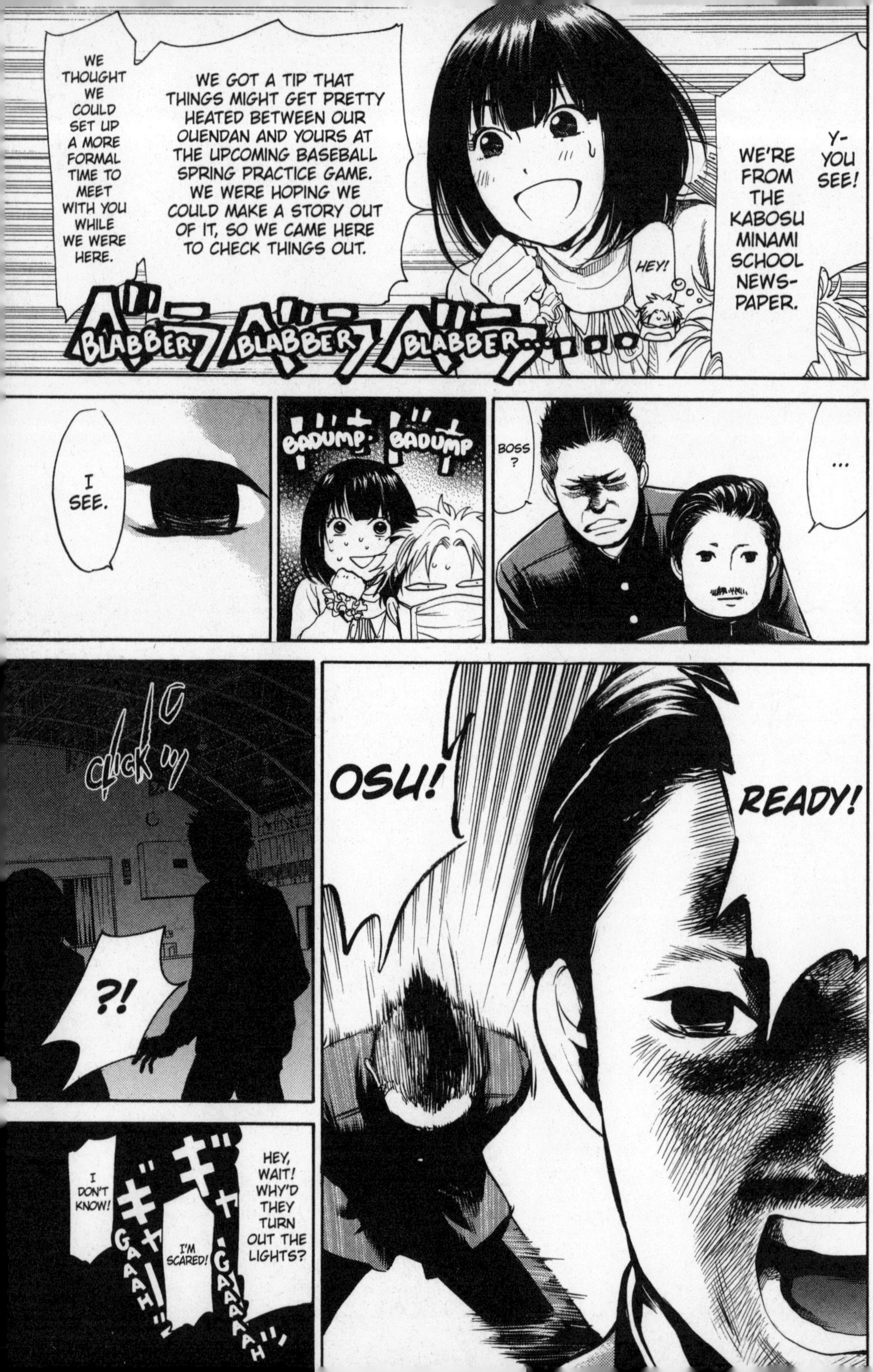
Y-YOU SEE!
WE'RE FROM THE KABOSU MINAMI SCHOOL NEWSPAPER.
HEY!
WE GOT A TIP THAT THINGS MIGHT GET PRETTY HEATED BETWEEN OUR OUENDAN AND YOURS AT THE UPCOMING BASEBALL SPRING PRACTICE GAME. WE WERE HOPING WE COULD MAKE A STORY OUT OF IT, SO WE CAME HERE TO CHECK THINGS OUT.
WE THOUGHT WE COULD SET UP A MORE FORMAL TIME TO MEET WITH YOU WHILE WE WERE HERE.
BLABBER BLABBER BLABBER...
...
BOSS?
BADUMP BADUMP
I SEE.
READY!
OSU!
CLICK
?!
HEY, WAIT! WHY'D THEY TURN OUT THE LIGHTS?
GAAAAAH
I'M SCARED!
I DON'T KNOW!
GAAAH

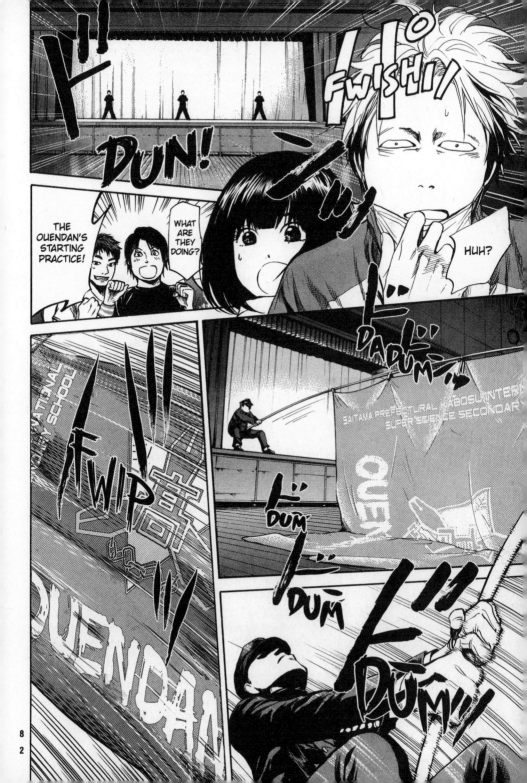

FWISH!!

DUN!

THE OUENDAN'S STARTING PRACTICE!

WHAT ARE THEY DOING?

HUH?

DA DUM

FWIP

DUM

DUM

DUM!!

OUENDAA

SAITAMA PREFECTURAL KABOSU INTERNA SUPER SCIENCE SECONDAR

OUEN

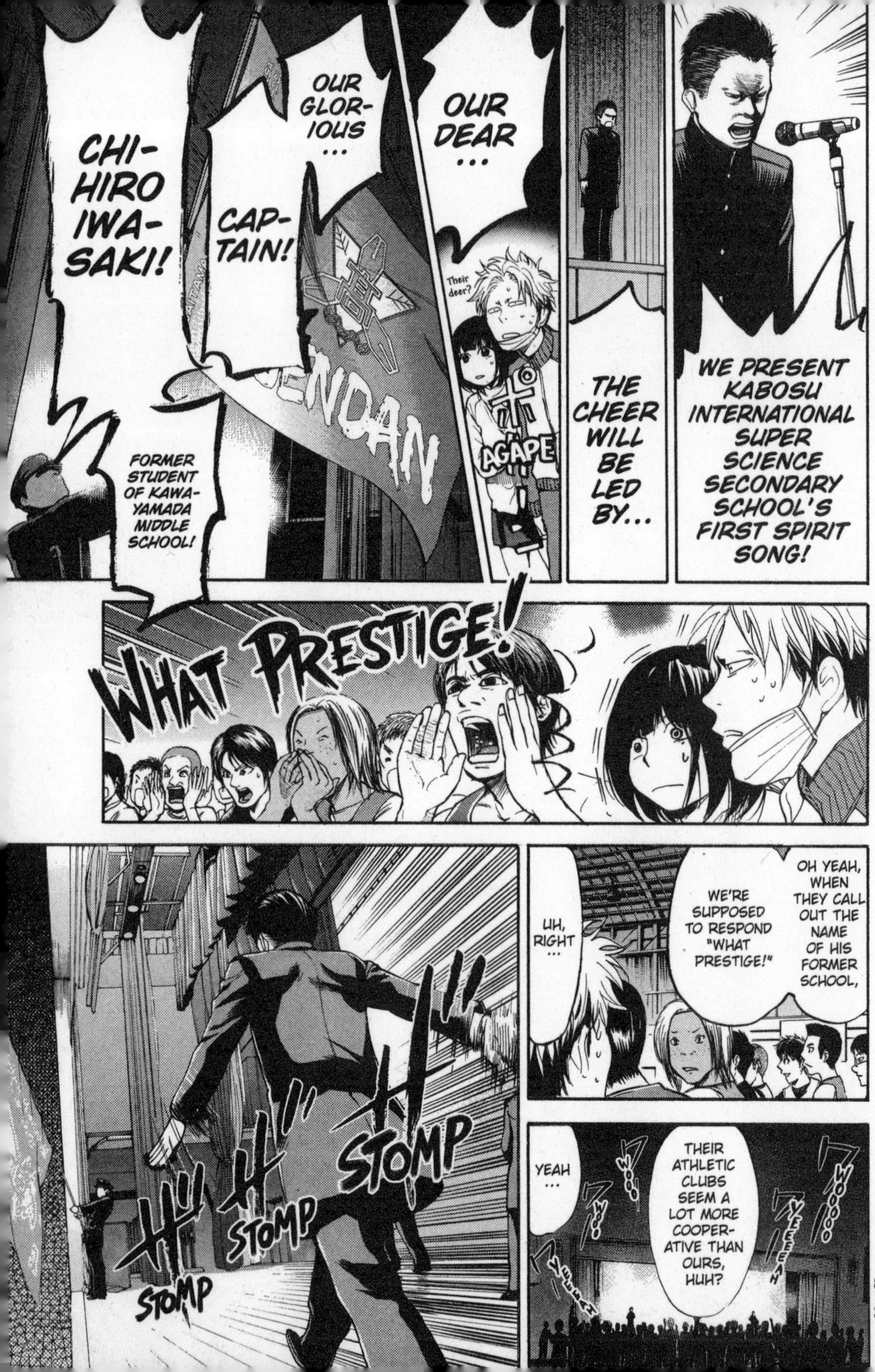
WE PRESENT KABOSU INTERNATIONAL SUPER SCIENCE SECONDARY SCHOOL'S FIRST SPIRIT SONG!
THE CHEER WILL BE LED BY...
OUR DEAR ...
Their deer?
AGAPE
OUR GLORIOUS ...
CAP-TAIN!
CHI-HIRO IWA-SAKI!
FORMER STUDENT OF KAWA-YAMADA MIDDLE SCHOOL!
WHAT PRESTIGE!
OH YEAH, WHEN THEY CALL OUT THE NAME OF HIS FORMER SCHOOL,
WE'RE SUPPOSED TO RESPOND "WHAT PRESTIGE!"
UH, RIGHT ...
THEIR ATHLETIC CLUBS SEEM A LOT MORE COOPERATIVE THAN OURS, HUH?
YEAH ...
WOOOOO
YEEEEAH
STOMP
STOMP
STOMP

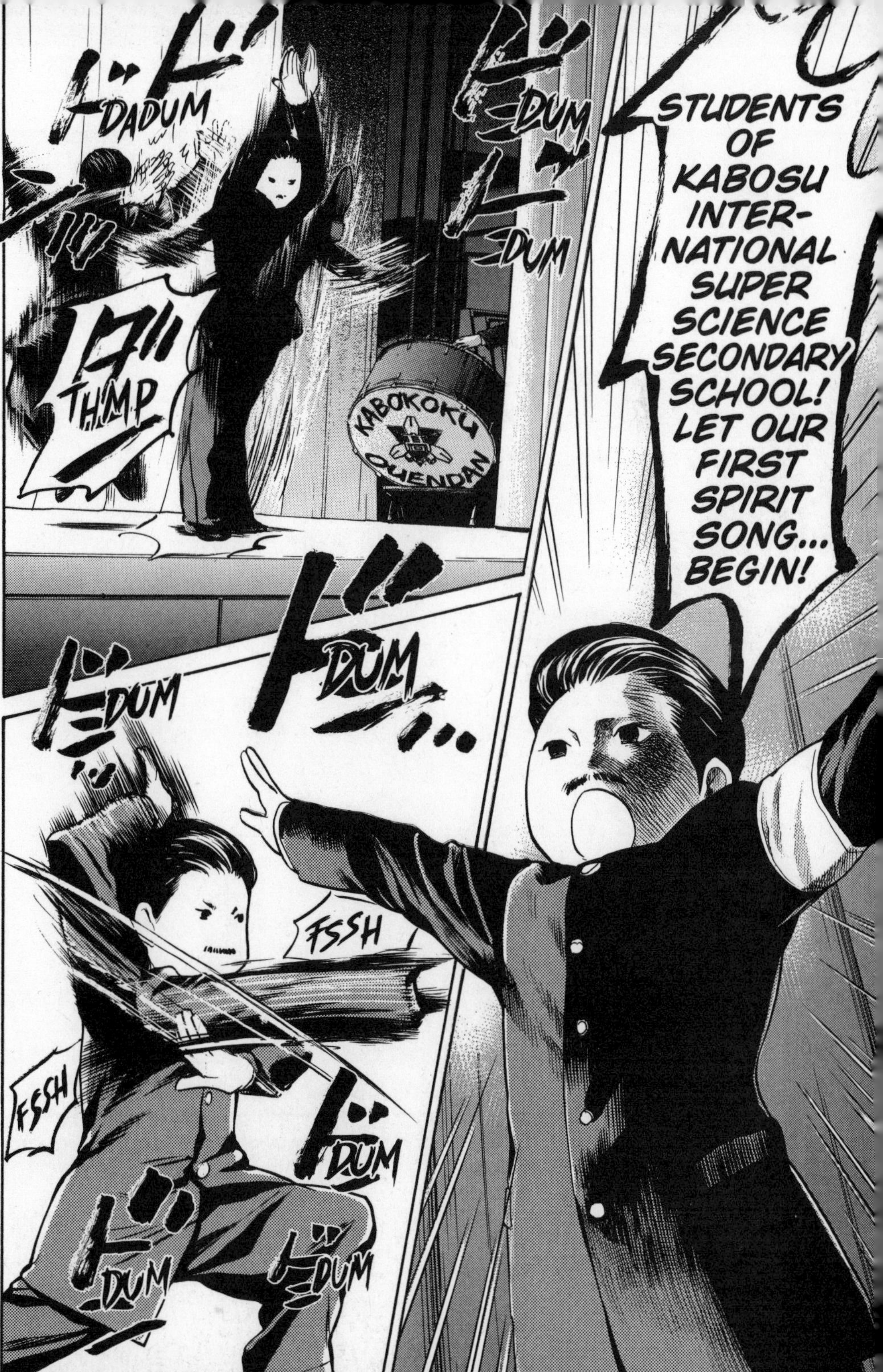
STUDENTS OF KABOSU INTER-NATIONAL SUPER SCIENCE SECONDARY SCHOOL! LET OUR FIRST SPIRIT SONG... BEGIN!
DUM
DUM
DADUM
KABOKOKU OUENDAN
THMP
DUM...
DUM
FSSH
FSSH
DUM
DUM
DUM

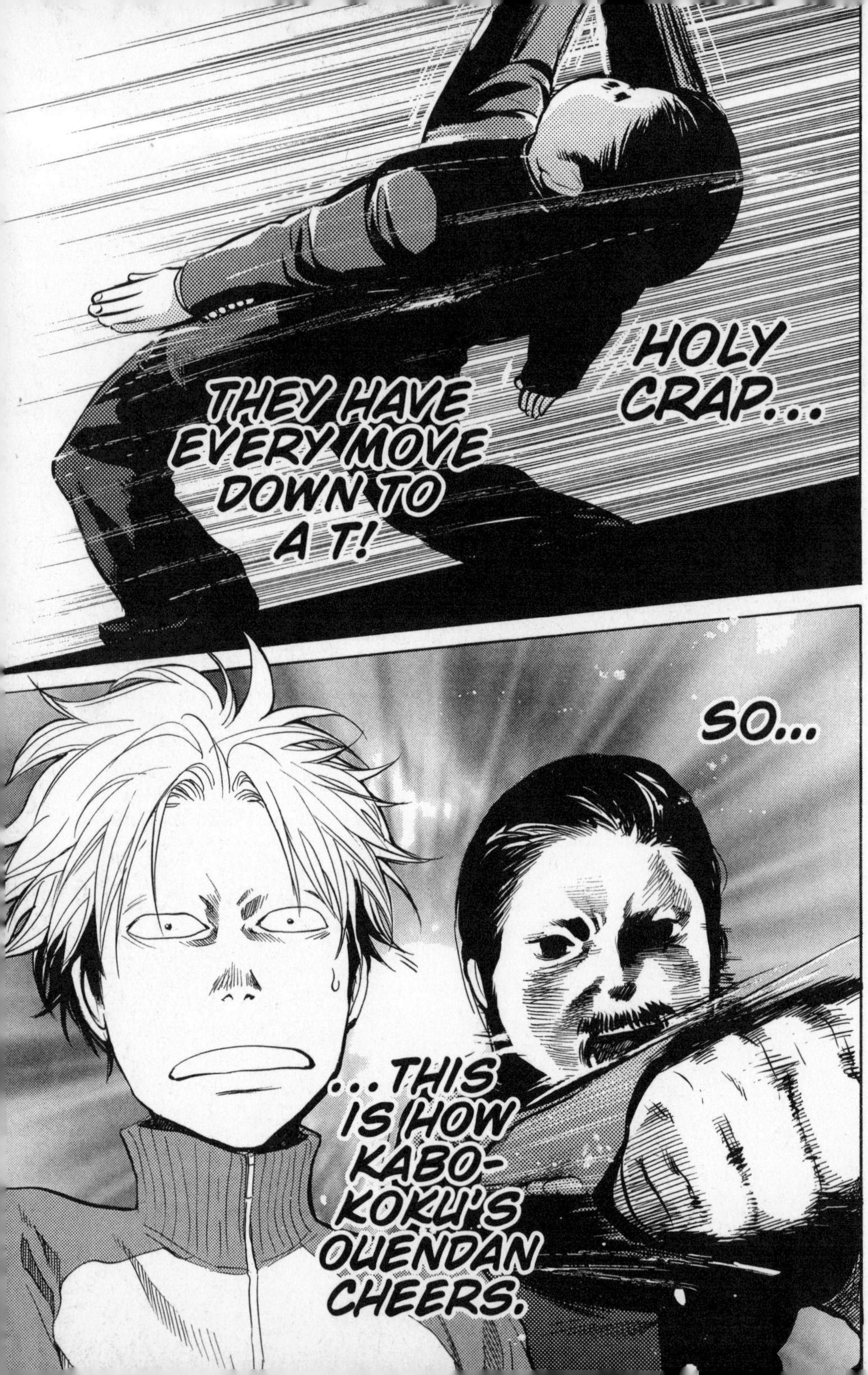
HOLY CRAP...
THEY HAVE EVERY MOVE DOWN TO A T!
SO...
...THIS IS HOW KABO-KOKU'S OUENDAN CHEERS.

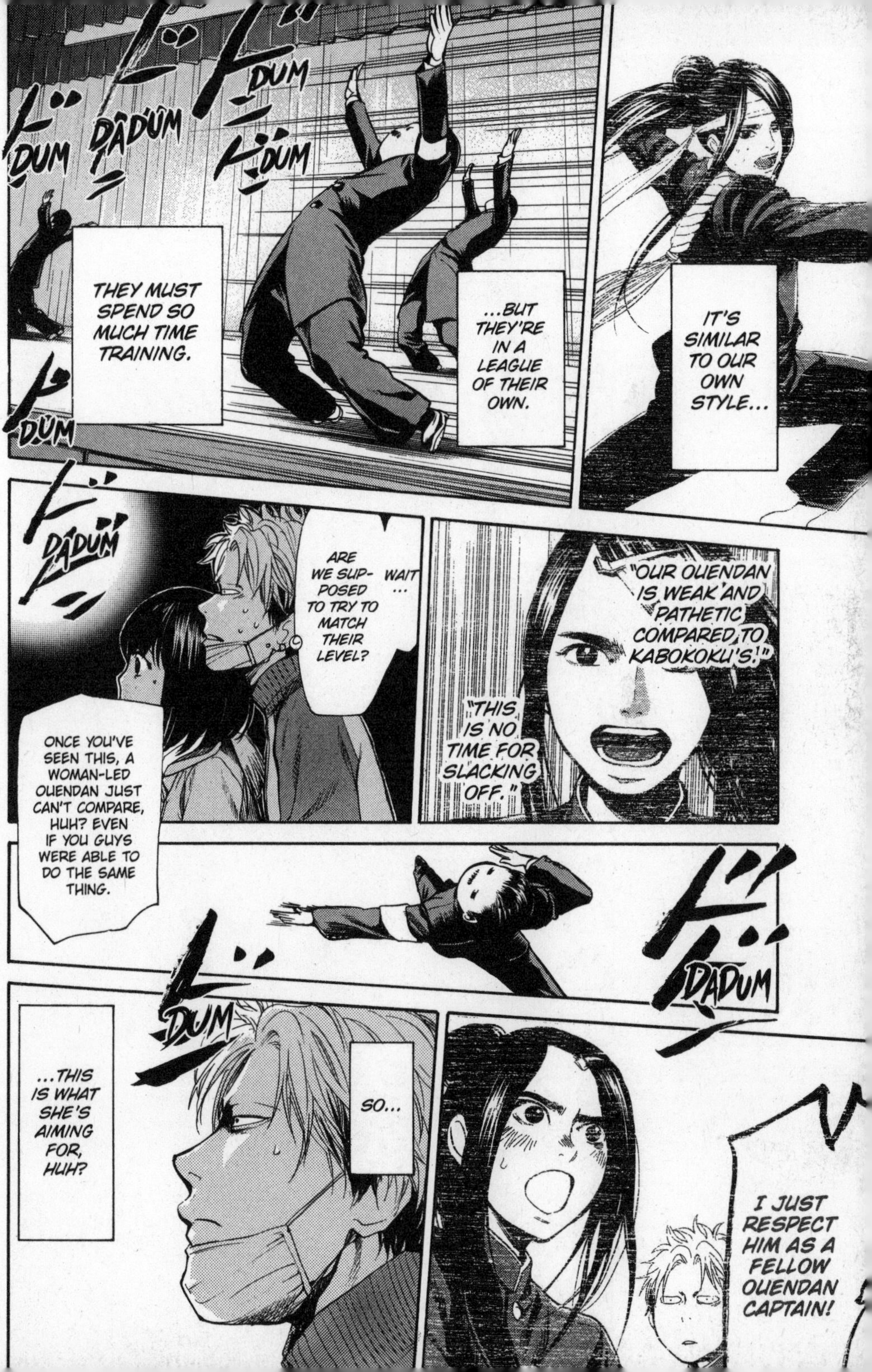
IT'S SIMILAR TO OUR OWN STYLE...
DUM
DUM
DADUM
DUM
...BUT THEY'RE IN A LEAGUE OF THEIR OWN.
THEY MUST SPEND SO MUCH TIME TRAINING.
DUM
"OUR OUENDAN IS WEAK AND PATHETIC COMPARED TO KABOKOKU'S!"
"THIS IS NO TIME FOR SLACKING OFF."
WAIT...
ARE WE SUPPOSED TO TRY TO MATCH THEIR LEVEL?
DADUM
ONCE YOU'VE SEEN THIS, A WOMAN-LED OUENDAN JUST CAN'T COMPARE, HUH? EVEN IF YOU GUYS WERE ABLE TO DO THE SAME THING.
DADUM
DUM
I JUST RESPECT HIM AS A FELLOW OUENDAN CAPTAIN!
SO...
...THIS IS WHAT SHE'S AIMING FOR, HUH?

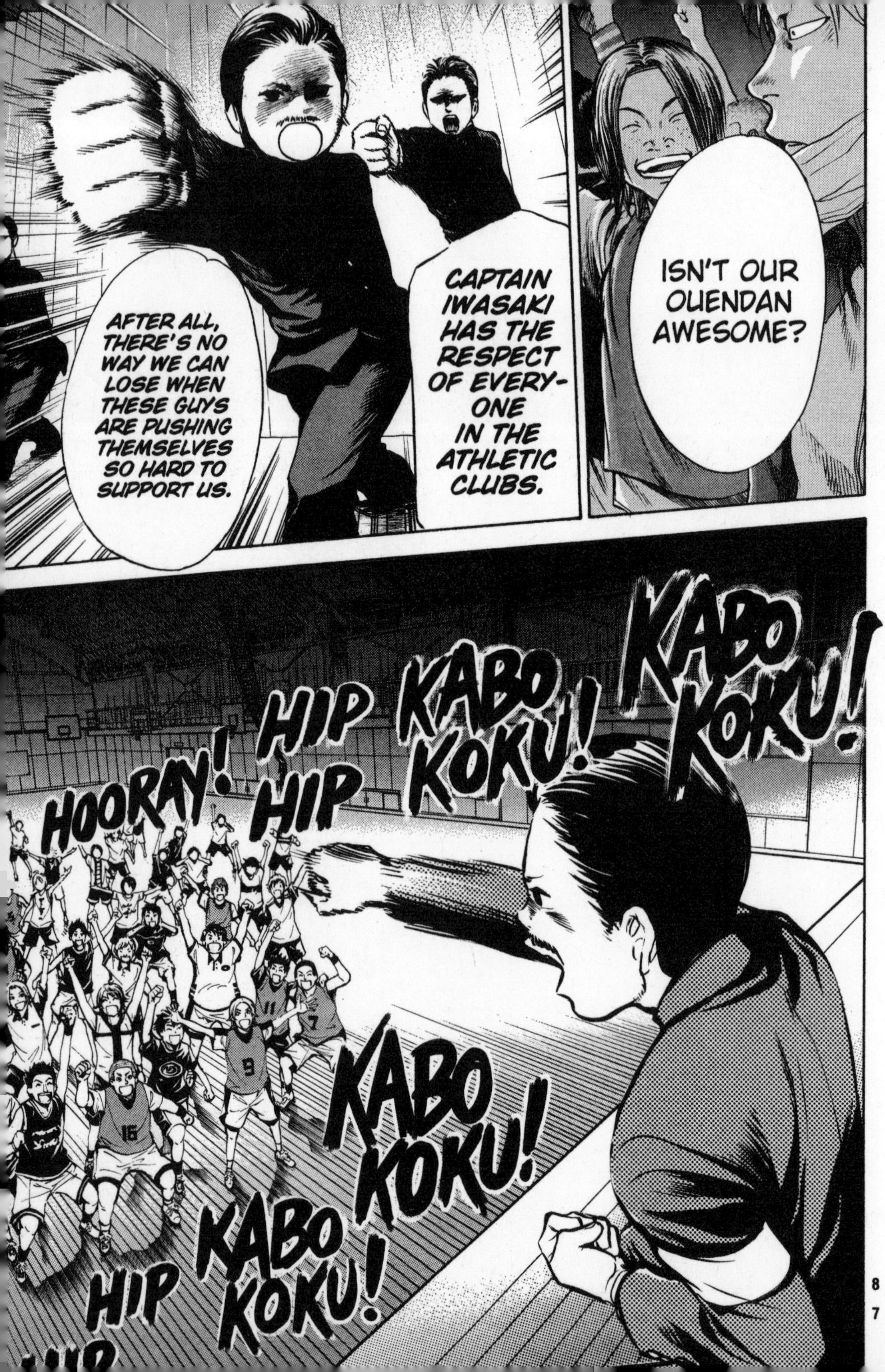
ISN'T OUR OUENDAN AWESOME?
CAPTAIN IWASAKI HAS THE RESPECT OF EVERY-ONE IN THE ATHLETIC CLUBS.
AFTER ALL, THERE'S NO WAY WE CAN LOSE WHEN THESE GUYS ARE PUSHING THEMSELVES SO HARD TO SUPPORT US.
KABO KOKU!
HIP HIP KABO KOKU!
HOORAY!
KABO KOKU!
HIP KABO KOKU!

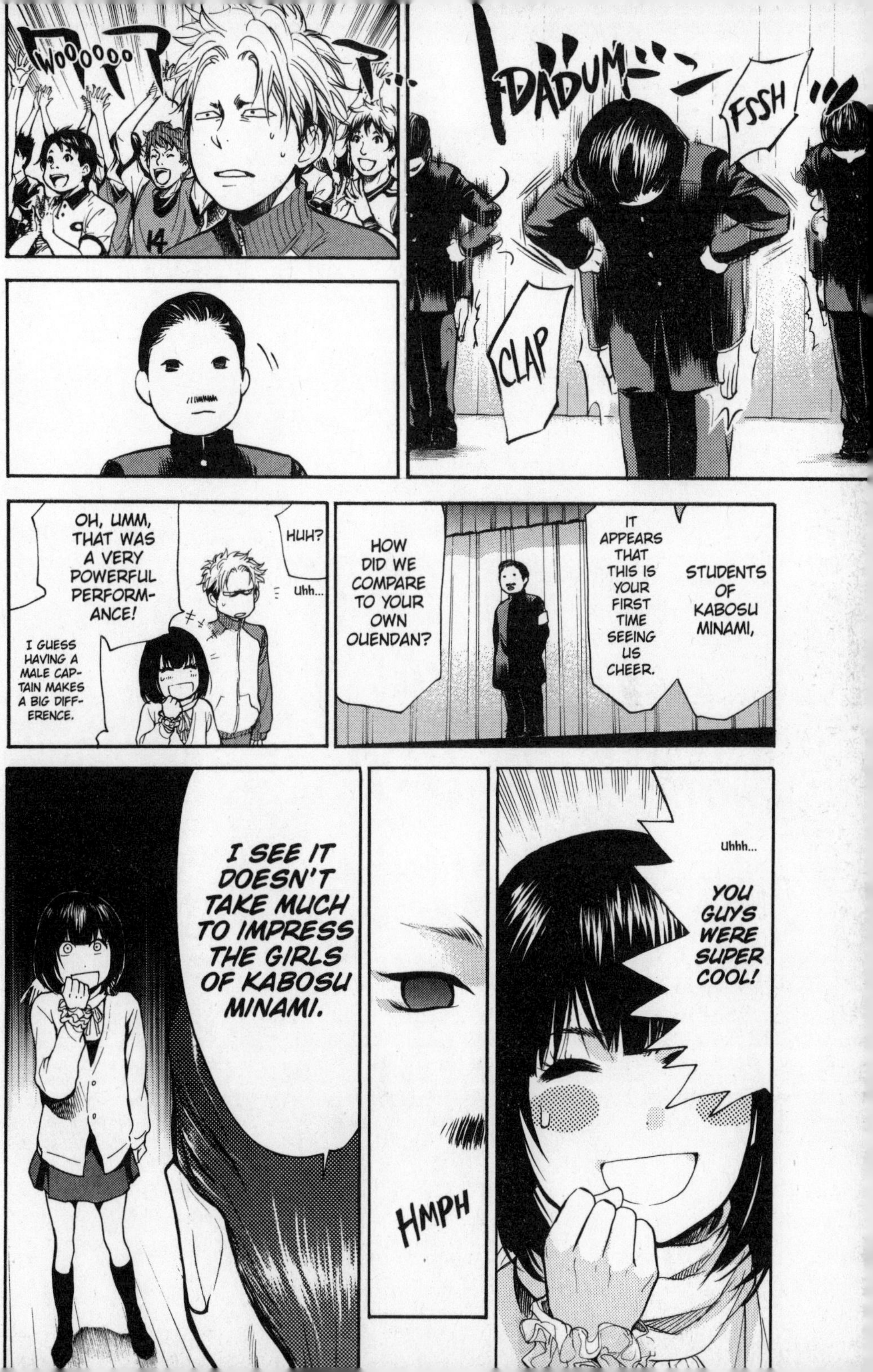
DADUM
FSSH
CLAP
WOOOOOO
STUDENTS OF KABOSU MINAMI,
IT APPEARS THAT THIS IS YOUR FIRST TIME SEEING US CHEER.
HOW DID WE COMPARE TO YOUR OWN OUENDAN?
HUH?
Uhh...
OH, UMM, THAT WAS A VERY POWERFUL PERFORMANCE!
I GUESS HAVING A MALE CAPTAIN MAKES A BIG DIFFERENCE.
Uhhh...
YOU GUYS WERE SUPER COOL!
HMPH
I SEE IT DOESN'T TAKE MUCH TO IMPRESS THE GIRLS OF KABOSU MINAMI.

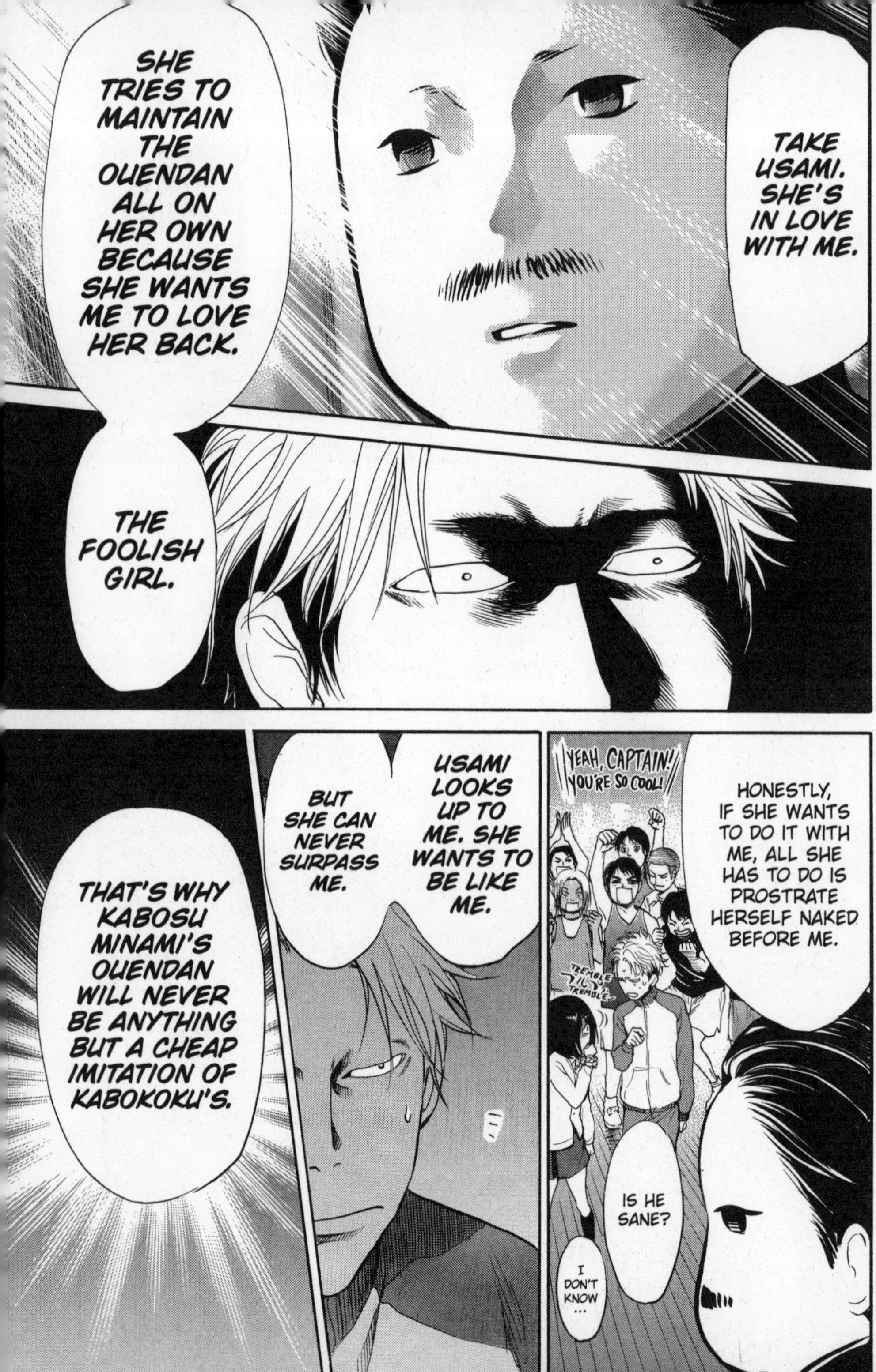
TAKE USAMI. SHE'S IN LOVE WITH ME.
SHE TRIES TO MAINTAIN THE OUENDAN ALL ON HER OWN BECAUSE SHE WANTS ME TO LOVE HER BACK.
THE FOOLISH GIRL.
HONESTLY, IF SHE WANTS TO DO IT WITH ME, ALL SHE HAS TO DO IS PROSTRATE HERSELF NAKED BEFORE ME.
YEAH, CAPTAIN! YOU'RE SO COOL!
TREMBLE TREMBLE
IS HE SANE?
I DON'T KNOW...
USAMI LOOKS UP TO ME. SHE WANTS TO BE LIKE ME.
BUT SHE CAN NEVER SURPASS ME.
THAT'S WHY KABOSU MINAMI'S OUENDAN WILL NEVER BE ANYTHING BUT A CHEAP IMITATION OF KABOKOKU'S.

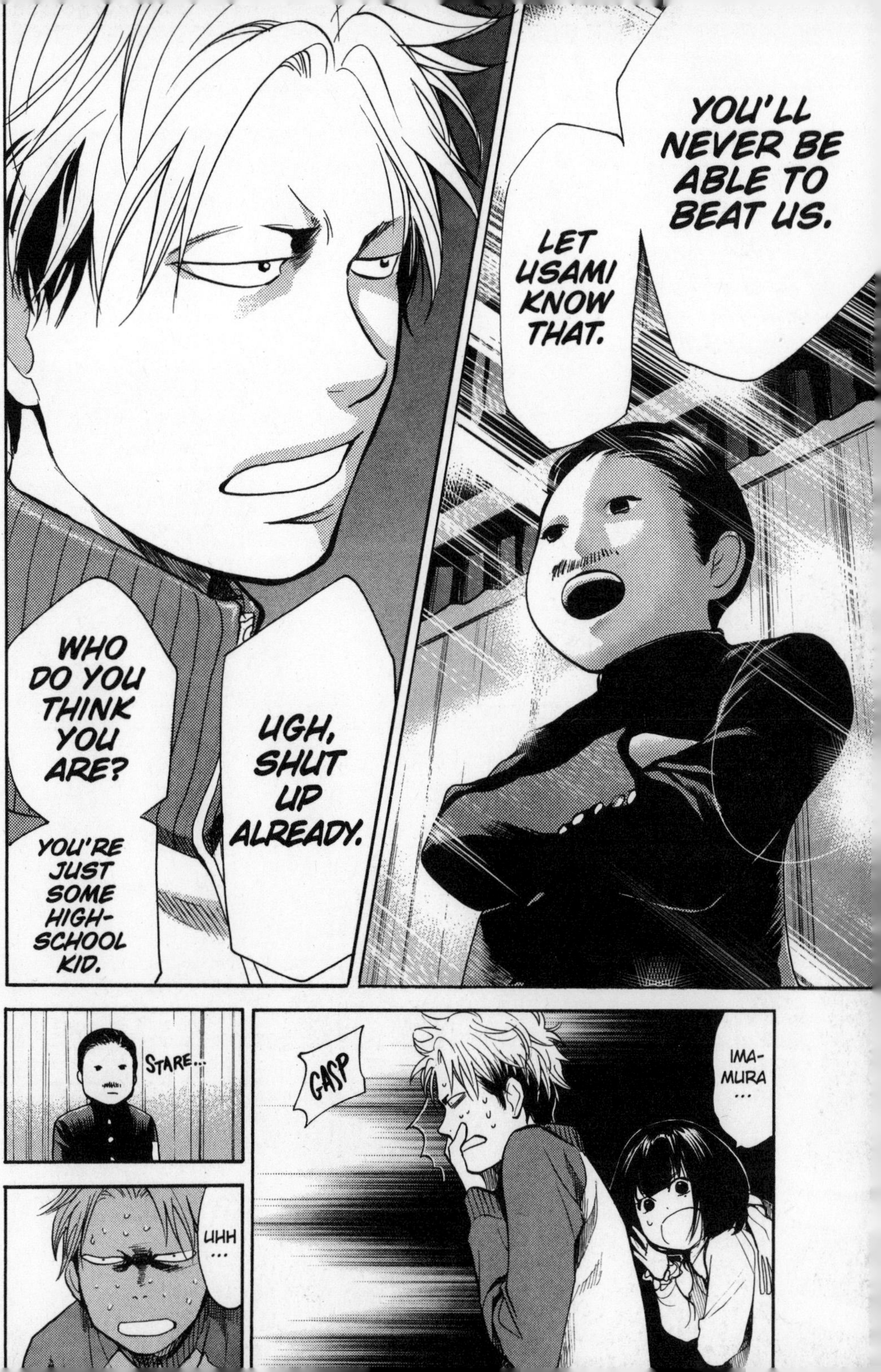
YOU'LL NEVER BE ABLE TO BEAT US.
LET USAMI KNOW THAT.
UGH, SHUT UP ALREADY.
WHO DO YOU THINK YOU ARE?
YOU'RE JUST SOME HIGH-SCHOOL KID.
IMA-MURA...
GASP
STARE...
UHH...

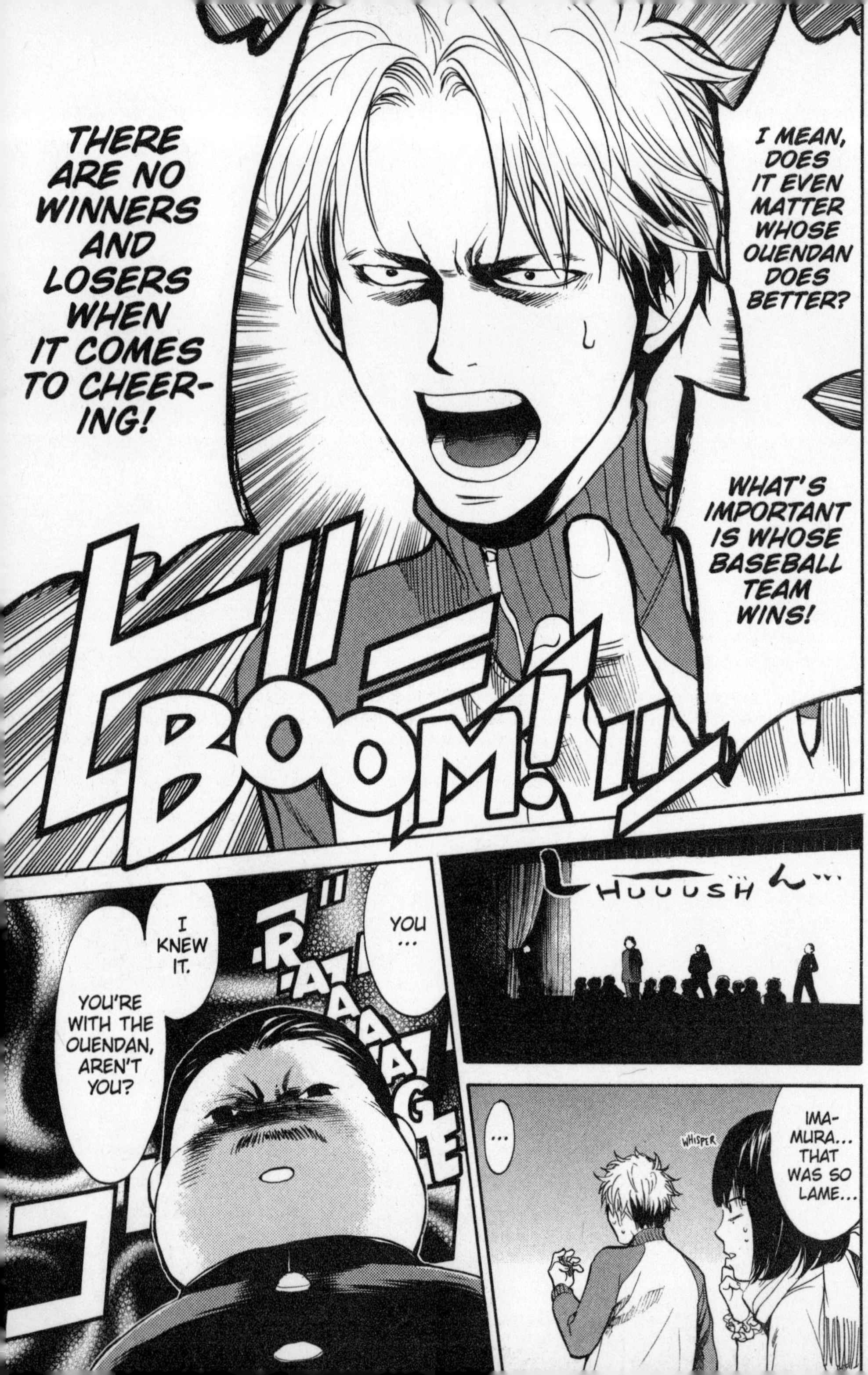
I MEAN, DOES IT EVEN MATTER WHOSE OUENDAN DOES BETTER?
THERE ARE NO WINNERS AND LOSERS WHEN IT COMES TO CHEER-ING!
WHAT'S IMPORTANT IS WHOSE BASEBALL TEAM WINS!
BOOM!
HUUUSH
IMA-MURA... THAT WAS SO LAME...
WHISPER
...
YOU ...
I KNEW IT.
YOU'RE WITH THE OUENDAN, AREN'T YOU?
RAAAAGE

Again!!
アゲイン!!

25. LET ME SLEEP IN YOUR ARMS

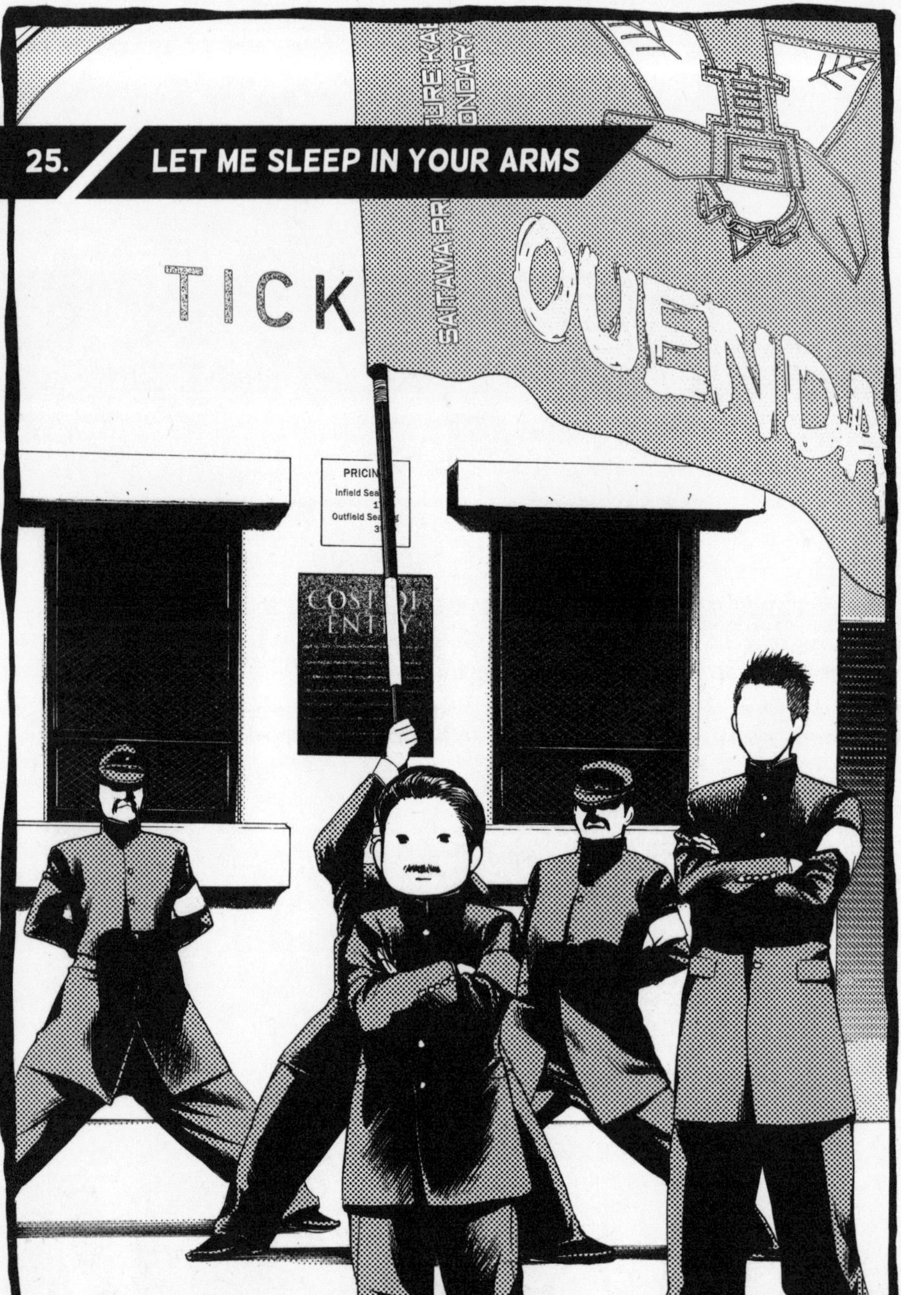

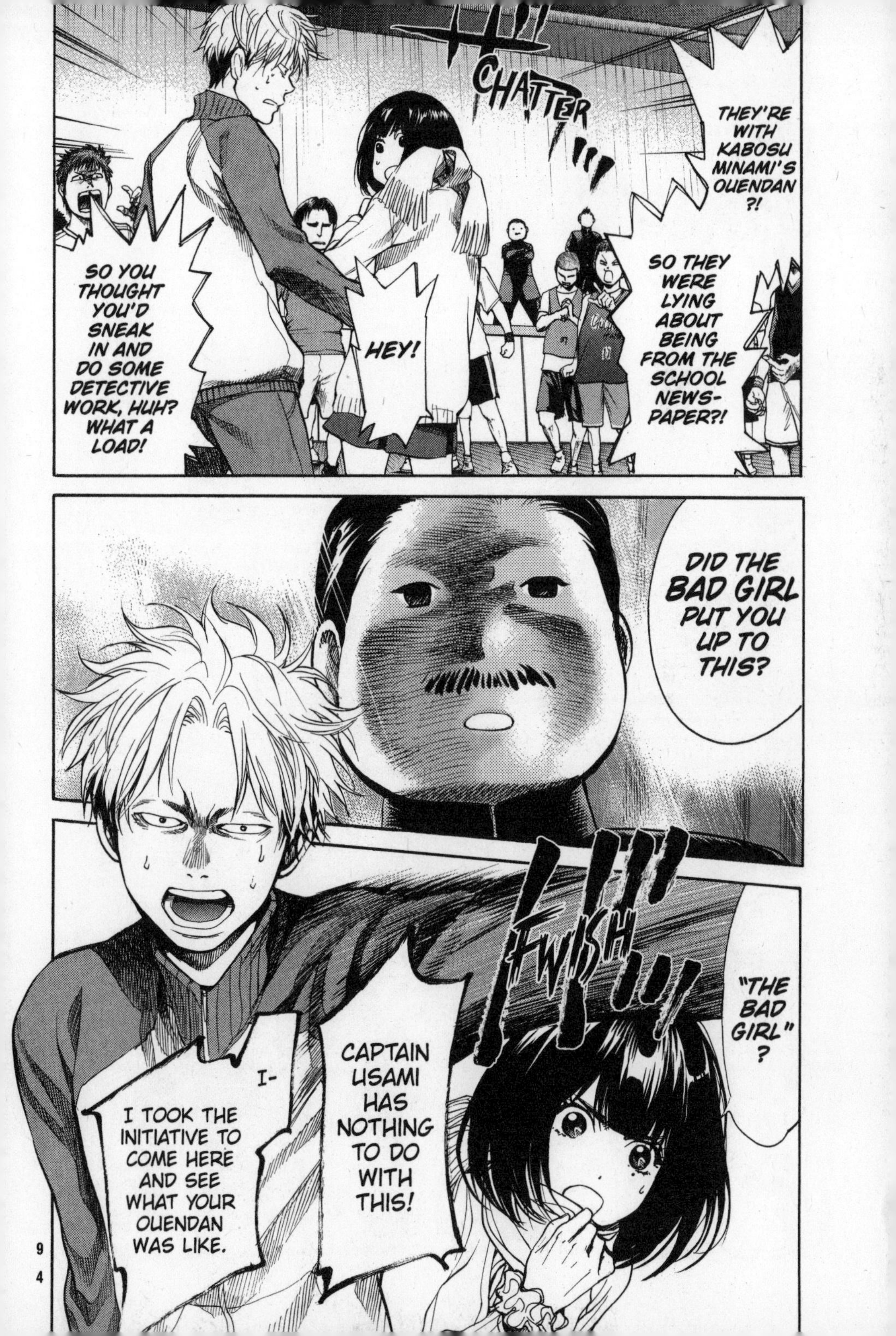
CHATTER
THEY'RE WITH KABOSU MINAMI'S OUENDAN ?!
SO THEY WERE LYING ABOUT BEING FROM THE SCHOOL NEWS-PAPER?!
HEY!
SO YOU THOUGHT YOU'D SNEAK IN AND DO SOME DETECTIVE WORK, HUH? WHAT A LOAD!
DID THE BAD GIRL PUT YOU UP TO THIS?
"THE BAD GIRL" ?
FWISH
CAPTAIN USAMI HAS NOTHING TO DO WITH THIS!
I-
I TOOK THE INITIATIVE TO COME HERE AND SEE WHAT YOUR OUENDAN WAS LIKE.

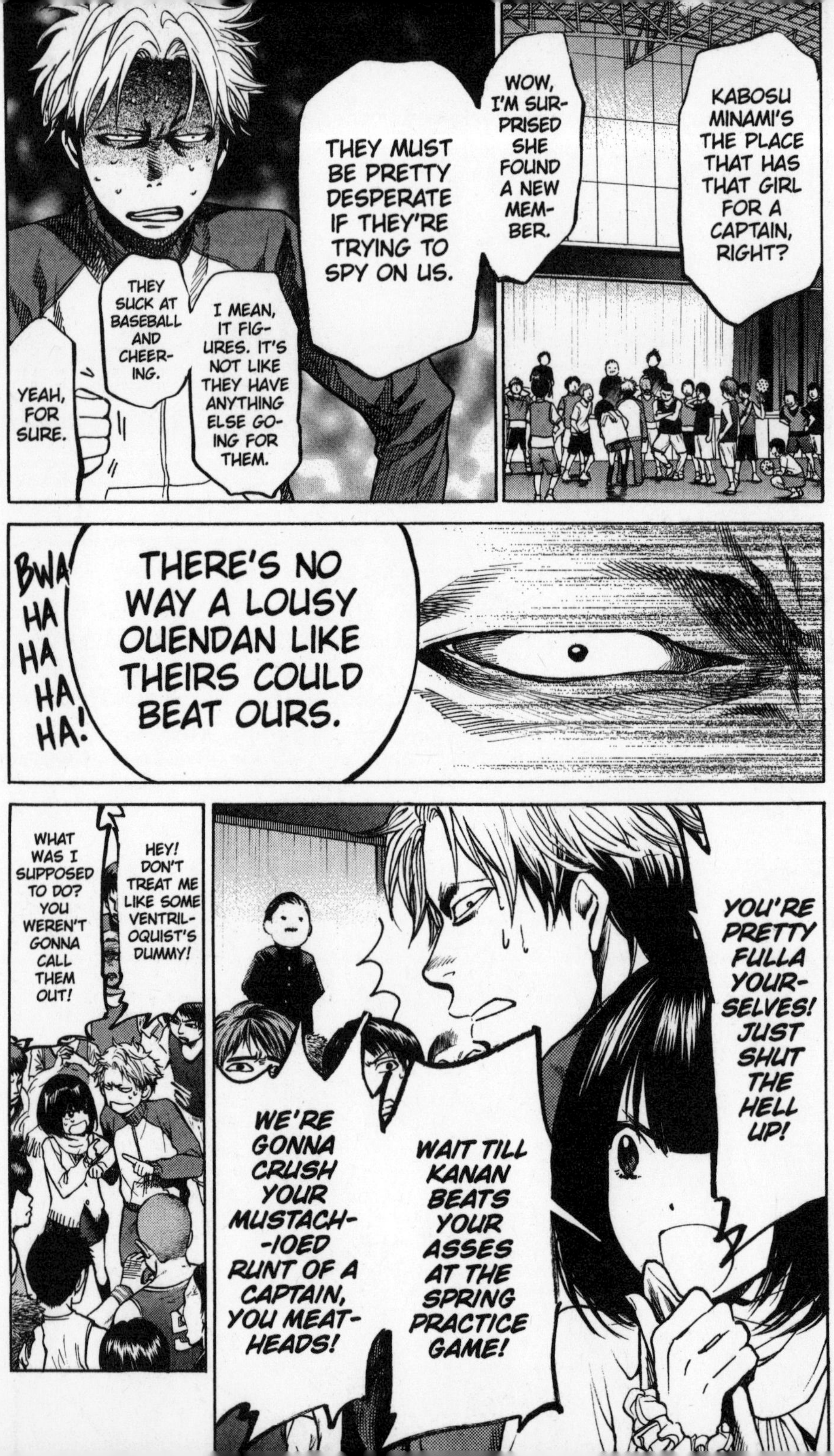
KABOSU MINAMI'S THE PLACE THAT HAS THAT GIRL FOR A CAPTAIN, RIGHT?
WOW, I'M SURPRISED SHE FOUND A NEW MEMBER.
THEY MUST BE PRETTY DESPERATE IF THEY'RE TRYING TO SPY ON US.
I MEAN, IT FIGURES. IT'S NOT LIKE THEY HAVE ANYTHING ELSE GOING FOR THEM.
THEY SUCK AT BASEBALL AND CHEERING.
YEAH, FOR SURE.
THERE'S NO WAY A LOUSY OUENDAN LIKE THEIRS COULD BEAT OURS.
BWAHAHAHAHAHA!
YOU'RE PRETTY FULLA YOURSELVES! JUST SHUT THE HELL UP!
WAIT TILL KANAN BEATS YOUR ASSES AT THE SPRING PRACTICE GAME!
WE'RE GONNA CRUSH YOUR MUSTACHIOED RUNT OF A CAPTAIN, YOU MEATHEADS!
HEY! DON'T TREAT ME LIKE SOME VENTRILOQUIST'S DUMMY!
WHAT WAS I SUPPOSED TO DO? YOU WEREN'T GONNA CALL THEM OUT!

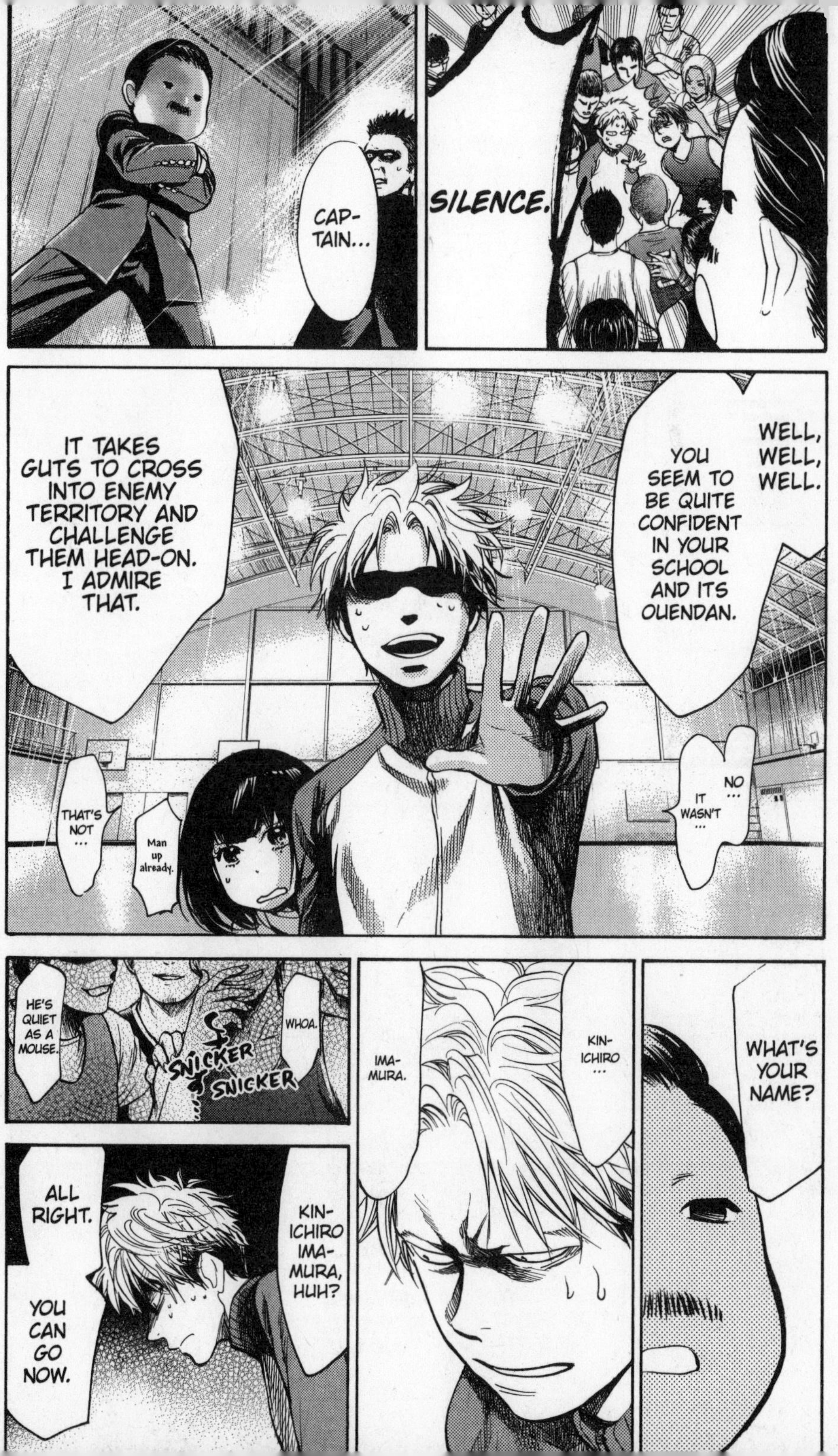
SILENCE.
CAP-TAIN...
WELL, WELL, WELL.
YOU SEEM TO BE QUITE CONFIDENT IN YOUR SCHOOL AND ITS OUENDAN.
IT TAKES GUTS TO CROSS INTO ENEMY TERRITORY AND CHALLENGE THEM HEAD-ON. I ADMIRE THAT.
NO...
IT WASN'T...
Man up already.
THAT'S NOT...
WHAT'S YOUR NAME?
KIN-ICHIRO...
IMA-MURA.
WHOA.
HE'S QUIET AS A MOUSE.
SNICKER SNICKER
KIN-ICHIRO IMA-MURA, HUH?
ALL RIGHT.
YOU CAN GO NOW.

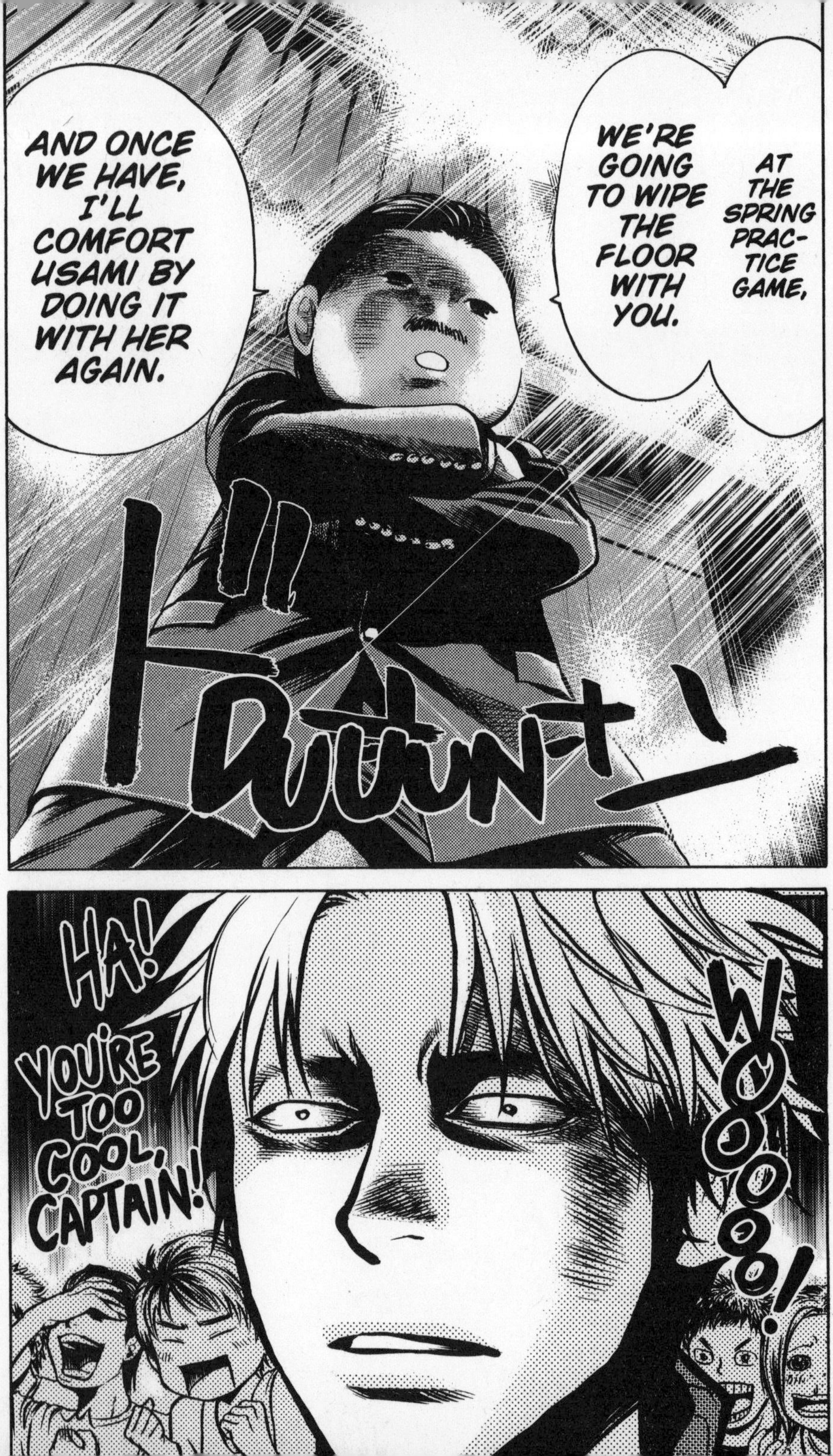
AT THE SPRING PRACTICE GAME,
WE'RE GOING TO WIPE THE FLOOR WITH YOU.
AND ONCE WE HAVE, I'LL COMFORT USAMI BY DOING IT WITH HER AGAIN.
DUTUN
WOOOOO!
HA! YOU'RE TOO COOL, CAPTAIN!

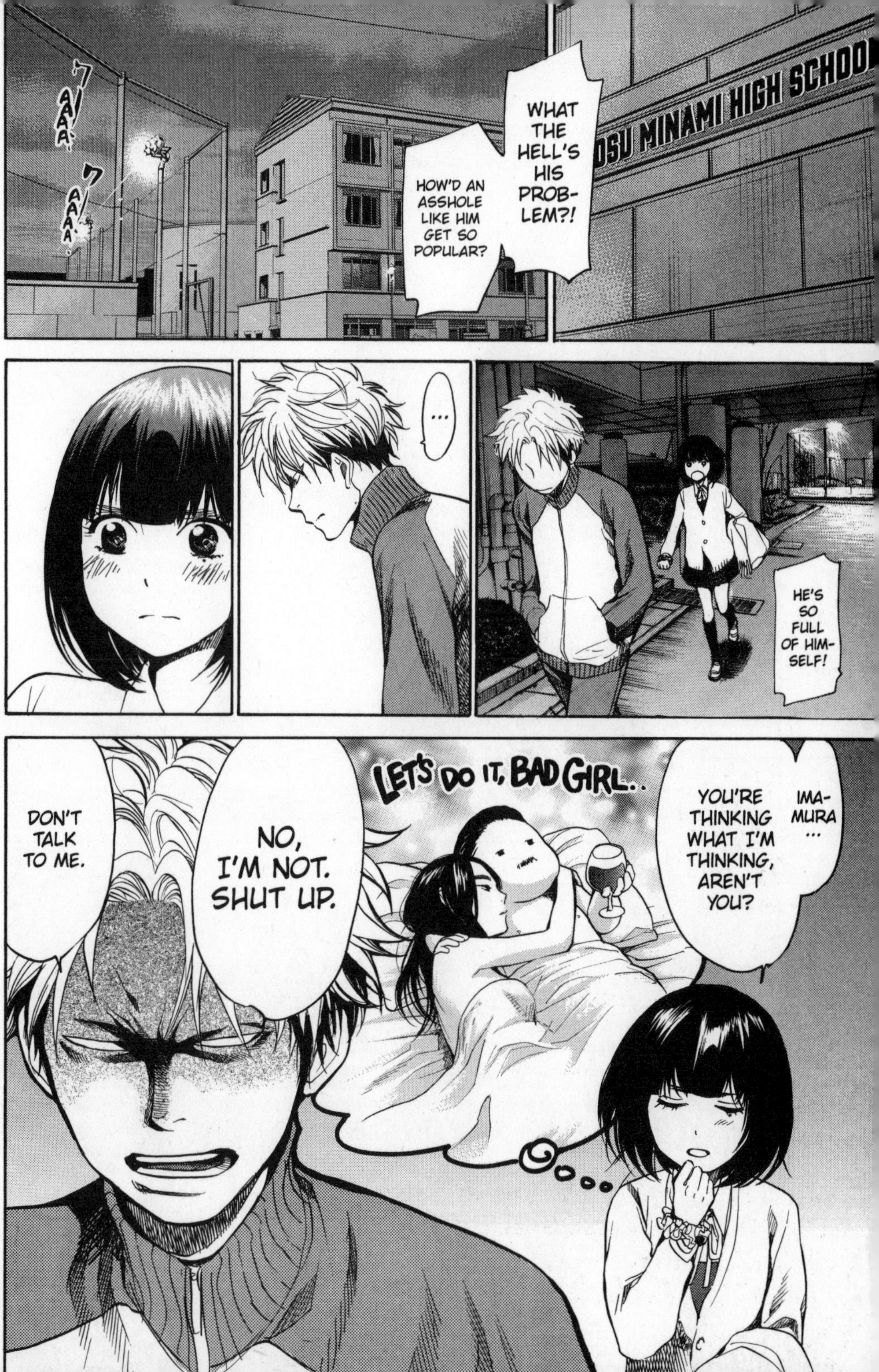

AAAA...
AAAA...
OSU MINAMI HIGH SCHOO
WHAT THE HELL'S HIS PROBLEM?!
HOW'D AN ASSHOLE LIKE HIM GET SO POPULAR?
HE'S SO FULL OF HIMSELF!
...
IMAMURA...
YOU'RE THINKING WHAT I'M THINKING, AREN'T YOU?
LET'S DO IT, BAD GIRL...
NO, I'M NOT. SHUT UP.
DON'T TALK TO ME.

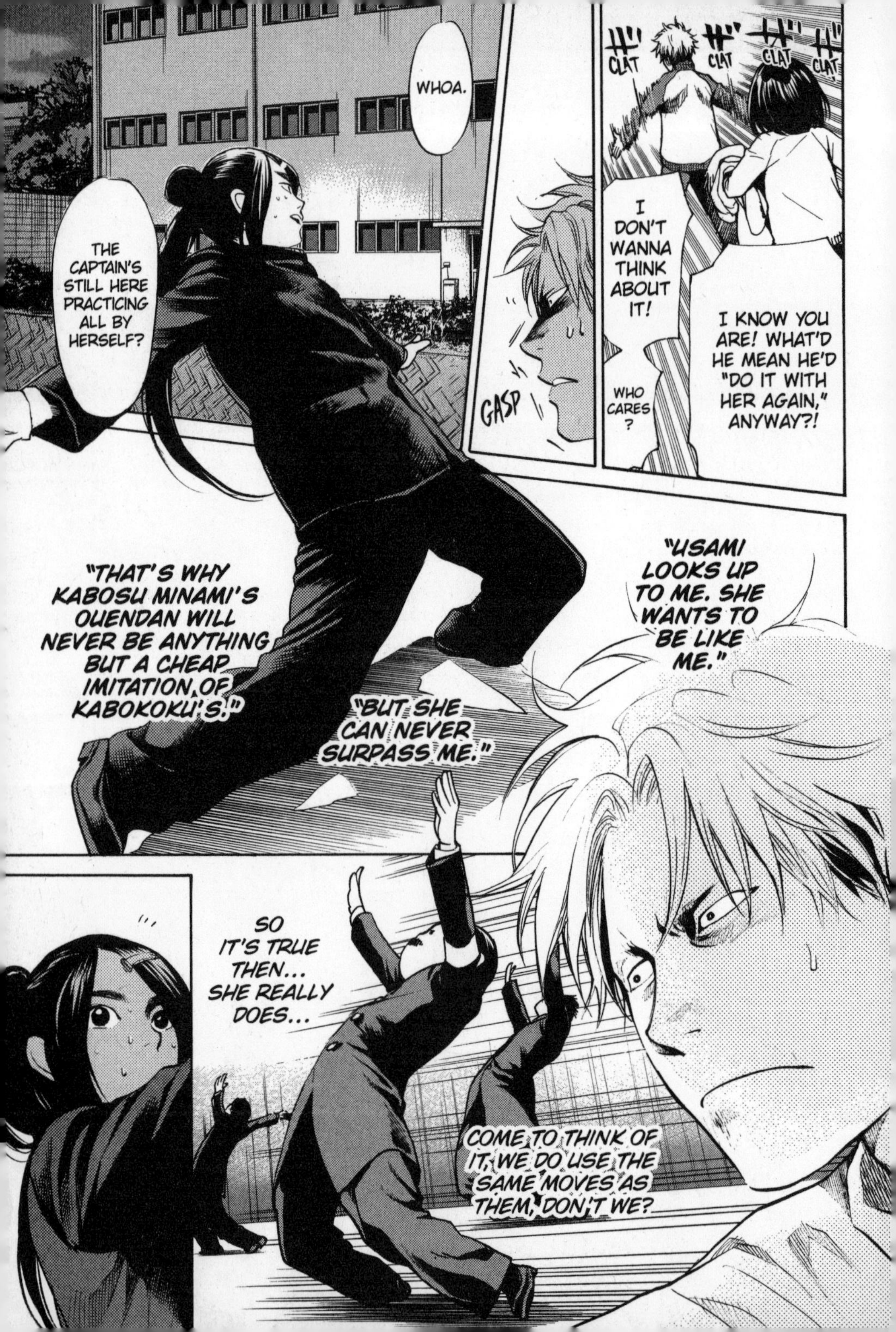
CLAT
CLAT
CLAT
CLAT
I DON'T WANNA THINK ABOUT IT!
I KNOW YOU ARE! WHAT'D HE MEAN HE'D "DO IT WITH HER AGAIN," ANYWAY?!
WHO CARES?
GASP
WHOA.
THE CAPTAIN'S STILL HERE PRACTICING ALL BY HERSELF?
"USAMI LOOKS UP TO ME. SHE WANTS TO BE LIKE ME."
"BUT SHE CAN NEVER SURPASS ME."
"THAT'S WHY KABOSU MINAMI'S OUENDAN WILL NEVER BE ANYTHING BUT A CHEAP IMITATION OF KABOKOKU'S."
COME TO THINK OF IT, WE DO USE THE SAME MOVES AS THEM, DON'T WE?
SO IT'S TRUE THEN... SHE REALLY DOES...

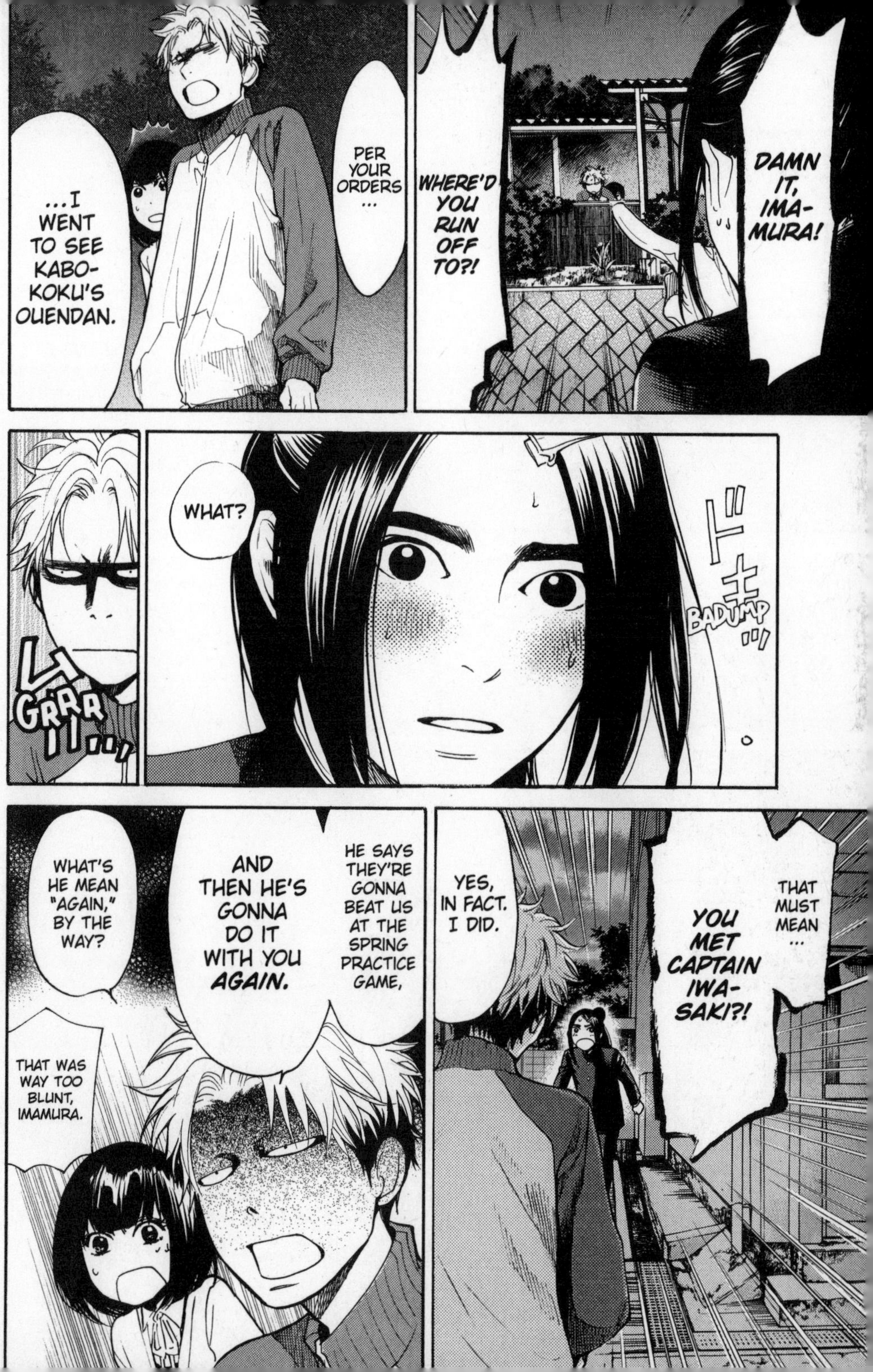
DAMN IT, IMAMURA!
WHERE'D YOU RUN OFF TO?!
PER YOUR ORDERS ...
...I WENT TO SEE KABOKOKU'S OUENDAN.
WHAT?
ドキ
BADUMP
GRRR
THAT MUST MEAN ...
YOU MET CAPTAIN IWASAKI?!
YES, IN FACT. I DID.
HE SAYS THEY'RE GONNA BEAT US AT THE SPRING PRACTICE GAME,
AND THEN HE'S GONNA DO IT WITH YOU AGAIN.
WHAT'S HE MEAN "AGAIN," BY THE WAY?
THAT WAS WAY TOO BLUNT, IMAMURA.

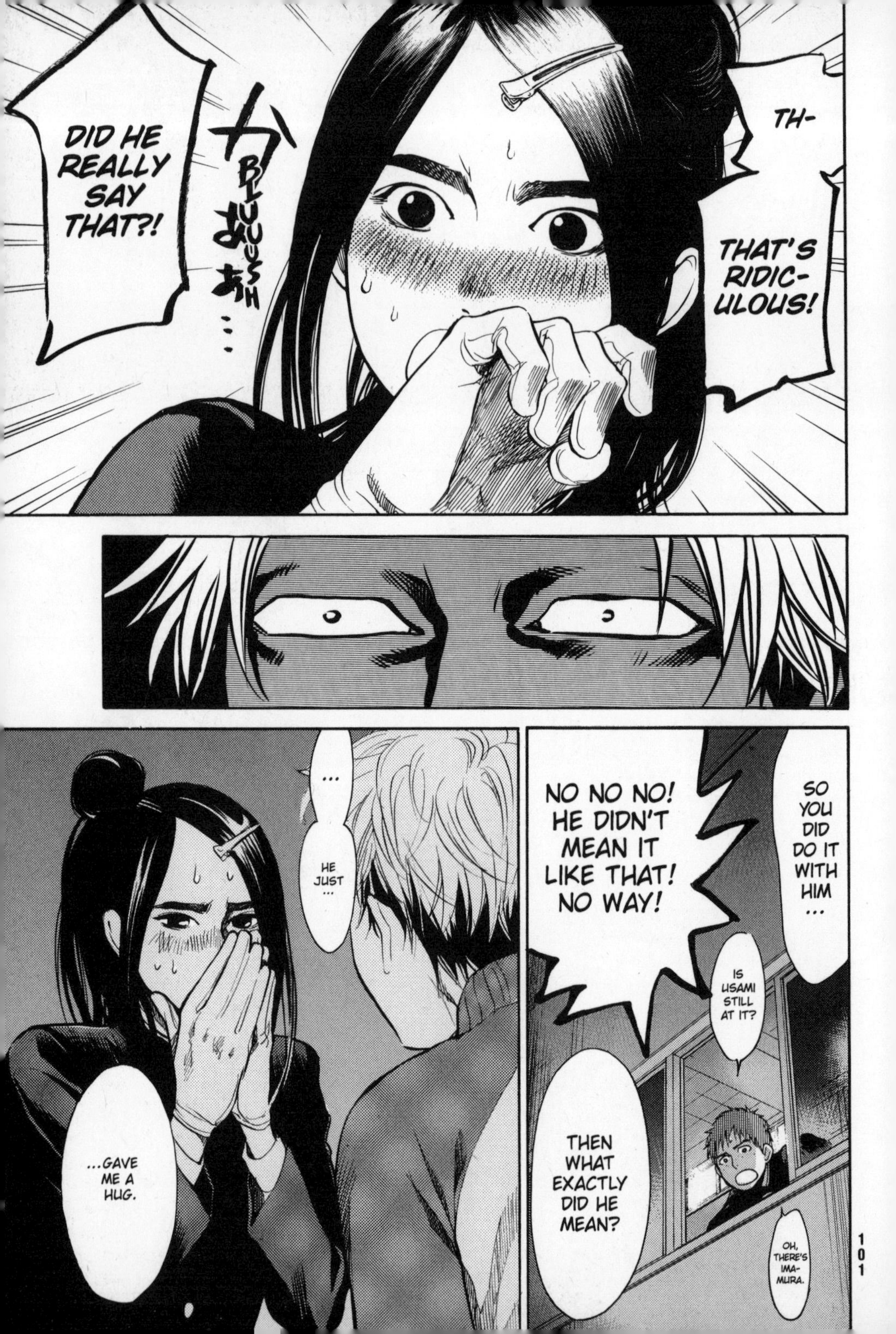
TH-
THAT'S RIDICULOUS!
BLUUUSH
DID HE REALLY SAY THAT?!
SO YOU DID DO IT WITH HIM...
NO NO NO! HE DIDN'T MEAN IT LIKE THAT! NO WAY!
IS USAMI STILL AT IT?
THEN WHAT EXACTLY DID HE MEAN?
OH, THERE'S IMAMURA.
...
HE JUST...
...GAVE ME A HUG.

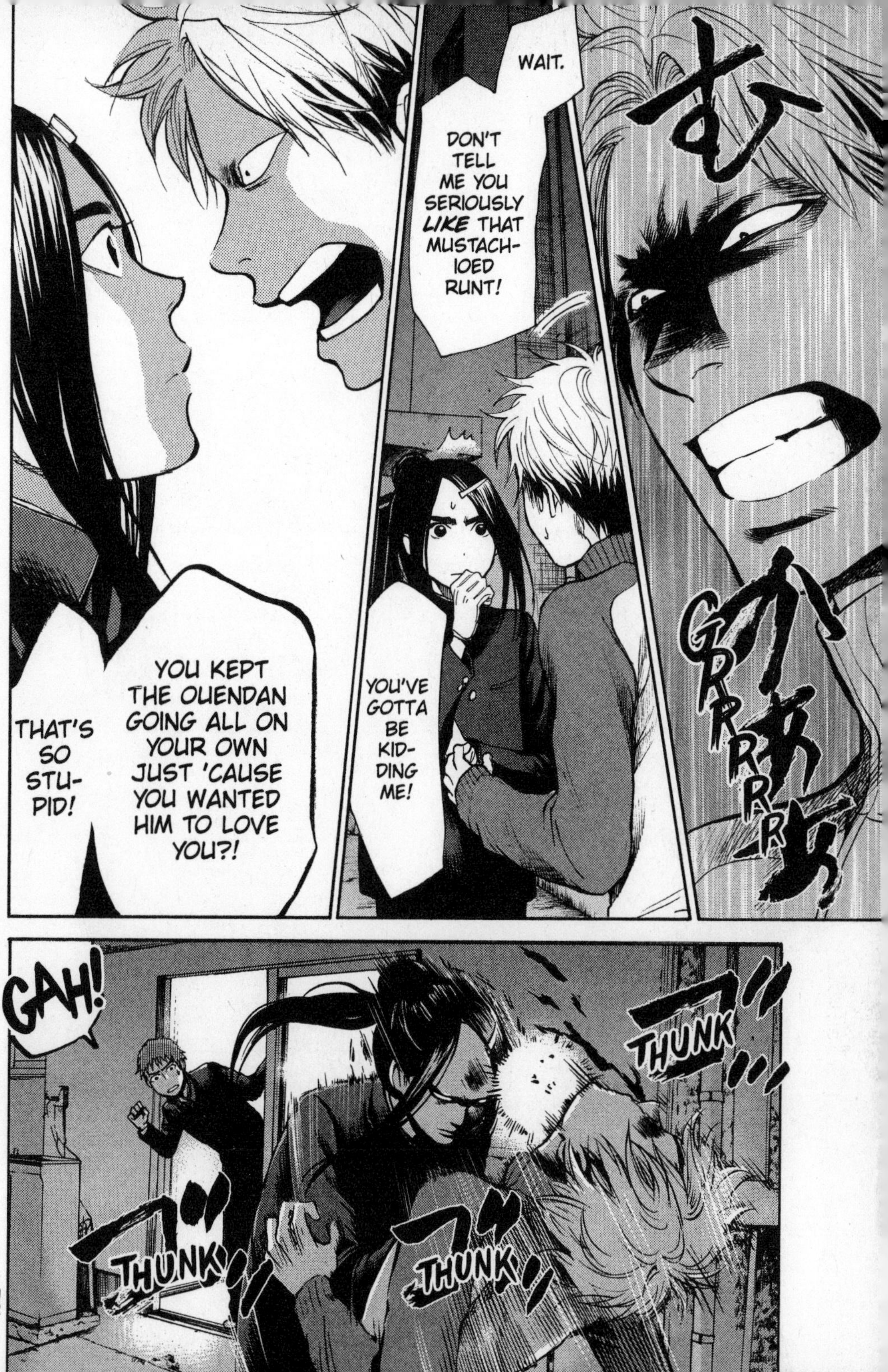
GRRRRR
WAIT.
DON'T TELL ME YOU SERIOUSLY *LIKE* THAT MUSTACHIOED RUNT!
YOU'VE GOTTA BE KIDDING ME!
YOU KEPT THE OUENDAN GOING ALL ON YOUR OWN JUST 'CAUSE YOU WANTED HIM TO LOVE YOU?!
THAT'S SO STUPID!
THUNK
GAH!
THUNK
THUNK

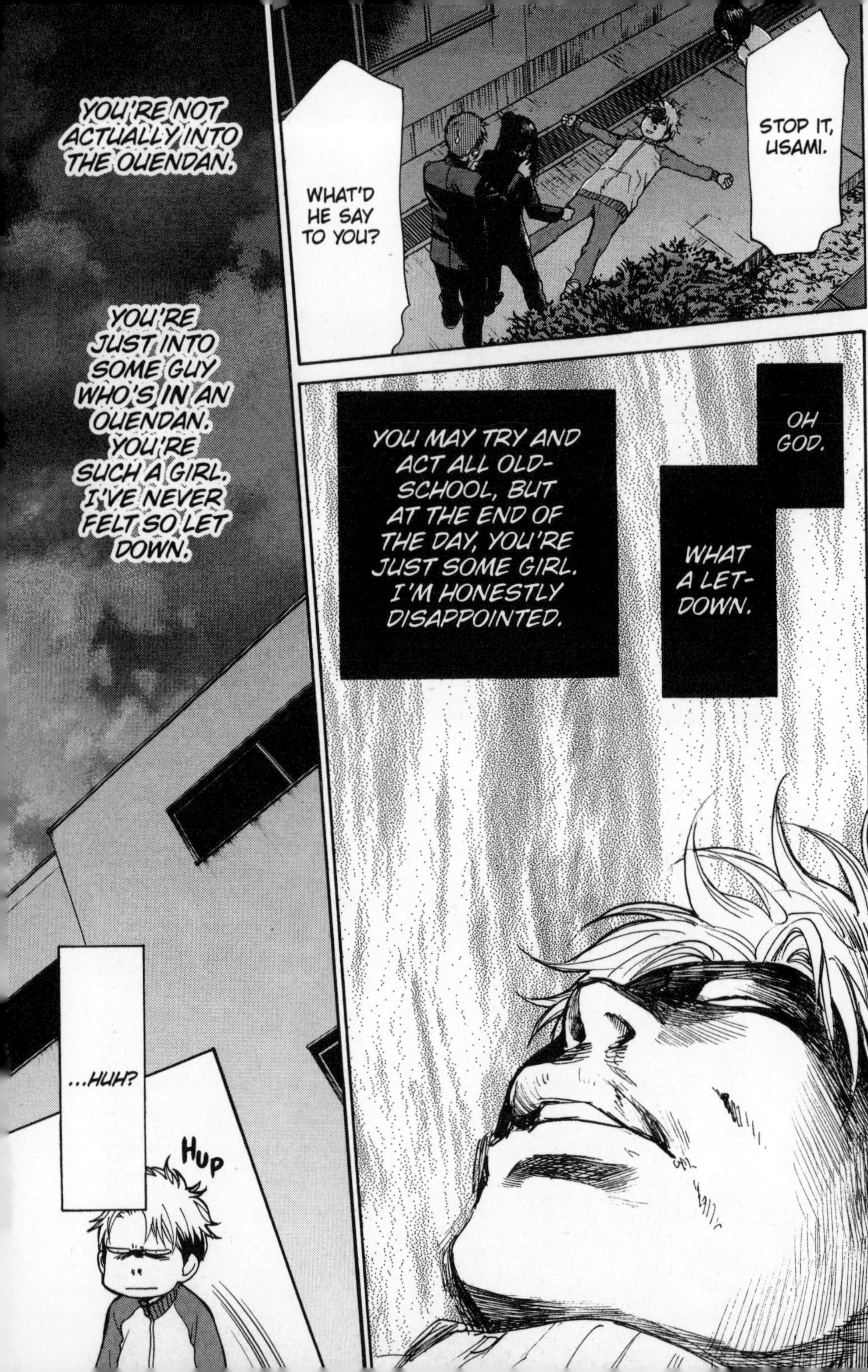
STOP IT, USAMI.
WHAT'D HE SAY TO YOU?
OH GOD.
WHAT A LET-DOWN.
YOU MAY TRY AND ACT ALL OLD-SCHOOL, BUT AT THE END OF THE DAY, YOU'RE JUST SOME GIRL. I'M HONESTLY DISAPPOINTED.
YOU'RE NOT ACTUALLY INTO THE OUENDAN.
YOU'RE JUST INTO SOME GUY WHO'S IN AN OUENDAN. YOU'RE SUCH A GIRL. I'VE NEVER FELT SO LET DOWN.
...HUH?
HUP

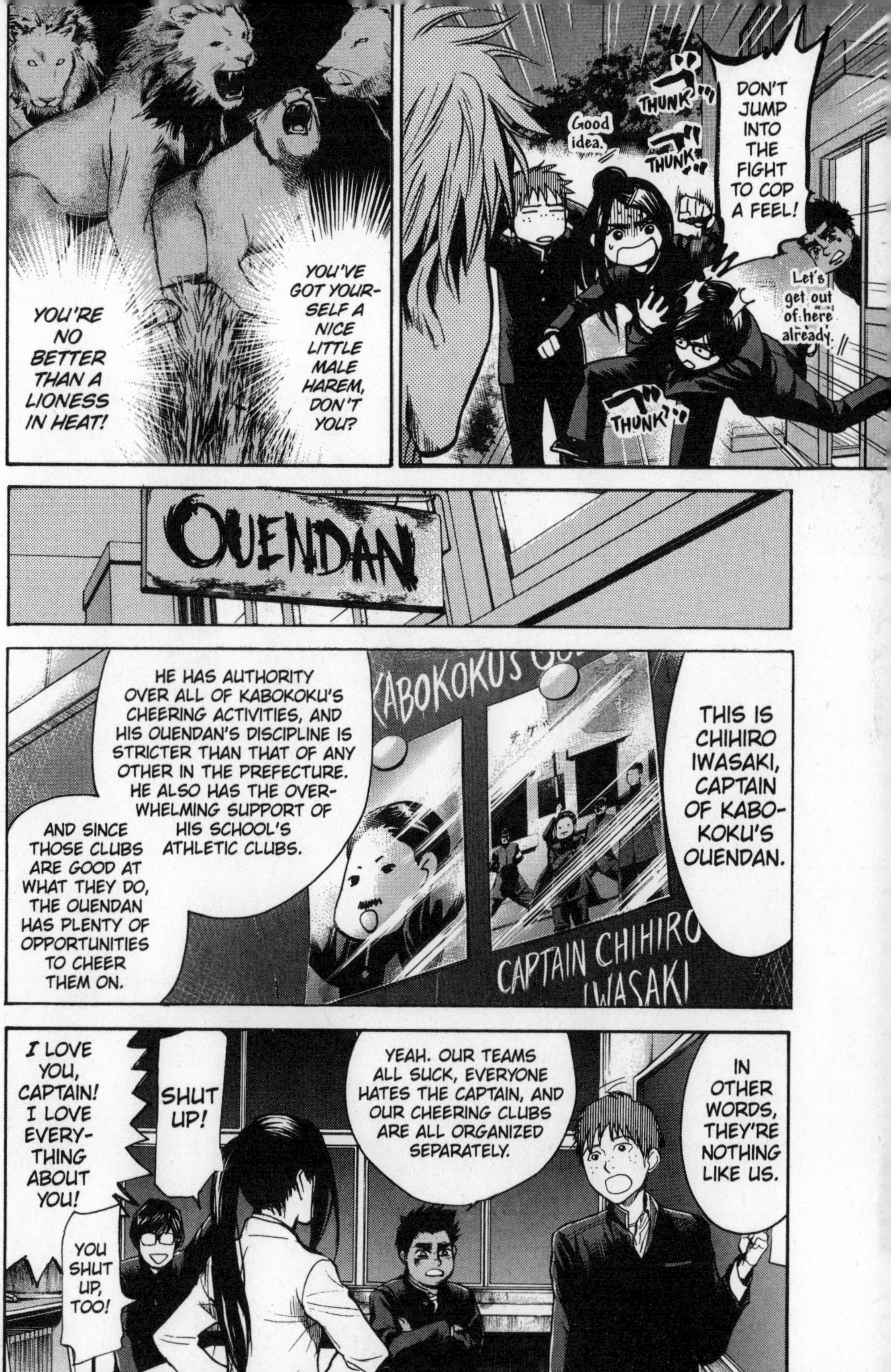
DON'T JUMP INTO THE FIGHT TO COP A FEEL!
THUNK
Good idea.
THUNK
Let's get out of here already.
THUNK
YOU'VE GOT YOURSELF A NICE LITTLE MALE HAREM, DON'T YOU?
YOU'RE NO BETTER THAN A LIONESS IN HEAT!
OUENDAN
THIS IS CHIHIRO IWASAKI, CAPTAIN OF KABOKOKU'S OUENDAN.
CAPTAIN CHIHIRO IWASAKI
HE HAS AUTHORITY OVER ALL OF KABOKOKU'S CHEERING ACTIVITIES, AND HIS OUENDAN'S DISCIPLINE IS STRICTER THAN THAT OF ANY OTHER IN THE PREFECTURE. HE ALSO HAS THE OVERWHELMING SUPPORT OF HIS SCHOOL'S ATHLETIC CLUBS.
AND SINCE THOSE CLUBS ARE GOOD AT WHAT THEY DO, THE OUENDAN HAS PLENTY OF OPPORTUNITIES TO CHEER THEM ON.
IN OTHER WORDS, THEY'RE NOTHING LIKE US.
YEAH. OUR TEAMS ALL SUCK, EVERYONE HATES THE CAPTAIN, AND OUR CHEERING CLUBS ARE ALL ORGANIZED SEPARATELY.
SHUT UP!
I LOVE YOU, CAPTAIN! I LOVE EVERYTHING ABOUT YOU!
YOU SHUT UP, TOO!

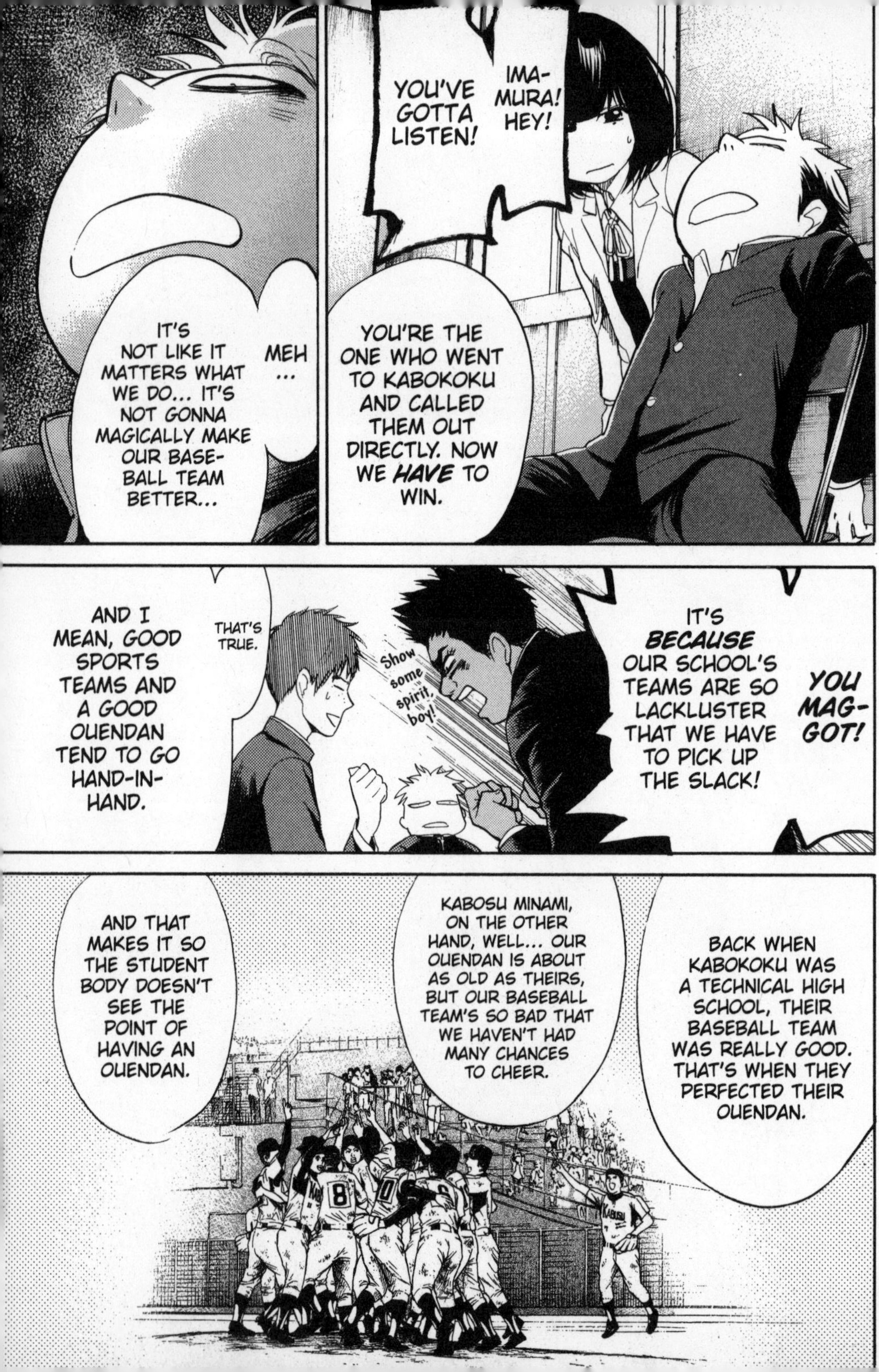
IMA-MURA! HEY!
YOU'VE GOTTA LISTEN!
YOU'RE THE ONE WHO WENT TO KABOKOKU AND CALLED THEM OUT DIRECTLY. NOW WE HAVE TO WIN.
MEH...
IT'S NOT LIKE IT MATTERS WHAT WE DO... IT'S NOT GONNA MAGICALLY MAKE OUR BASE-BALL TEAM BETTER...
YOU MAG-GOT!
IT'S BECAUSE OUR SCHOOL'S TEAMS ARE SO LACKLUSTER THAT WE HAVE TO PICK UP THE SLACK!
Show some spirit, boy!
THAT'S TRUE.
AND I MEAN, GOOD SPORTS TEAMS AND A GOOD OUENDAN TEND TO GO HAND-IN-HAND.
BACK WHEN KABOKOKU WAS A TECHNICAL HIGH SCHOOL, THEIR BASEBALL TEAM WAS REALLY GOOD. THAT'S WHEN THEY PERFECTED THEIR OUENDAN.
KABOSU MINAMI, ON THE OTHER HAND, WELL... OUR OUENDAN IS ABOUT AS OLD AS THEIRS, BUT OUR BASEBALL TEAM'S SO BAD THAT WE HAVEN'T HAD MANY CHANCES TO CHEER.
AND THAT MAKES IT SO THE STUDENT BODY DOESN'T SEE THE POINT OF HAVING AN OUENDAN.

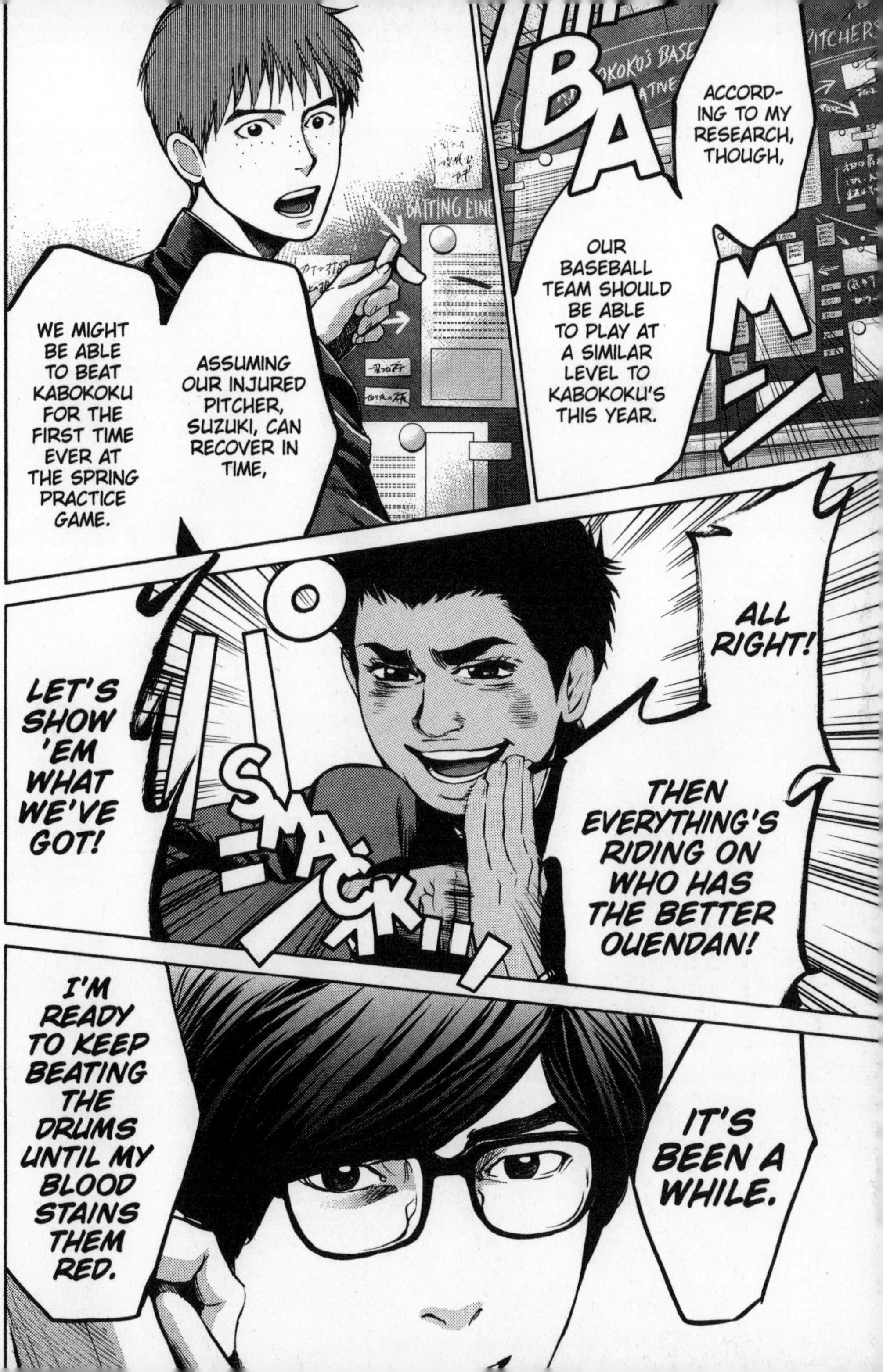
BAM!
ACCORDING TO MY RESEARCH, THOUGH,
OUR BASEBALL TEAM SHOULD BE ABLE TO PLAY AT A SIMILAR LEVEL TO KABOKOKU'S THIS YEAR.
ASSUMING OUR INJURED PITCHER, SUZUKI, CAN RECOVER IN TIME,
WE MIGHT BE ABLE TO BEAT KABOKOKU FOR THE FIRST TIME EVER AT THE SPRING PRACTICE GAME.
ALL RIGHT!
THEN EVERYTHING'S RIDING ON WHO HAS THE BETTER OUENDAN!
LET'S SHOW 'EM WHAT WE'VE GOT!
SMACK!
IT'S BEEN A WHILE.
I'M READY TO KEEP BEATING THE DRUMS UNTIL MY BLOOD STAINS THEM RED.

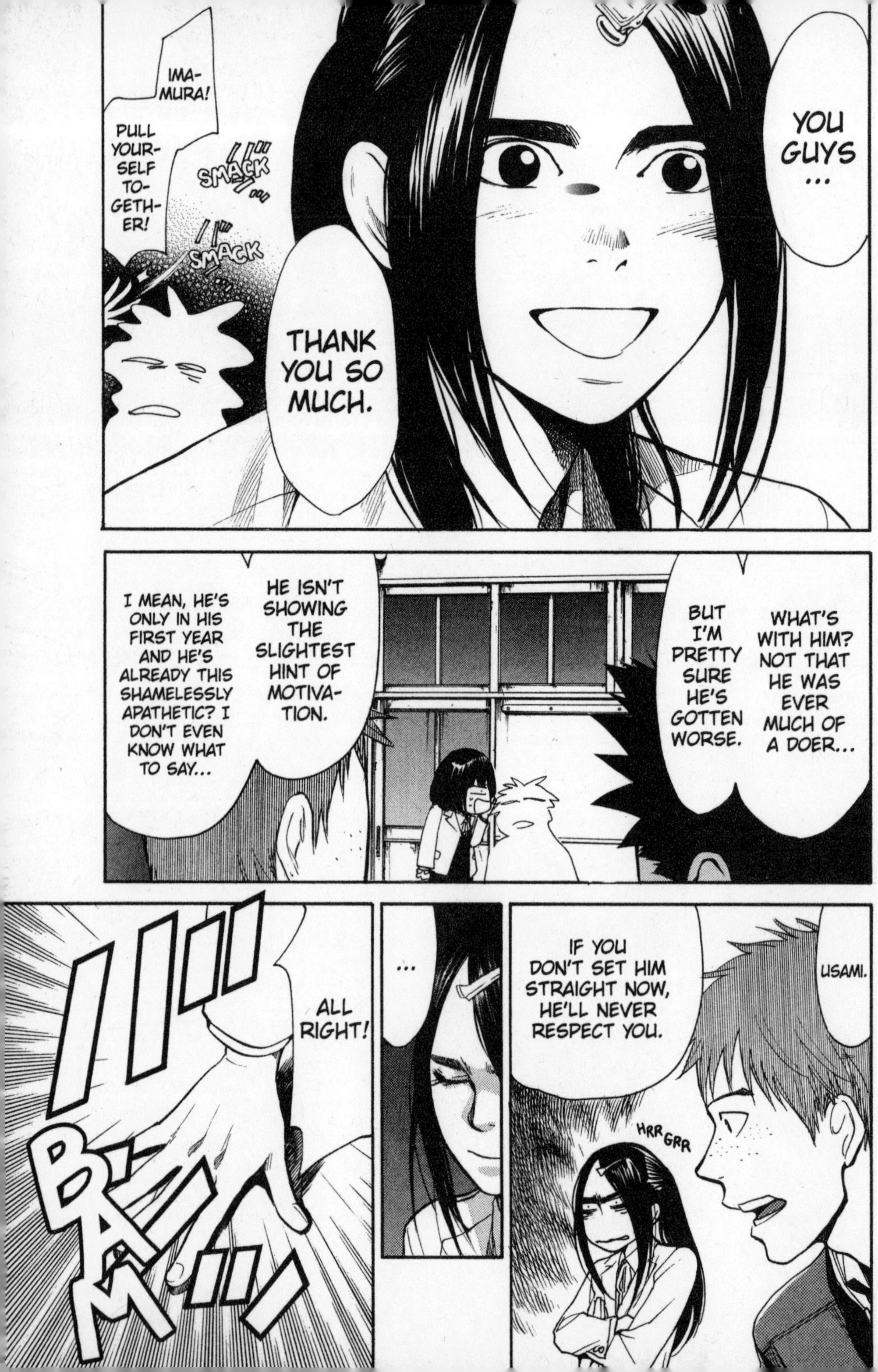
YOU GUYS ...
THANK YOU SO MUCH.
IMA-MURA!
PULL YOUR-SELF TO-GETH-ER!
SMACK
SMACK
WHAT'S WITH HIM? NOT THAT HE WAS EVER MUCH OF A DOER...
BUT I'M PRETTY SURE HE'S GOTTEN WORSE.
HE ISN'T SHOWING THE SLIGHTEST HINT OF MOTIVA-TION.
I MEAN, HE'S ONLY IN HIS FIRST YEAR AND HE'S ALREADY THIS SHAMELESSLY APATHETIC? I DON'T EVEN KNOW WHAT TO SAY...
USAMI.
IF YOU DON'T SET HIM STRAIGHT NOW, HE'LL NEVER RESPECT YOU.
HRR GRR
...
ALL RIGHT!
BAM

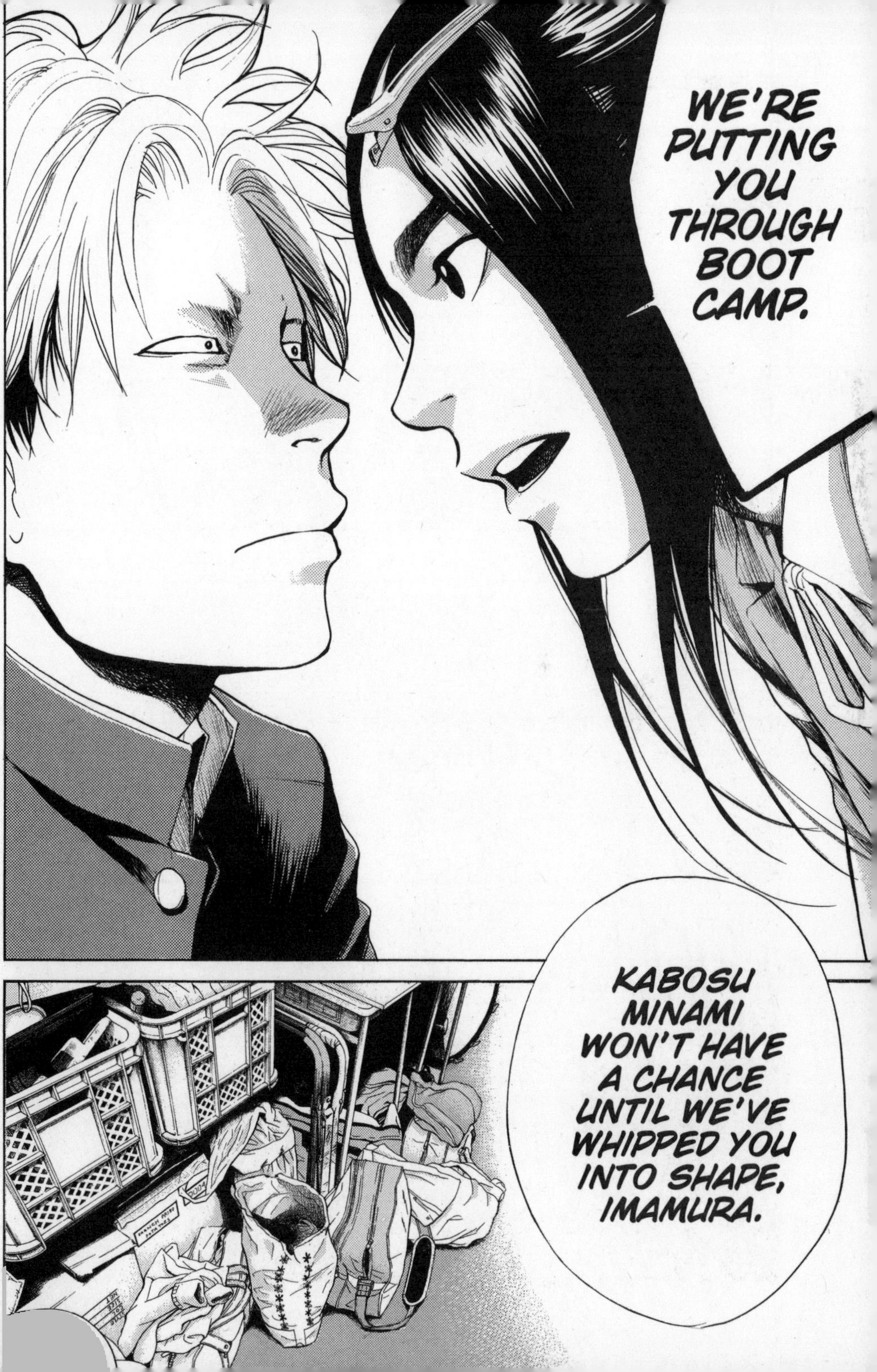
WE'RE PUTTING YOU THROUGH BOOT CAMP.
KABOSU MINAMI WON'T HAVE A CHANCE UNTIL WE'VE WHIPPED YOU INTO SHAPE, IMAMURA.

26. OUENDAN BOOT CAMP!

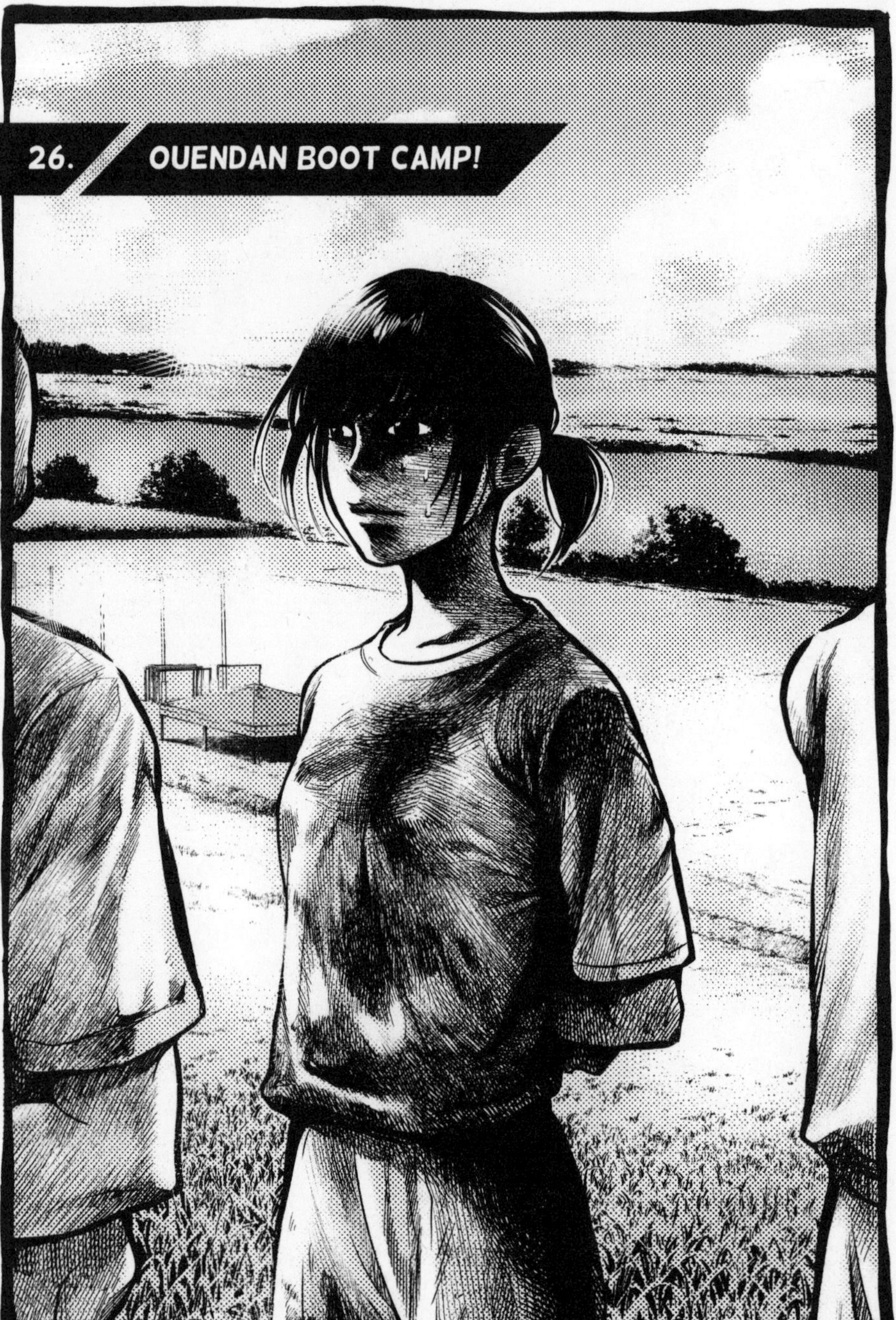

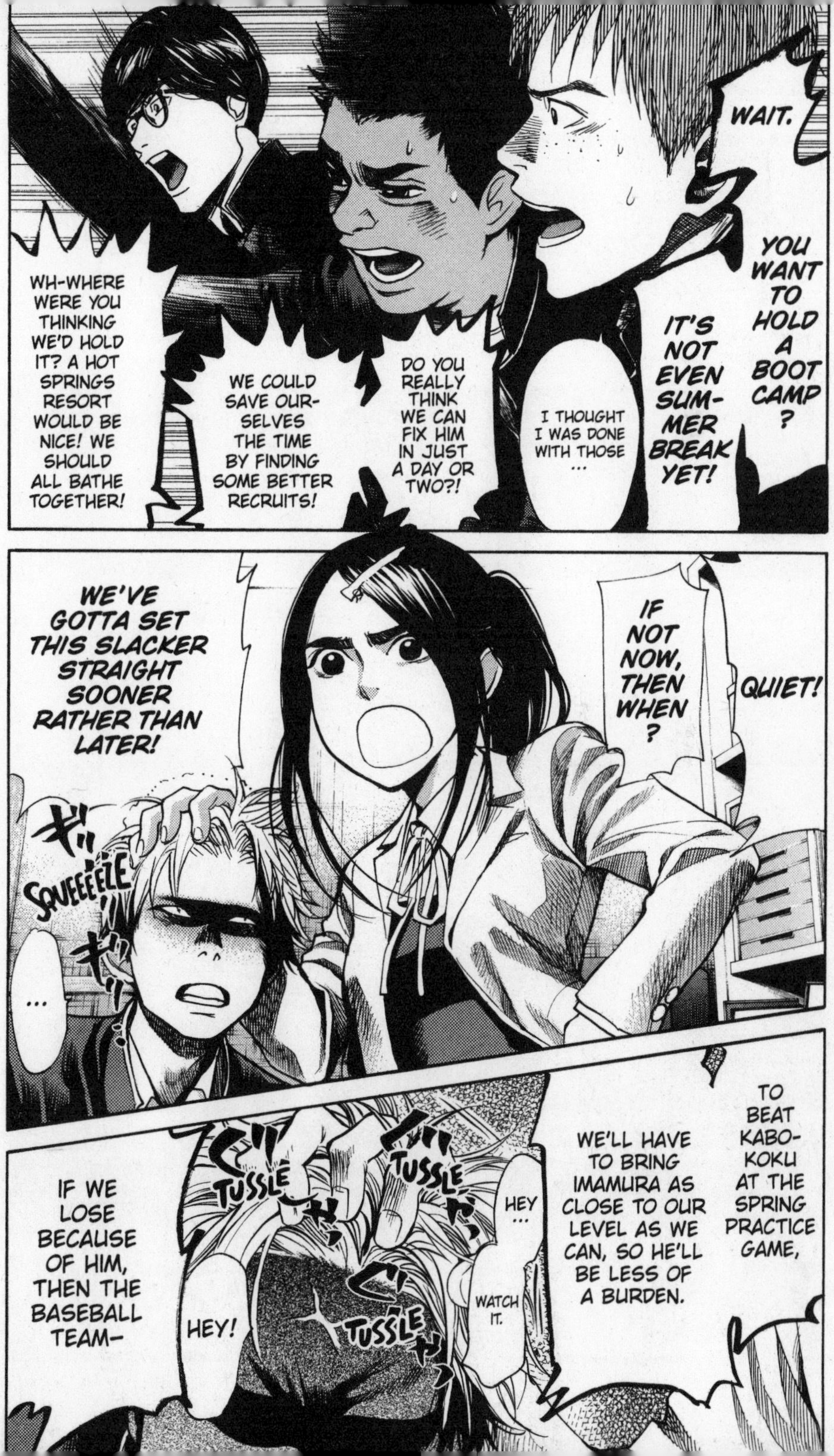

WAIT.
YOU WANT TO HOLD A BOOT CAMP?
IT'S NOT EVEN SUMMER BREAK YET!
I THOUGHT I WAS DONE WITH THOSE...
DO YOU REALLY THINK WE CAN FIX HIM IN JUST A DAY OR TWO?!
WE COULD SAVE OURSELVES THE TIME BY FINDING SOME BETTER RECRUITS!
WH-WHERE WERE YOU THINKING WE'D HOLD IT? A HOT SPRINGS RESORT WOULD BE NICE! WE SHOULD ALL BATHE TOGETHER!
QUIET!
IF NOT NOW, THEN WHEN?
WE'VE GOTTA SET THIS SLACKER STRAIGHT SOONER RATHER THAN LATER!
SQUEEEEEZE
...
TO BEAT KABOKOKU AT THE SPRING PRACTICE GAME,
WE'LL HAVE TO BRING IMAMURA AS CLOSE TO OUR LEVEL AS WE CAN, SO HE'LL BE LESS OF A BURDEN.
WATCH IT.
HEY...
TUSSLE
TUSSLE
TUSSLE
HEY!
IF WE LOSE BECAUSE OF HIM, THEN THE BASEBALL TEAM-

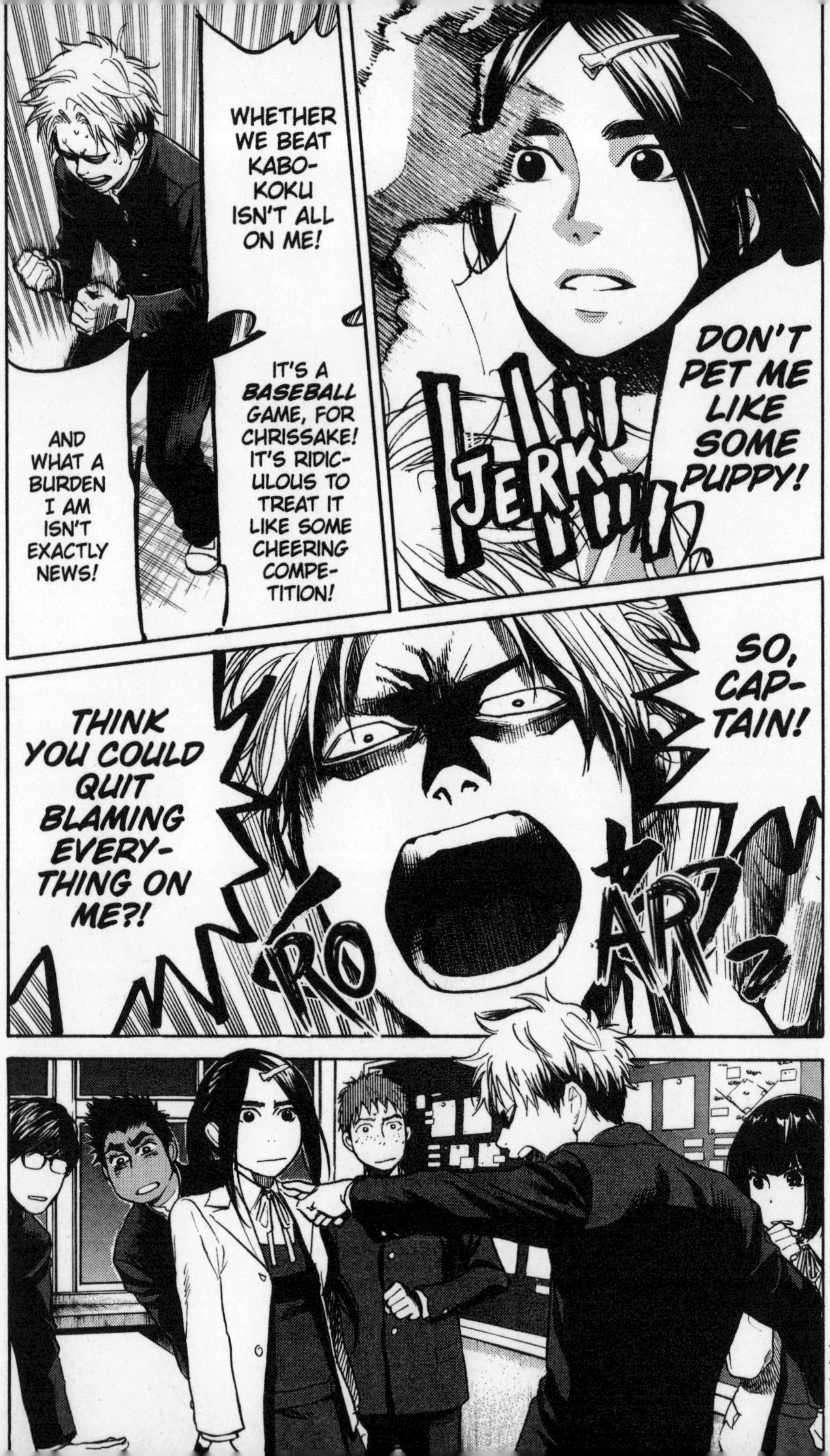
DON'T PET ME LIKE SOME PUPPY!
JERK
WHETHER WE BEAT KABO-KOKU ISN'T ALL ON ME!
IT'S A BASEBALL GAME, FOR CHRISSAKE! IT'S RIDIC-ULOUS TO TREAT IT LIKE SOME CHEERING COMPE-TITION!
AND WHAT A BURDEN I AM ISN'T EXACTLY NEWS!
SO, CAP-TAIN!
THINK YOU COULD QUIT BLAMING EVERY-THING ON ME?!
ROAR

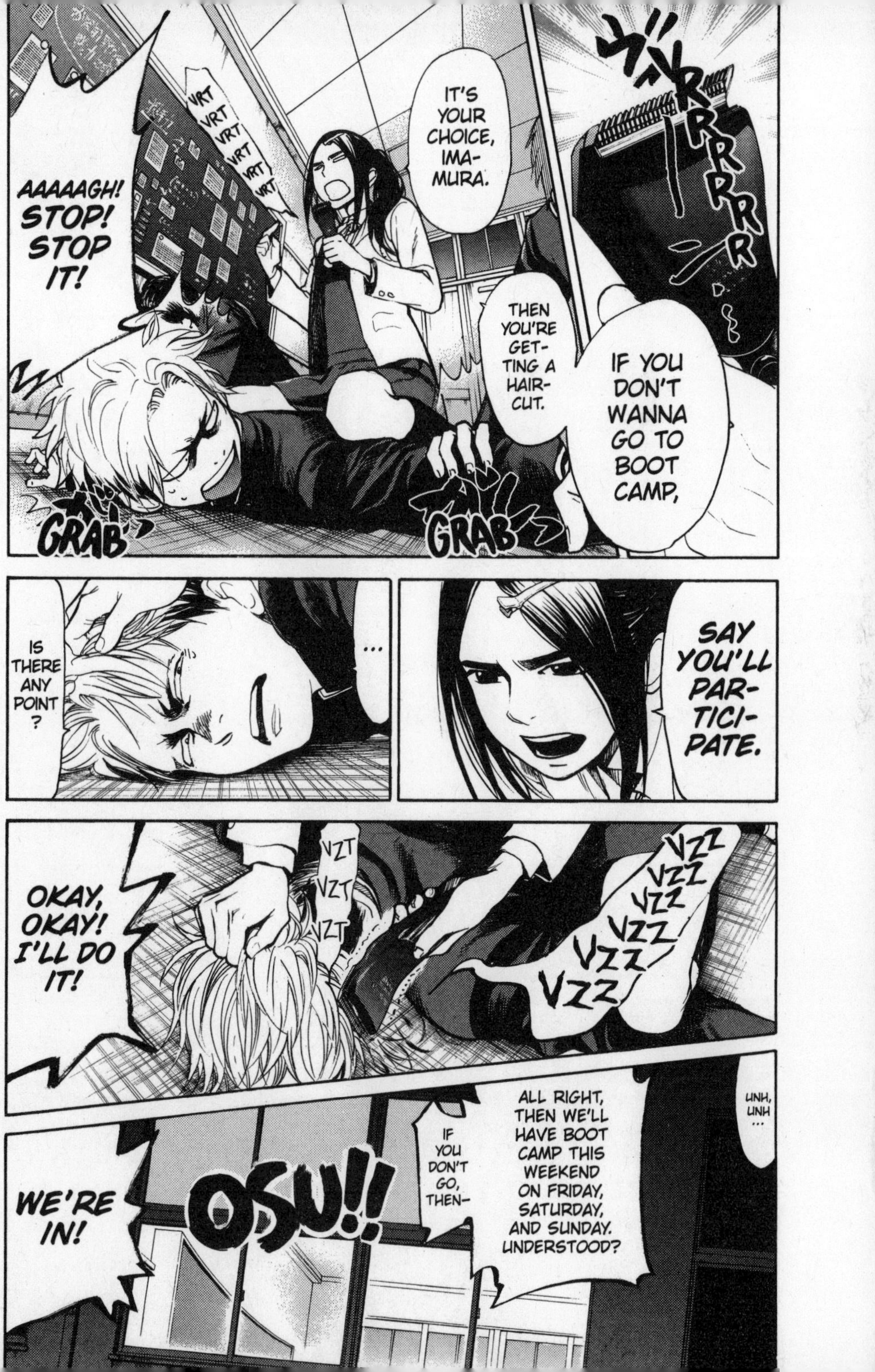
RRRRR
IT'S YOUR CHOICE, IMA-MURA.
VRT VRT VRT VRT VRT VRT
AAAAAGH! STOP! STOP IT!
IF YOU DON'T WANNA GO TO BOOT CAMP,
THEN YOU'RE GET-TING A HAIR-CUT.
GRAB
GRAB
SAY YOU'LL PAR-TICI-PATE.
...
IS THERE ANY POINT ?
VZZ VZZ VZZ VZZ VZZ VZZ
VZT VZT VZT
OKAY, OKAY! I'LL DO IT!
UNH, UNH ...
ALL RIGHT, THEN WE'LL HAVE BOOT CAMP THIS WEEKEND ON FRIDAY, SATURDAY, AND SUNDAY. UNDERSTOOD?
IF YOU DON'T GO, THEN–
OSU!!
WE'RE IN!

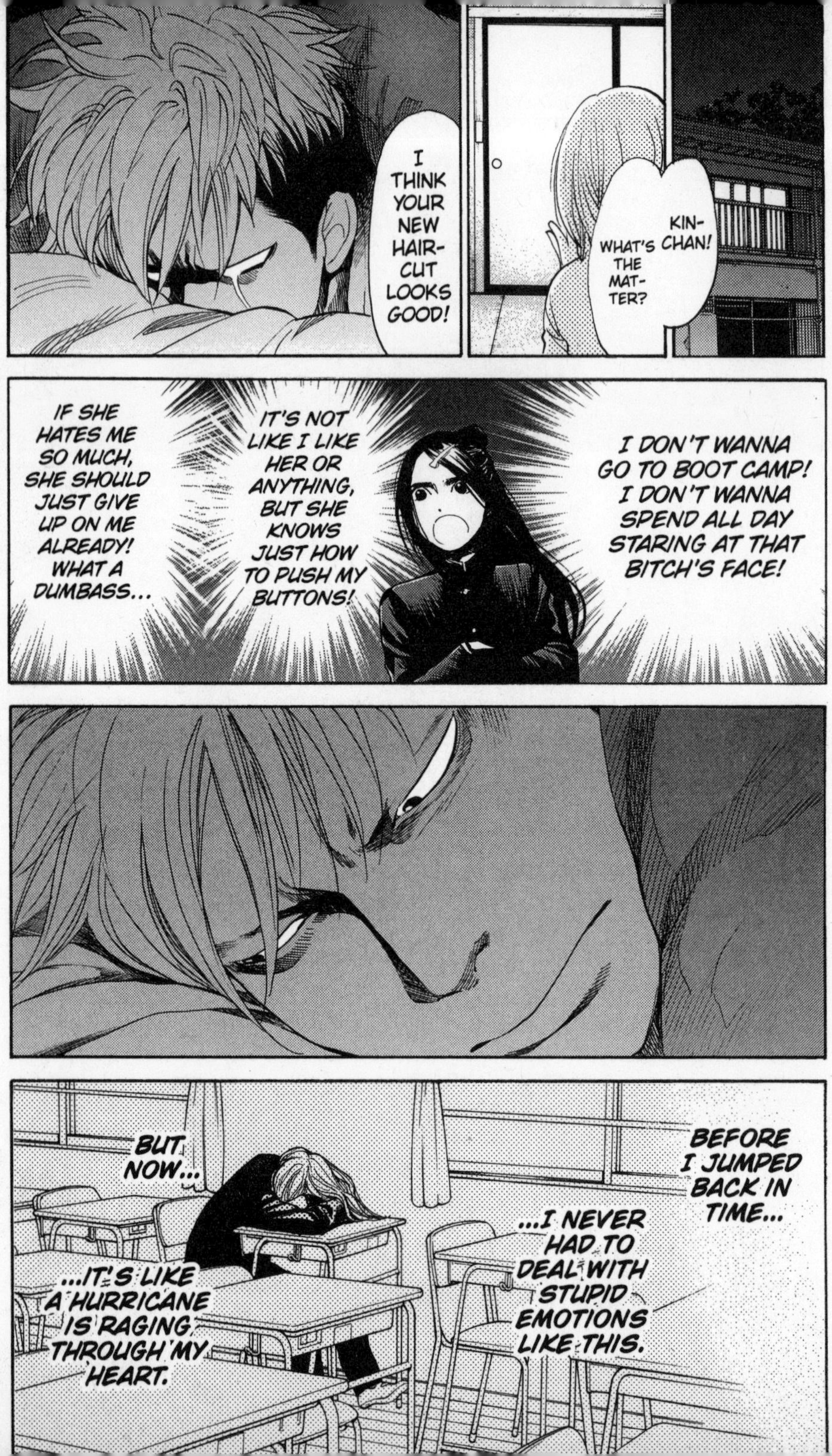
KIN-CHAN!
WHAT'S THE MATTER?
I THINK YOUR NEW HAIRCUT LOOKS GOOD!
I DON'T WANNA GO TO BOOT CAMP! I DON'T WANNA SPEND ALL DAY STARING AT THAT BITCH'S FACE!
IT'S NOT LIKE I LIKE HER OR ANYTHING, BUT SHE KNOWS JUST HOW TO PUSH MY BUTTONS!
IF SHE HATES ME SO MUCH, SHE SHOULD JUST GIVE UP ON ME ALREADY! WHAT A DUMBASS...
BEFORE I JUMPED BACK IN TIME...
...I NEVER HAD TO DEAL WITH STUPID EMOTIONS LIKE THIS.
BUT NOW...
...IT'S LIKE A HURRICANE IS RAGING THROUGH MY HEART.

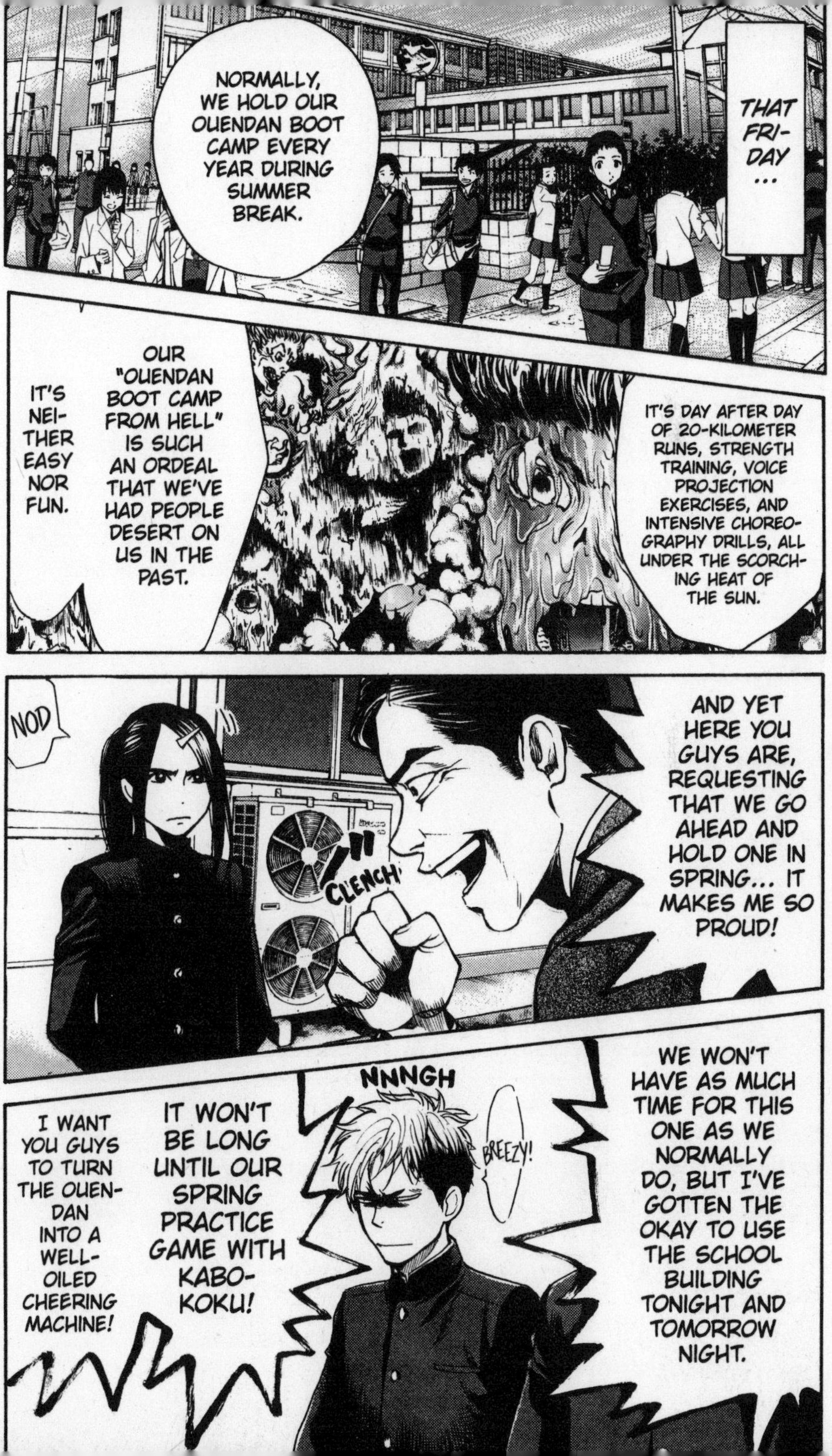
THAT FRI-DAY...
NORMALLY, WE HOLD OUR OUENDAN BOOT CAMP EVERY YEAR DURING SUMMER BREAK.
IT'S DAY AFTER DAY OF 20-KILOMETER RUNS, STRENGTH TRAINING, VOICE PROJECTION EXERCISES, AND INTENSIVE CHOREOGRAPHY DRILLS, ALL UNDER THE SCORCHING HEAT OF THE SUN.
OUR "OUENDAN BOOT CAMP FROM HELL" IS SUCH AN ORDEAL THAT WE'VE HAD PEOPLE DESERT ON US IN THE PAST.
IT'S NEITHER EASY NOR FUN.
AND YET HERE YOU GUYS ARE, REQUESTING THAT WE GO AHEAD AND HOLD ONE IN SPRING... IT MAKES ME SO PROUD!
CLENCH
NOD
WE WON'T HAVE AS MUCH TIME FOR THIS ONE AS WE NORMALLY DO, BUT I'VE GOTTEN THE OKAY TO USE THE SCHOOL BUILDING TONIGHT AND TOMORROW NIGHT.
BREEZY!
NNNGH
IT WON'T BE LONG UNTIL OUR SPRING PRACTICE GAME WITH KABOKOKU!
I WANT YOU GUYS TO TURN THE OUENDAN INTO A WELL-OILED CHEERING MACHINE!

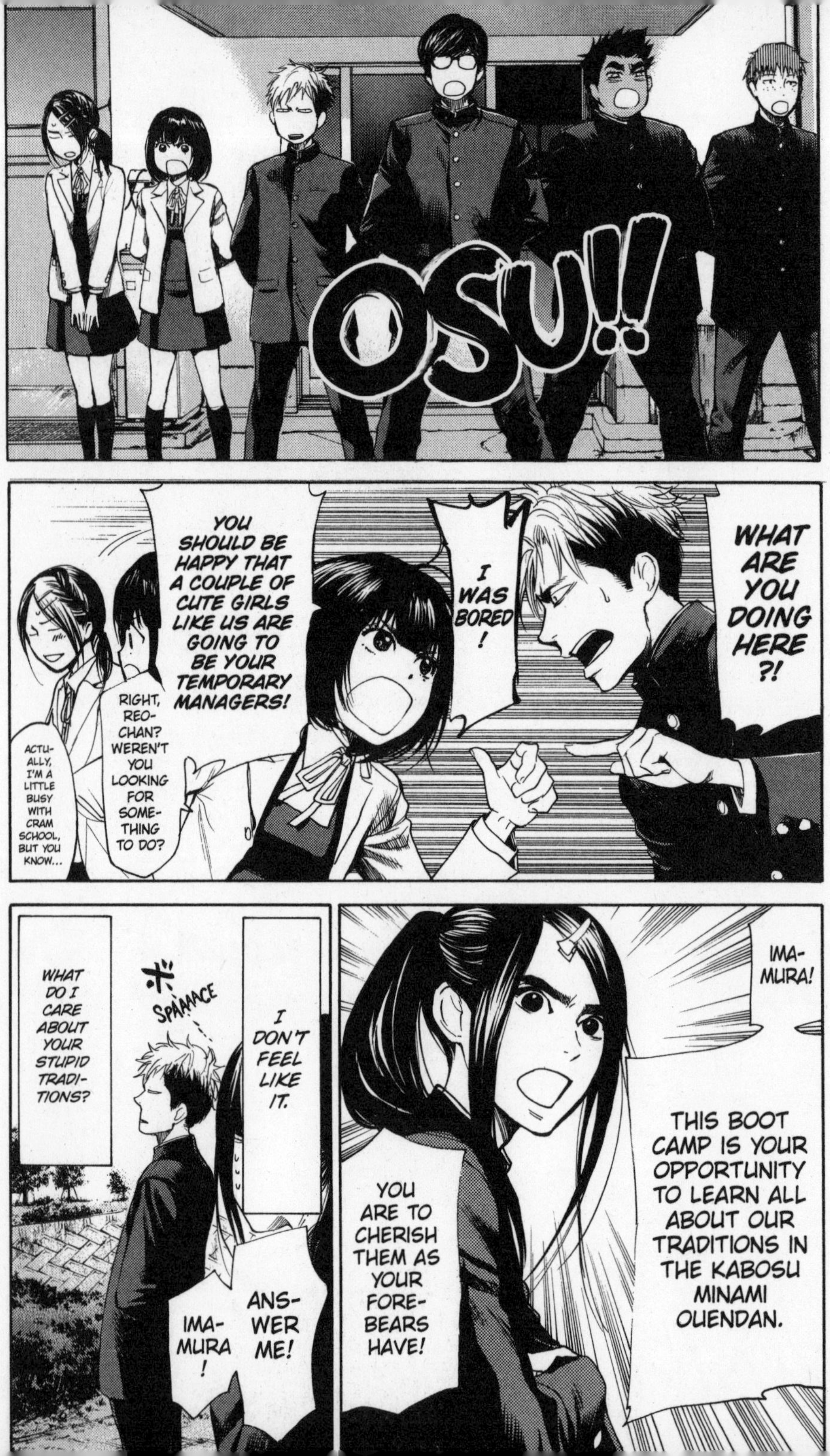
OSU!!
WHAT ARE YOU DOING HERE?!
I WAS BORED!
YOU SHOULD BE HAPPY THAT A COUPLE OF CUTE GIRLS LIKE US ARE GOING TO BE YOUR TEMPORARY MANAGERS!
RIGHT, REO-CHAN? WEREN'T YOU LOOKING FOR SOMETHING TO DO?
ACTUALLY, I'M A LITTLE BUSY WITH CRAM SCHOOL, BUT YOU KNOW...
IMAMURA!
THIS BOOT CAMP IS YOUR OPPORTUNITY TO LEARN ALL ABOUT OUR TRADITIONS IN THE KABOSU MINAMI OUENDAN.
YOU ARE TO CHERISH THEM AS YOUR FOREBEARS HAVE!
ANSWER ME!
IMAMURA!
I DON'T FEEL LIKE IT.
ボ
SPAAAACE
WHAT DO I CARE ABOUT YOUR STUPID TRADITIONS?

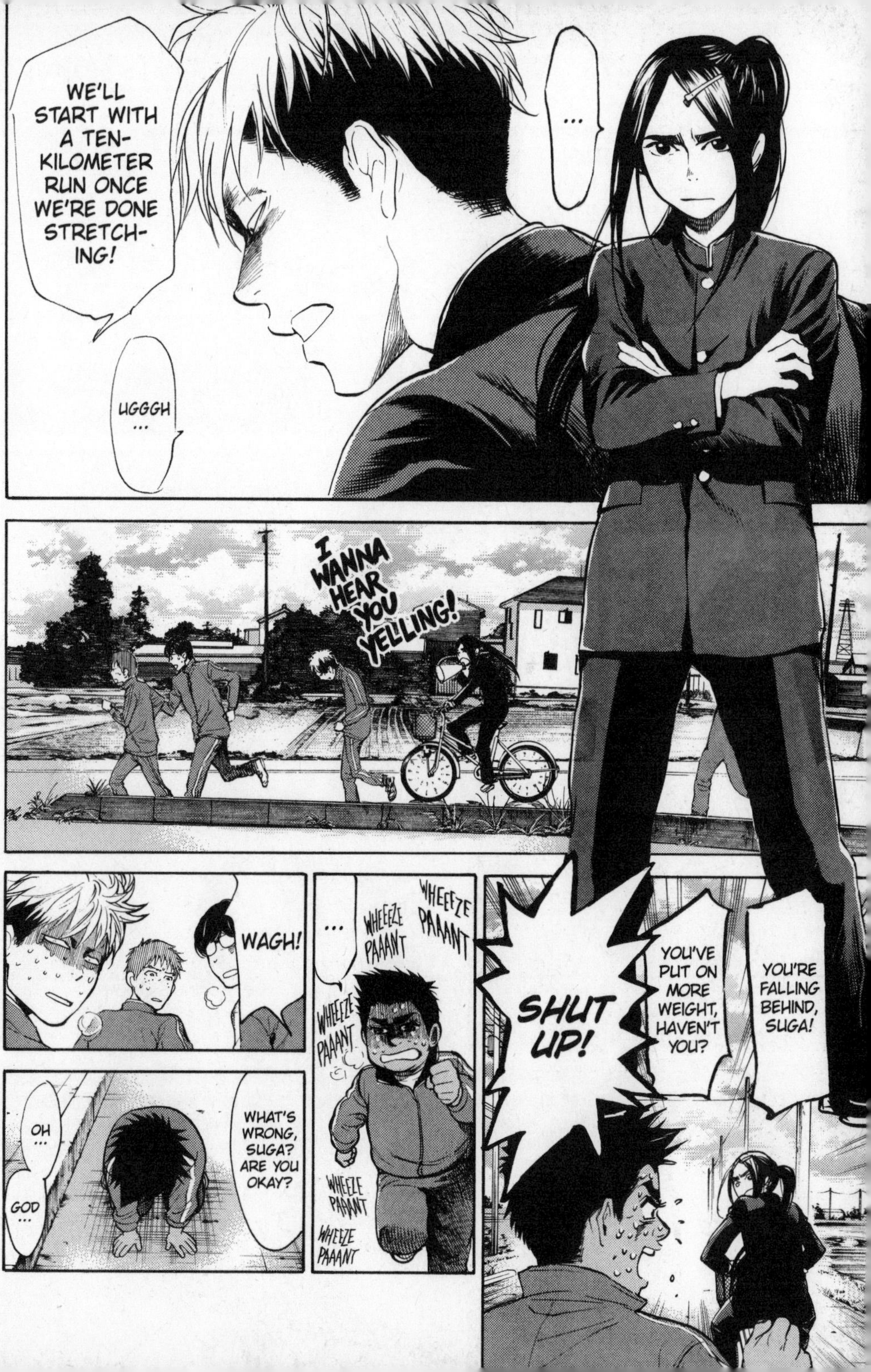
...
WE'LL START WITH A TEN-KILOMETER RUN ONCE WE'RE DONE STRETCH-ING!
UGGGH...
I WANNA HEAR YOU YELLING!
YOU'RE FALLING BEHIND, SUGA!
YOU'VE PUT ON MORE WEIGHT, HAVEN'T YOU?
SHUT UP!
WHEEEZE PAAANT
WHEEEZE PAAANT
...
WHEEEZE PAAANT
WAGH!
WHEEZE PAAANT
WHEEZE PAAANT
WHAT'S WRONG, SUGA? ARE YOU OKAY?
OH...
GOD...

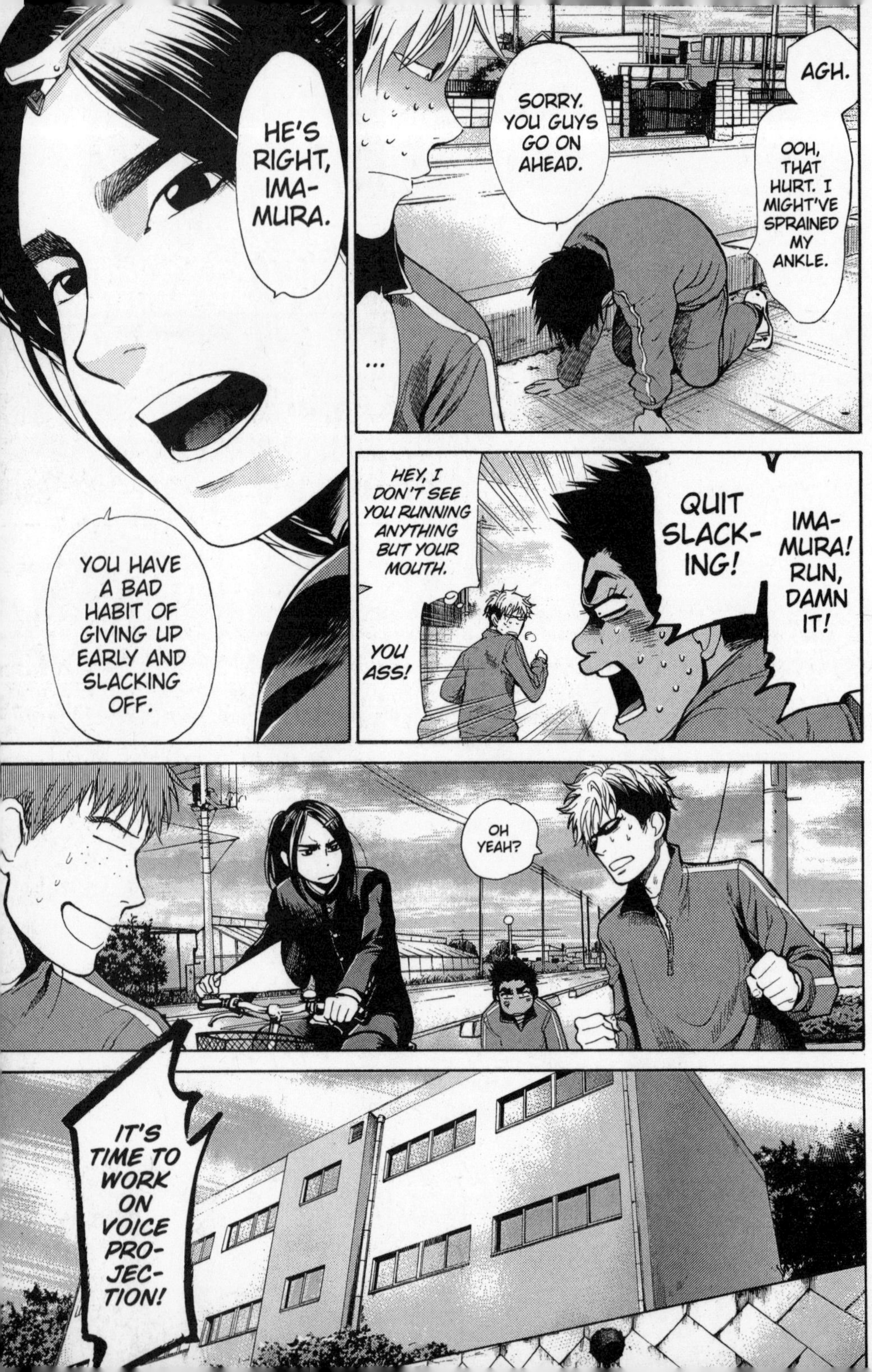
AGH.
OOH, THAT HURT. I MIGHT'VE SPRAINED MY ANKLE.
SORRY. YOU GUYS GO ON AHEAD.
...
IMA-MURA! RUN, DAMN IT!
QUIT SLACK-ING!
HEY, I DON'T SEE YOU RUNNING ANYTHING BUT YOUR MOUTH.
YOU ASS!
HE'S RIGHT, IMA-MURA.
YOU HAVE A BAD HABIT OF GIVING UP EARLY AND SLACKING OFF.
OH YEAH?
IT'S TIME TO WORK ON VOICE PRO-JEC-TION!

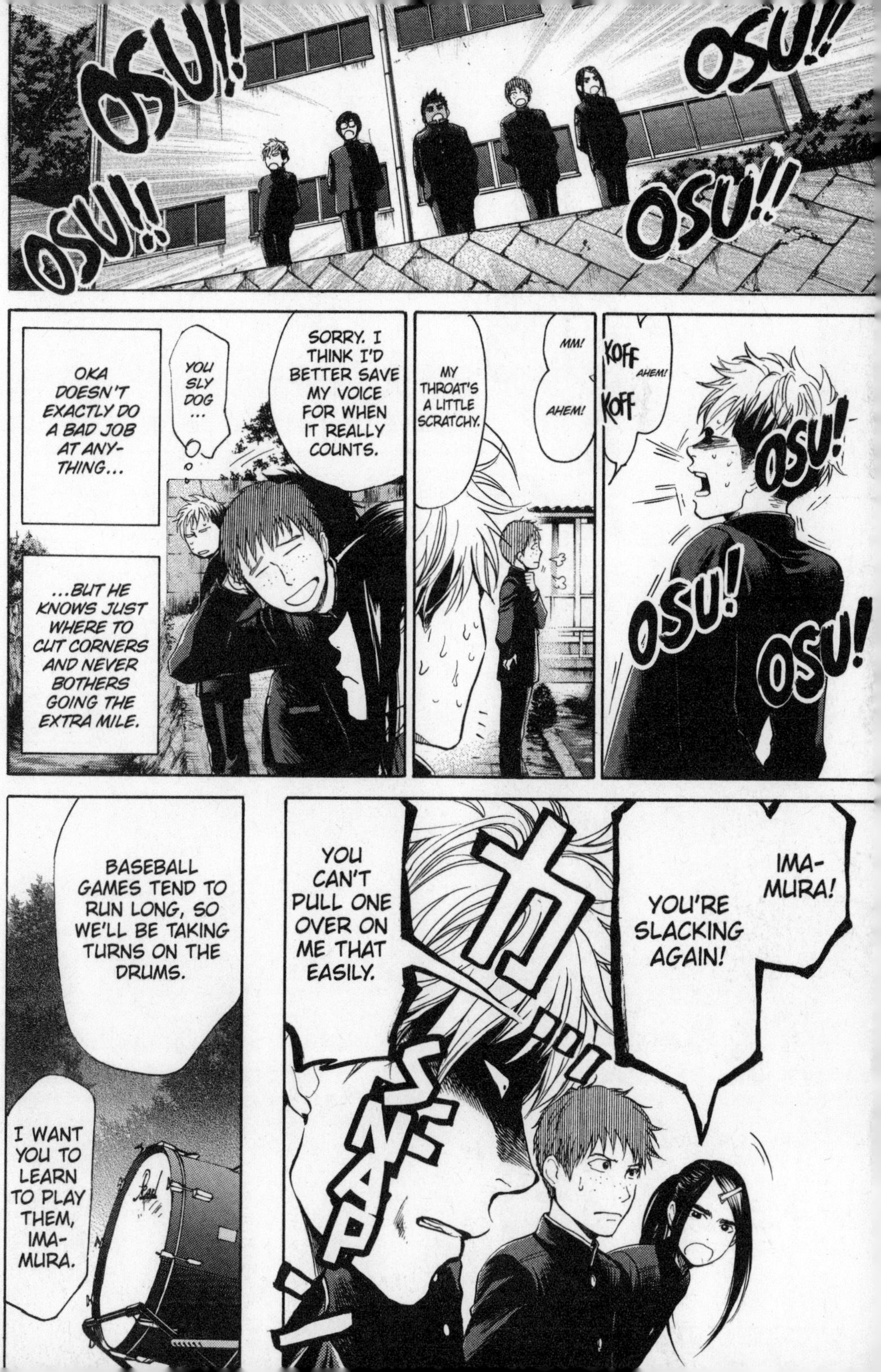
OSU!!
OSU!!
OSU!!
OSU!!
OSU!
OSU!
OSU!
KOFF AHEM! KOFF
MM! AHEM!
MY THROAT'S A LITTLE SCRATCHY.
SORRY. I THINK I'D BETTER SAVE MY VOICE FOR WHEN IT REALLY COUNTS.
YOU SLY DOG ...
OKA DOESN'T EXACTLY DO A BAD JOB AT ANY-THING...
...BUT HE KNOWS JUST WHERE TO CUT CORNERS AND NEVER BOTHERS GOING THE EXTRA MILE.
IMA-MURA!
YOU'RE SLACKING AGAIN!
カッ
SNAP!
YOU CAN'T PULL ONE OVER ON ME THAT EASILY.
BASEBALL GAMES TEND TO RUN LONG, SO WE'LL BE TAKING TURNS ON THE DRUMS.
I WANT YOU TO LEARN TO PLAY THEM, IMA-MURA.

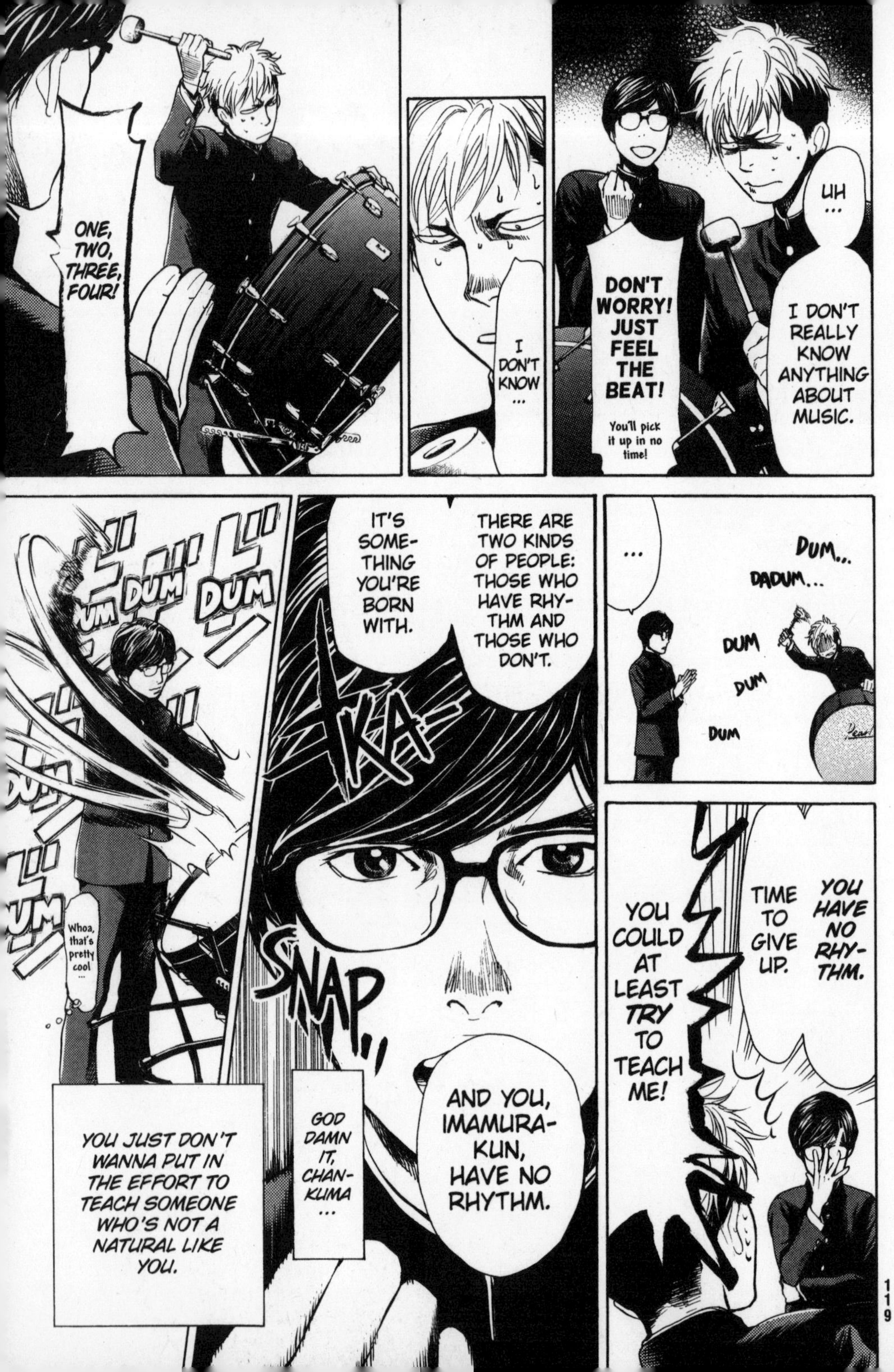
UH ...
I DON'T REALLY KNOW ANYTHING ABOUT MUSIC.
DON'T WORRY! JUST FEEL THE BEAT!
You'll pick it up in no time!
I DON'T KNOW ...
ONE, TWO, THREE, FOUR!
...
DUM... DADUM...
DUM
DUM
DUM
YOU HAVE NO RHY-THM.
TIME TO GIVE UP.
YOU COULD AT LEAST TRY TO TEACH ME!
THERE ARE TWO KINDS OF PEOPLE: THOSE WHO HAVE RHY-THM AND THOSE WHO DON'T.
IT'S SOME-THING YOU'RE BORN WITH.
KA-
SNAP
AND YOU, IMAMURA-KUN, HAVE NO RHYTHM.
GOD DAMN IT, CHAN-KUMA ...
DUM DUM DUM
Whoa, that's pretty cool ...
YOU JUST DON'T WANNA PUT IN THE EFFORT TO TEACH SOMEONE WHO'S NOT A NATURAL LIKE YOU.

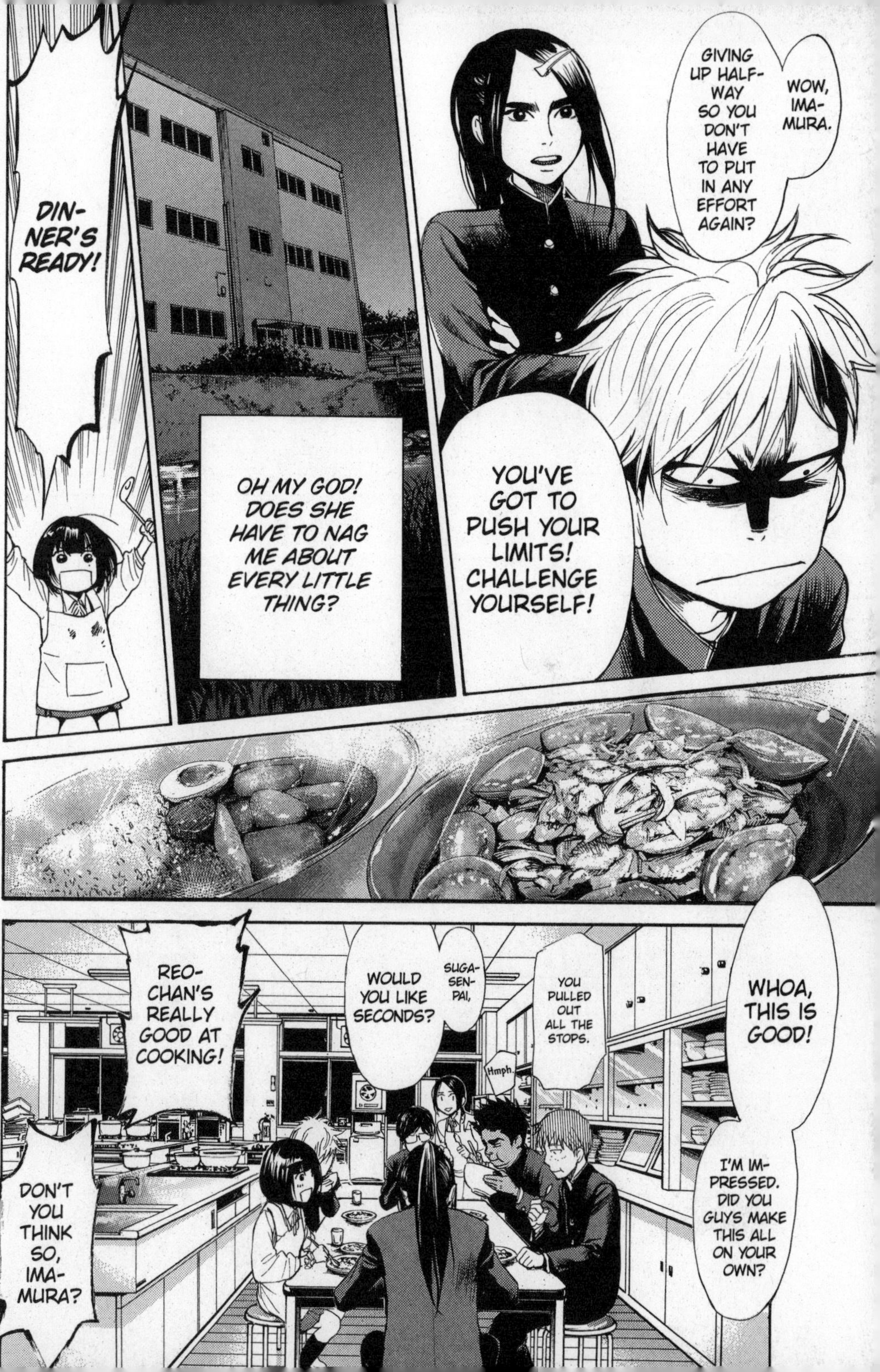
WOW, IMAMURA.
GIVING UP HALFWAY SO YOU DON'T HAVE TO PUT IN ANY EFFORT AGAIN?
YOU'VE GOT TO PUSH YOUR LIMITS! CHALLENGE YOURSELF!
OH MY GOD! DOES SHE HAVE TO NAG ME ABOUT EVERY LITTLE THING?
DINNER'S READY!
WHOA, THIS IS GOOD!
I'M IMPRESSED. DID YOU GUYS MAKE THIS ALL ON YOUR OWN?
YOU PULLED OUT ALL THE STOPS.
Hmph.
SUGA-SENPAI,
WOULD YOU LIKE SECONDS?
REO-CHAN'S REALLY GOOD AT COOKING!
DON'T YOU THINK SO, IMAMURA?

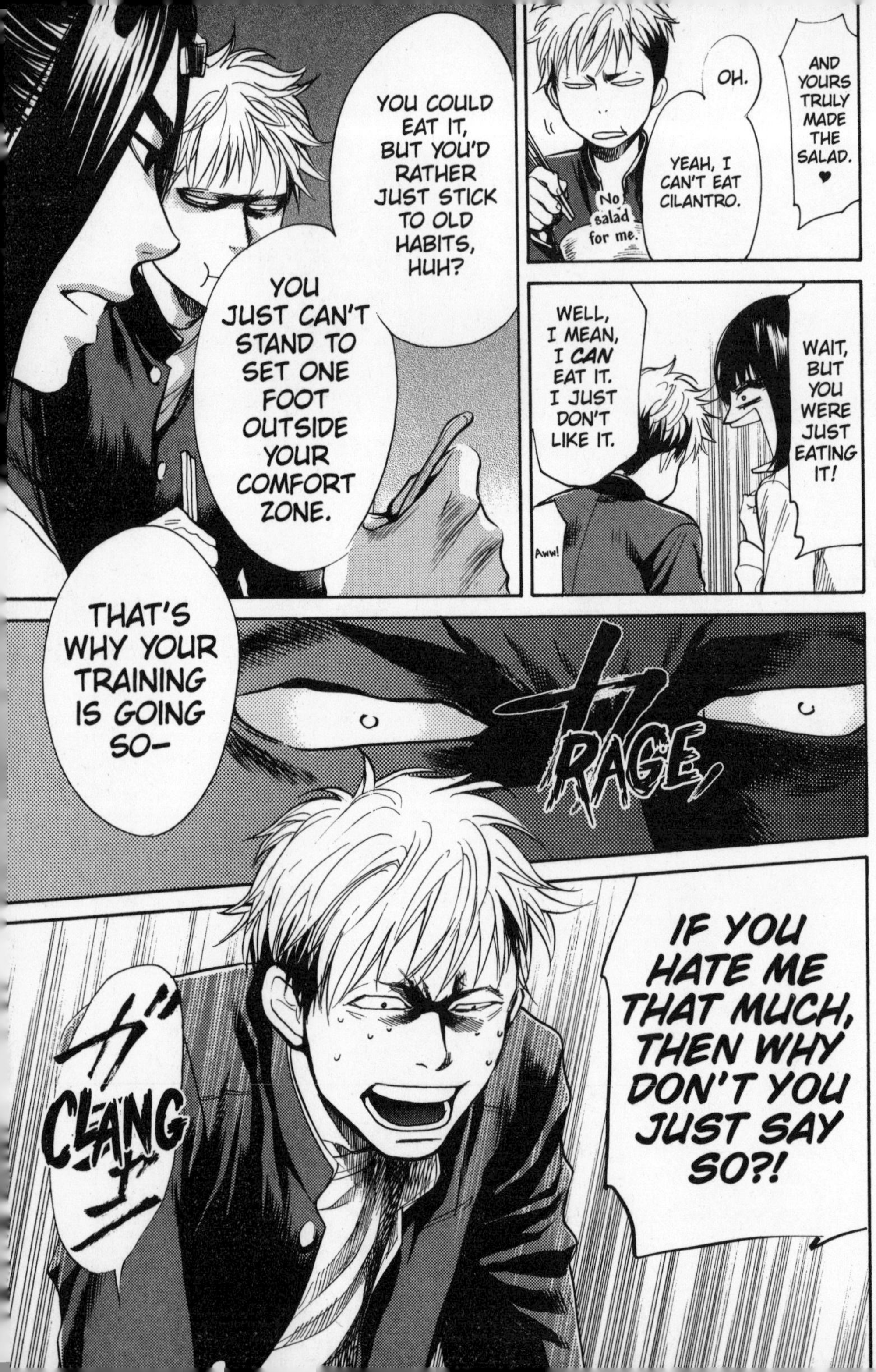
AND YOURS TRULY MADE THE SALAD. ♥
OH.
YEAH, I CAN'T EAT CILANTRO.
No salad for me.
WAIT, BUT YOU WERE JUST EATING IT!
WELL, I MEAN, I *CAN* EAT IT. I JUST DON'T LIKE IT.
Aww!
YOU COULD EAT IT, BUT YOU'D RATHER JUST STICK TO OLD HABITS, HUH?
YOU JUST CAN'T STAND TO SET ONE FOOT OUTSIDE YOUR COMFORT ZONE.
THAT'S WHY YOUR TRAINING IS GOING SO–
RAGE
IF YOU HATE ME THAT MUCH, THEN WHY DON'T YOU JUST SAY SO?!
CLANG

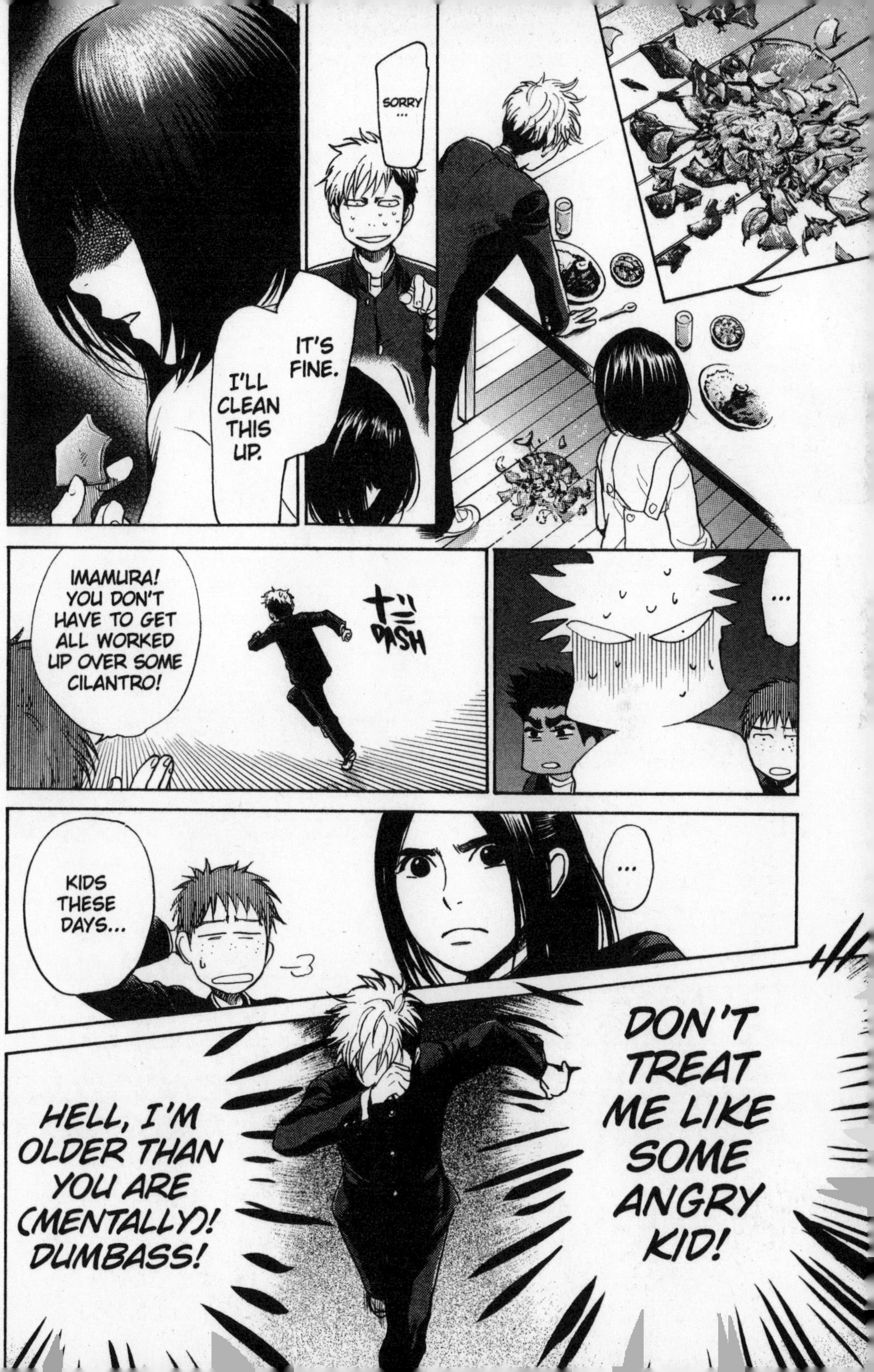
SORRY ...
IT'S FINE.
I'LL CLEAN THIS UP.
...
IMAMURA! YOU DON'T HAVE TO GET ALL WORKED UP OVER SOME CILANTRO!
DASH
...
KIDS THESE DAYS...
DON'T TREAT ME LIKE SOME ANGRY KID!
HELL, I'M OLDER THAN YOU ARE (MENTALLY)! DUMBASS!

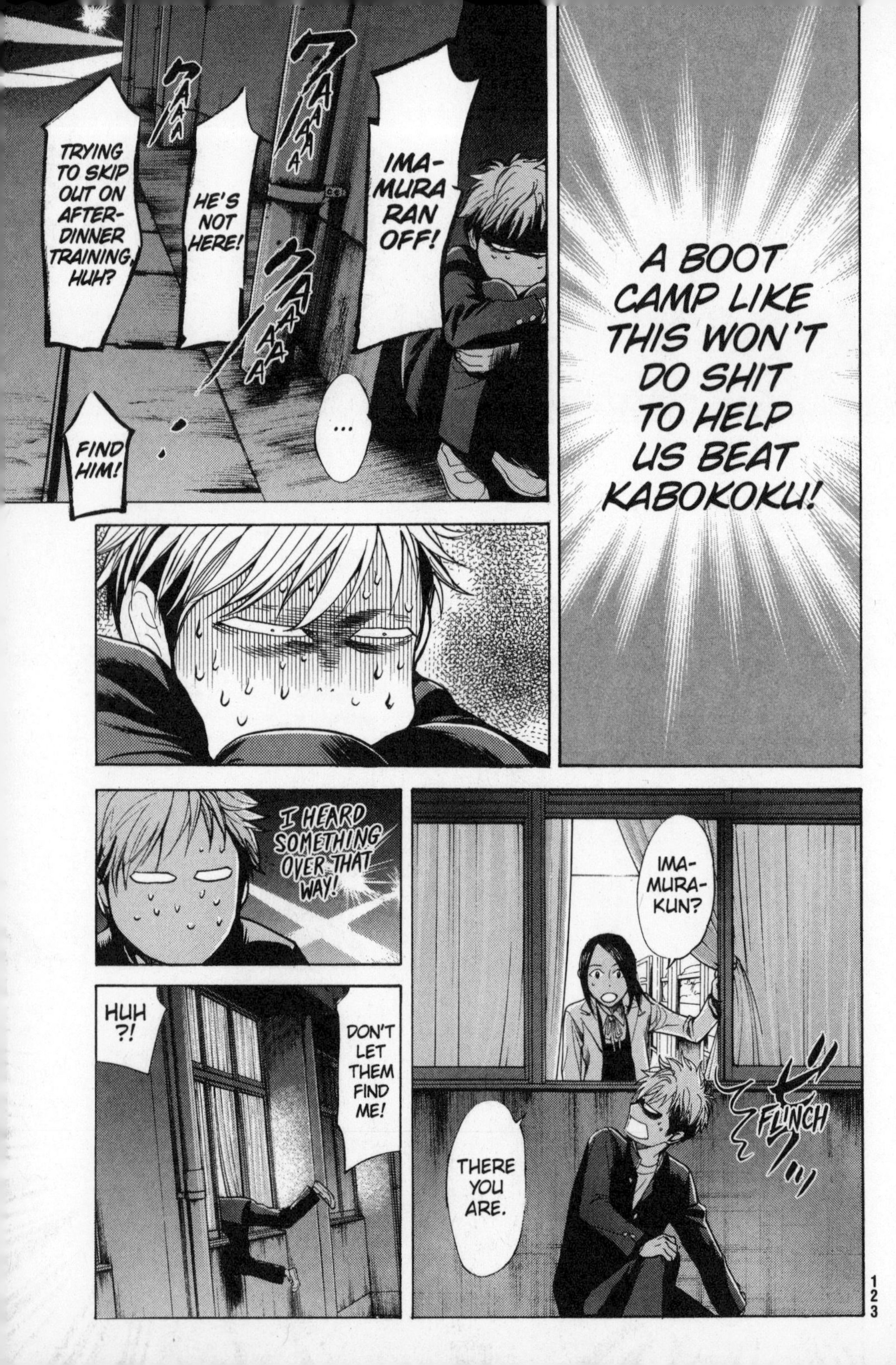
A BOOT CAMP LIKE THIS WON'T DO SHIT TO HELP US BEAT KABOKOKU!
IMA-MURA RAN OFF!
...
HE'S NOT HERE!
TRYING TO SKIP OUT ON AFTER-DINNER TRAINING, HUH?
FIND HIM!
IMA-MURA-KUN?
FLINCH
THERE YOU ARE.
I HEARD SOMETHING OVER THAT WAY!
DON'T LET THEM FIND ME!
HUH ?!

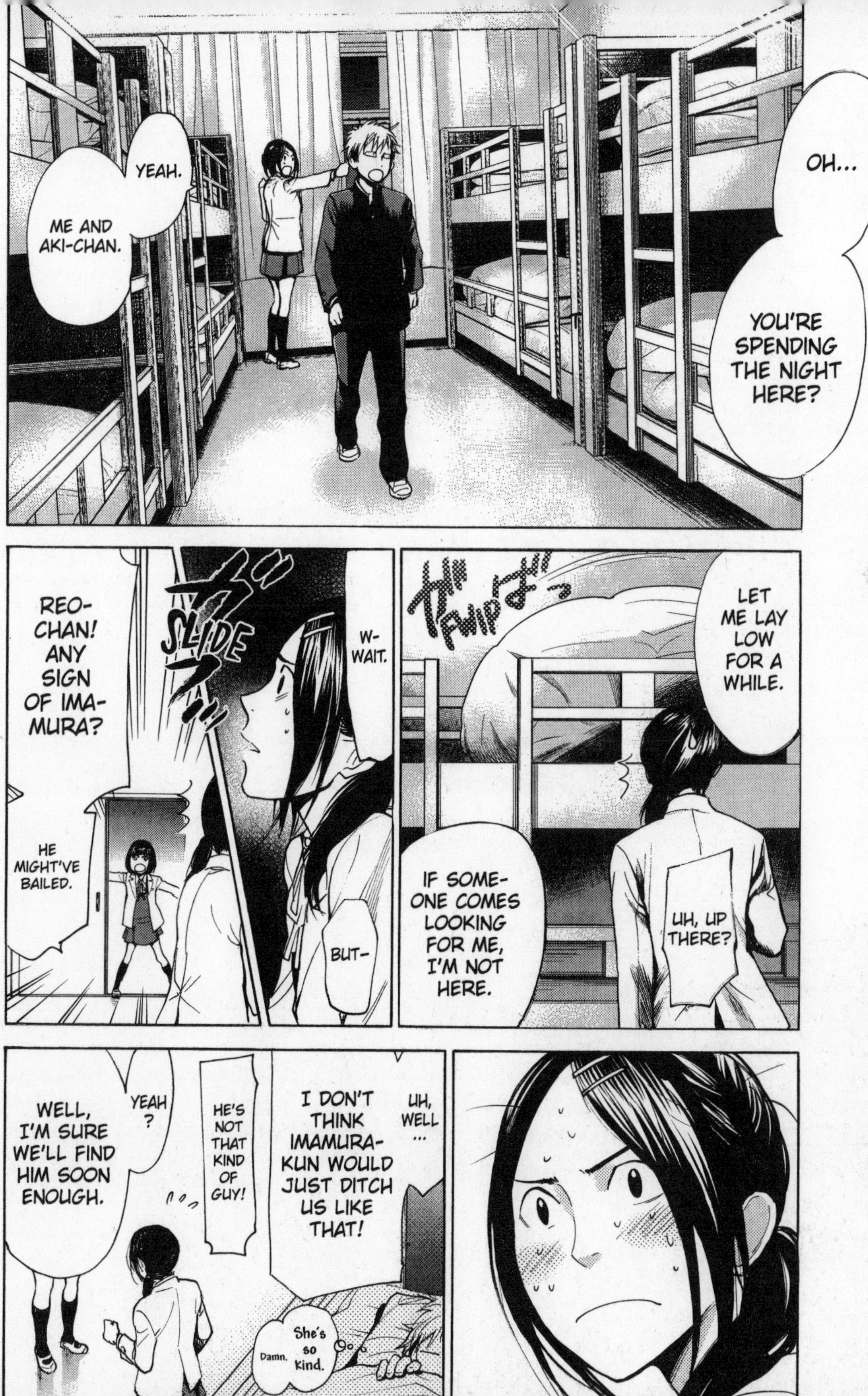
OH...
YOU'RE SPENDING THE NIGHT HERE?
YEAH.
ME AND AKI-CHAN.
FWIP
LET ME LAY LOW FOR A WHILE.
UH, UP THERE?
IF SOME-ONE COMES LOOKING FOR ME, I'M NOT HERE.
W-WAIT.
SLIDE
BUT-
REO-CHAN! ANY SIGN OF IMA-MURA?
HE MIGHT'VE BAILED.
UH, WELL ...
I DON'T THINK IMAMURA-KUN WOULD JUST DITCH US LIKE THAT!
HE'S NOT THAT KIND OF GUY!
YEAH ?
WELL, I'M SURE WE'LL FIND HIM SOON ENOUGH.
She's so kind.
Damn.

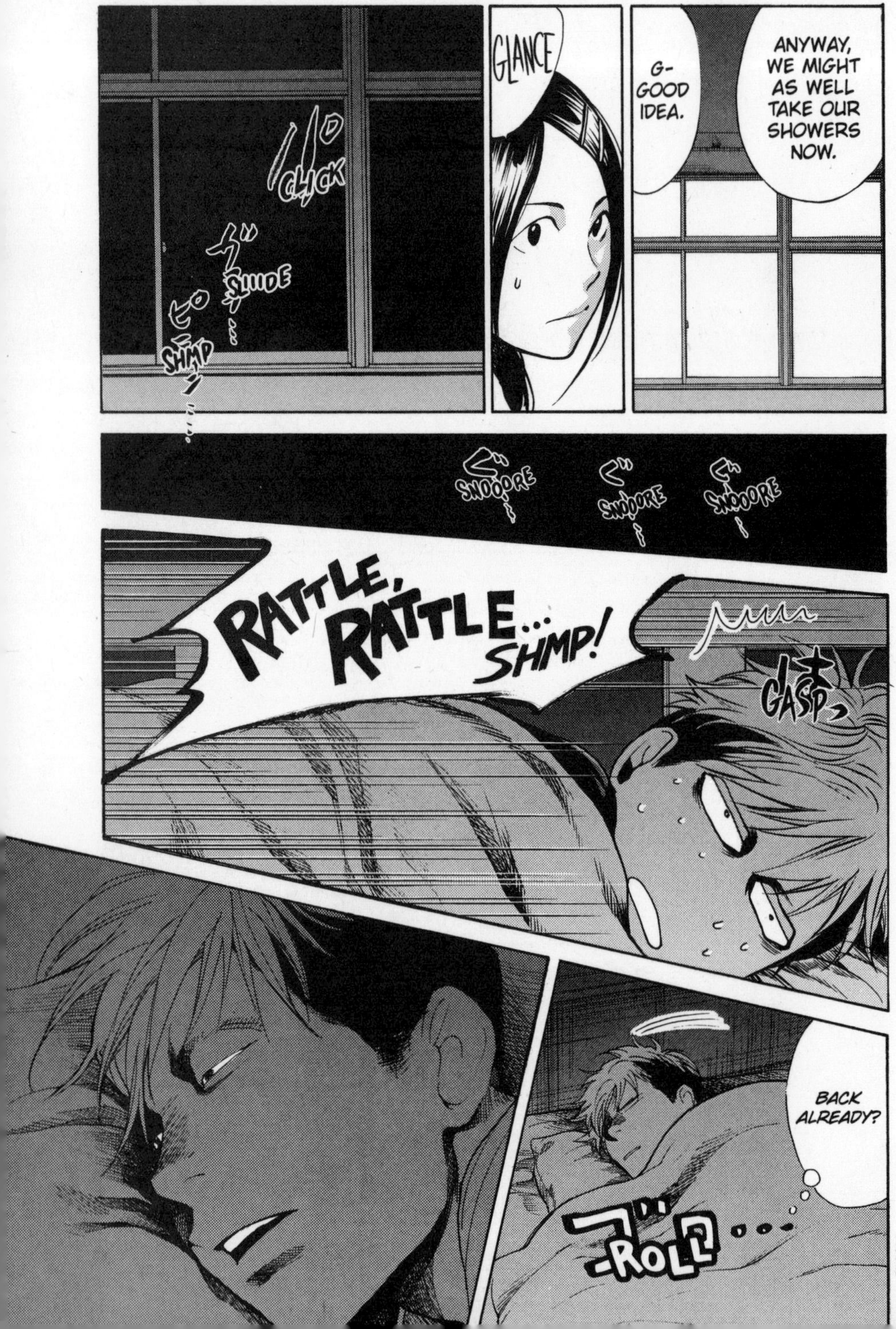
ANYWAY, WE MIGHT AS WELL TAKE OUR SHOWERS NOW.
G-GOOD IDEA.
GLANCE
CLICK
SLIIDE
SHMP
SNOOORE
SNOOORE
SNOOORE
RATTLE, RATTLE... SHMP!
GASP
BACK ALREADY?
ROLL...

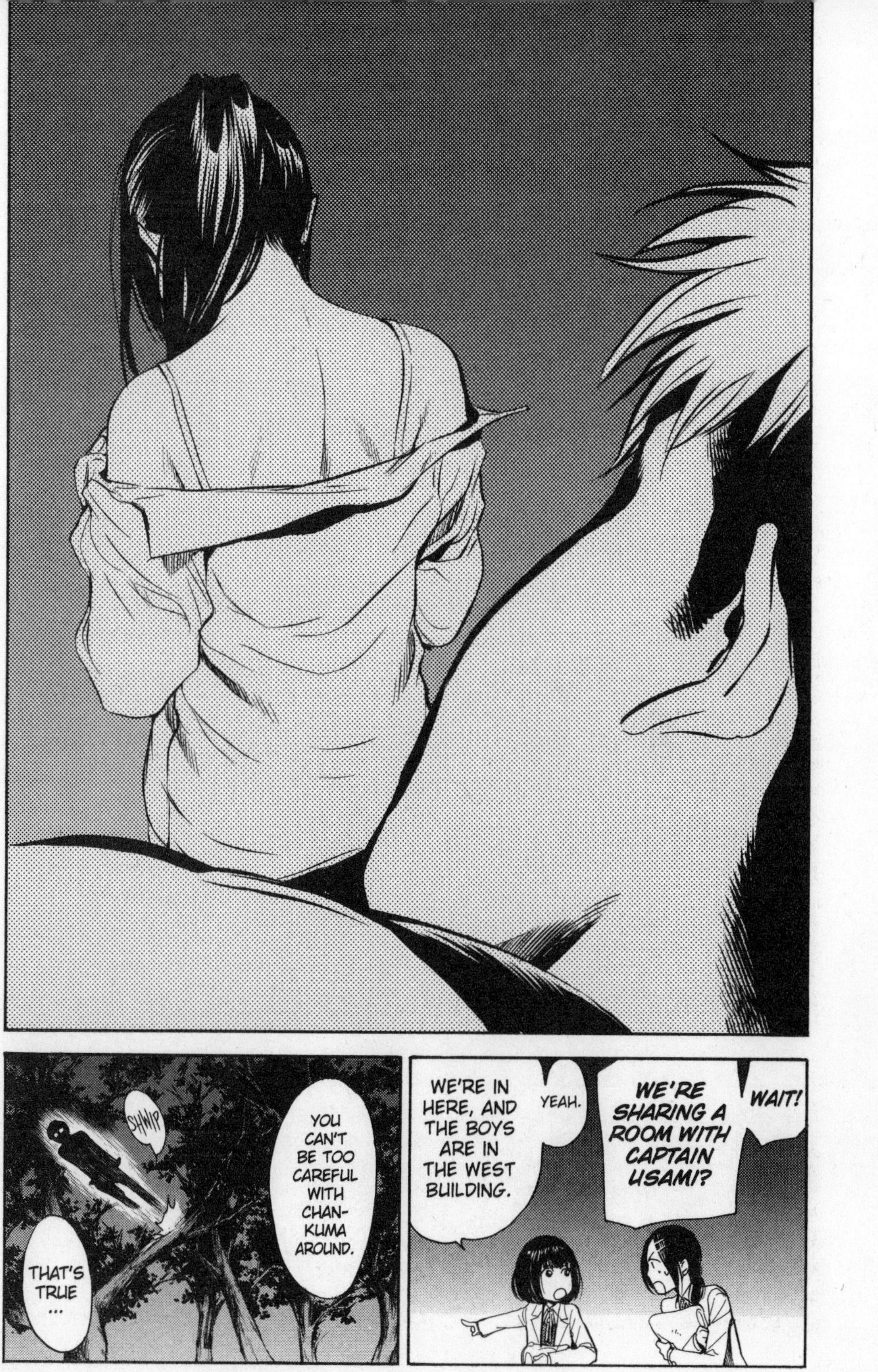
WAIT!
WE'RE SHARING A ROOM WITH CAPTAIN USAMI?
YEAH.
WE'RE IN HERE, AND THE BOYS ARE IN THE WEST BUILDING.
YOU CAN'T BE TOO CAREFUL WITH CHAN-KUMA AROUND.
SHWIP
THAT'S TRUE ...

27. A HARD DAY'S NIGHT

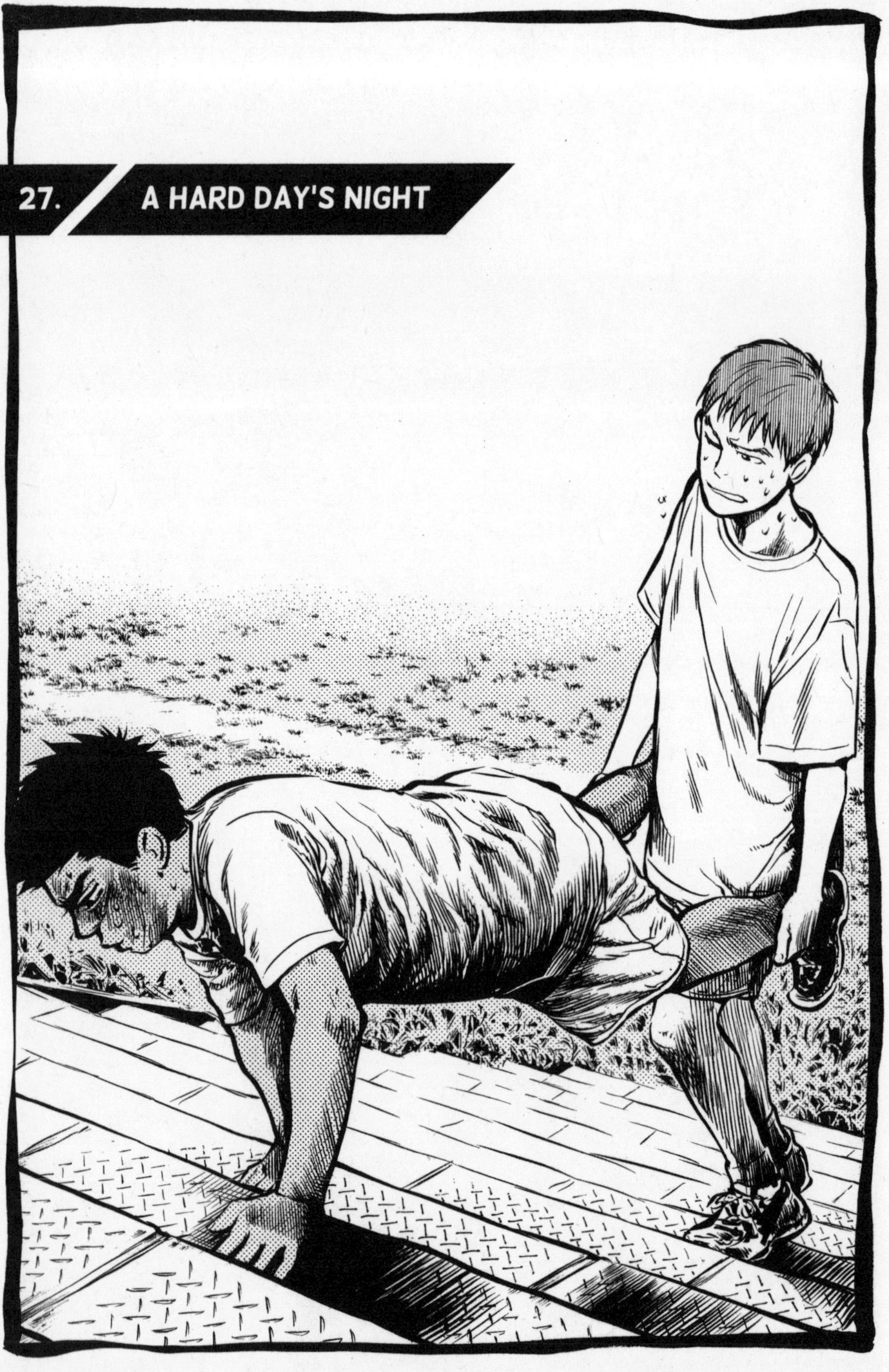

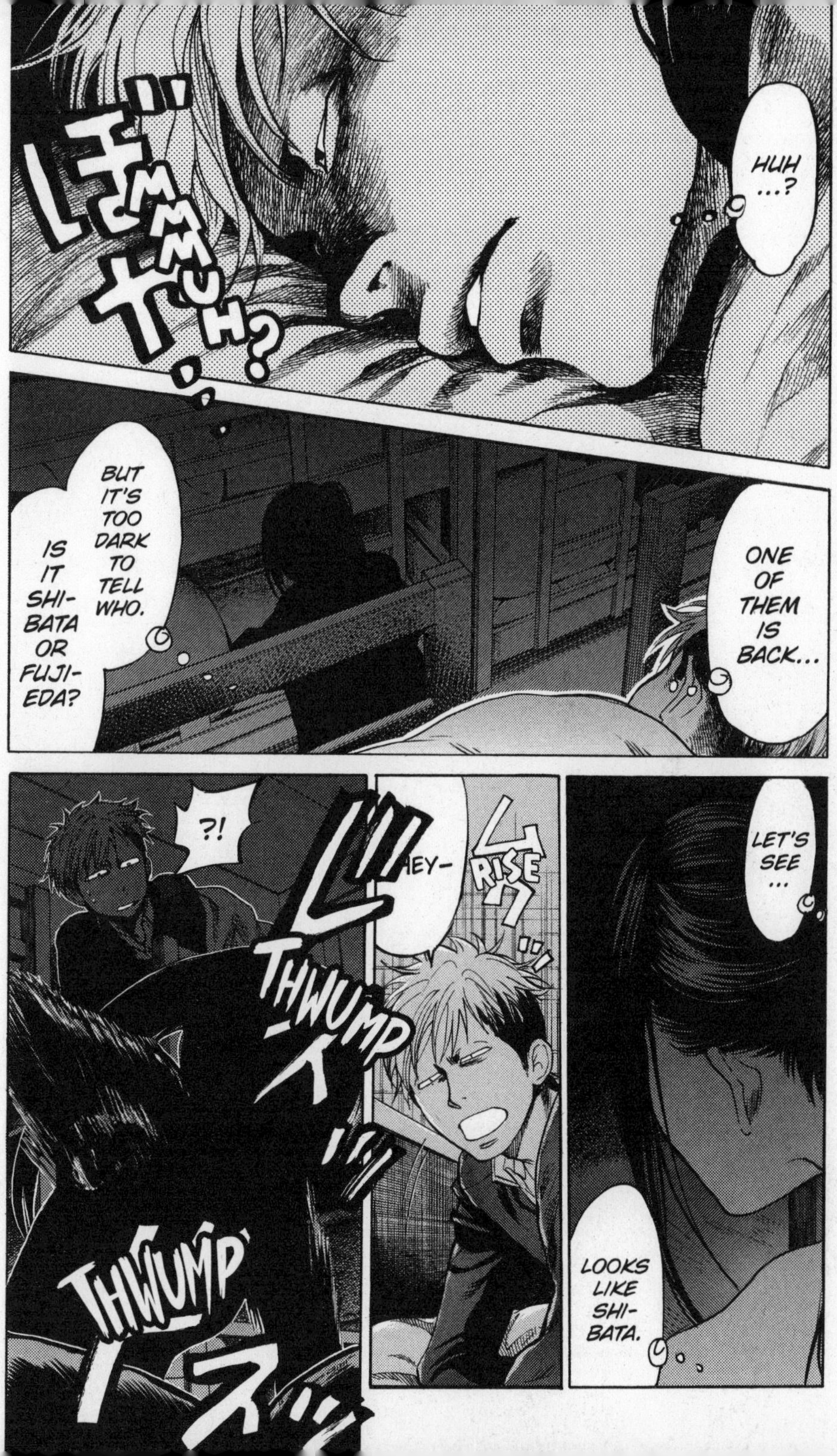
HUH ...?
MMMUH?
ONE OF THEM IS BACK...
BUT IT'S TOO DARK TO TELL WHO.
IS IT SHI-BATA OR FUJI-EDA?
LET'S SEE ...
LOOKS LIKE SHI-BATA.
RISE
HEY-
?!
THWUMP
THWUMP

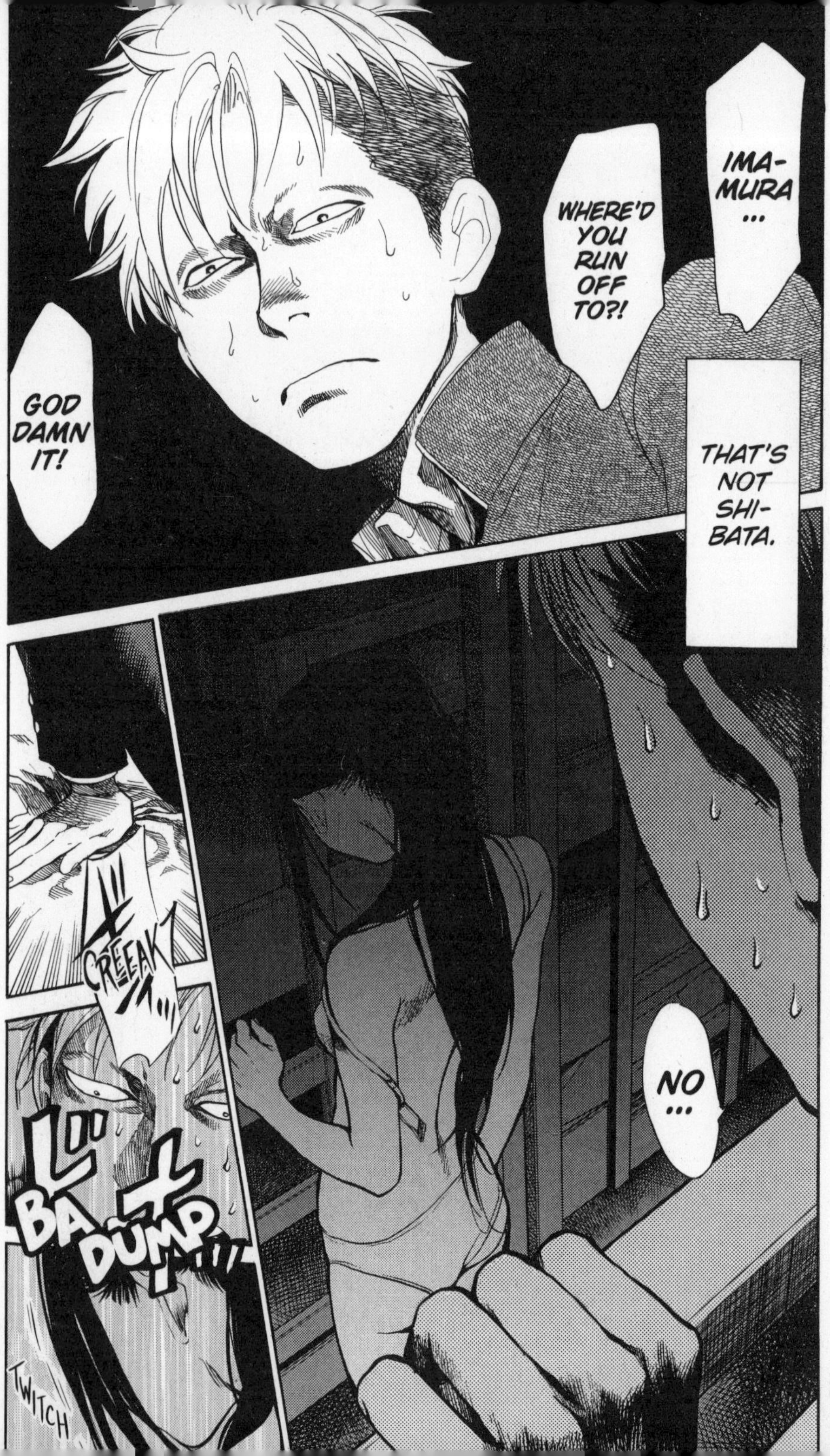
IMA-MURA...
WHERE'D YOU RUN OFF TO?!
GOD DAMN IT!
THAT'S NOT SHI-BATA.
NO...
CREEAK
BA-DUMP
TWITCH

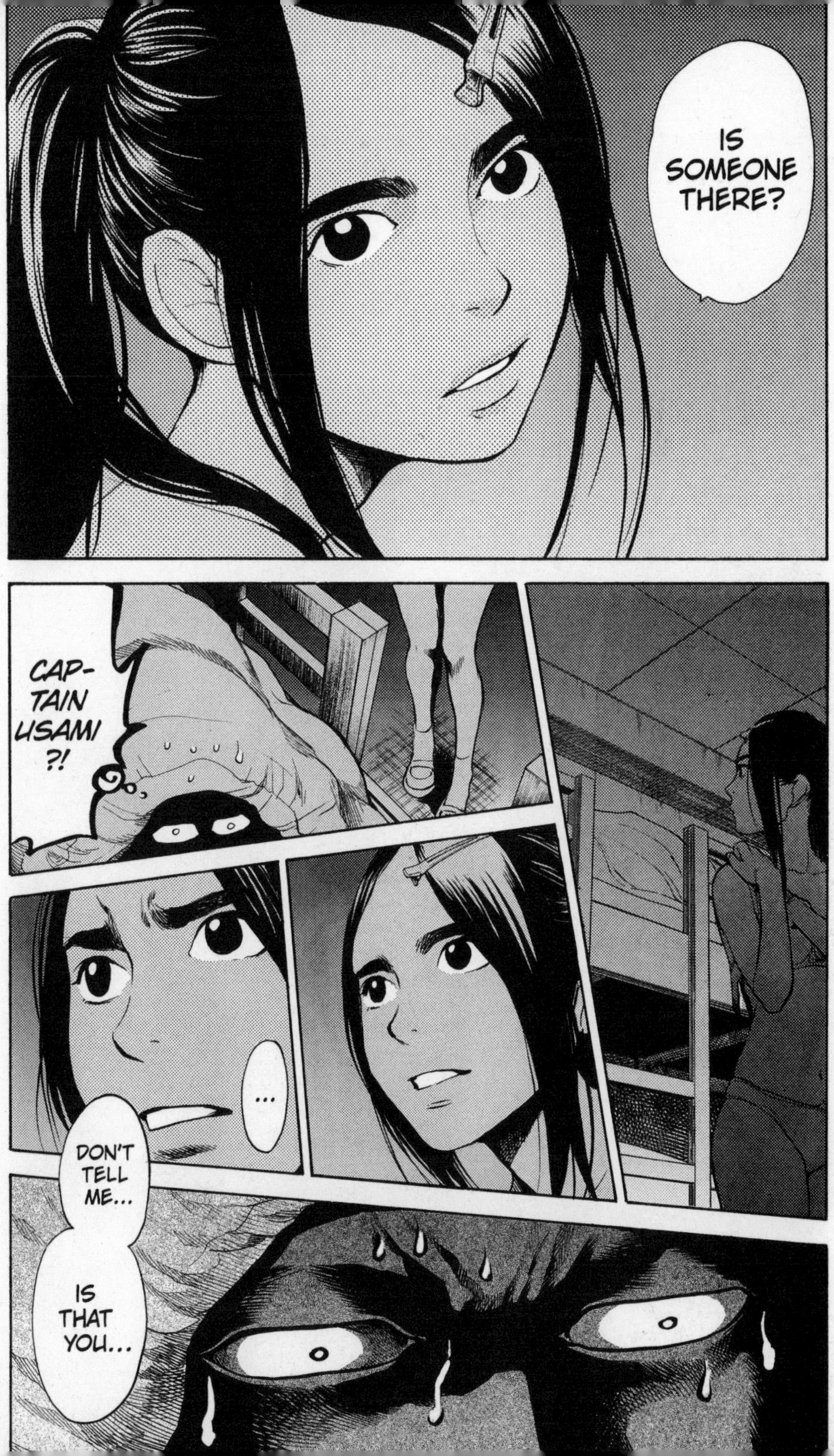
IS SOMEONE THERE?
CAP-TAIN USAMI ?!
...
DON'T TELL ME...
IS THAT YOU...

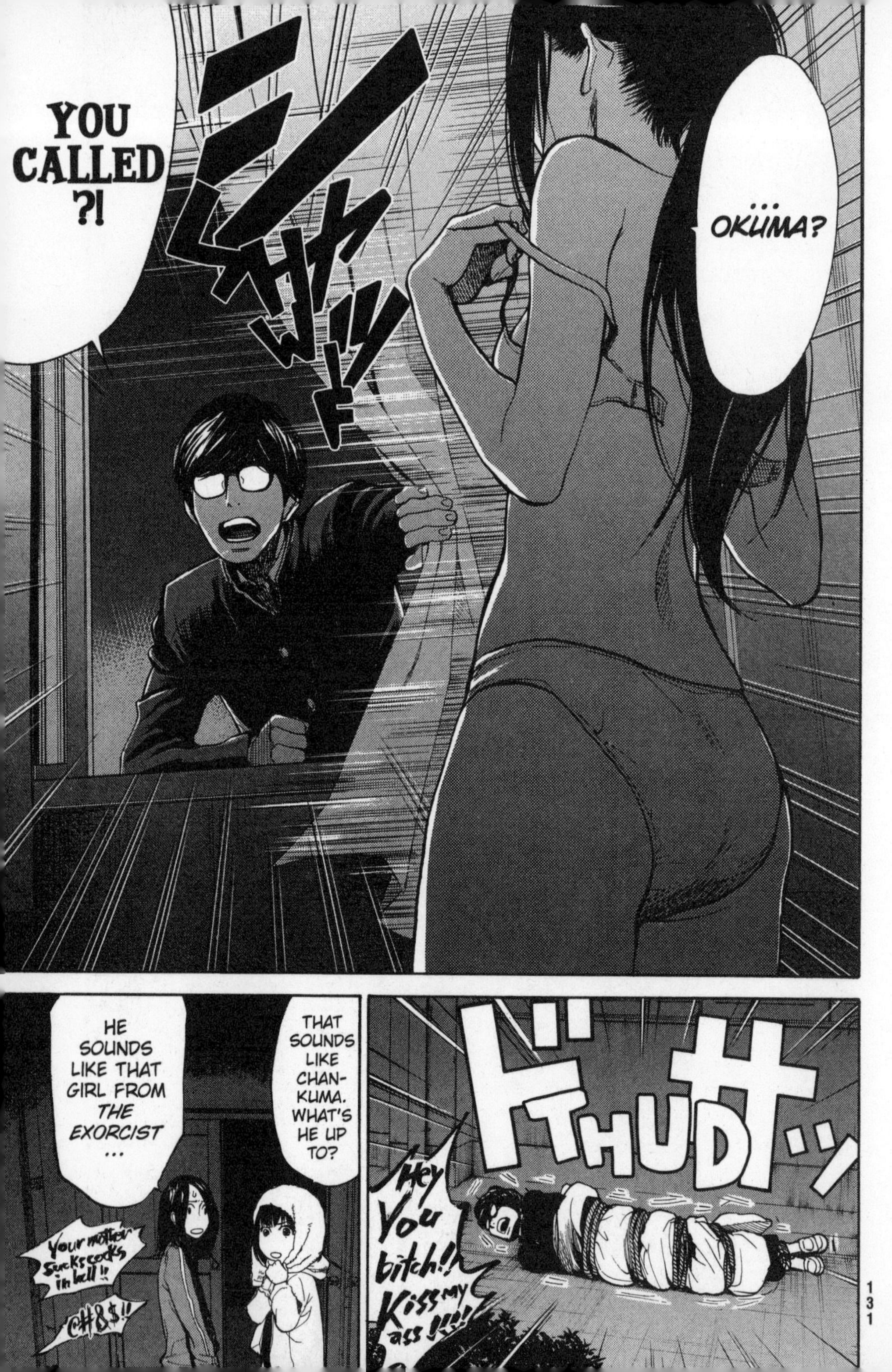
...OKUMA?
YOU CALLED ?!
THUD
Hey You bitch!! Kiss my ass!!!
THAT SOUNDS LIKE CHAN-KUMA. WHAT'S HE UP TO?
HE SOUNDS LIKE THAT GIRL FROM *THE EXORCIST* ...
Your mother sucks cocks in hell!!
C#&$!!

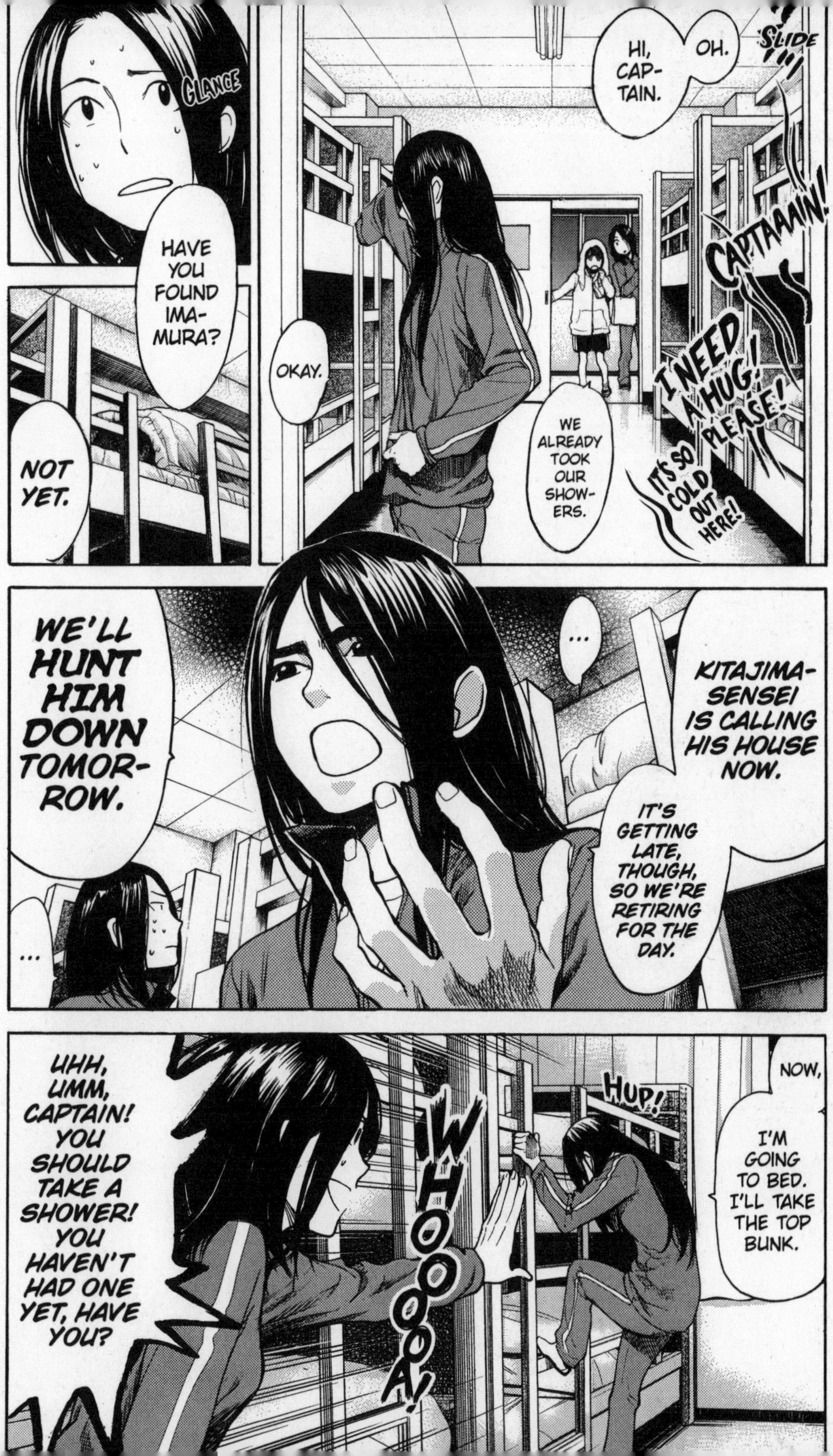
SLIDE
OH.
HI, CAPTAIN.
CAPTAAAIN!
I NEED A HUG! PLEASE!
IT'S SO COLD OUT HERE!
WE ALREADY TOOK OUR SHOWERS.
OKAY.
GLANCE
HAVE YOU FOUND IMAMURA?
NOT YET.
...
KITAJIMA-SENSEI IS CALLING HIS HOUSE NOW.
IT'S GETTING LATE, THOUGH, SO WE'RE RETIRING FOR THE DAY.
WE'LL HUNT HIM DOWN TOMORROW.
...
NOW,
I'M GOING TO BED. I'LL TAKE THE TOP BUNK.
HUP!
WHOOOOA!
UHH, UMM, CAPTAIN! YOU SHOULD TAKE A SHOWER! YOU HAVEN'T HAD ONE YET, HAVE YOU?

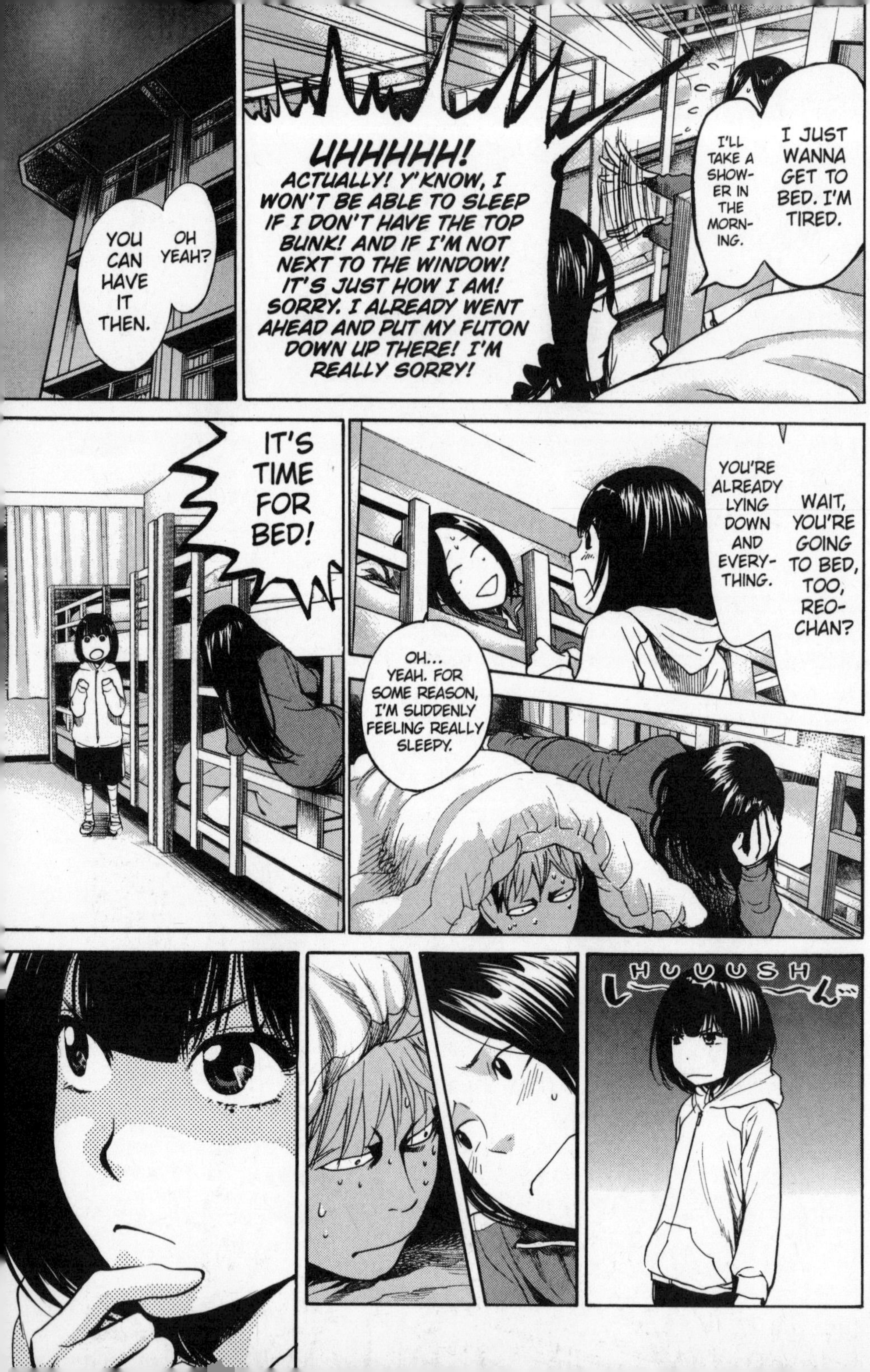
I JUST WANNA GET TO BED. I'M TIRED.
I'LL TAKE A SHOWER IN THE MORNING.
UHHHHH! ACTUALLY! Y'KNOW, I WON'T BE ABLE TO SLEEP IF I DON'T HAVE THE TOP BUNK! AND IF I'M NOT NEXT TO THE WINDOW! IT'S JUST HOW I AM! SORRY. I ALREADY WENT AHEAD AND PUT MY FUTON DOWN UP THERE! I'M REALLY SORRY!
OH YEAH?
YOU CAN HAVE IT THEN.
WAIT, YOU'RE GOING TO BED, TOO, REO-CHAN?
YOU'RE ALREADY LYING DOWN AND EVERYTHING.
OH... YEAH. FOR SOME REASON, I'M SUDDENLY FEELING REALLY SLEEPY.
IT'S TIME FOR BED!
HUUUSH

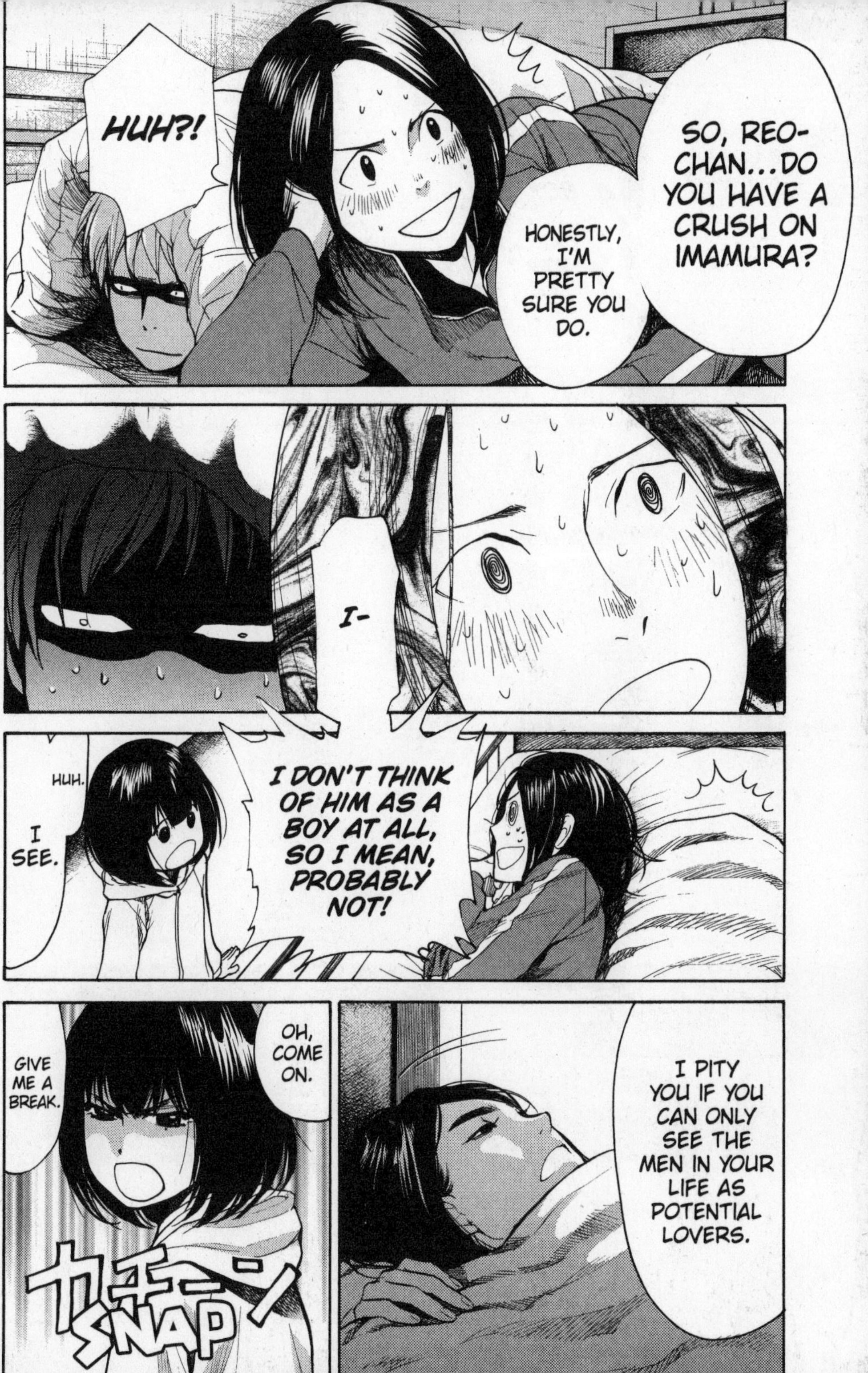
SO, REO-CHAN...DO YOU HAVE A CRUSH ON IMAMURA?
HONESTLY, I'M PRETTY SURE YOU DO.
HUH?!
I-
I DON'T THINK OF HIM AS A BOY AT ALL, SO I MEAN, PROBABLY NOT!
HUH.
I SEE.
I PITY YOU IF YOU CAN ONLY SEE THE MEN IN YOUR LIFE AS POTENTIAL LOVERS.
OH, COME ON.
GIVE ME A BREAK.
カチーン
SNAP

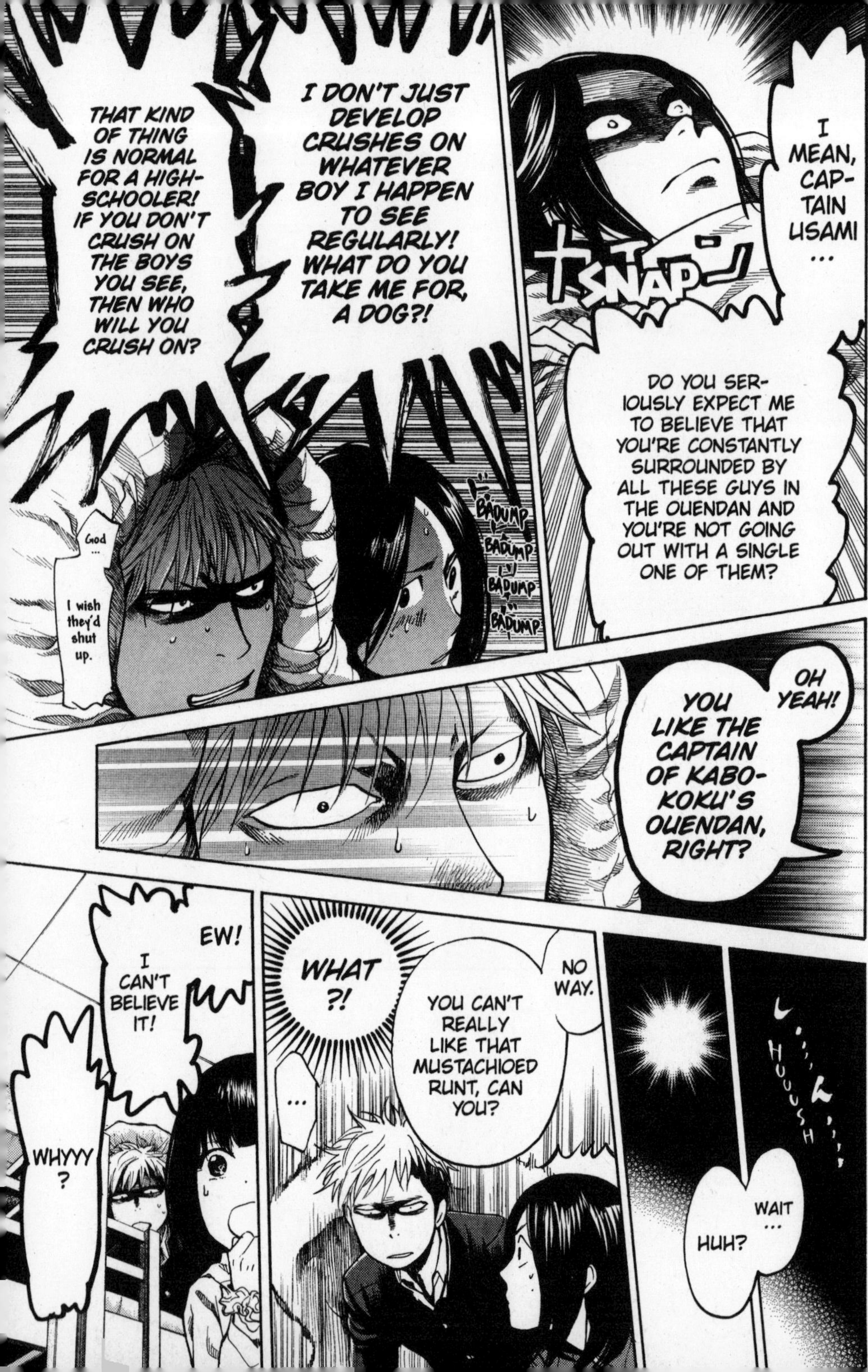
I MEAN, CAP-TAIN USAMI ...
SNAP
DO YOU SER-IOUSLY EXPECT ME TO BELIEVE THAT YOU'RE CONSTANTLY SURROUNDED BY ALL THESE GUYS IN THE OUENDAN AND YOU'RE NOT GOING OUT WITH A SINGLE ONE OF THEM?
I DON'T JUST DEVELOP CRUSHES ON WHATEVER BOY I HAPPEN TO SEE REGULARLY! WHAT DO YOU TAKE ME FOR, A DOG?!
THAT KIND OF THING IS NORMAL FOR A HIGH-SCHOOLER! IF YOU DON'T CRUSH ON THE BOYS YOU SEE, THEN WHO WILL YOU CRUSH ON?
BADUMP BADUMP BADUMP BADUMP
God ...
I wish they'd shut up.
OH YEAH!
YOU LIKE THE CAPTAIN OF KABO-KOKU'S OUENDAN, RIGHT?
HUUUSH
WAIT ...
HUH?
NO WAY.
YOU CAN'T REALLY LIKE THAT MUSTACHIOED RUNT, CAN YOU?
WHAT ?!
...
EW!
I CAN'T BELIEVE IT!
WHYYY ?

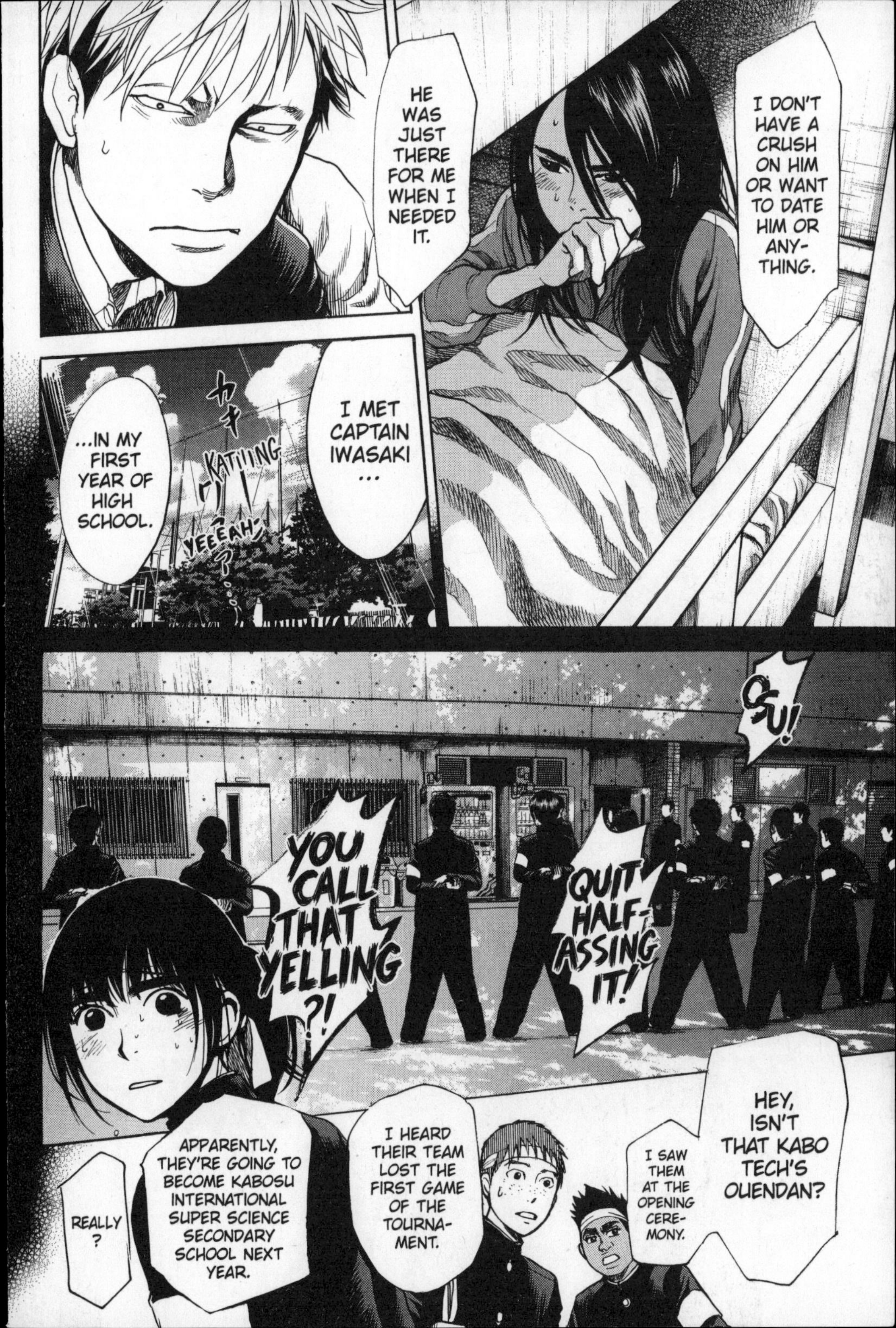
I DON'T HAVE A CRUSH ON HIM OR WANT TO DATE HIM OR ANY-THING.
HE WAS JUST THERE FOR ME WHEN I NEEDED IT.
I MET CAPTAIN IWASAKI...
...IN MY FIRST YEAR OF HIGH SCHOOL.
カキ
KATIIING
YEEEAH
OSU!
QUIT HALF-ASSING IT!
YOU CALL THAT YELLING?!
HEY, ISN'T THAT KABO TECH'S OUENDAN?
I SAW THEM AT THE OPENING CEREMONY.
I HEARD THEIR TEAM LOST THE FIRST GAME OF THE TOURNA-MENT.
APPARENTLY, THEY'RE GOING TO BECOME KABOSU INTERNATIONAL SUPER SCIENCE SECONDARY SCHOOL NEXT YEAR.
REALLY?

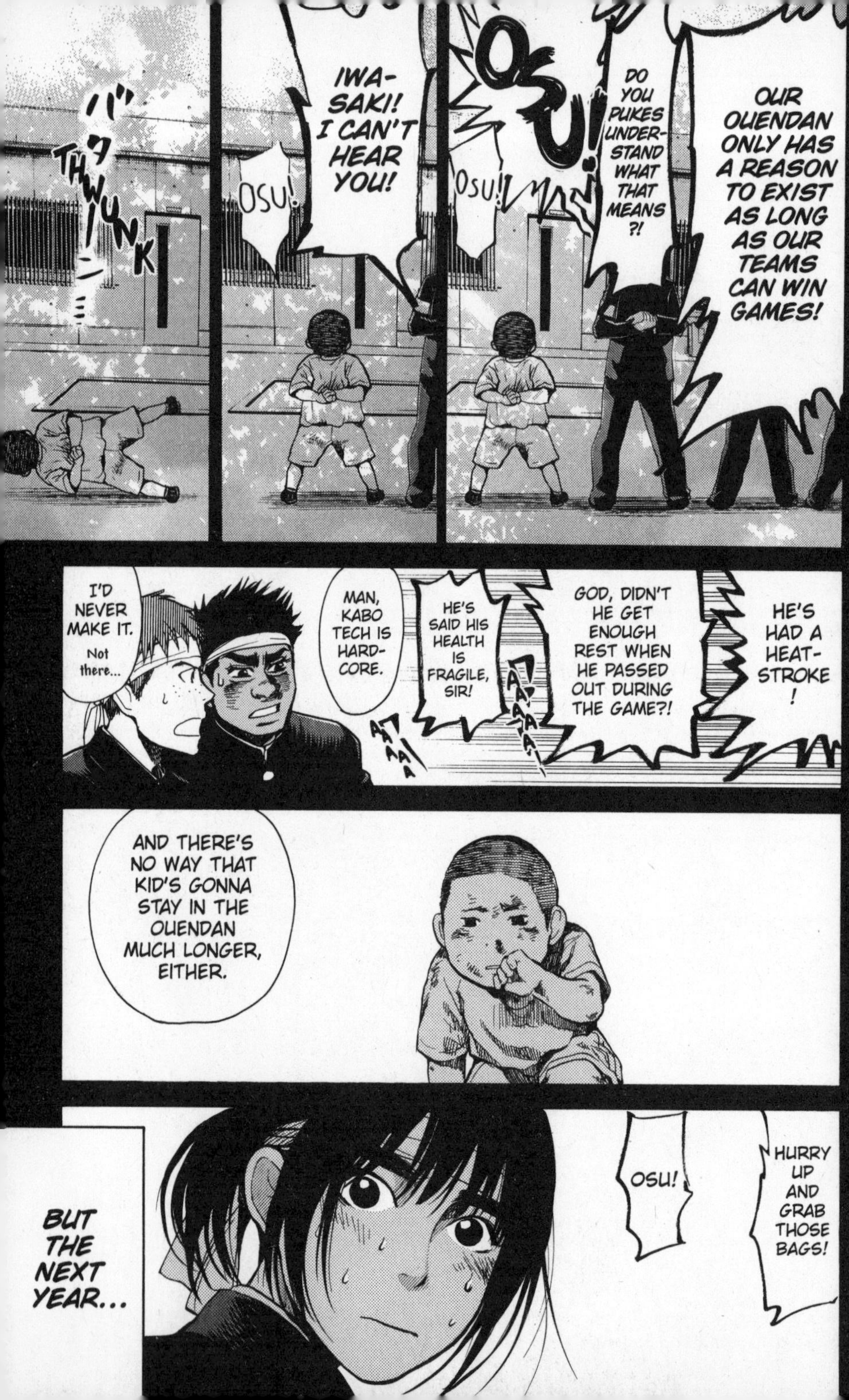
OUR OUENDAN ONLY HAS A REASON TO EXIST AS LONG AS OUR TEAMS CAN WIN GAMES!
DO YOU PUKES UNDERSTAND WHAT THAT MEANS ?!
OSU!
OSU!
IWA-SAKI! I CAN'T HEAR YOU!
OSU!
THWUNK
HE'S HAD A HEAT-STROKE!
GOD, DIDN'T HE GET ENOUGH REST WHEN HE PASSED OUT DURING THE GAME?!
AAAAAA
HE'S SAID HIS HEALTH IS FRAGILE, SIR!
MAN, KABO TECH IS HARD-CORE.
AAAAA
I'D NEVER MAKE IT.
Not there...
AND THERE'S NO WAY THAT KID'S GONNA STAY IN THE OUENDAN MUCH LONGER, EITHER.
HURRY UP AND GRAB THOSE BAGS!
OSU!
BUT THE NEXT YEAR...

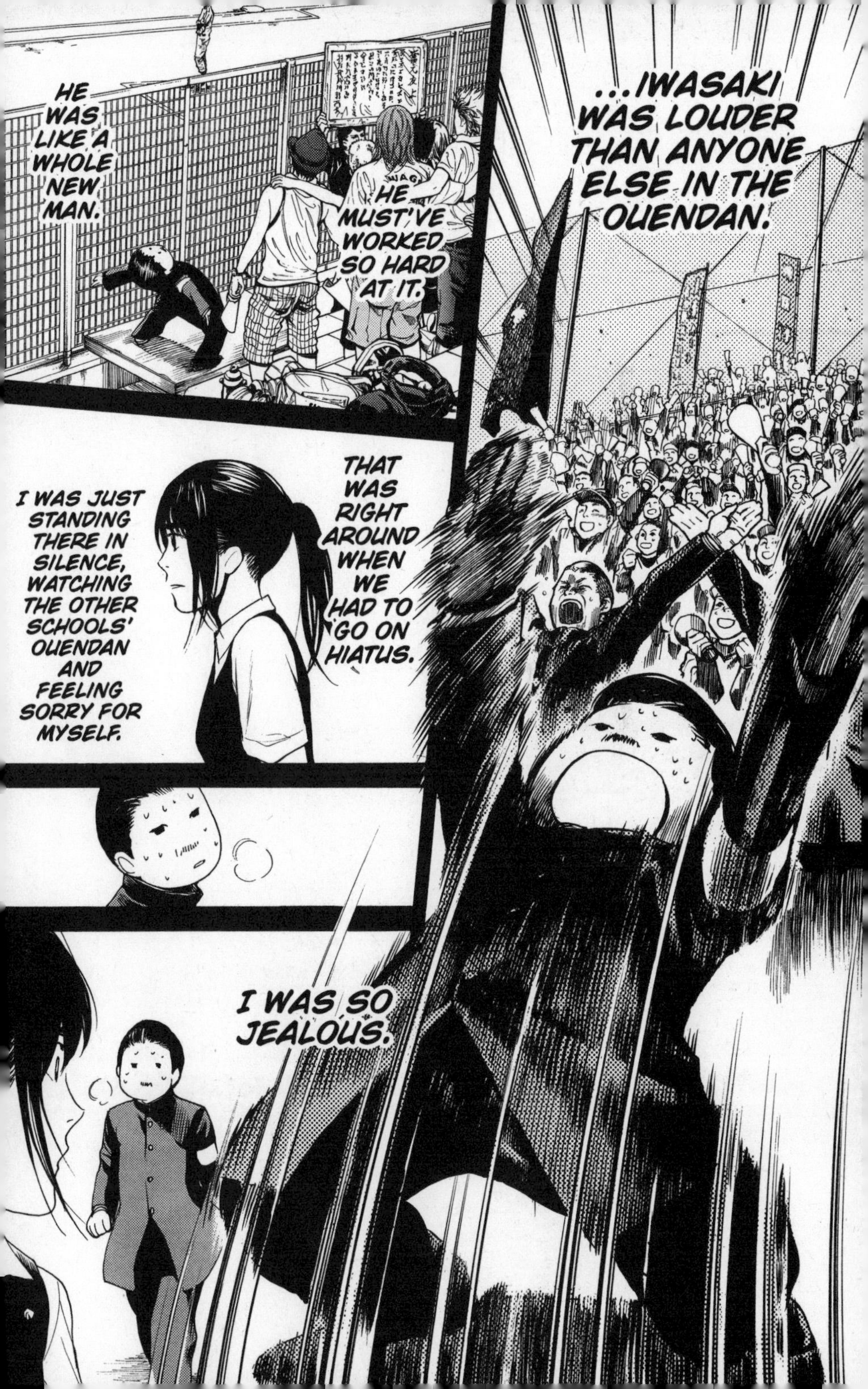
...IWASAKI WAS LOUDER THAN ANYONE ELSE IN THE OUENDAN.
HE WAS LIKE A WHOLE NEW MAN.
HE MUST'VE WORKED SO HARD AT IT.
THAT WAS RIGHT AROUND WHEN WE HAD TO GO ON HIATUS.
I WAS JUST STANDING THERE IN SILENCE, WATCHING THE OTHER SCHOOLS' OUENDAN AND FEELING SORRY FOR MYSELF.
I WAS SO JEALOUS.

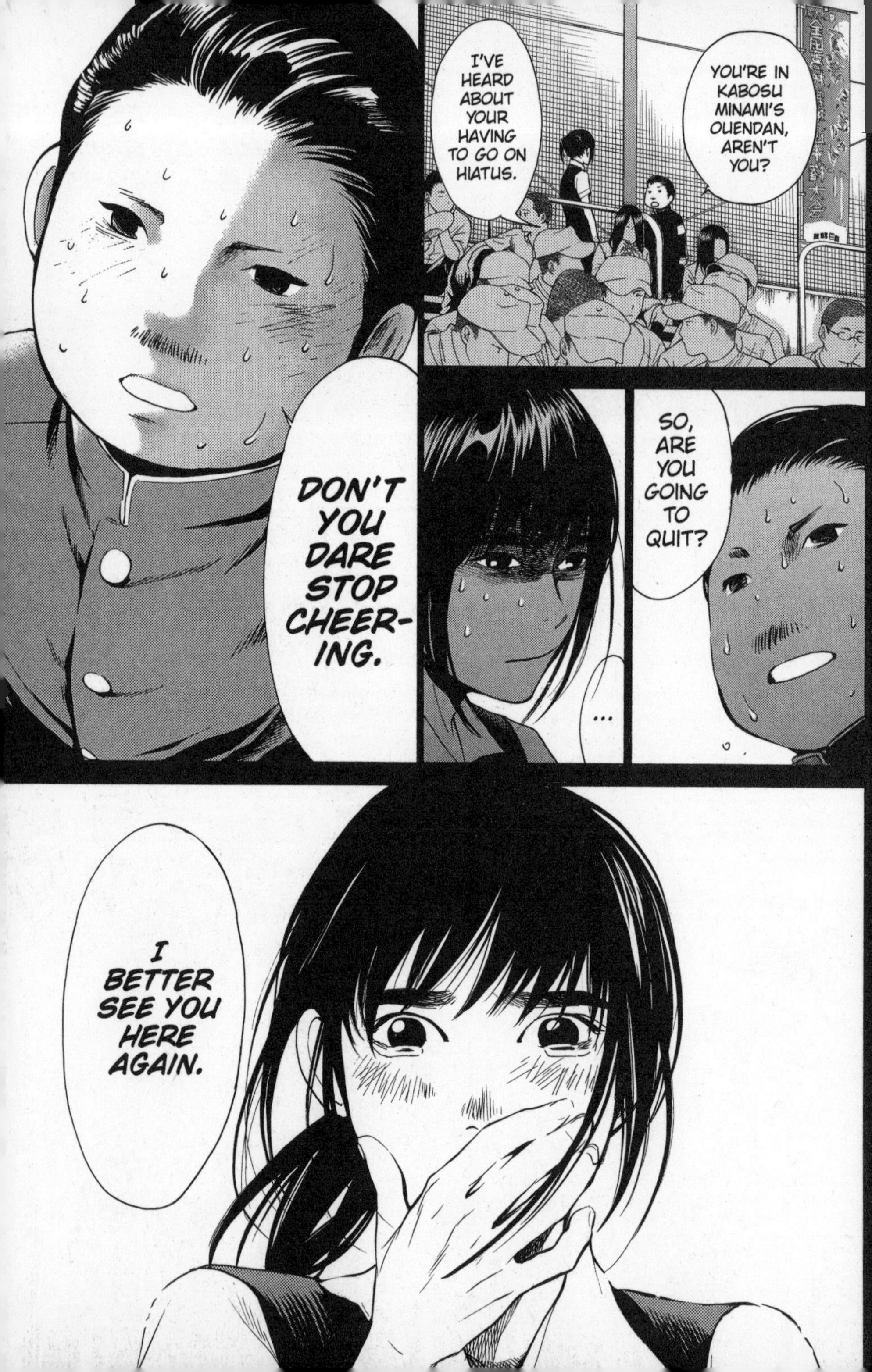
YOU'RE IN KABOSU MINAMI'S OUENDAN, AREN'T YOU?
I'VE HEARD ABOUT YOUR HAVING TO GO ON HIATUS.
SO, ARE YOU GOING TO QUIT?
...
DON'T YOU DARE STOP CHEERING.
I BETTER SEE YOU HERE AGAIN.

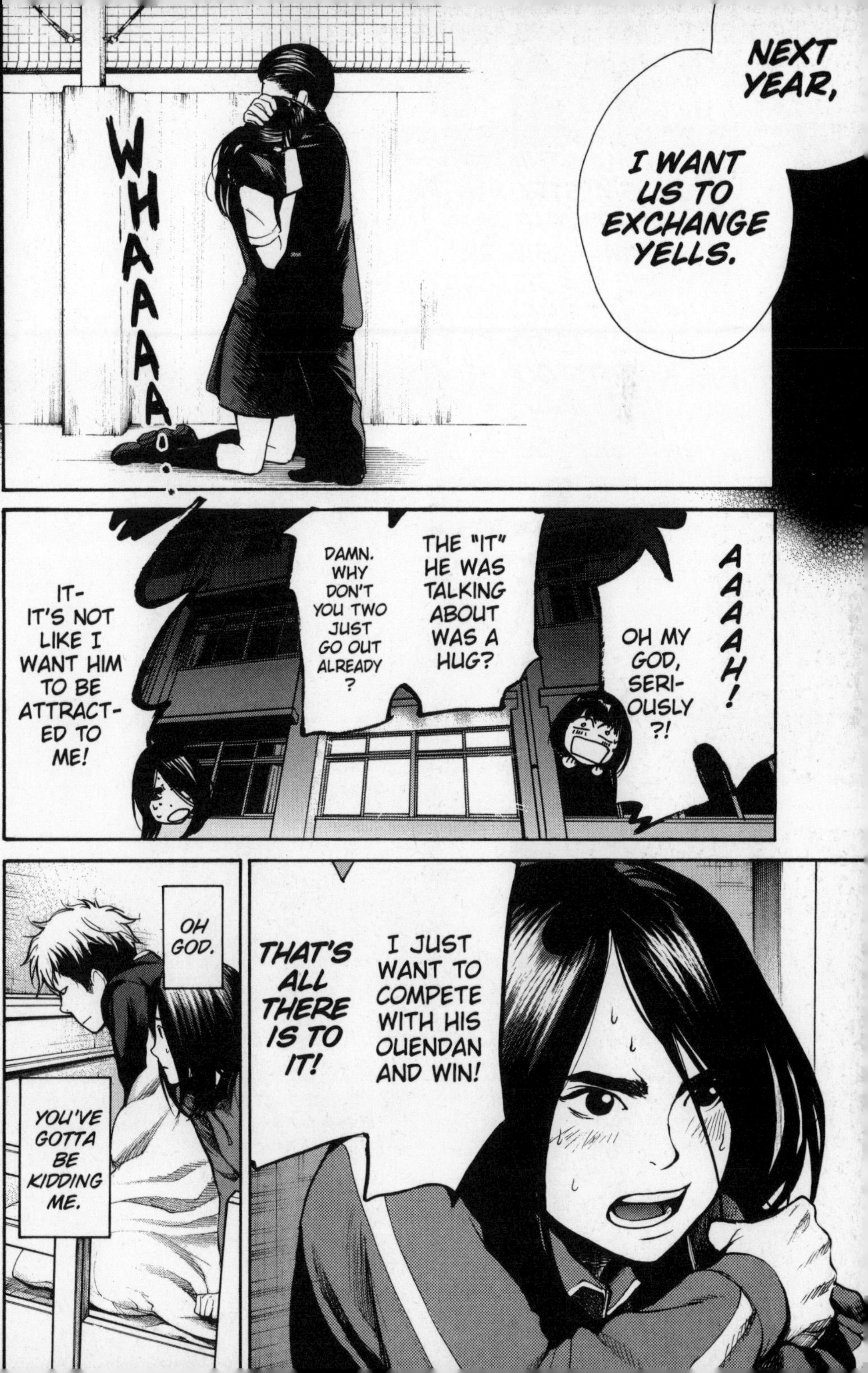
NEXT YEAR,
I WANT US TO EXCHANGE YELLS.
WHAAAAA
AAAAH!
OH MY GOD, SERIOUSLY?!
THE "IT" HE WAS TALKING ABOUT WAS A HUG?
DAMN. WHY DON'T YOU TWO JUST GO OUT ALREADY?
IT- IT'S NOT LIKE I WANT HIM TO BE ATTRACTED TO ME!
I JUST WANT TO COMPETE WITH HIS OUENDAN AND WIN!
THAT'S ALL THERE IS TO IT!
OH GOD.
YOU'VE GOTTA BE KIDDING ME.

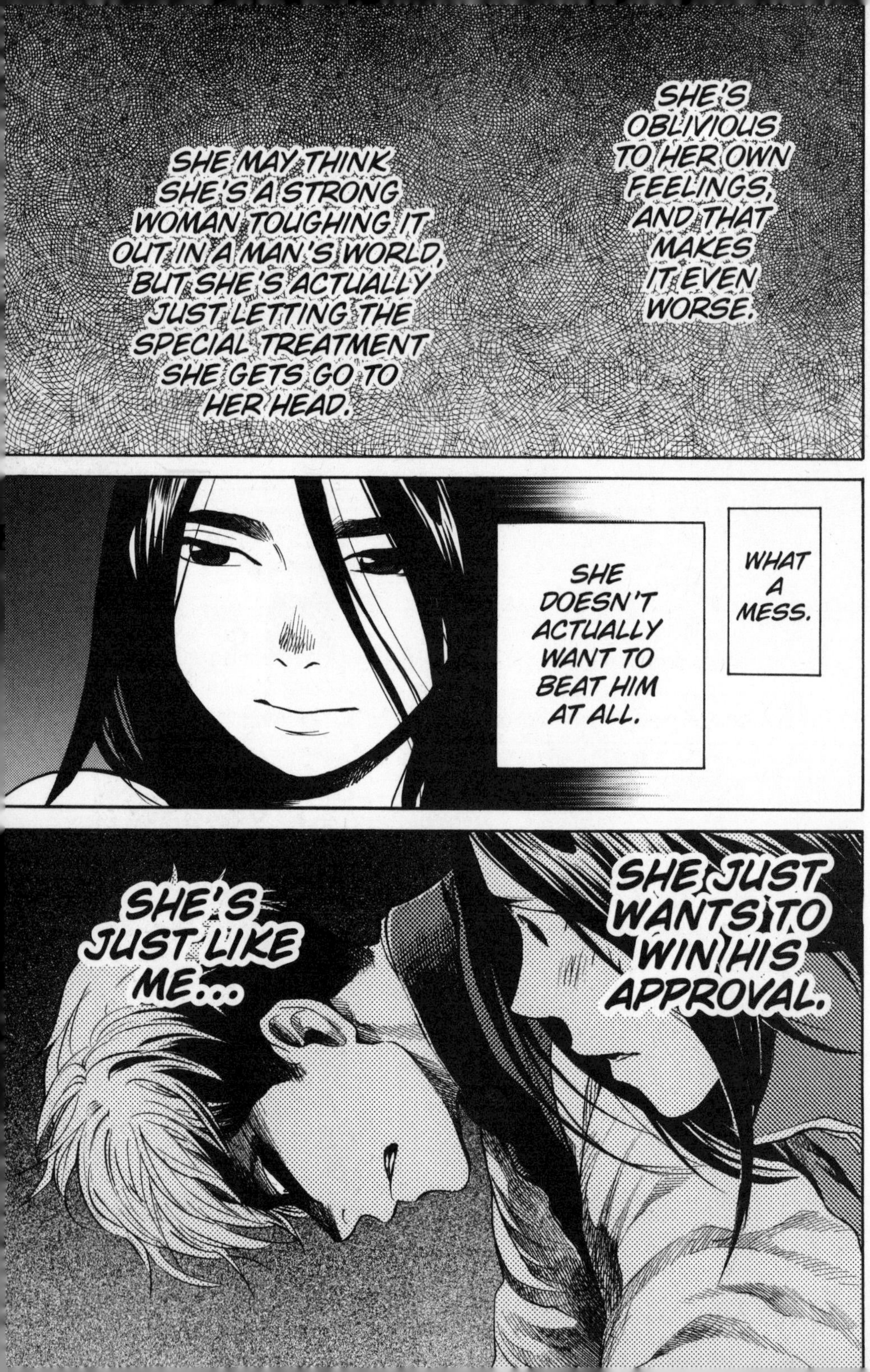
SHE'S OBLIVIOUS TO HER OWN FEELINGS, AND THAT MAKES IT EVEN WORSE.
SHE MAY THINK SHE'S A STRONG WOMAN TOUGHING IT OUT IN A MAN'S WORLD, BUT SHE'S ACTUALLY JUST LETTING THE SPECIAL TREATMENT SHE GETS GO TO HER HEAD.
WHAT A MESS.
SHE DOESN'T ACTUALLY WANT TO BEAT HIM AT ALL.
SHE JUST WANTS TO WIN HIS APPROVAL.
SHE'S JUST LIKE ME...

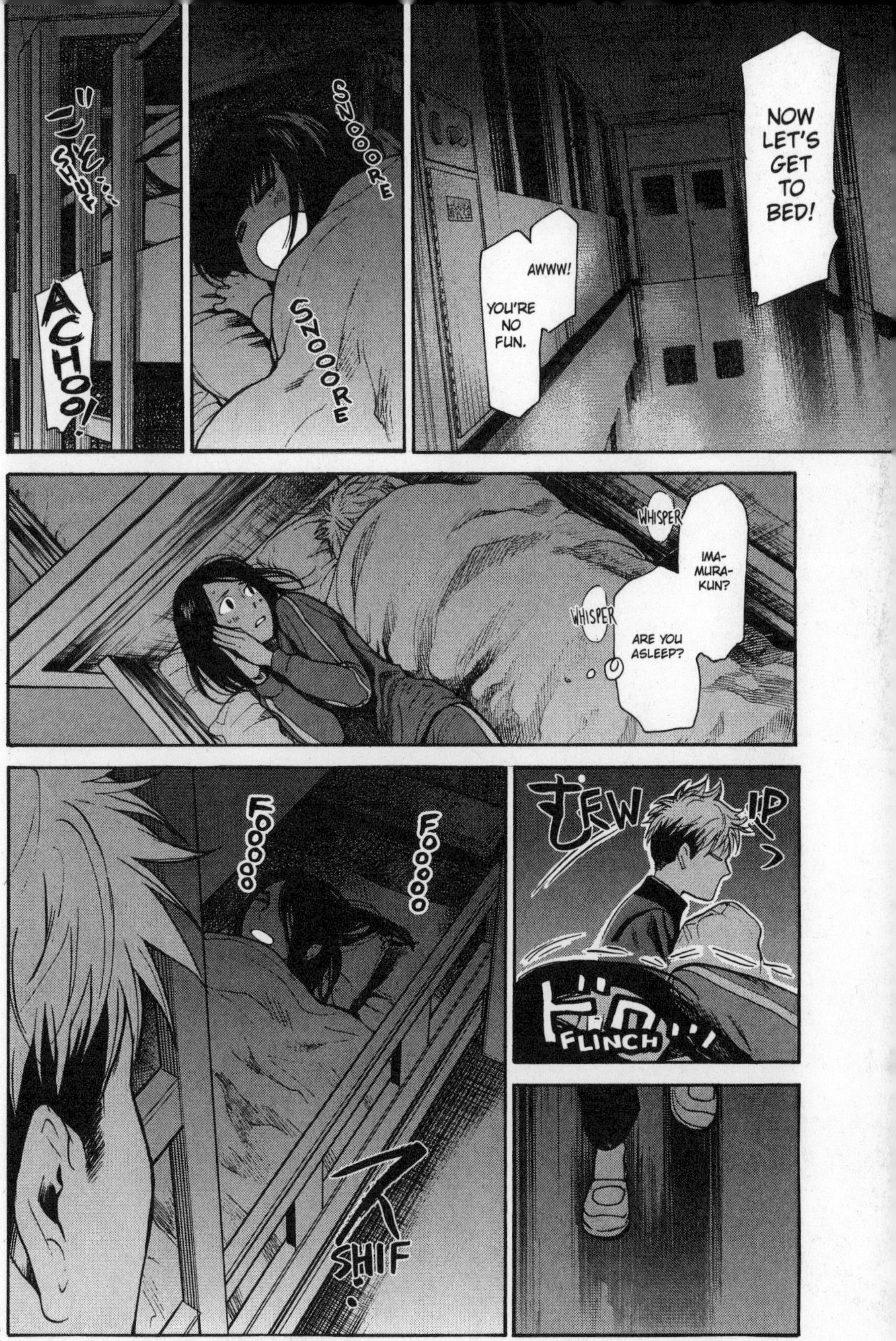
NOW LET'S GET TO BED!
AWWW!
YOU'RE NO FUN.
SNOOORE
SNOOORE
SHUF
ACHOO!
WHISPER
IMA-MURA-KUN?
WHISPER
ARE YOU ASLEEP?
FWIP
FLINCH
FOOOOO
FOOOOO
SHIF

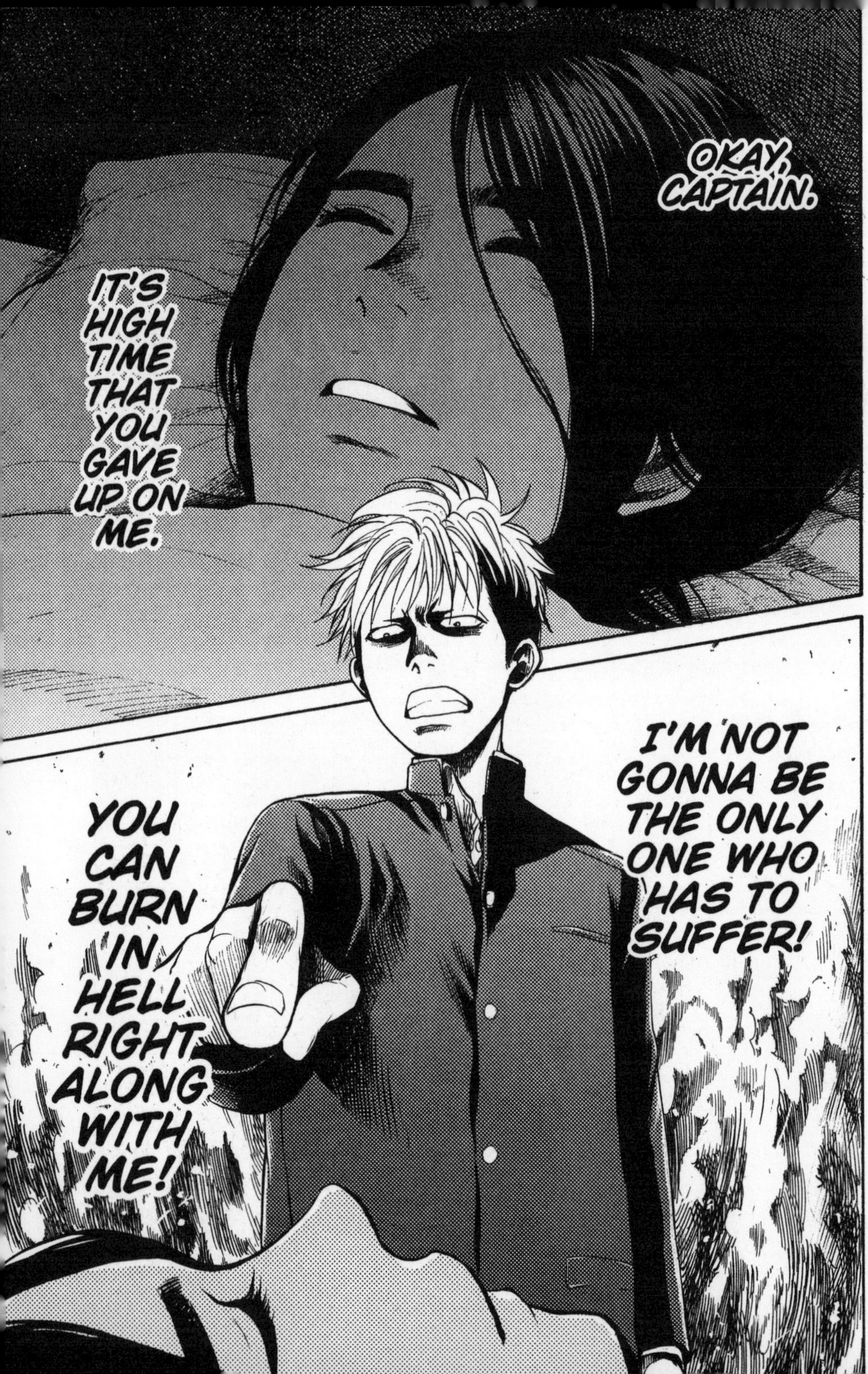
OKAY, CAPTAIN.
IT'S HIGH TIME THAT YOU GAVE UP ON ME.
I'M NOT GONNA BE THE ONLY ONE WHO HAS TO SUFFER!
YOU CAN BURN IN HELL RIGHT ALONG WITH ME!

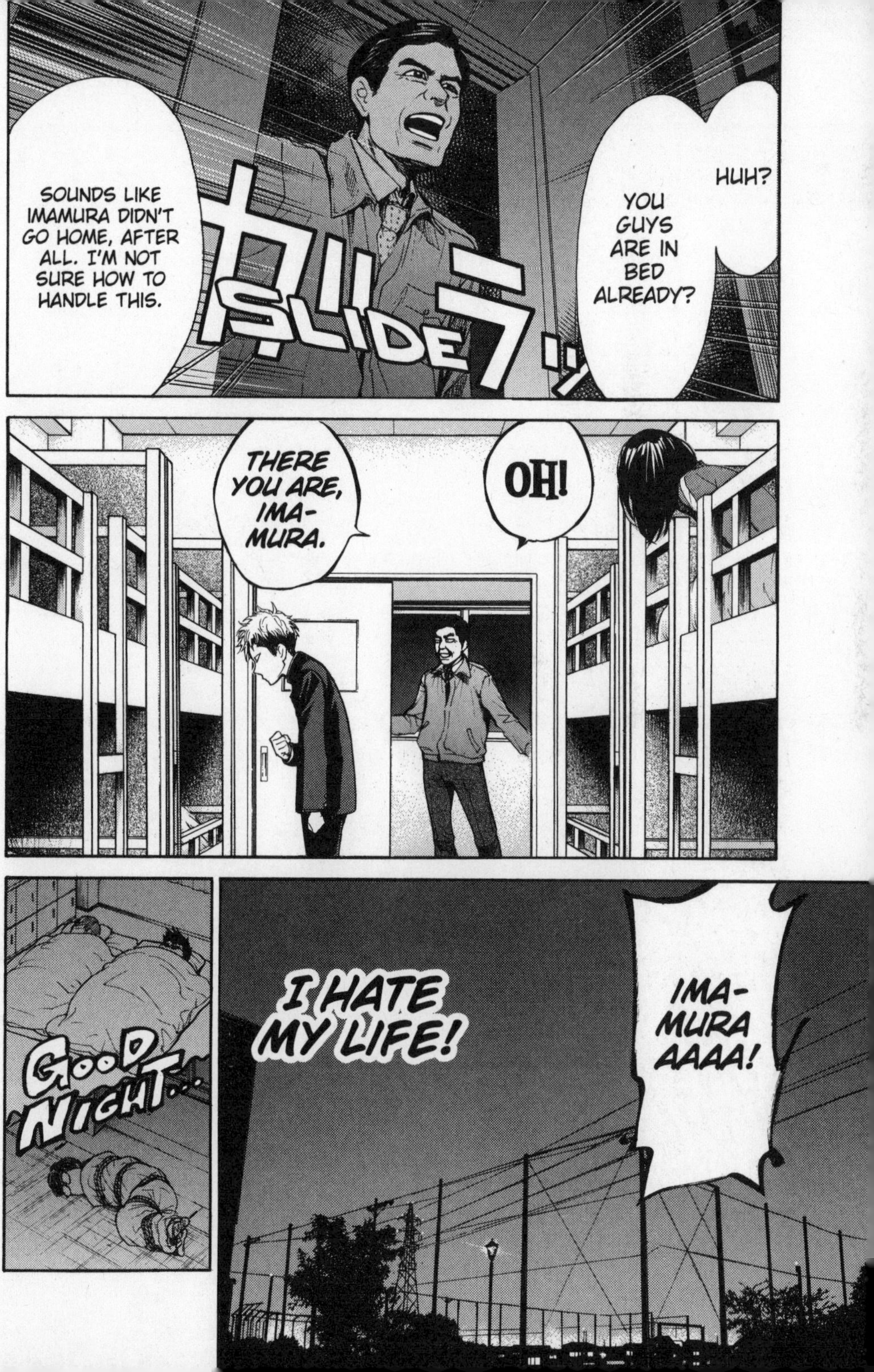
HUH?
YOU GUYS ARE IN BED ALREADY?
SLIDE
SOUNDS LIKE IMAMURA DIDN'T GO HOME, AFTER ALL. I'M NOT SURE HOW TO HANDLE THIS.
OH!
THERE YOU ARE, IMA-MURA.
IMA-MURA AAAA!
I HATE MY LIFE!
GOOD NIGHT...

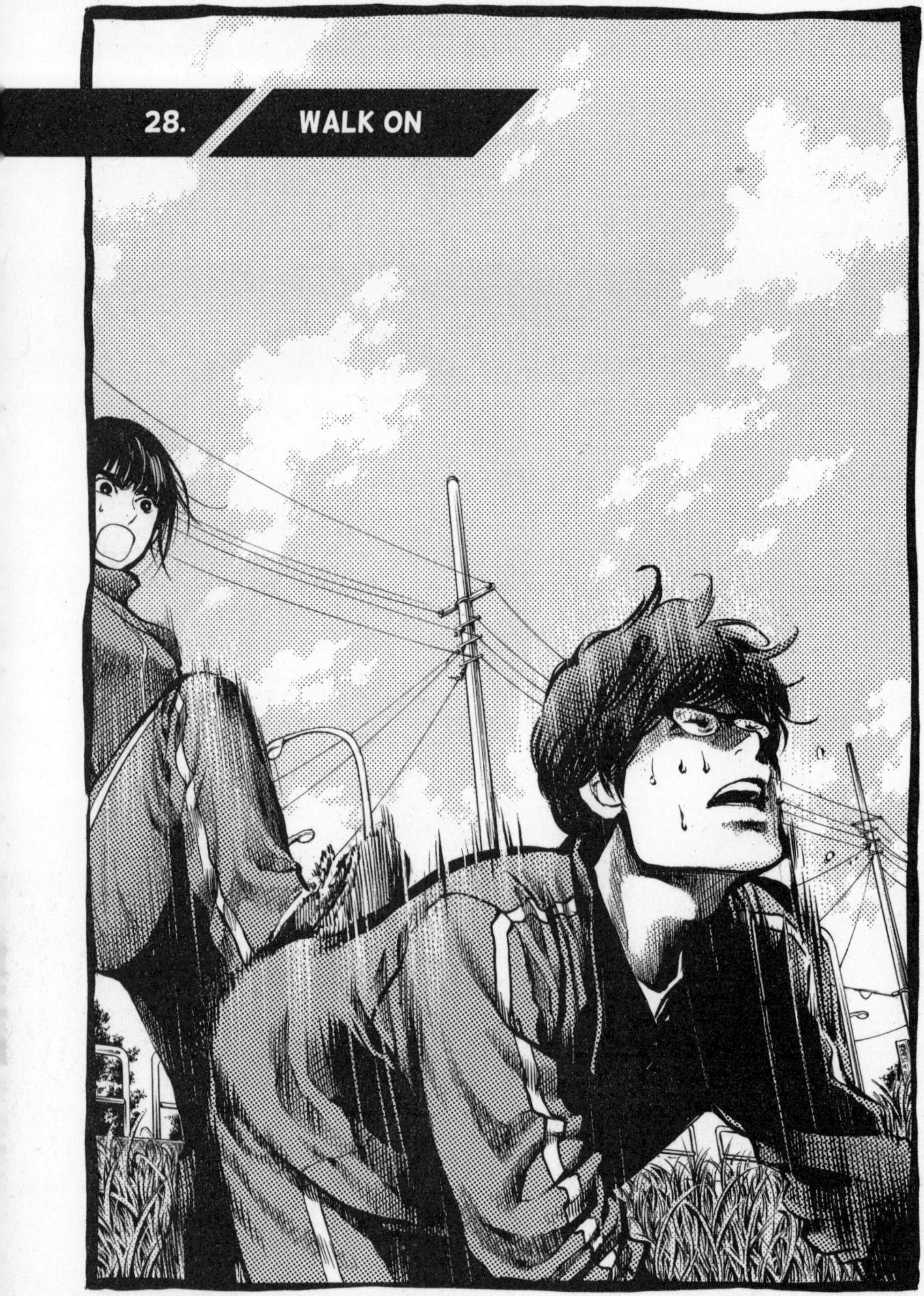
28.
WALK ON

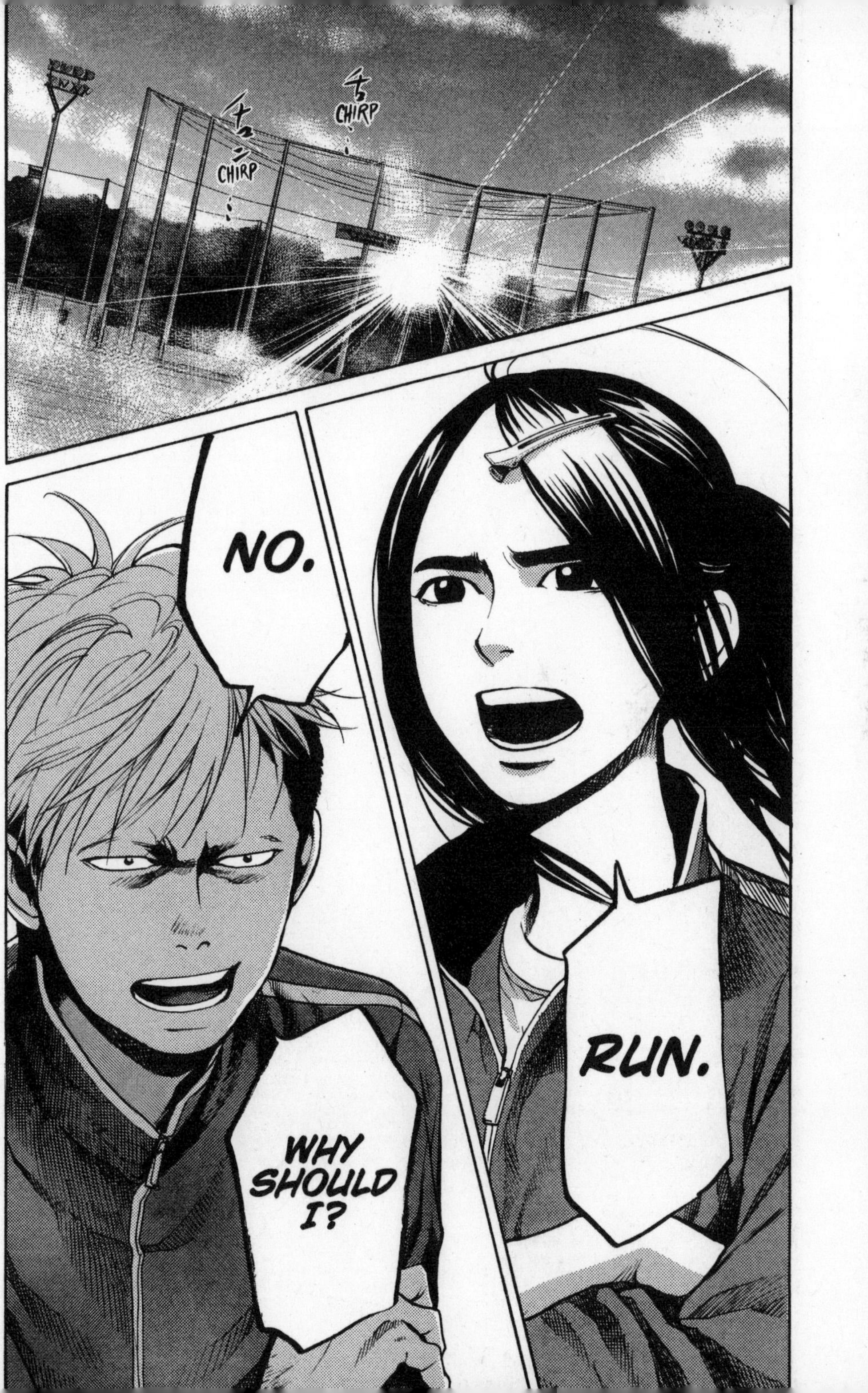
CHIRP
CHIRP
RUN.
NO.
WHY SHOULD I?

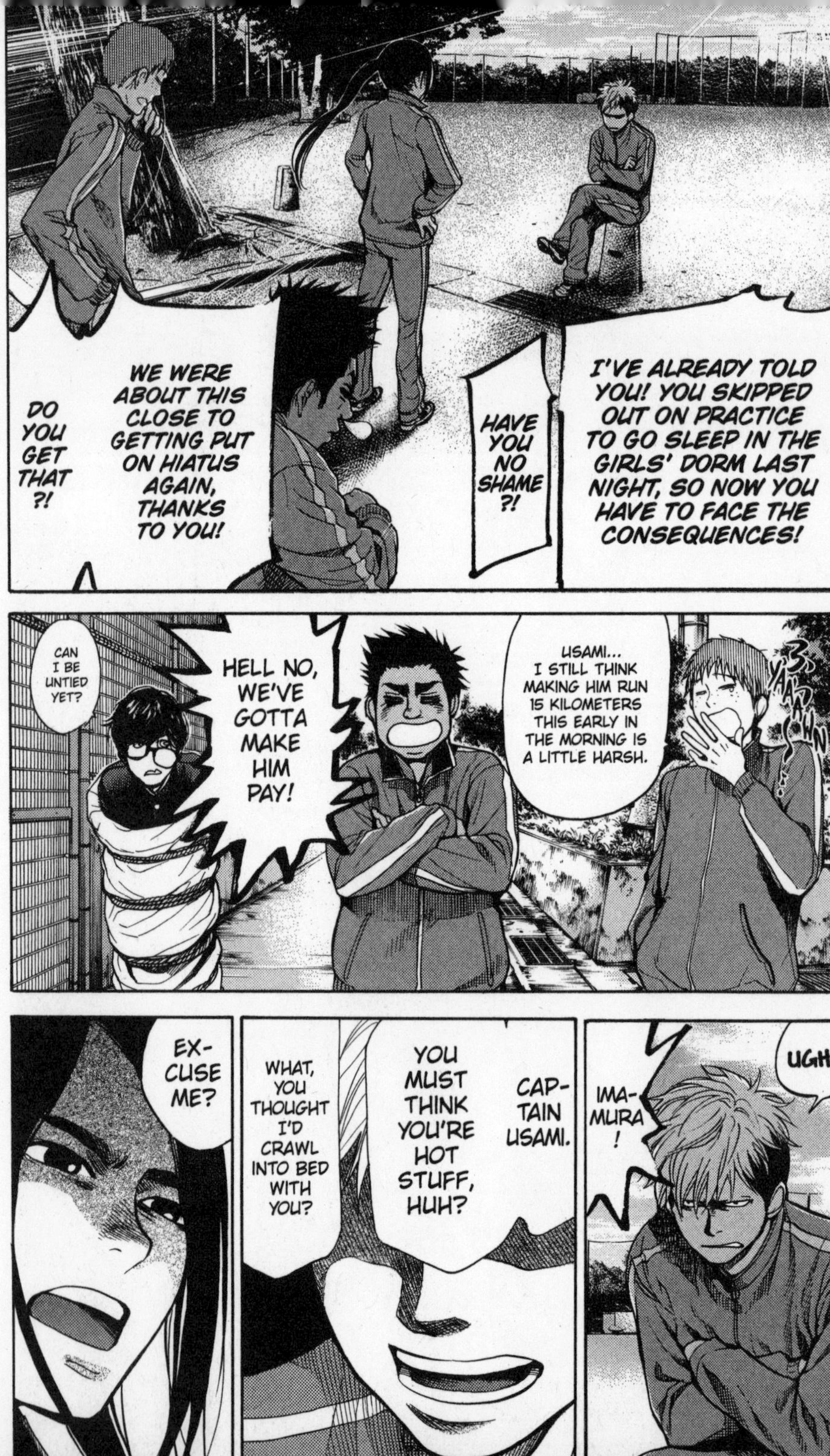
I'VE ALREADY TOLD YOU! YOU SKIPPED OUT ON PRACTICE TO GO SLEEP IN THE GIRLS' DORM LAST NIGHT, SO NOW YOU HAVE TO FACE THE CONSEQUENCES!
HAVE YOU NO SHAME ?!
WE WERE ABOUT THIS CLOSE TO GETTING PUT ON HIATUS AGAIN, THANKS TO YOU!
DO YOU GET THAT ?!
YAAAWN
USAMI... I STILL THINK MAKING HIM RUN 15 KILOMETERS THIS EARLY IN THE MORNING IS A LITTLE HARSH.
HELL NO, WE'VE GOTTA MAKE HIM PAY!
CAN I BE UNTIED YET?
UGH.
IMA-MURA !
CAP-TAIN USAMI.
YOU MUST THINK YOU'RE HOT STUFF, HUH?
WHAT, YOU THOUGHT I'D CRAWL INTO BED WITH YOU?
EX-CUSE ME?

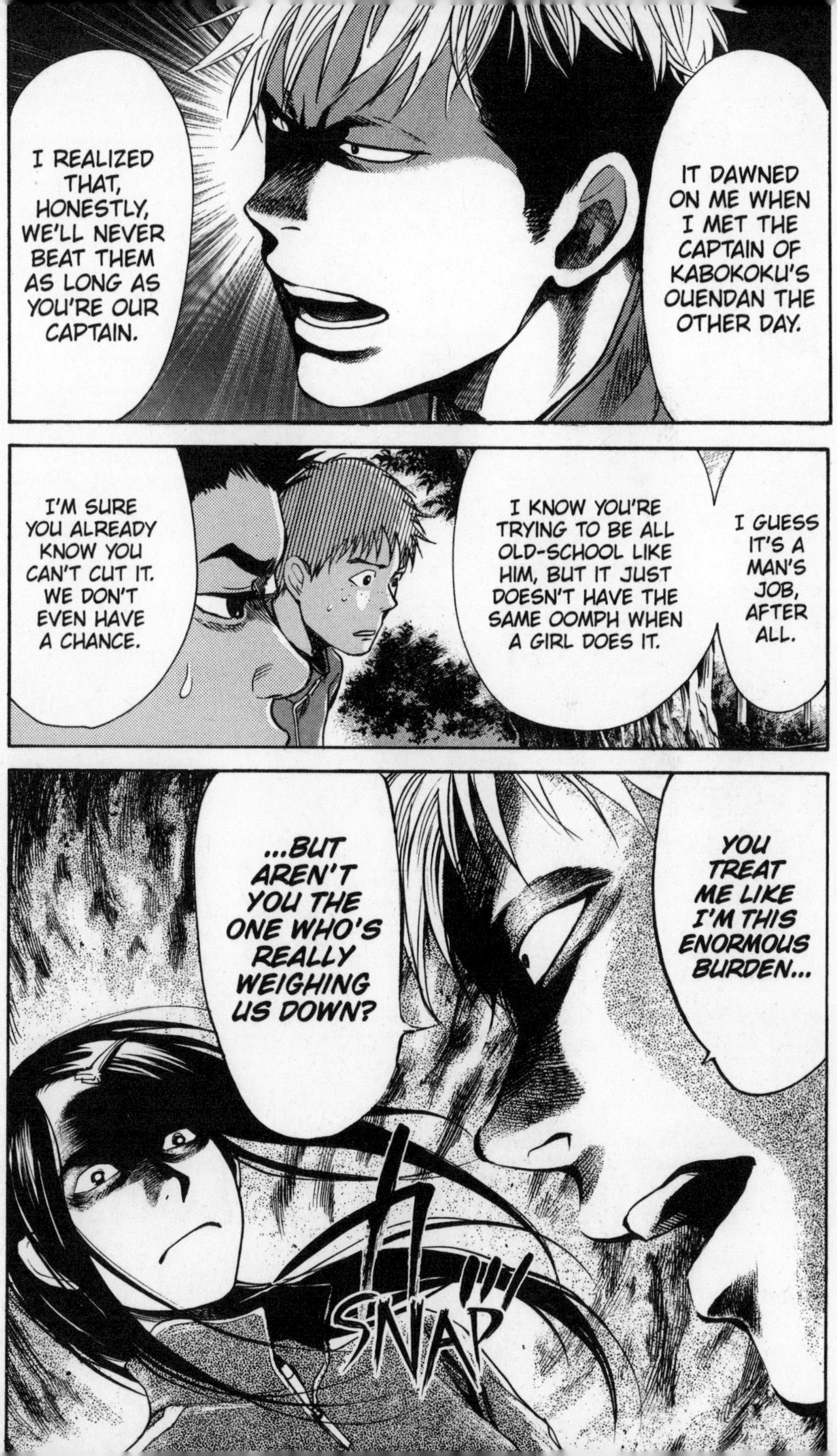
IT DAWNED ON ME WHEN I MET THE CAPTAIN OF KABOKOKU'S OUENDAN THE OTHER DAY.
I REALIZED THAT, HONESTLY, WE'LL NEVER BEAT THEM AS LONG AS YOU'RE OUR CAPTAIN.
I GUESS IT'S A MAN'S JOB, AFTER ALL.
I KNOW YOU'RE TRYING TO BE ALL OLD-SCHOOL LIKE HIM, BUT IT JUST DOESN'T HAVE THE SAME OOMPH WHEN A GIRL DOES IT.
I'M SURE YOU ALREADY KNOW YOU CAN'T CUT IT. WE DON'T EVEN HAVE A CHANCE.
YOU TREAT ME LIKE I'M THIS ENORMOUS BURDEN...
...BUT AREN'T YOU THE ONE WHO'S REALLY WEIGHING US DOWN?
SNAP

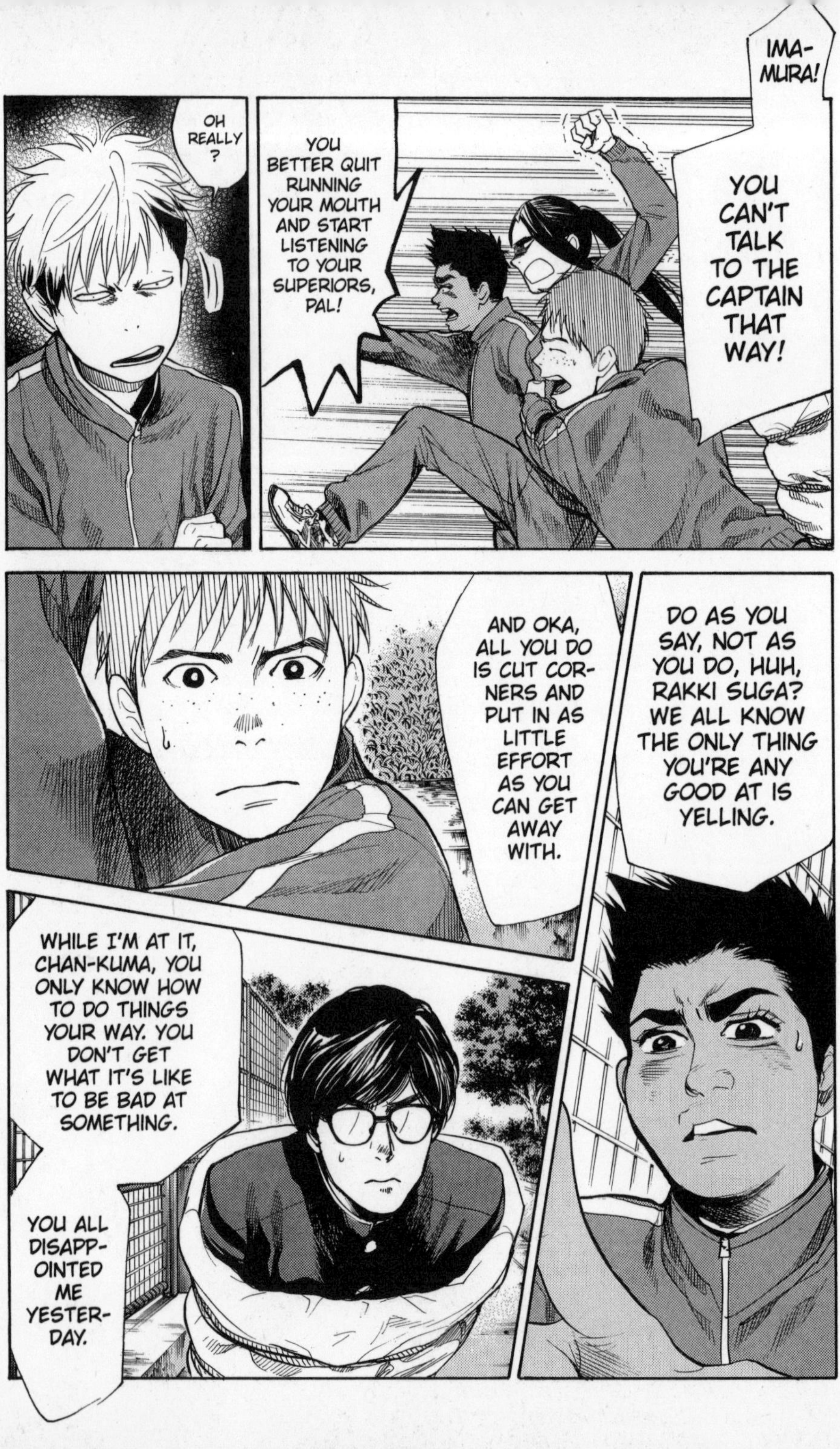
IMA-MURA!
YOU CAN'T TALK TO THE CAPTAIN THAT WAY!
YOU BETTER QUIT RUNNING YOUR MOUTH AND START LISTENING TO YOUR SUPERIORS, PAL!
OH REALLY?
DO AS YOU SAY, NOT AS YOU DO, HUH, RAKKI SUGA? WE ALL KNOW THE ONLY THING YOU'RE ANY GOOD AT IS YELLING.
AND OKA, ALL YOU DO IS CUT COR-NERS AND PUT IN AS LITTLE EFFORT AS YOU CAN GET AWAY WITH.
WHILE I'M AT IT, CHAN-KUMA, YOU ONLY KNOW HOW TO DO THINGS YOUR WAY. YOU DON'T GET WHAT IT'S LIKE TO BE BAD AT SOMETHING.
YOU ALL DISAPP-OINTED ME YESTER-DAY.

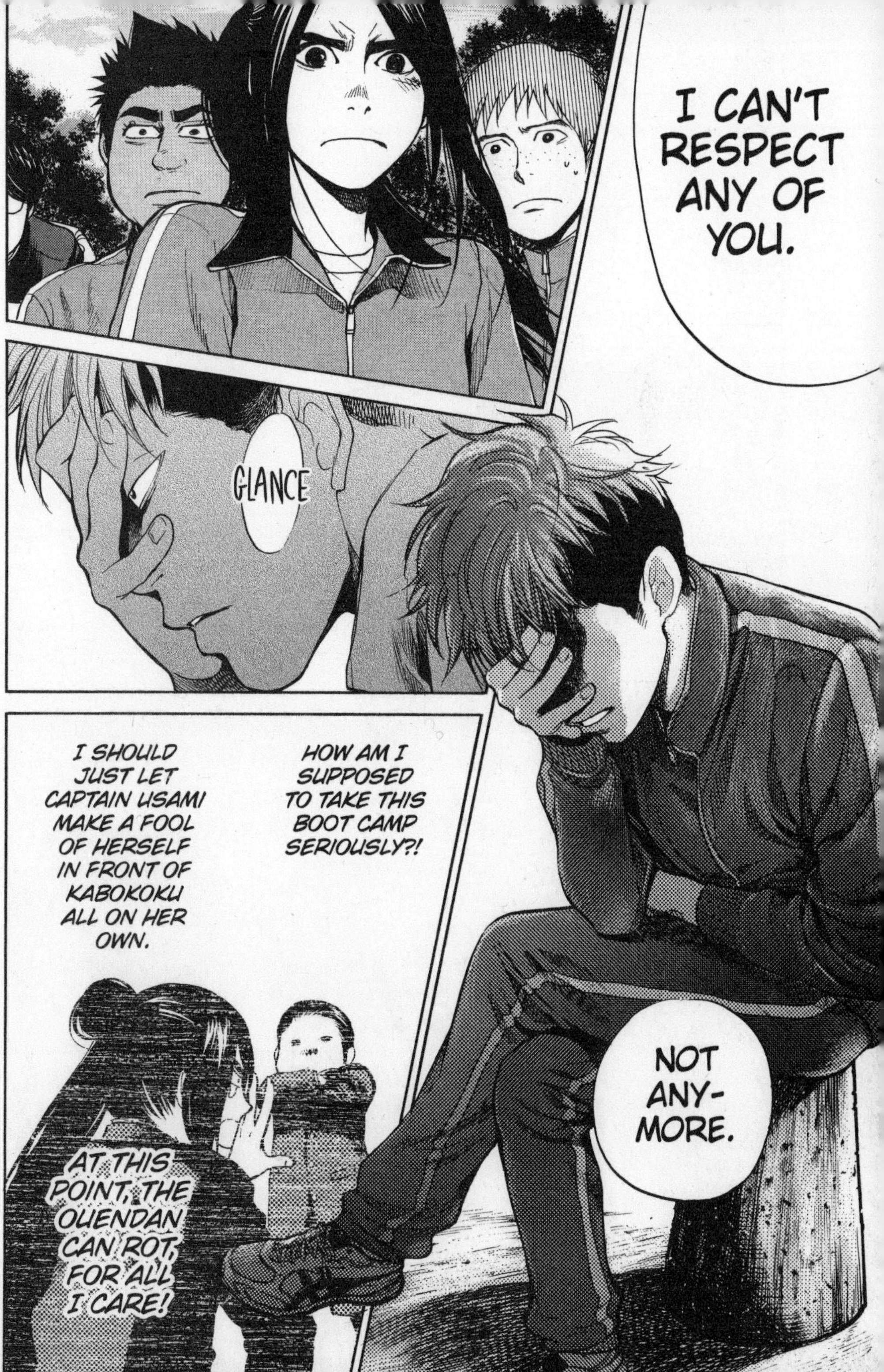
I CAN'T RESPECT ANY OF YOU.
GLANCE
HOW AM I SUPPOSED TO TAKE THIS BOOT CAMP SERIOUSLY?!
I SHOULD JUST LET CAPTAIN USAMI MAKE A FOOL OF HERSELF IN FRONT OF KABOKOKU ALL ON HER OWN.
NOT ANY-MORE.
AT THIS POINT, THE OUENDAN CAN ROT, FOR ALL I CARE!

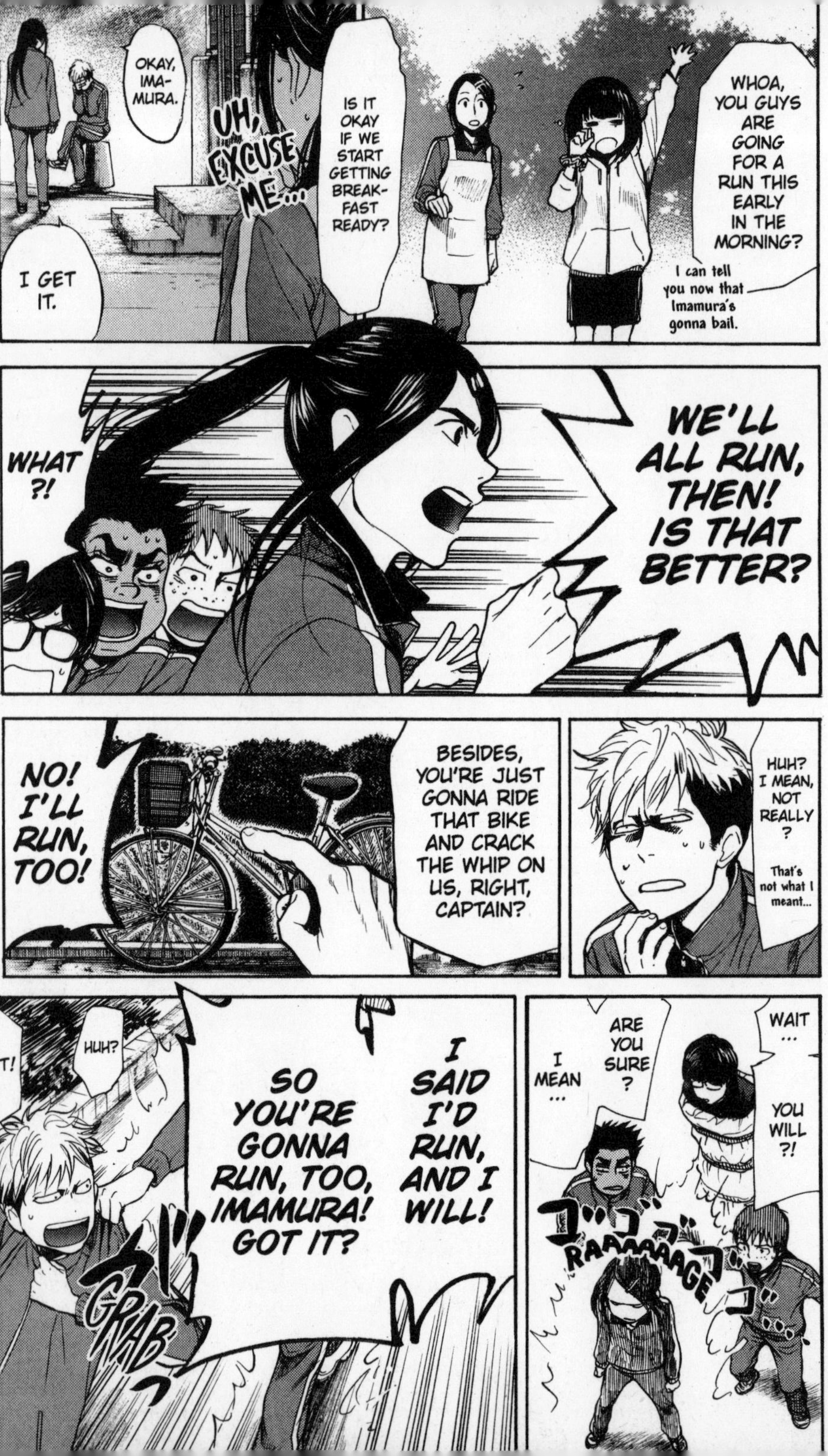
WHOA, YOU GUYS ARE GOING FOR A RUN THIS EARLY IN THE MORNING?
I can tell you now that Imamura's gonna bail.
IS IT OKAY IF WE START GETTING BREAK-FAST READY?
UH, EXCUSE ME...
OKAY, IMA-MURA.
I GET IT.
WE'LL ALL RUN, THEN! IS THAT BETTER?
WHAT ?!
HUH? I MEAN, NOT REALLY ?
That's not what I meant...
BESIDES, YOU'RE JUST GONNA RIDE THAT BIKE AND CRACK THE WHIP ON US, RIGHT, CAPTAIN?
NO! I'LL RUN, TOO!
WAIT ...
YOU WILL ?!
ARE YOU SURE ?
I MEAN ...
RAAAAAAGE
I SAID I'D RUN, AND I WILL!
SO YOU'RE GONNA RUN, TOO, IMAMURA! GOT IT?
HUH?
WAIT!
GRAB

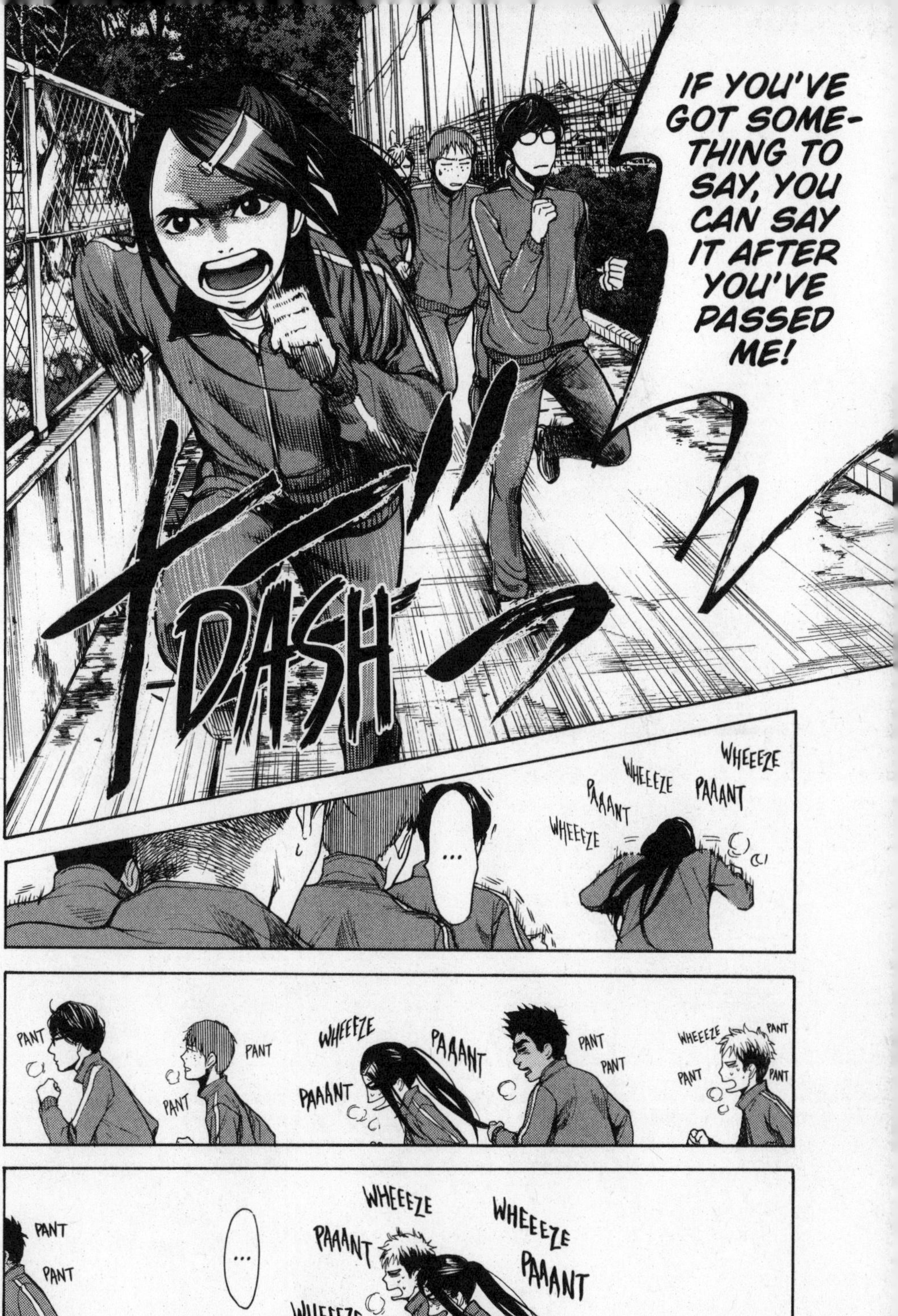
IF YOU'VE GOT SOMETHING TO SAY, YOU CAN SAY IT AFTER YOU'VE PASSED ME!
DASH
WHEEEZE
PAAANT
WHEEEZE
PAAANT
WHEEEZE
...
PANT
PANT
WHEEEZE
PANT
PANT
PANT
PAAANT
WHEEEZE
PAAANT
PANT
PANT
PANT
WHEEEZE
PAAANT
WHEEEZE
PAAANT
...
WHEEEZE
PANT
PANT

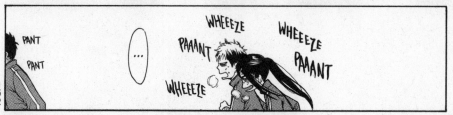

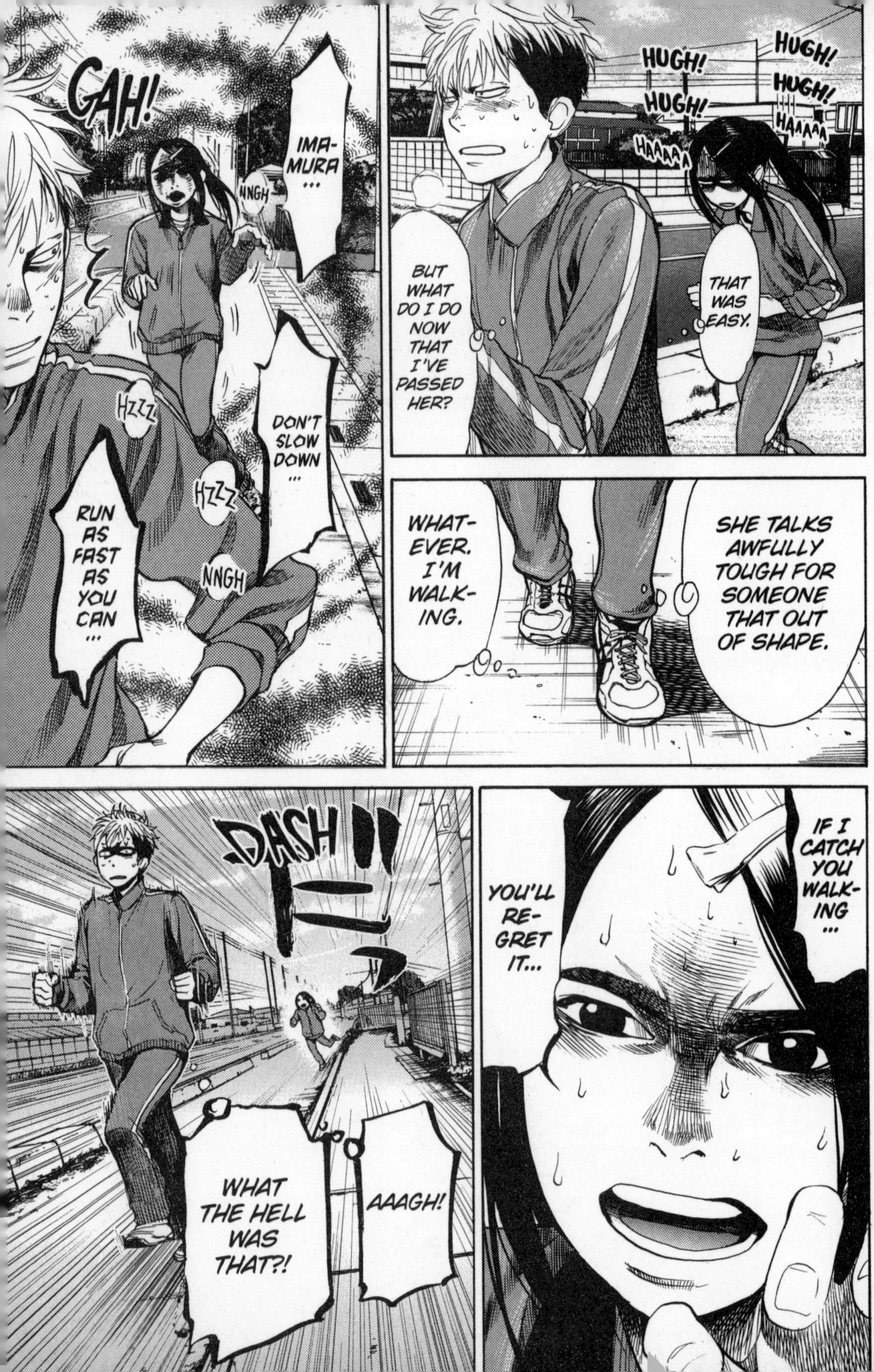
HUGH!
HUGH!
HUGH!
HUGH!
HAAAAA
HAAAAA
THAT WAS EASY.
BUT WHAT DO I DO NOW THAT I'VE PASSED HER?
SHE TALKS AWFULLY TOUGH FOR SOMEONE THAT OUT OF SHAPE.
WHAT-EVER. I'M WALK-ING.
IMA-MURA ...
GAH!
NNGH
DON'T SLOW DOWN ...
RUN AS FAST AS YOU CAN ...
HZZZ
HZZZ
NNGH
IF I CATCH YOU WALK-ING ...
YOU'LL RE-GRET IT...
DASH!!
AAAGH!
WHAT THE HELL WAS THAT?!

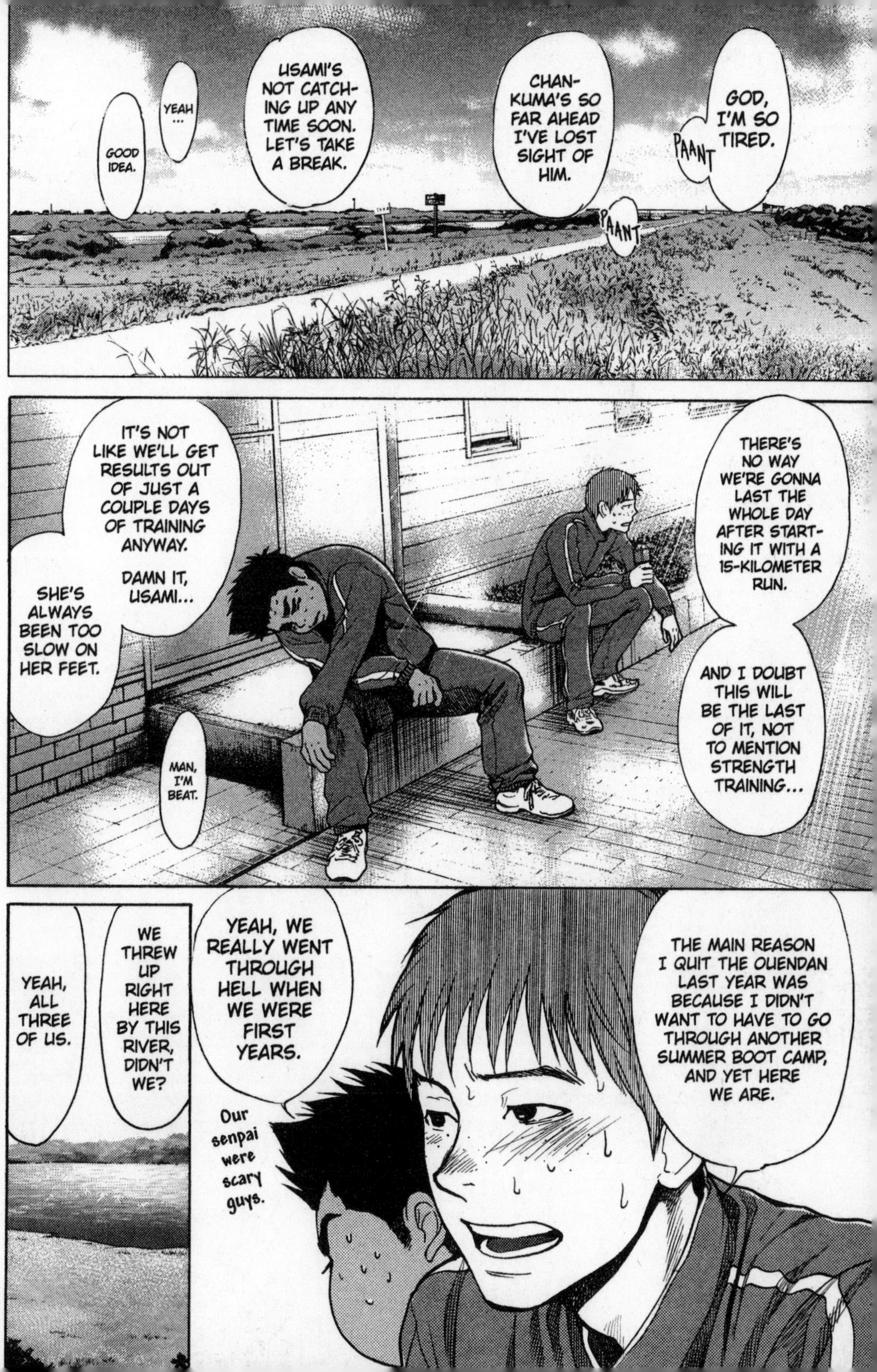
GOD, I'M SO TIRED.
PAANT
PAANT
CHAN-KUMA'S SO FAR AHEAD I'VE LOST SIGHT OF HIM.
USAMI'S NOT CATCHING UP ANY TIME SOON. LET'S TAKE A BREAK.
YEAH ...
GOOD IDEA.
THERE'S NO WAY WE'RE GONNA LAST THE WHOLE DAY AFTER STARTING IT WITH A 15-KILOMETER RUN.
AND I DOUBT THIS WILL BE THE LAST OF IT, NOT TO MENTION STRENGTH TRAINING...
IT'S NOT LIKE WE'LL GET RESULTS OUT OF JUST A COUPLE DAYS OF TRAINING ANYWAY.
DAMN IT, USAMI...
SHE'S ALWAYS BEEN TOO SLOW ON HER FEET.
MAN, I'M BEAT.
THE MAIN REASON I QUIT THE OUENDAN LAST YEAR WAS BECAUSE I DIDN'T WANT TO HAVE TO GO THROUGH ANOTHER SUMMER BOOT CAMP, AND YET HERE WE ARE.
YEAH, WE REALLY WENT THROUGH HELL WHEN WE WERE FIRST YEARS.
Our senpai were scary guys.
WE THREW UP RIGHT HERE BY THIS RIVER, DIDN'T WE?
YEAH, ALL THREE OF US.

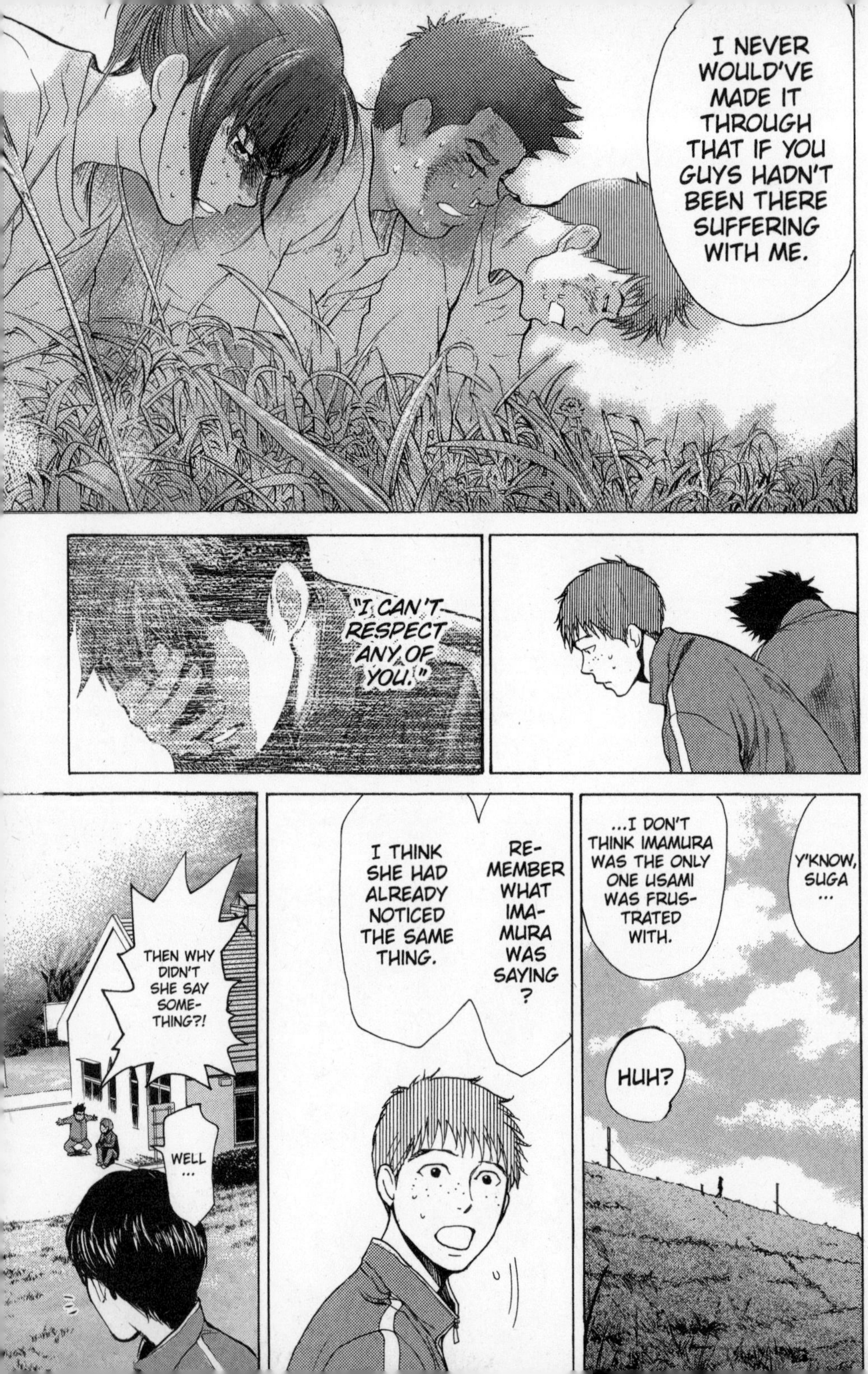
I NEVER WOULD'VE MADE IT THROUGH THAT IF YOU GUYS HADN'T BEEN THERE SUFFERING WITH ME.
"I CAN'T RESPECT ANY OF YOU."
Y'KNOW, SUGA ...
...I DON'T THINK IMAMURA WAS THE ONLY ONE USAMI WAS FRUS-TRATED WITH.
HUH?
RE-MEMBER WHAT IMA-MURA WAS SAYING ?
I THINK SHE HAD ALREADY NOTICED THE SAME THING.
THEN WHY DIDN'T SHE SAY SOME-THING?!
WELL ...

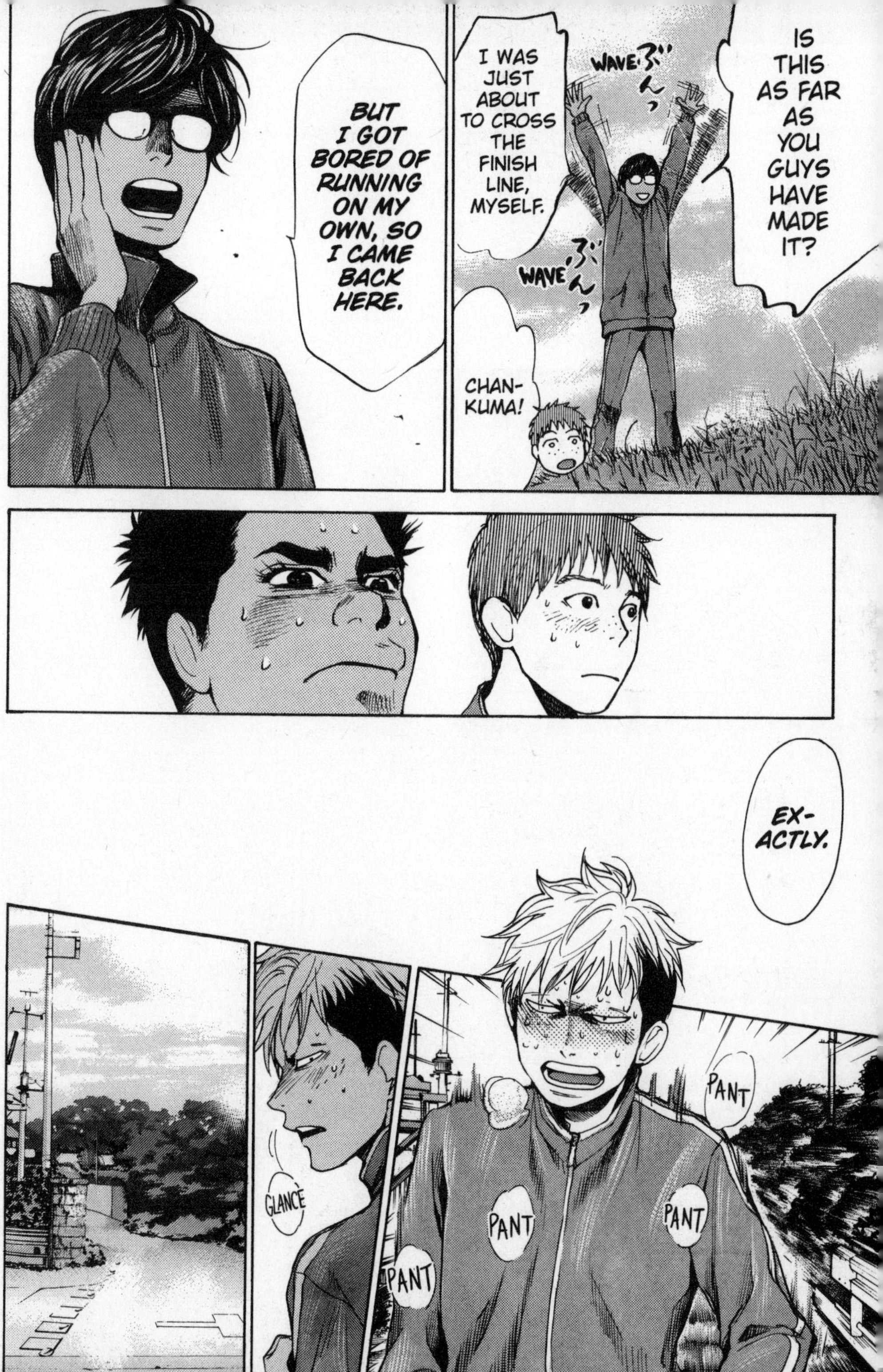
IS THIS AS FAR AS YOU GUYS HAVE MADE IT?
I WAS JUST ABOUT TO CROSS THE FINISH LINE, MYSELF.
WAVE ぶん
WAVE ぶん
CHAN-KUMA!
BUT I GOT BORED OF RUNNING ON MY OWN, SO I CAME BACK HERE.
EX-ACTLY.
PANT
PANT
PANT
PANT
GLANCE

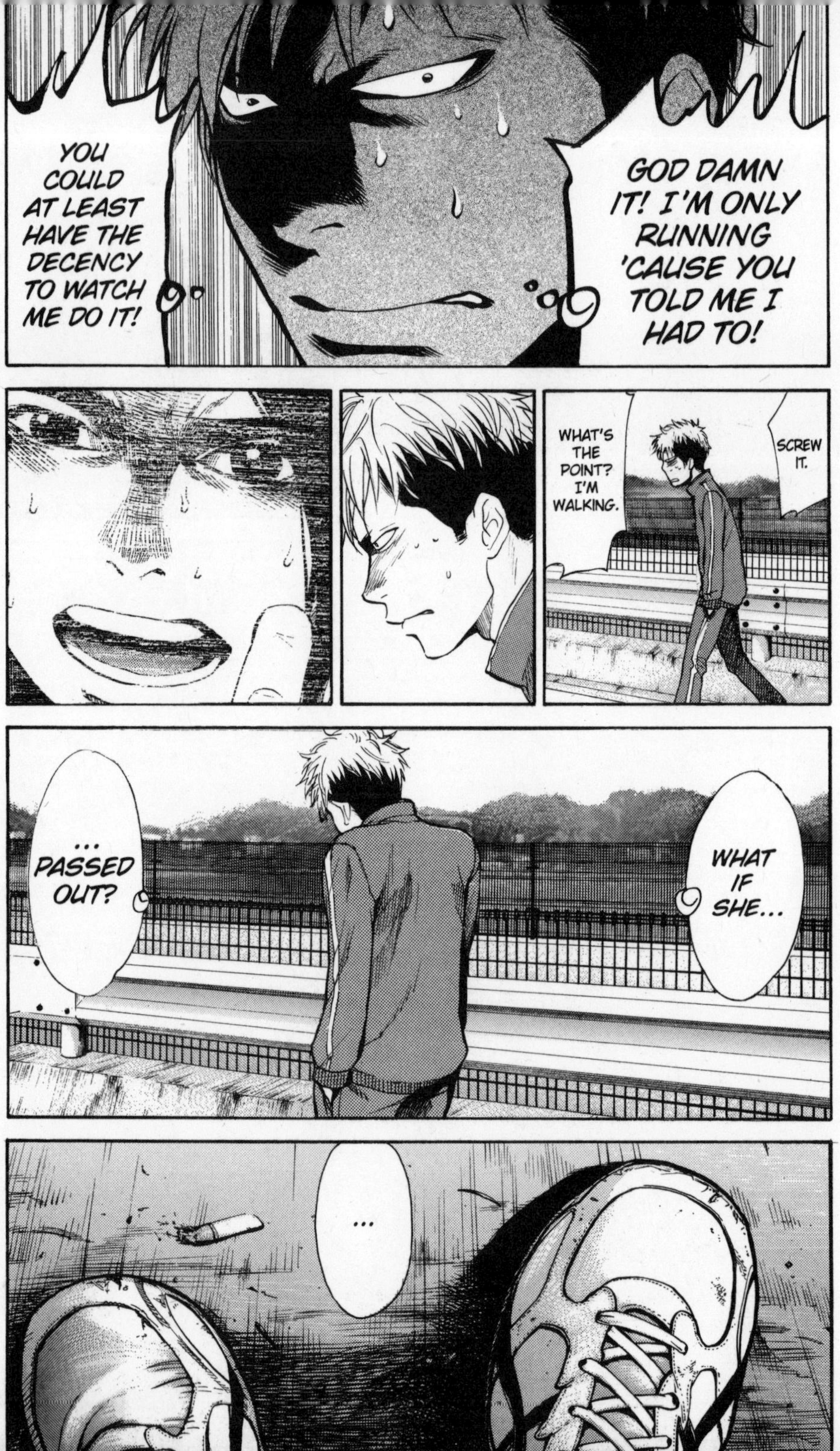
GOD DAMN IT! I'M ONLY RUNNING 'CAUSE YOU TOLD ME I HAD TO!
YOU COULD AT LEAST HAVE THE DECENCY TO WATCH ME DO IT!
SCREW IT.
WHAT'S THE POINT? I'M WALKING.
WHAT IF SHE...
...PASSED OUT?
...

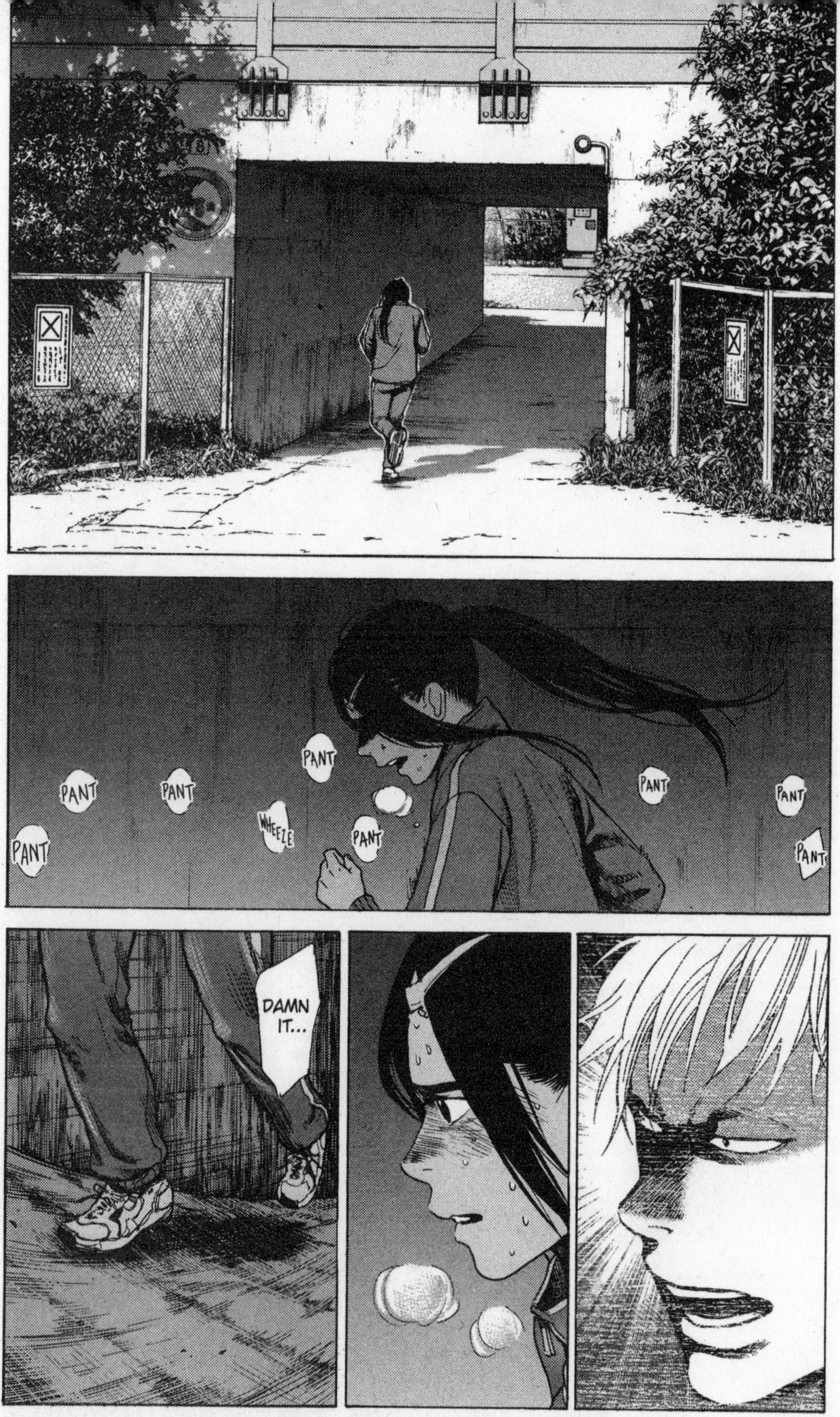

PANT
PANT
PANT
PANT
PANT
WHEEZE
PANT
PANT
PANT
DAMN IT...

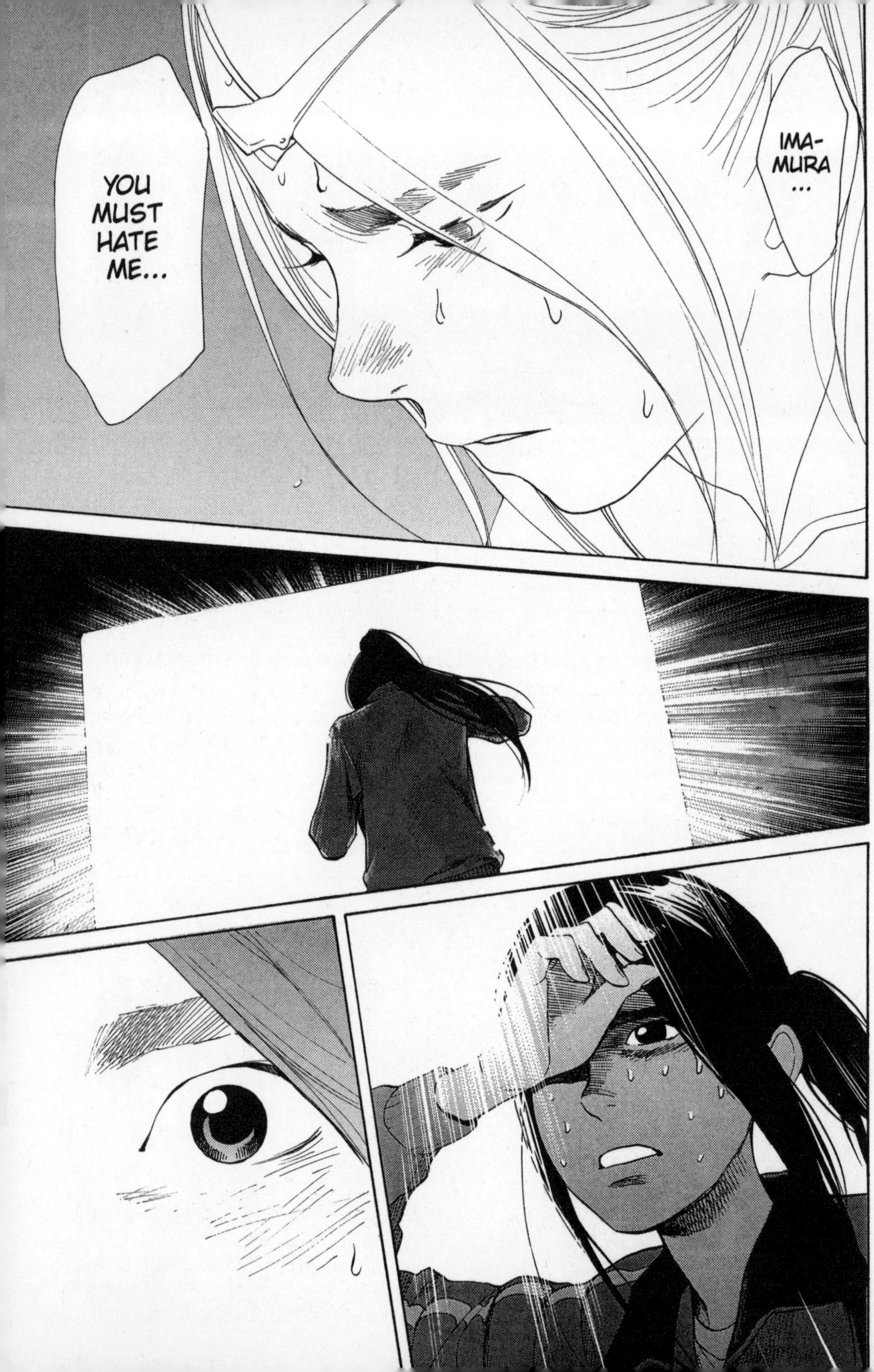
IMA-
MURA
...
YOU
MUST
HATE
ME...

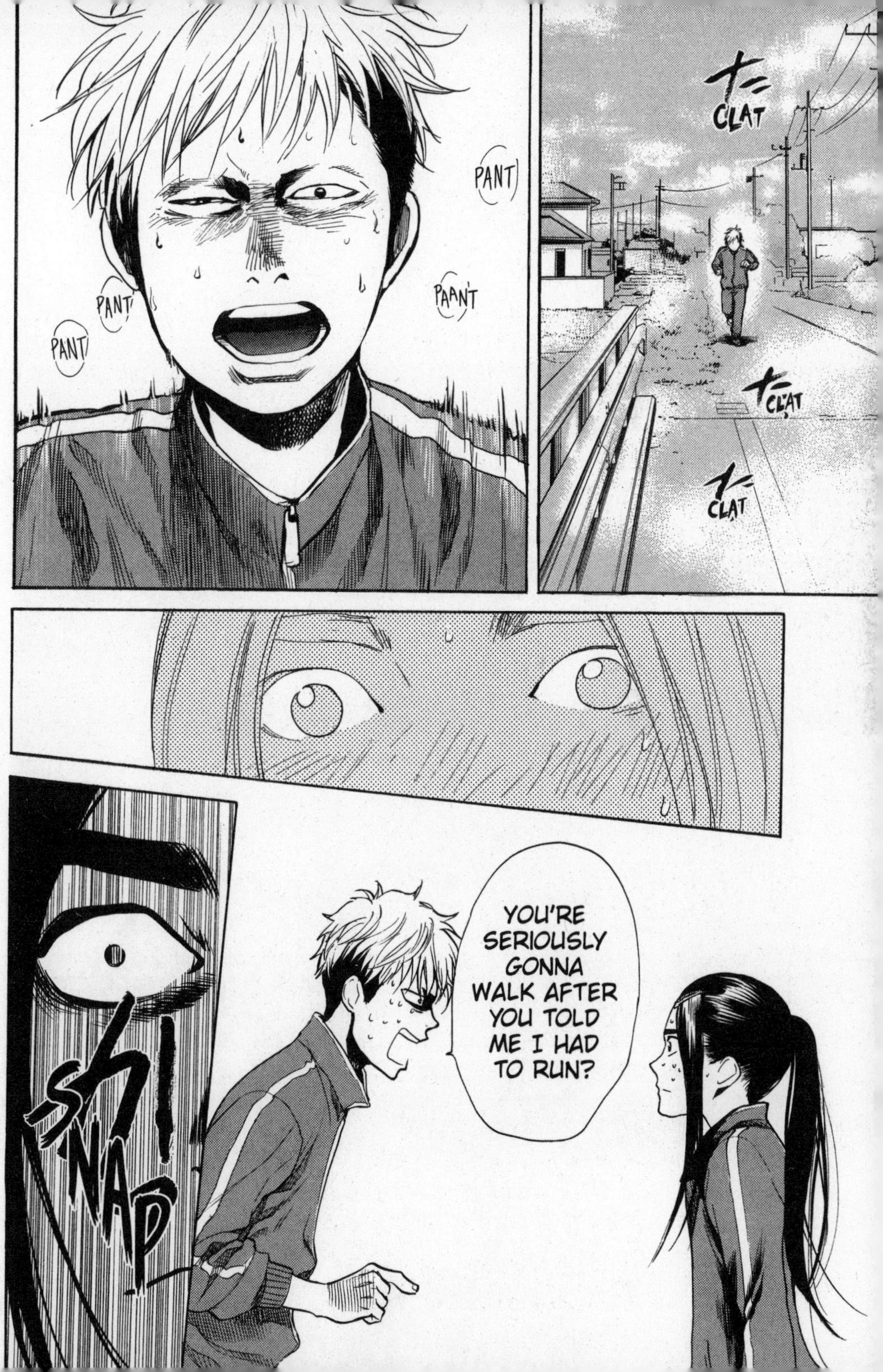
CLAT
CLAT
CLAT
PANT
PAAN'T
PANT
PANT
YOU'RE SERIOUSLY GONNA WALK AFTER YOU TOLD ME I HAD TO RUN?
SNAP

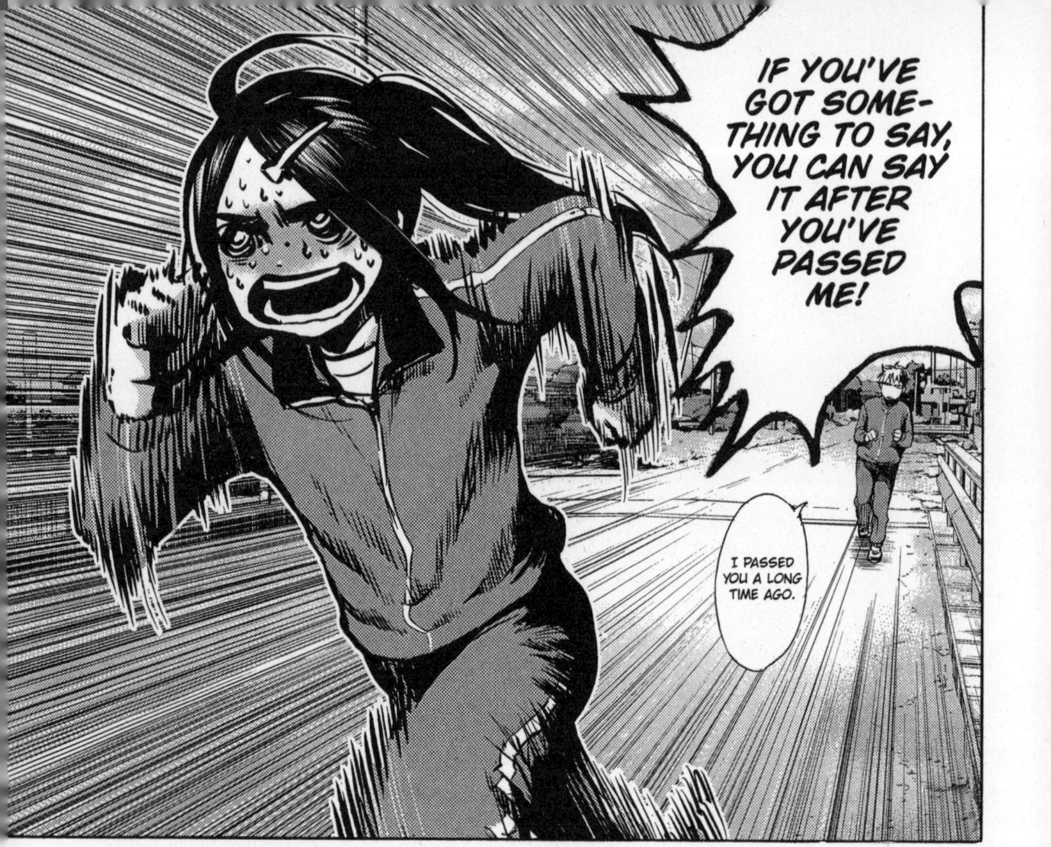
IF YOU'VE GOT SOME-THING TO SAY, YOU CAN SAY IT AFTER YOU'VE PASSED ME!
I PASSED YOU A LONG TIME AGO.

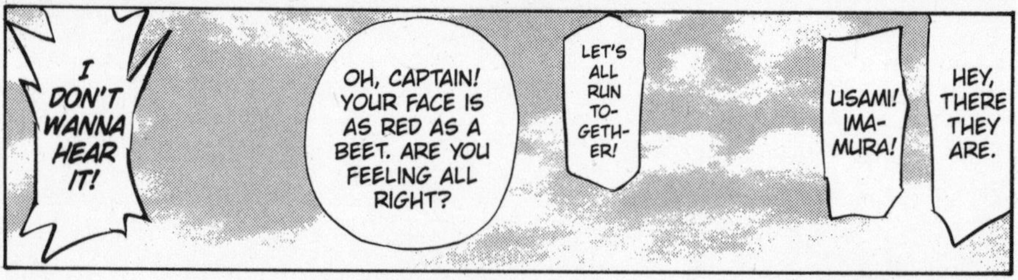
HEY, THERE THEY ARE.
USAMI! IMA-MURA!
LET'S ALL RUN TO-GETH-ER!
OH, CAPTAIN! YOUR FACE IS AS RED AS A BEET. ARE YOU FEELING ALL RIGHT?
I DON'T WANNA HEAR IT!

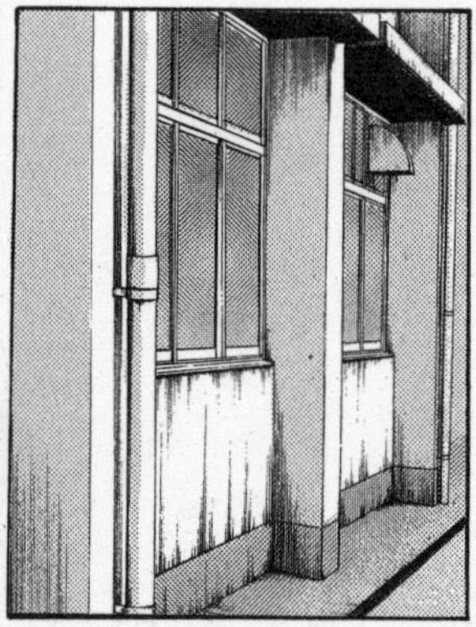

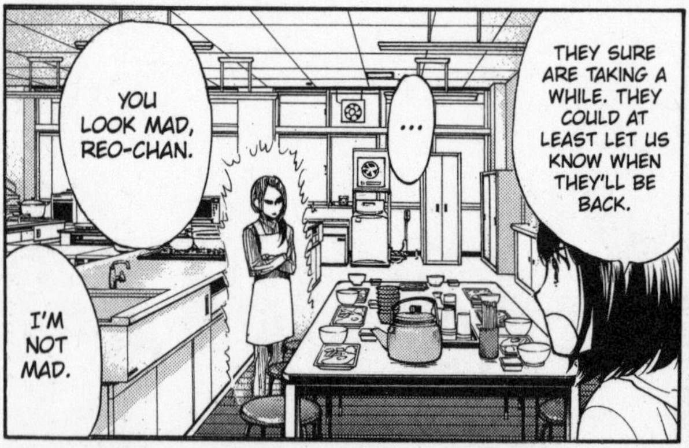
THEY SURE ARE TAKING A WHILE. THEY COULD AT LEAST LET US KNOW WHEN THEY'LL BE BACK.
...
YOU LOOK MAD, REO-CHAN.
I'M NOT MAD.

Again!!

アゲイン!!

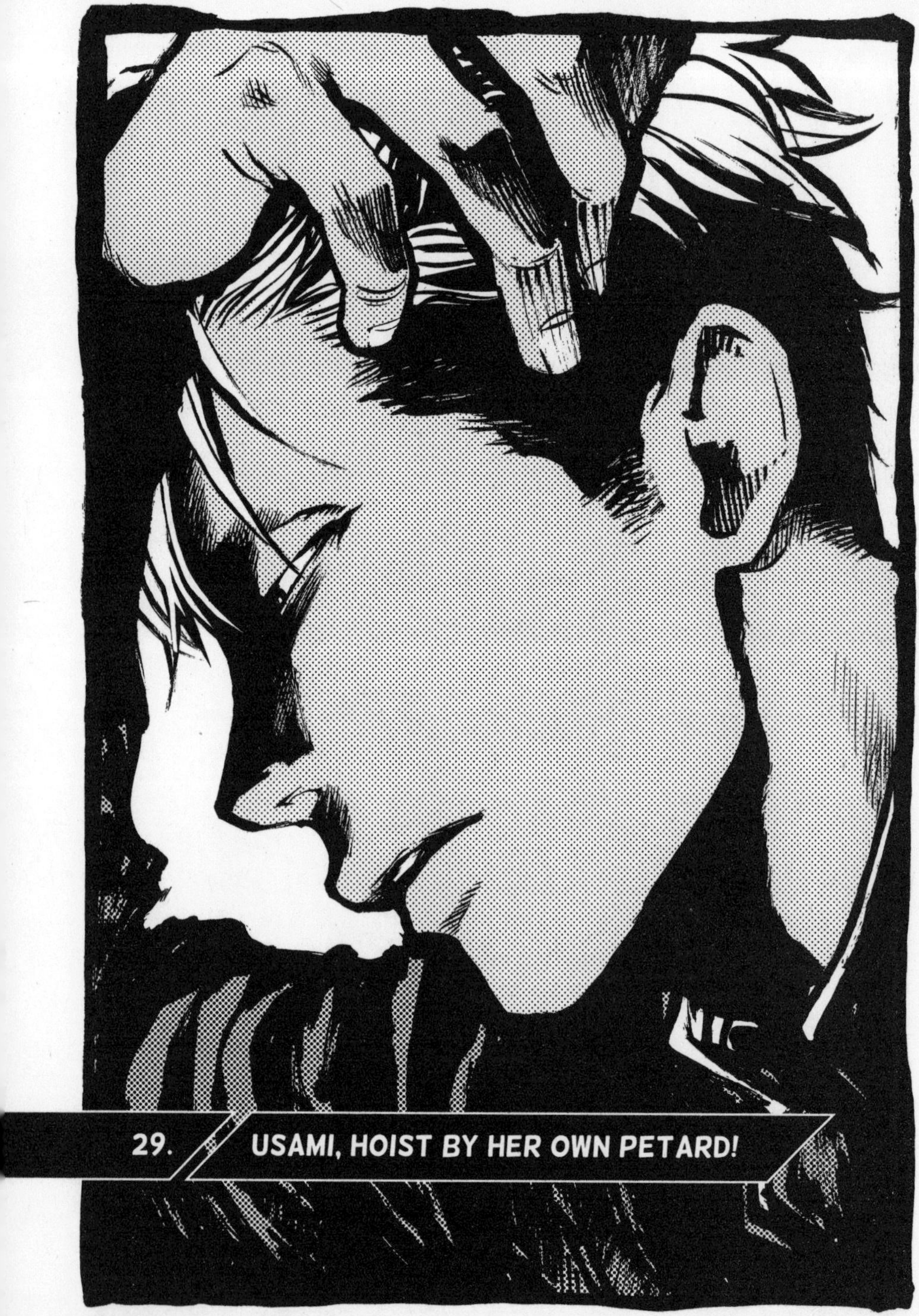

29. USAMI, HOIST BY HER OWN PETARD!

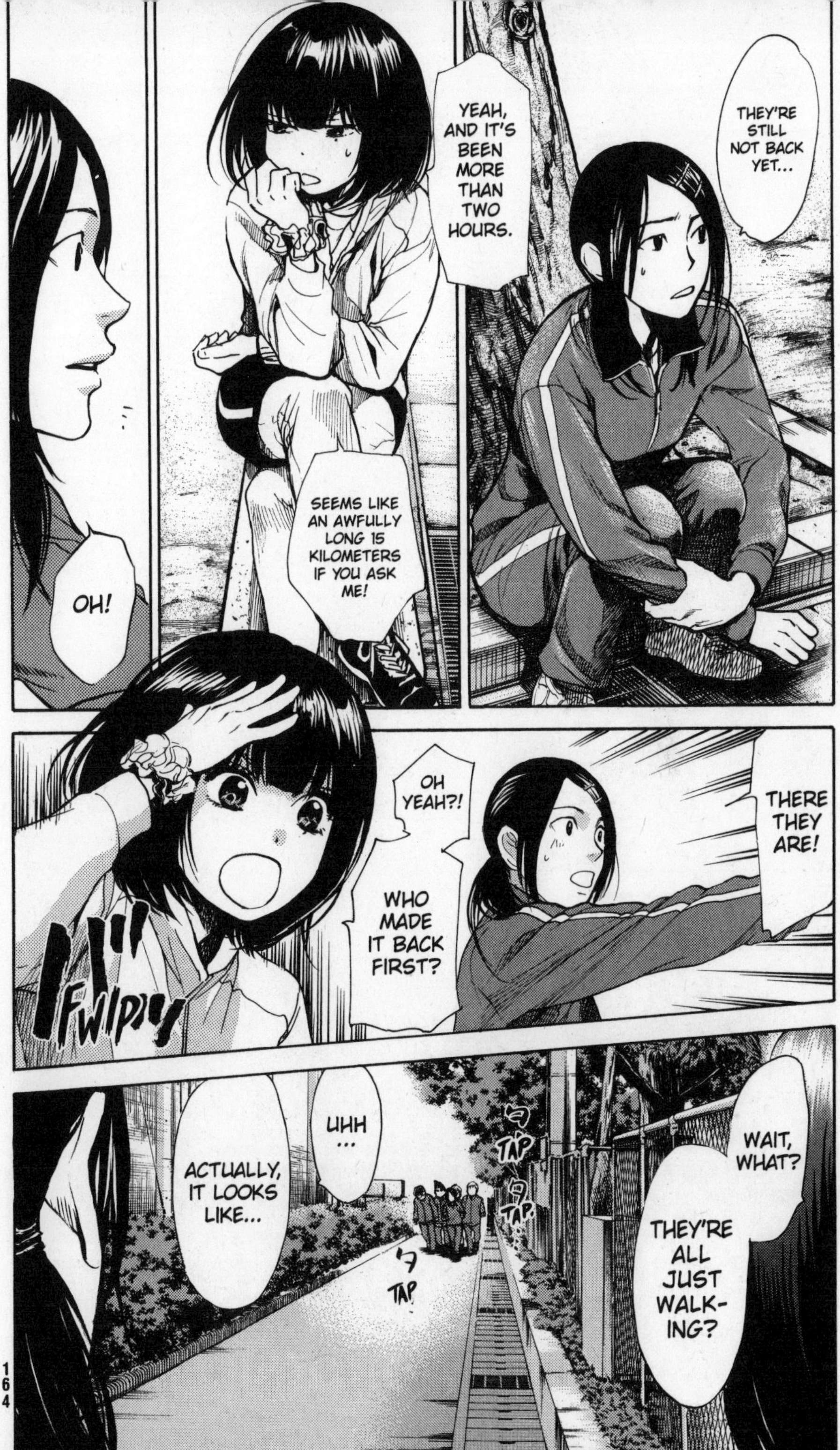

THEY'RE STILL NOT BACK YET...
YEAH, AND IT'S BEEN MORE THAN TWO HOURS.
SEEMS LIKE AN AWFULLY LONG 15 KILOMETERS IF YOU ASK ME!
OH!
THERE THEY ARE!
OH YEAH?!
WHO MADE IT BACK FIRST?
FWIP
WAIT, WHAT?
THEY'RE ALL JUST WALKING?
TAP
TAP
TAP
UHH...
ACTUALLY, IT LOOKS LIKE...

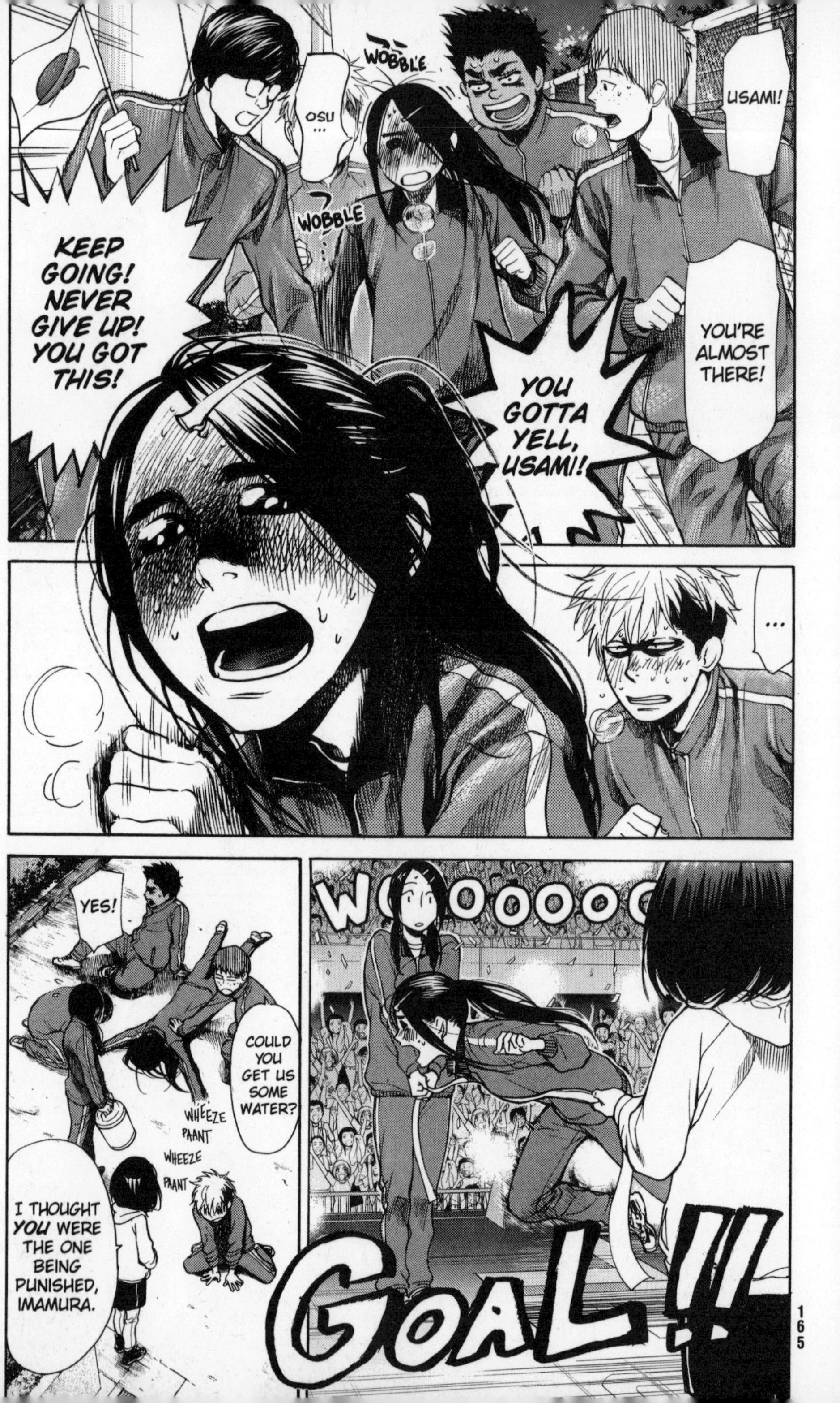

USAMI!
YOU'RE ALMOST THERE!
WOBBLE
OSU ...
WOBBLE
YOU GOTTA YELL, USAMI!!
KEEP GOING! NEVER GIVE UP! YOU GOT THIS!
...
WOOOOO
GOAL!!
YES!
COULD YOU GET US SOME WATER?
WHEEZE
PAANT
WHEEZE
PAANT
I THOUGHT YOU WERE THE ONE BEING PUNISHED, IMAMURA.

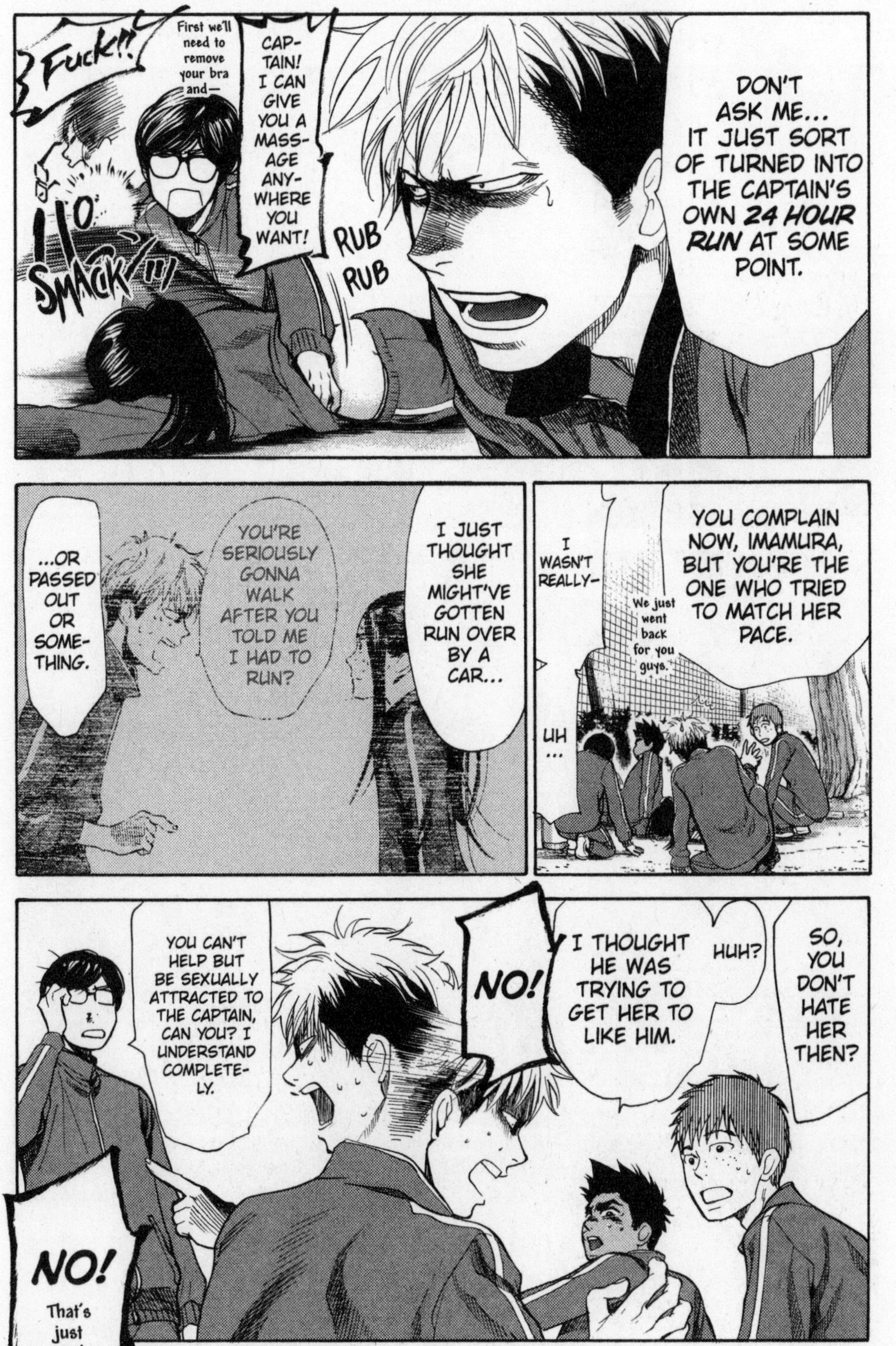
DON'T ASK ME... IT JUST SORT OF TURNED INTO THE CAPTAIN'S OWN **24 HOUR RUN** AT SOME POINT.
RUB RUB
CAP-TAIN! I CAN GIVE YOU A MASS-AGE ANY-WHERE YOU WANT!
First we'll need to remove your bra and—
FUCK!!
O...
SMACK!!
YOU COMPLAIN NOW, IMAMURA, BUT YOU'RE THE ONE WHO TRIED TO MATCH HER PACE.
I WASN'T REALLY—
We just went back for you guys.
UH ...
I JUST THOUGHT SHE MIGHT'VE GOTTEN RUN OVER BY A CAR...
YOU'RE SERIOUSLY GONNA WALK AFTER YOU TOLD ME I HAD TO RUN?
...OR PASSED OUT OR SOME-THING.
SO, YOU DON'T HATE HER THEN?
HUH?
I THOUGHT HE WAS TRYING TO GET HER TO LIKE HIM.
NO!
YOU CAN'T HELP BUT BE SEXUALLY ATTRACTED TO THE CAPTAIN, CAN YOU? I UNDERSTAND COMPLETE-LY.
NO! That's just you!

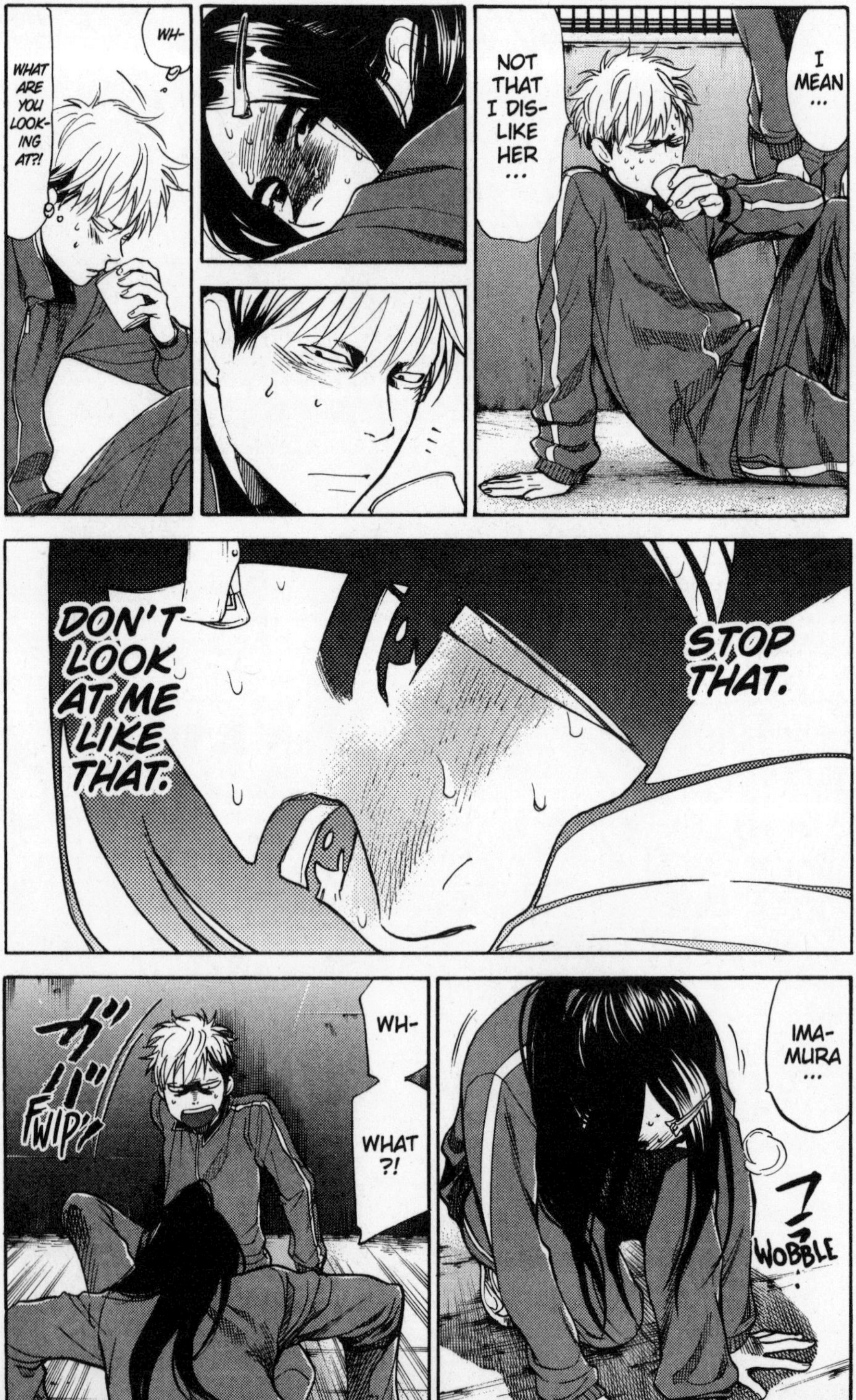
I MEAN ...
NOT THAT I DIS-LIKE HER ...
WH-
WHAT ARE YOU LOOK-ING AT?!
STOP THAT.
DON'T LOOK AT ME LIKE THAT.
IMA-MURA ...
WOBBLE
WH-
WHAT ?!
FWIP!!

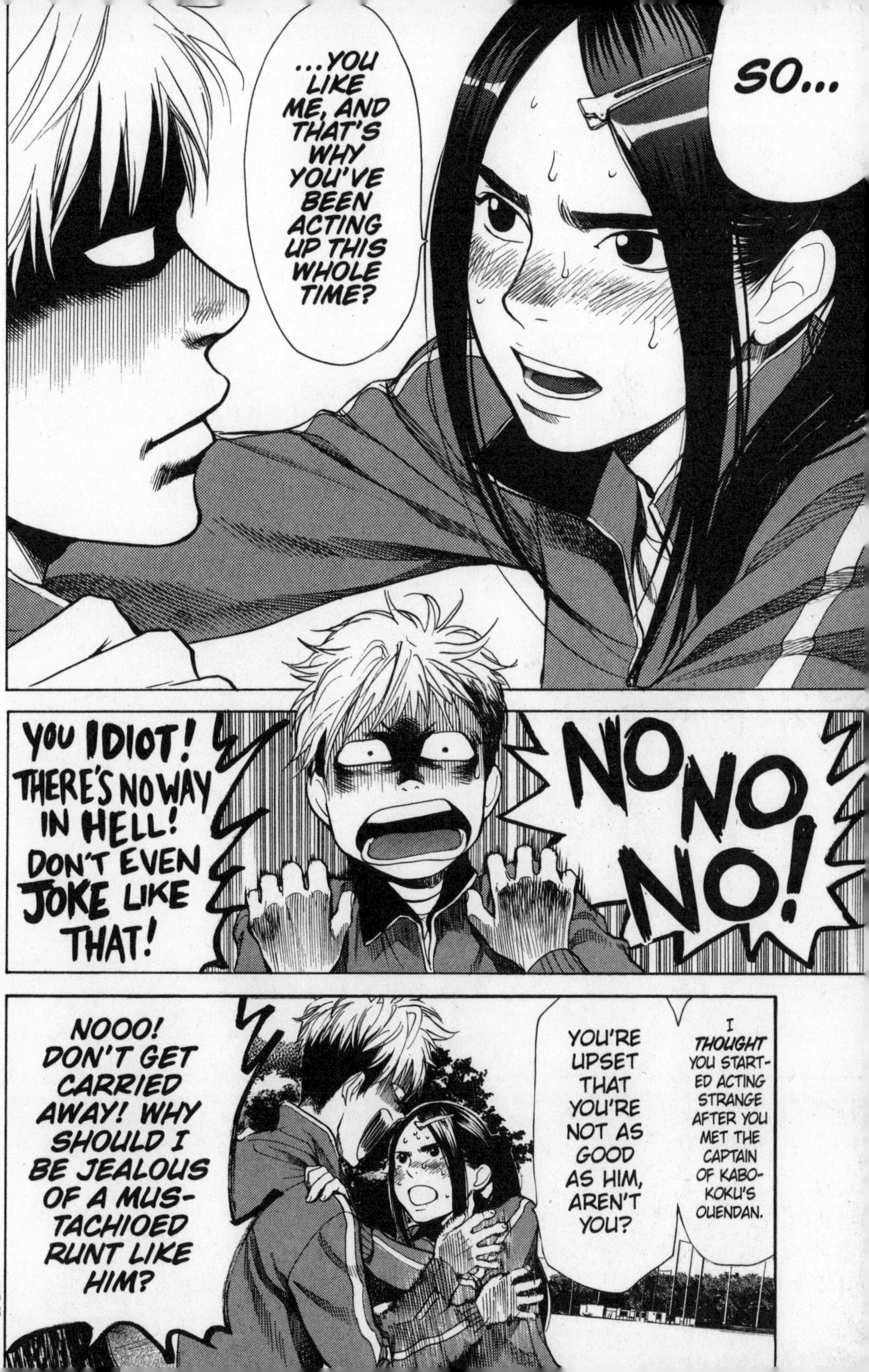
SO...
...YOU LIKE ME, AND THAT'S WHY YOU'VE BEEN ACTING UP THIS WHOLE TIME?
NO NO NO!
YOU IDIOT! THERE'S NO WAY IN HELL! DON'T EVEN JOKE LIKE THAT!
I THOUGHT YOU STARTED ACTING STRANGE AFTER YOU MET THE CAPTAIN OF KABOKOKU'S OUENDAN.
YOU'RE UPSET THAT YOU'RE NOT AS GOOD AS HIM, AREN'T YOU?
NOOO! DON'T GET CARRIED AWAY! WHY SHOULD I BE JEALOUS OF A MUSTACHIOED RUNT LIKE HIM?

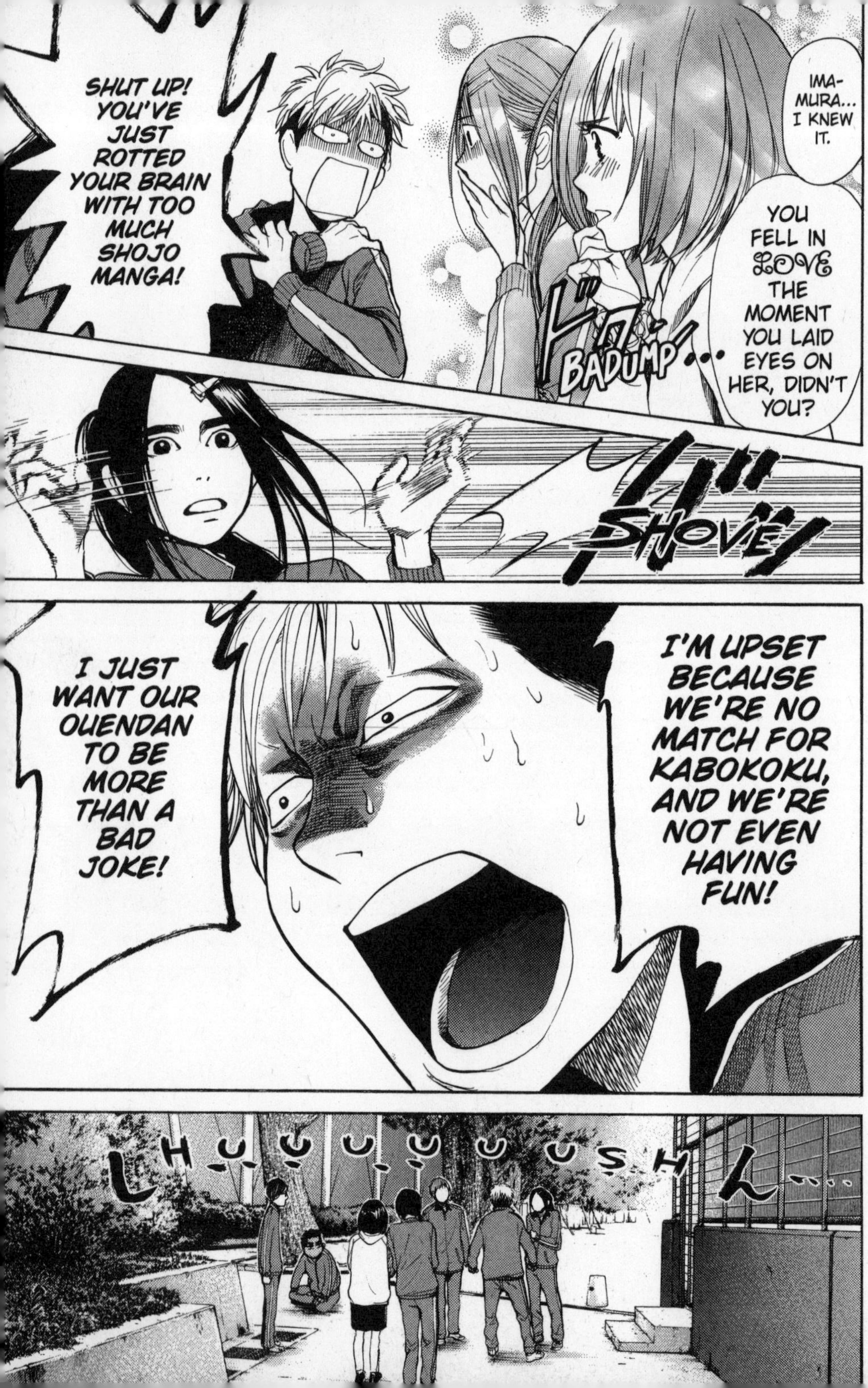
IMA-MURA... I KNEW IT.
YOU FELL IN LOVE THE MOMENT YOU LAID EYES ON HER, DIDN'T YOU?
BADUMP...
SHUT UP! YOU'VE JUST ROTTED YOUR BRAIN WITH TOO MUCH SHOJO MANGA!
SHOVE!
I'M UPSET BECAUSE WE'RE NO MATCH FOR KABOKOKU, AND WE'RE NOT EVEN HAVING FUN!
I JUST WANT OUR OUENDAN TO BE MORE THAN A BAD JOKE!
HUUUUUUSH...

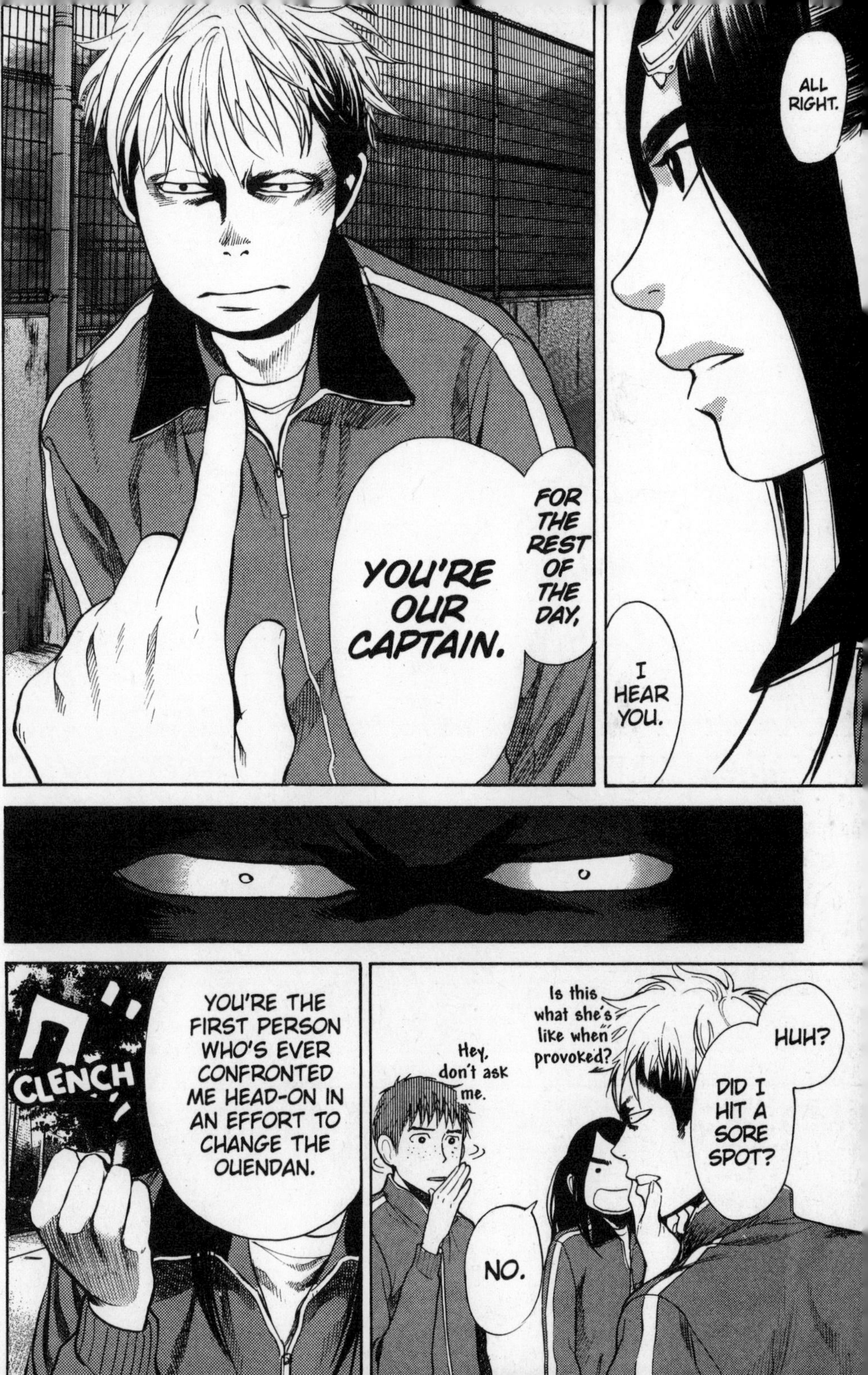
ALL RIGHT.
I HEAR YOU.
FOR THE REST OF THE DAY,
YOU'RE OUR CAPTAIN.
HUH?
DID I HIT A SORE SPOT?
Is this what she's like when provoked?
Hey, don't ask me.
NO.
CLENCH
YOU'RE THE FIRST PERSON WHO'S EVER CONFRONTED ME HEAD-ON IN AN EFFORT TO CHANGE THE OUENDAN.

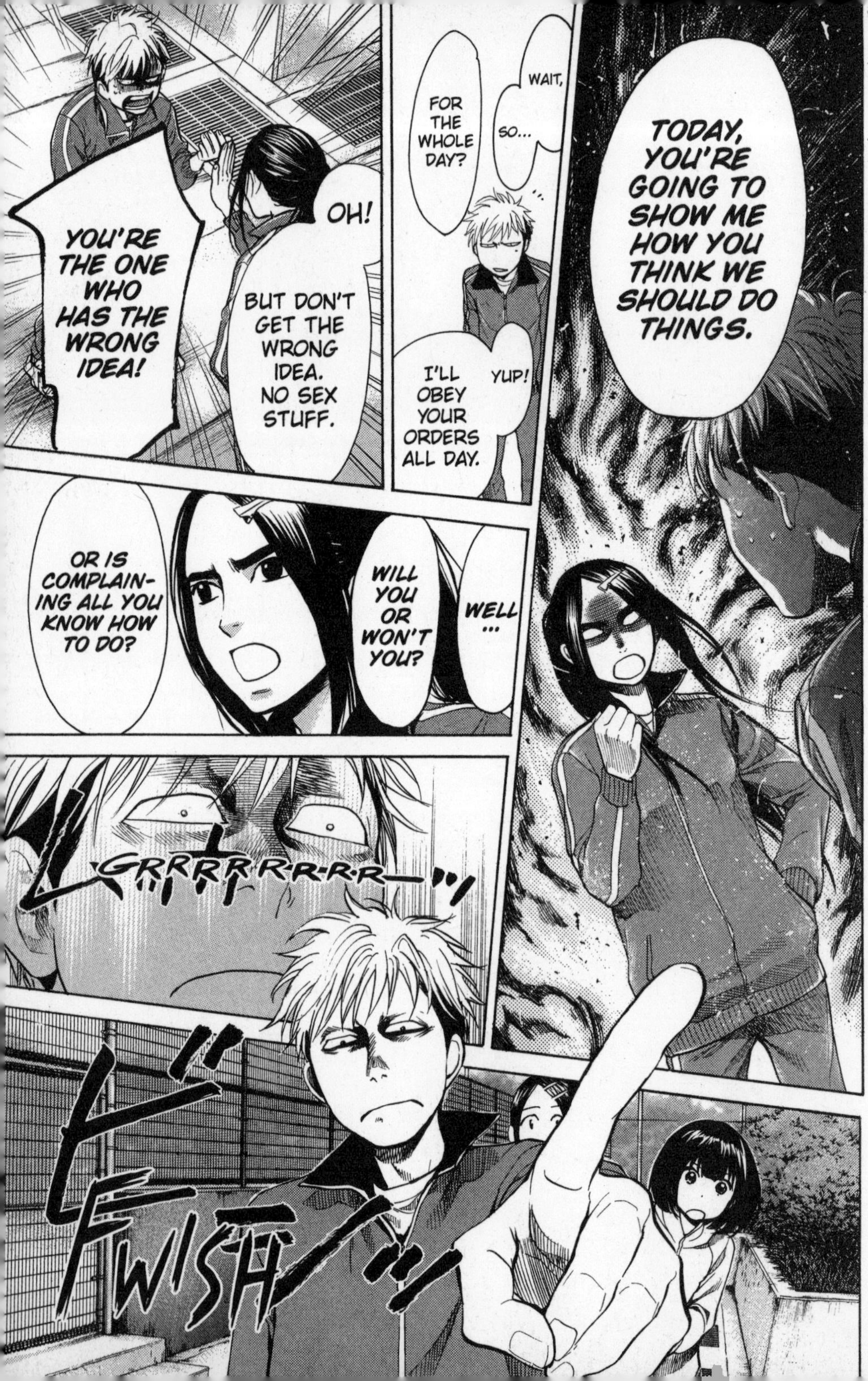
TODAY, YOU'RE GOING TO SHOW ME HOW YOU THINK WE SHOULD DO THINGS.
WAIT, SO...
FOR THE WHOLE DAY?
YUP!
I'LL OBEY YOUR ORDERS ALL DAY.
OH!
BUT DON'T GET THE WRONG IDEA. NO SEX STUFF.
YOU'RE THE ONE WHO HAS THE WRONG IDEA!
WELL...
WILL YOU OR WON'T YOU?
OR IS COMPLAINING ALL YOU KNOW HOW TO DO?
GRRRRRR-R-R-R--
FWISH

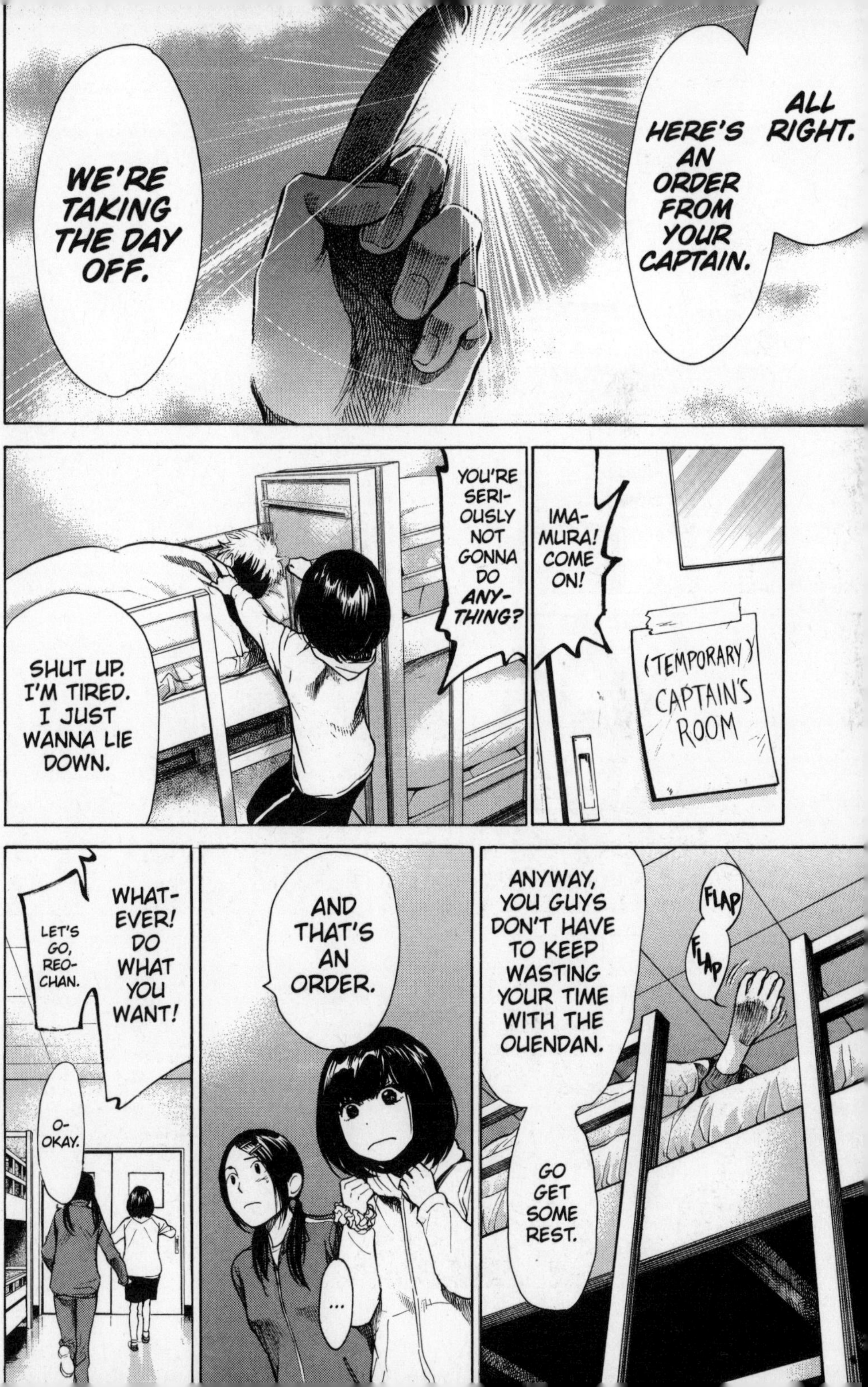
ALL RIGHT. HERE'S AN ORDER FROM YOUR CAPTAIN.
WE'RE TAKING THE DAY OFF.
(TEMPORARY) CAPTAIN'S ROOM
IMAMURA! COME ON!
YOU'RE SERIOUSLY NOT GONNA DO ANYTHING?
SHUT UP. I'M TIRED. I JUST WANNA LIE DOWN.
FLAP
FLAP
ANYWAY, YOU GUYS DON'T HAVE TO KEEP WASTING YOUR TIME WITH THE OUENDAN.
GO GET SOME REST.
AND THAT'S AN ORDER.
...
WHATEVER! DO WHAT YOU WANT!
LET'S GO, REO-CHAN.
O-OKAY.

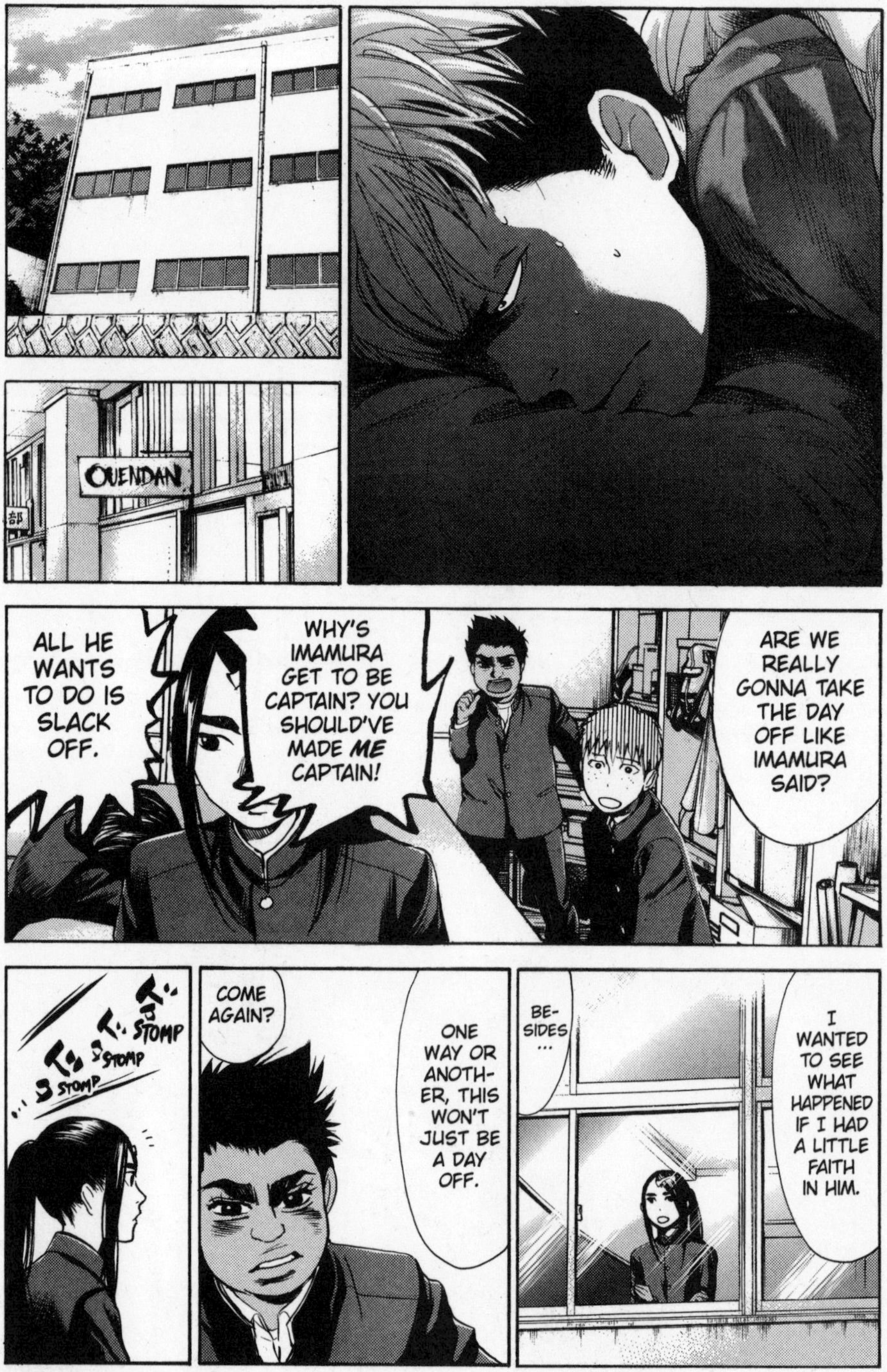
OUENDAN
ARE WE REALLY GONNA TAKE THE DAY OFF LIKE IMAMURA SAID?
WHY'S IMAMURA GET TO BE CAPTAIN? YOU SHOULD'VE MADE *ME* CAPTAIN!
ALL HE WANTS TO DO IS SLACK OFF.
I WANTED TO SEE WHAT HAPPENED IF I HAD A LITTLE FAITH IN HIM.
BE-SIDES...
ONE WAY OR ANOTH-ER, THIS WON'T JUST BE A DAY OFF.
COME AGAIN?
STOMP
STOMP
STOMP

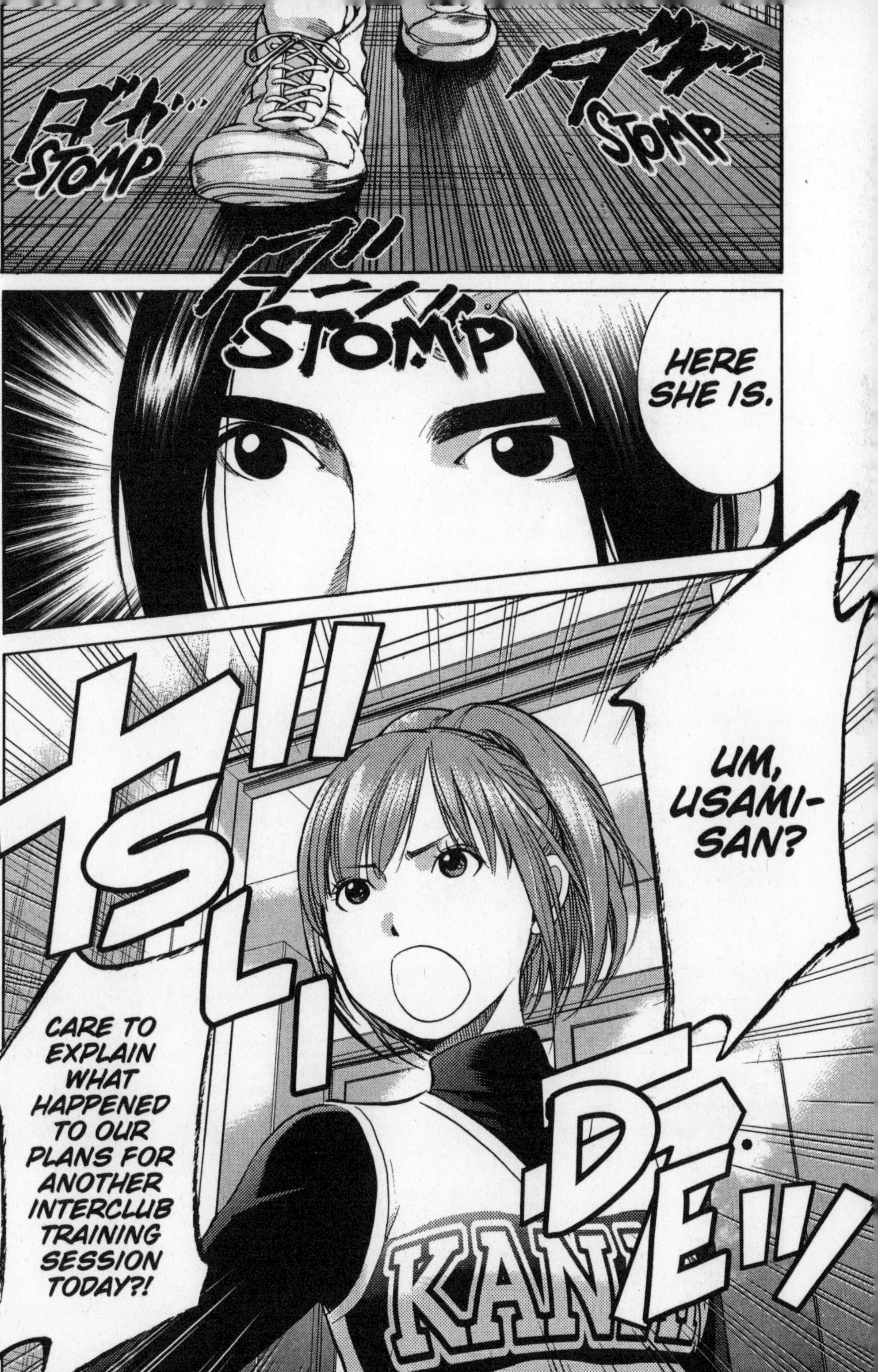
STOMP
STOMP
STOMP
HERE SHE IS.
UM, USAMI-SAN?
SLIDE
CARE TO EXPLAIN WHAT HAPPENED TO OUR PLANS FOR ANOTHER INTERCLUB TRAINING SESSION TODAY?!

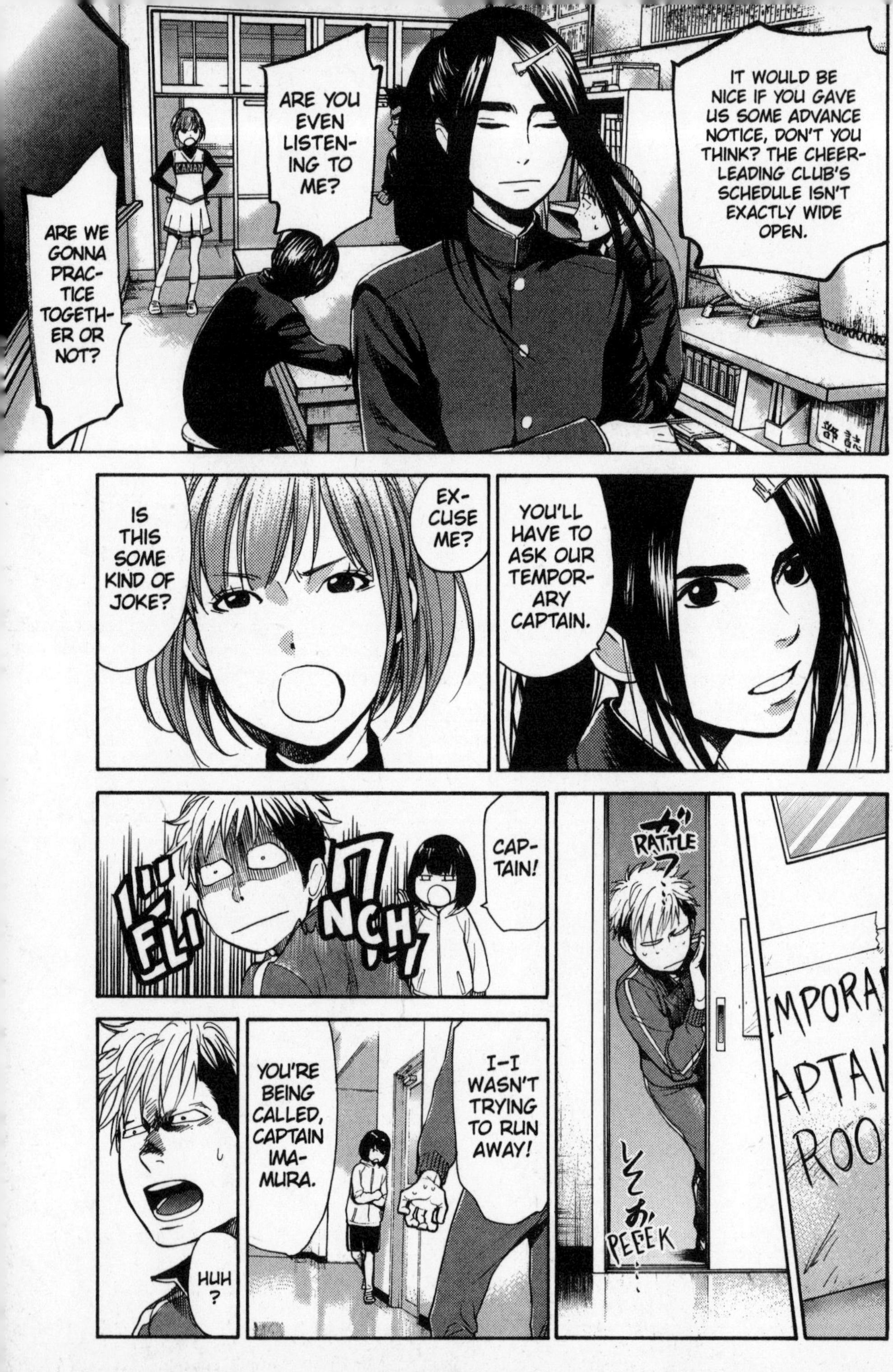

IT WOULD BE NICE IF YOU GAVE US SOME ADVANCE NOTICE, DON'T YOU THINK? THE CHEER-LEADING CLUB'S SCHEDULE ISN'T EXACTLY WIDE OPEN.
ARE YOU EVEN LISTENING TO ME?
KANAN
ARE WE GONNA PRAC-TICE TOGETH-ER OR NOT?
部誌
YOU'LL HAVE TO ASK OUR TEMPOR-ARY CAPTAIN.
EX-CUSE ME?
IS THIS SOME KIND OF JOKE?
ガ RATTLE
MPORA
APTAI
ROO
そぉ PEEEK
CAP-TAIN!
FLINCH
I-I WASN'T TRYING TO RUN AWAY!
YOU'RE BEING CALLED, CAPTAIN IMA-MURA.
HUH?

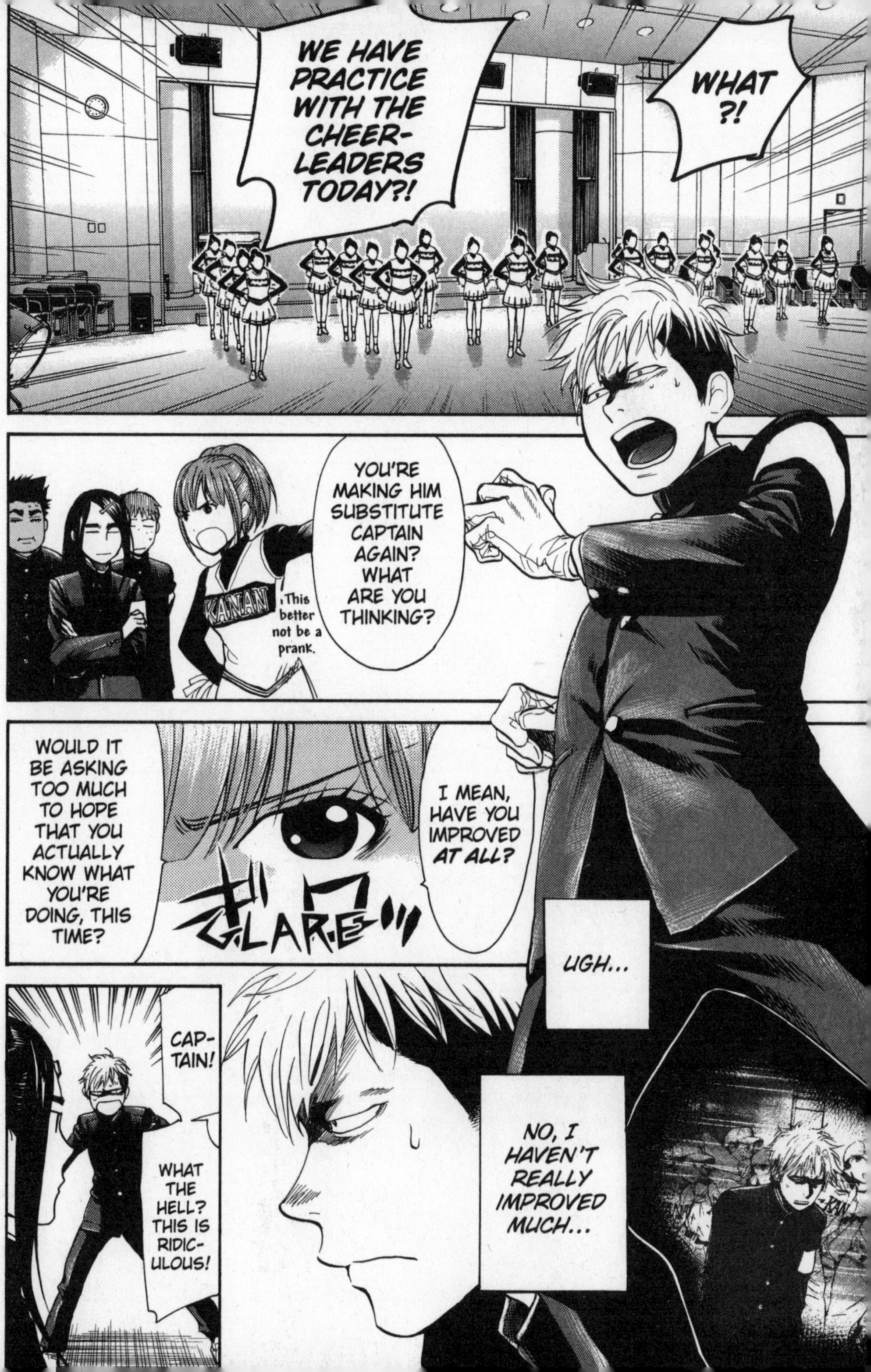
WHAT ?!
WE HAVE PRACTICE WITH THE CHEER-LEADERS TODAY?!
YOU'RE MAKING HIM SUBSTITUTE CAPTAIN AGAIN? WHAT ARE YOU THINKING?
This better not be a prank.
I MEAN, HAVE YOU IMPROVED AT ALL?
WOULD IT BE ASKING TOO MUCH TO HOPE THAT YOU ACTUALLY KNOW WHAT YOU'RE DOING, THIS TIME?
GLARE
UGH...
NO, I HAVEN'T REALLY IMPROVED MUCH...
CAP-TAIN!
WHAT THE HELL? THIS IS RIDIC-ULOUS!

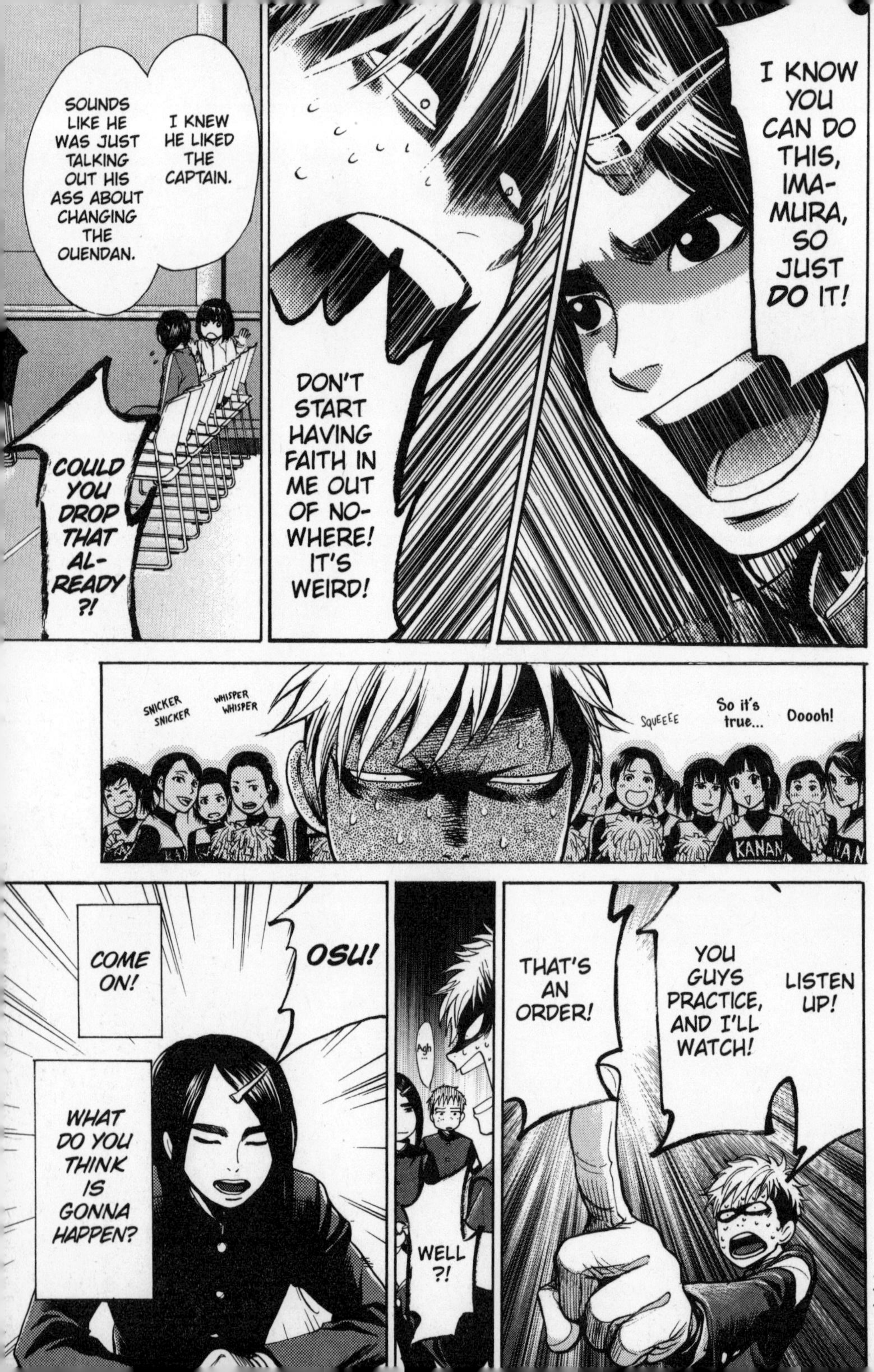
I KNOW YOU CAN DO THIS, IMA-MURA, SO JUST DO IT!
DON'T START HAVING FAITH IN ME OUT OF NO-WHERE! IT'S WEIRD!
I KNEW HE LIKED THE CAPTAIN.
SOUNDS LIKE HE WAS JUST TALKING OUT HIS ASS ABOUT CHANGING THE OUENDAN.
COULD YOU DROP THAT AL-READY ?!
Ooooh!
So it's true...
SQUEEEE
WHISPER WHISPER
SNICKER SNICKER
KANAN
LISTEN UP!
YOU GUYS PRACTICE, AND I'LL WATCH!
THAT'S AN ORDER!
Agh ...
WELL ?!
OSU!
COME ON!
WHAT DO YOU THINK IS GONNA HAPPEN?

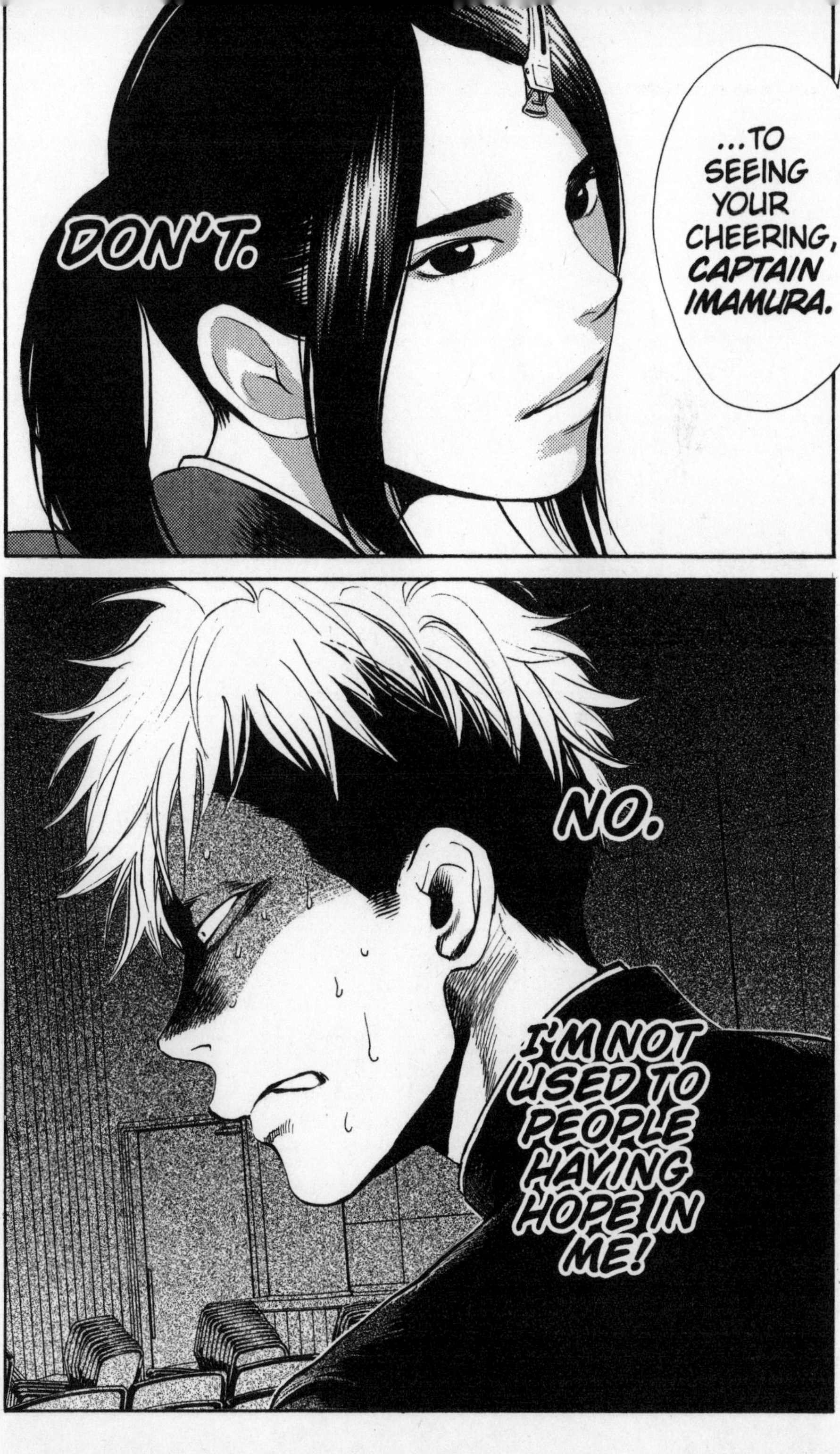
I LOOK FOR-WARD...
...TO SEEING YOUR CHEERING, CAPTAIN IMAMURA.
DON'T.
NO.
I'M NOT USED TO PEOPLE HAVING HOPE IN ME!

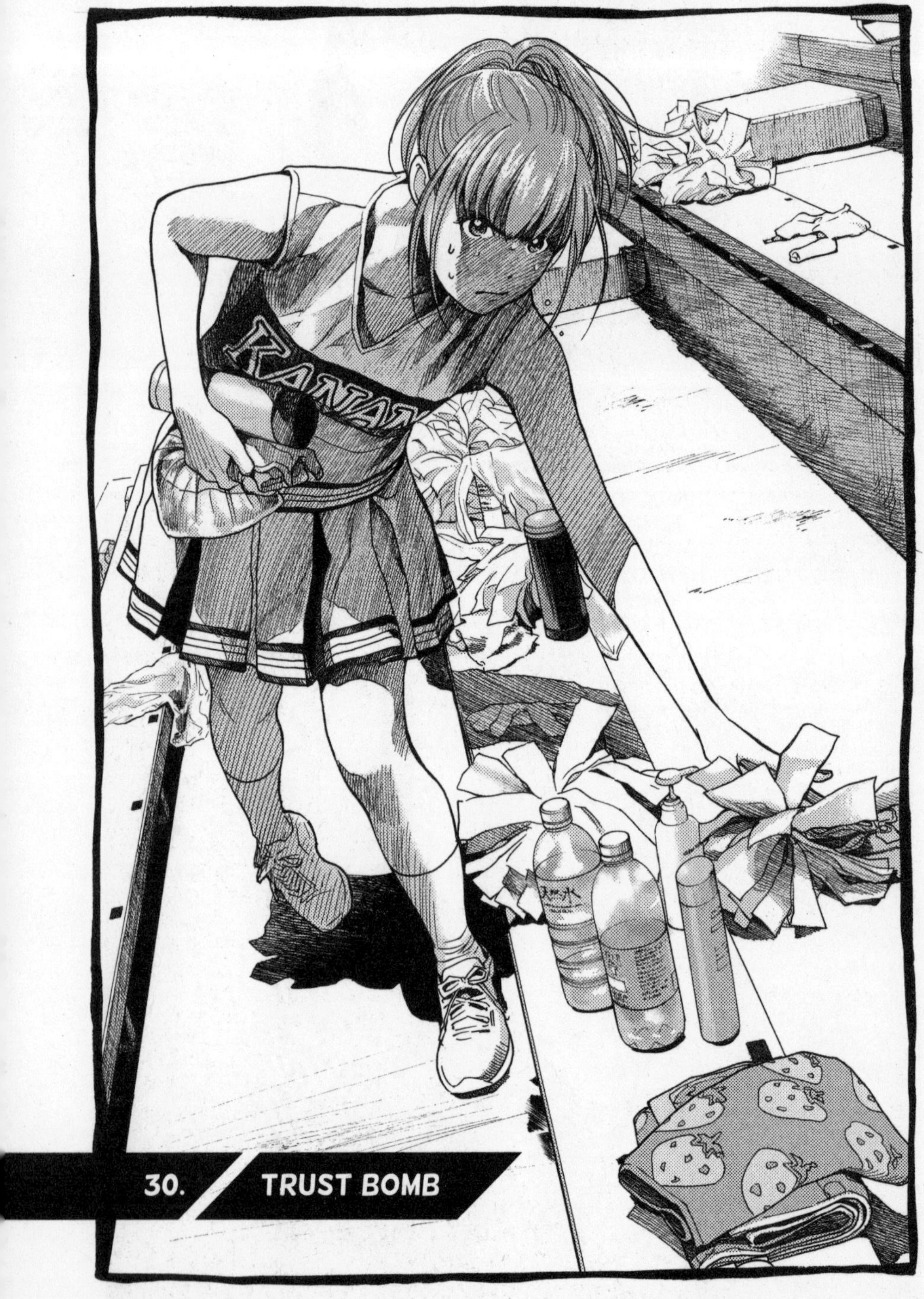

30. TRUST BOMB

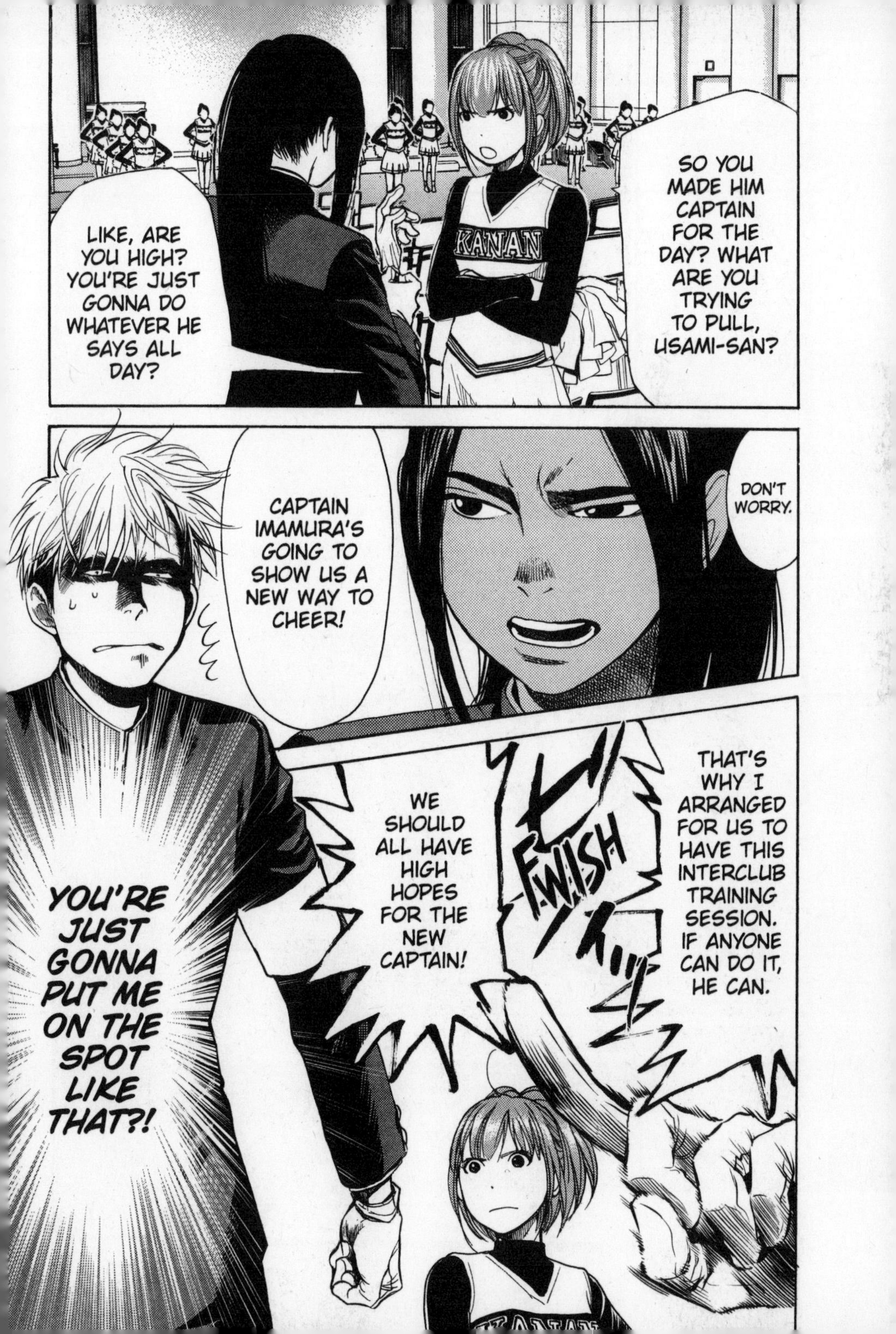
SO YOU MADE HIM CAPTAIN FOR THE DAY? WHAT ARE YOU TRYING TO PULL, USAMI-SAN?
KANAN
LIKE, ARE YOU HIGH? YOU'RE JUST GONNA DO WHATEVER HE SAYS ALL DAY?
DON'T WORRY.
CAPTAIN IMAMURA'S GOING TO SHOW US A NEW WAY TO CHEER!
THAT'S WHY I ARRANGED FOR US TO HAVE THIS INTERCLUB TRAINING SESSION. IF ANYONE CAN DO IT, HE CAN.
FWISH
WE SHOULD ALL HAVE HIGH HOPES FOR THE NEW CAPTAIN!
YOU'RE JUST GONNA PUT ME ON THE SPOT LIKE THAT?!

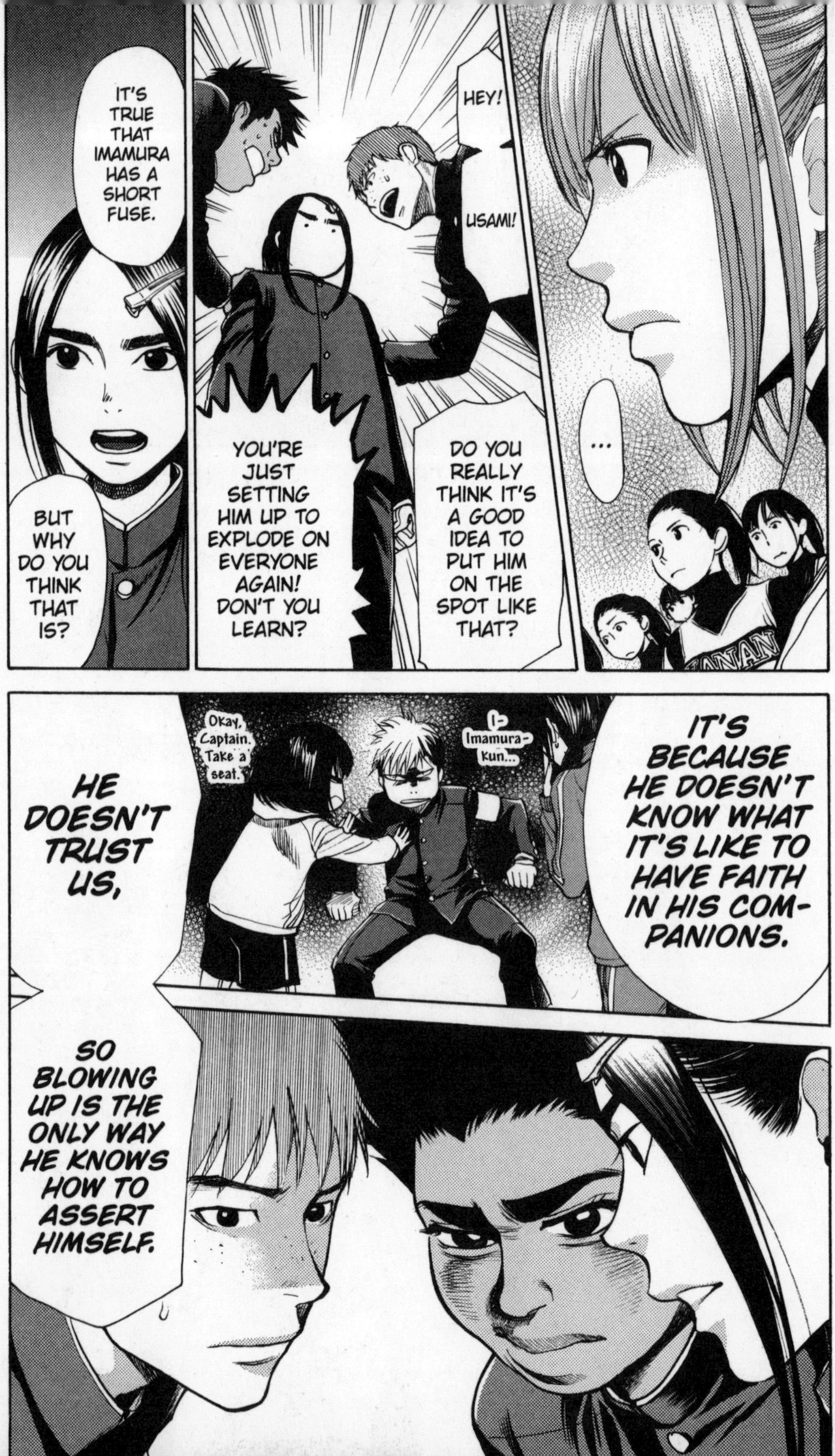
...
HEY!
USAMI!
DO YOU REALLY THINK IT'S A GOOD IDEA TO PUT HIM ON THE SPOT LIKE THAT?
YOU'RE JUST SETTING HIM UP TO EXPLODE ON EVERYONE AGAIN! DON'T YOU LEARN?
IT'S TRUE THAT IMAMURA HAS A SHORT FUSE.
BUT WHY DO YOU THINK THAT IS?
IT'S BECAUSE HE DOESN'T KNOW WHAT IT'S LIKE TO HAVE FAITH IN HIS COMPANIONS.
I- Imamura-kun...
Okay, Captain. Take a seat.
HE DOESN'T TRUST US,
SO BLOWING UP IS THE ONLY WAY HE KNOWS HOW TO ASSERT HIMSELF.

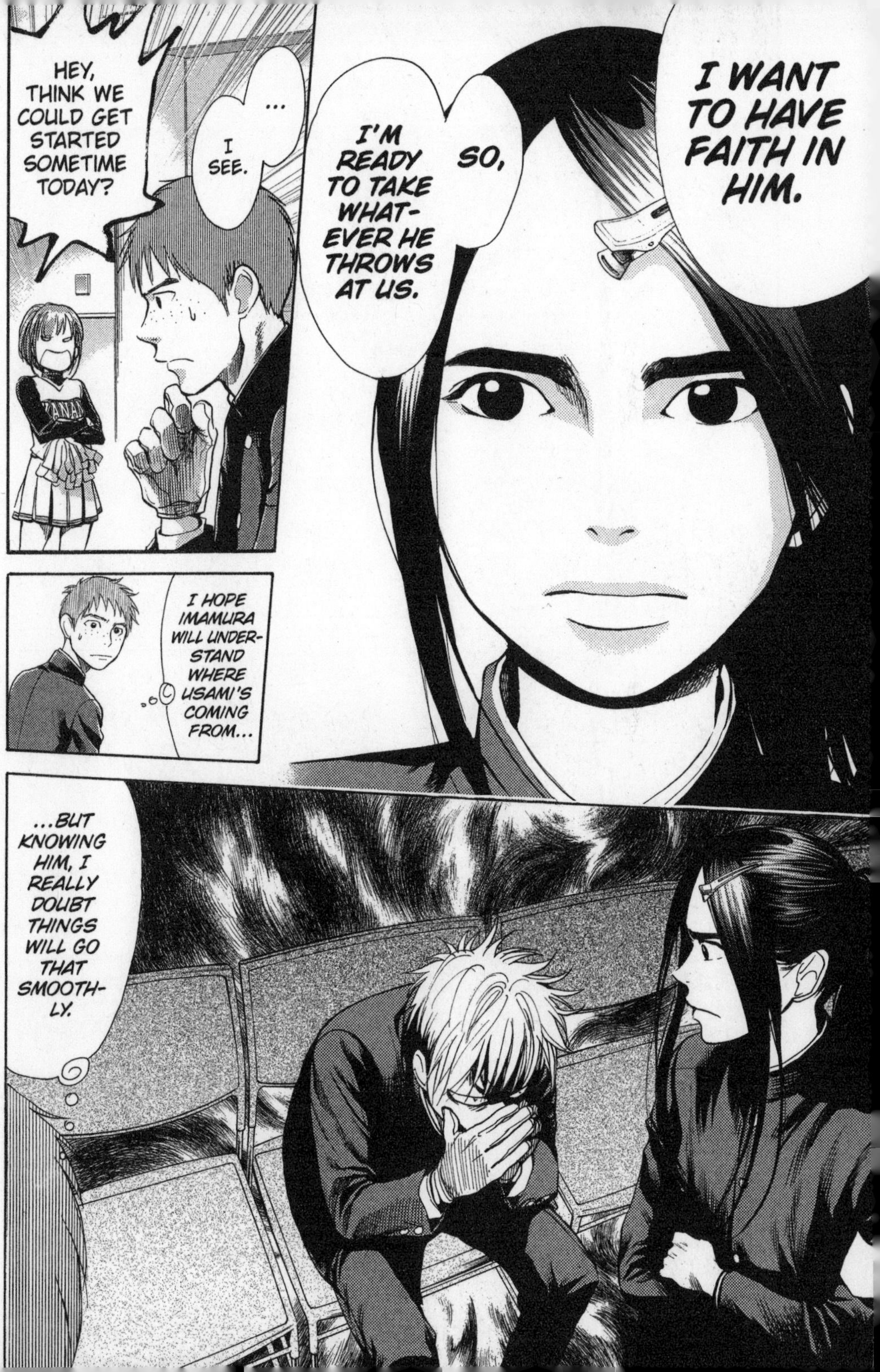
I WANT TO HAVE FAITH IN HIM.
SO,
I'M READY TO TAKE WHATEVER HE THROWS AT US.
...
I SEE.
HEY, THINK WE COULD GET STARTED SOMETIME TODAY?
I HOPE IMAMURA WILL UNDERSTAND WHERE USAMI'S COMING FROM...
...BUT KNOWING HIM, I REALLY DOUBT THINGS WILL GO THAT SMOOTHLY.

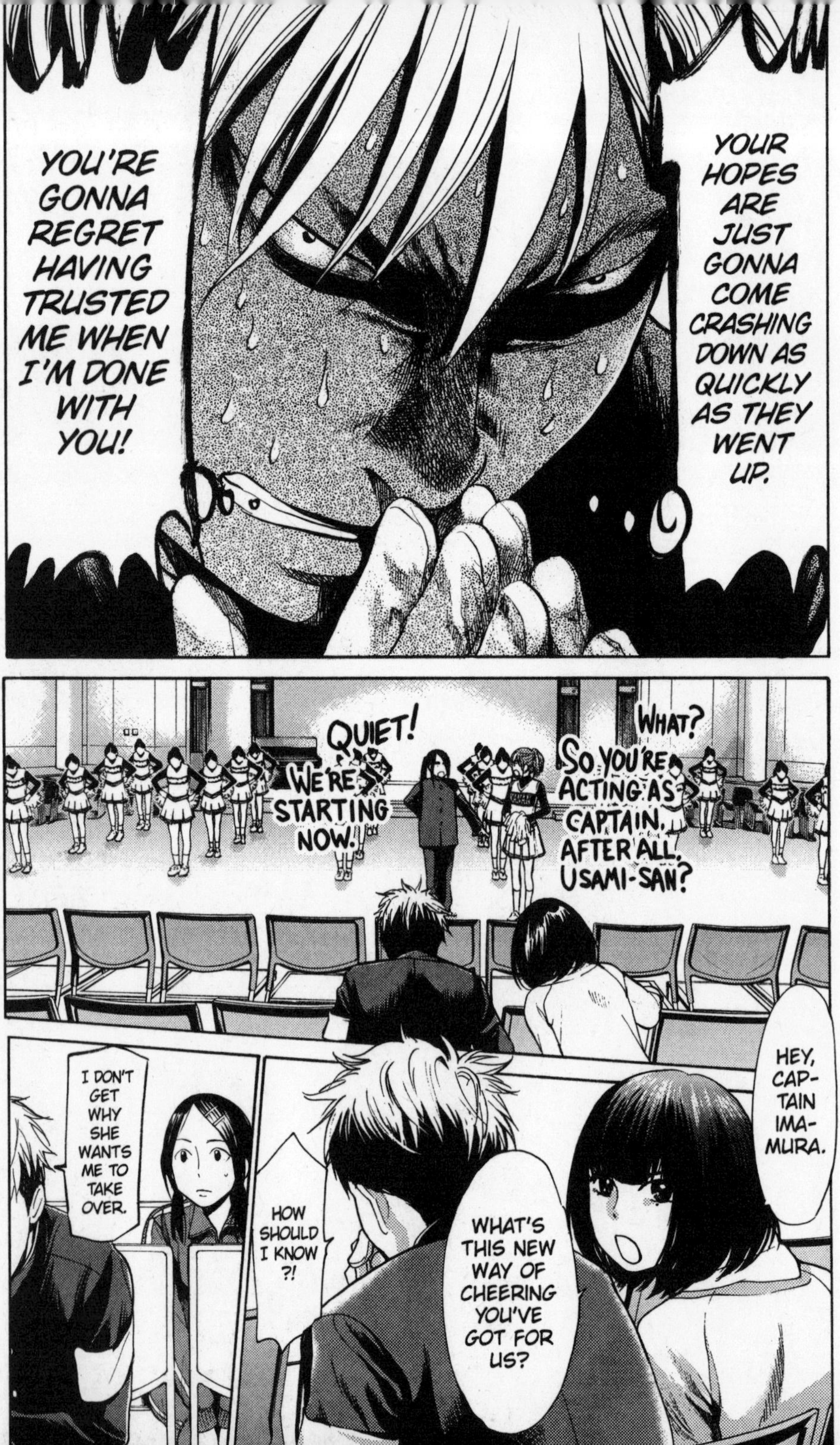
YOUR HOPES ARE JUST GONNA COME CRASHING DOWN AS QUICKLY AS THEY WENT UP.
YOU'RE GONNA REGRET HAVING TRUSTED ME WHEN I'M DONE WITH YOU!
WHAT?
SO YOU'RE ACTING AS CAPTAIN, AFTER ALL, USAMI-SAN?
QUIET!
WE'RE STARTING NOW.
HEY, CAPTAIN IMAMURA.
WHAT'S THIS NEW WAY OF CHEERING YOU'VE GOT FOR US?
HOW SHOULD I KNOW ?!
I DON'T GET WHY SHE WANTS ME TO TAKE OVER.

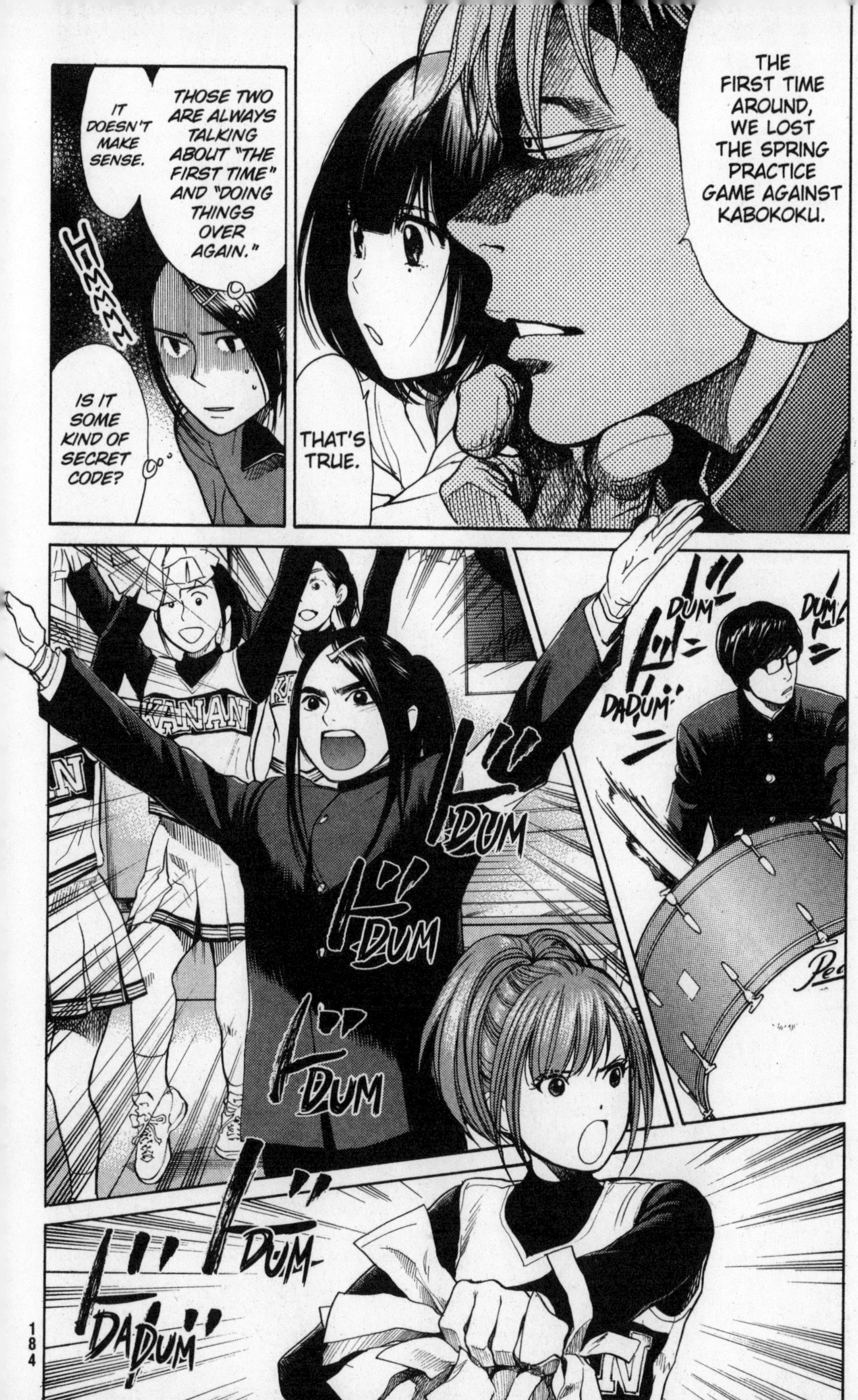
THE FIRST TIME AROUND, WE LOST THE SPRING PRACTICE GAME AGAINST KABOKOKU.
THAT'S TRUE.
THOSE TWO ARE ALWAYS TALKING ABOUT "THE FIRST TIME" AND "DOING THINGS OVER AGAIN."
IT DOESN'T MAKE SENSE.
IS IT SOME KIND OF SECRET CODE?
DUM
DUM
DADUM
DUM
DUM
DUM
DUM-
DADUM

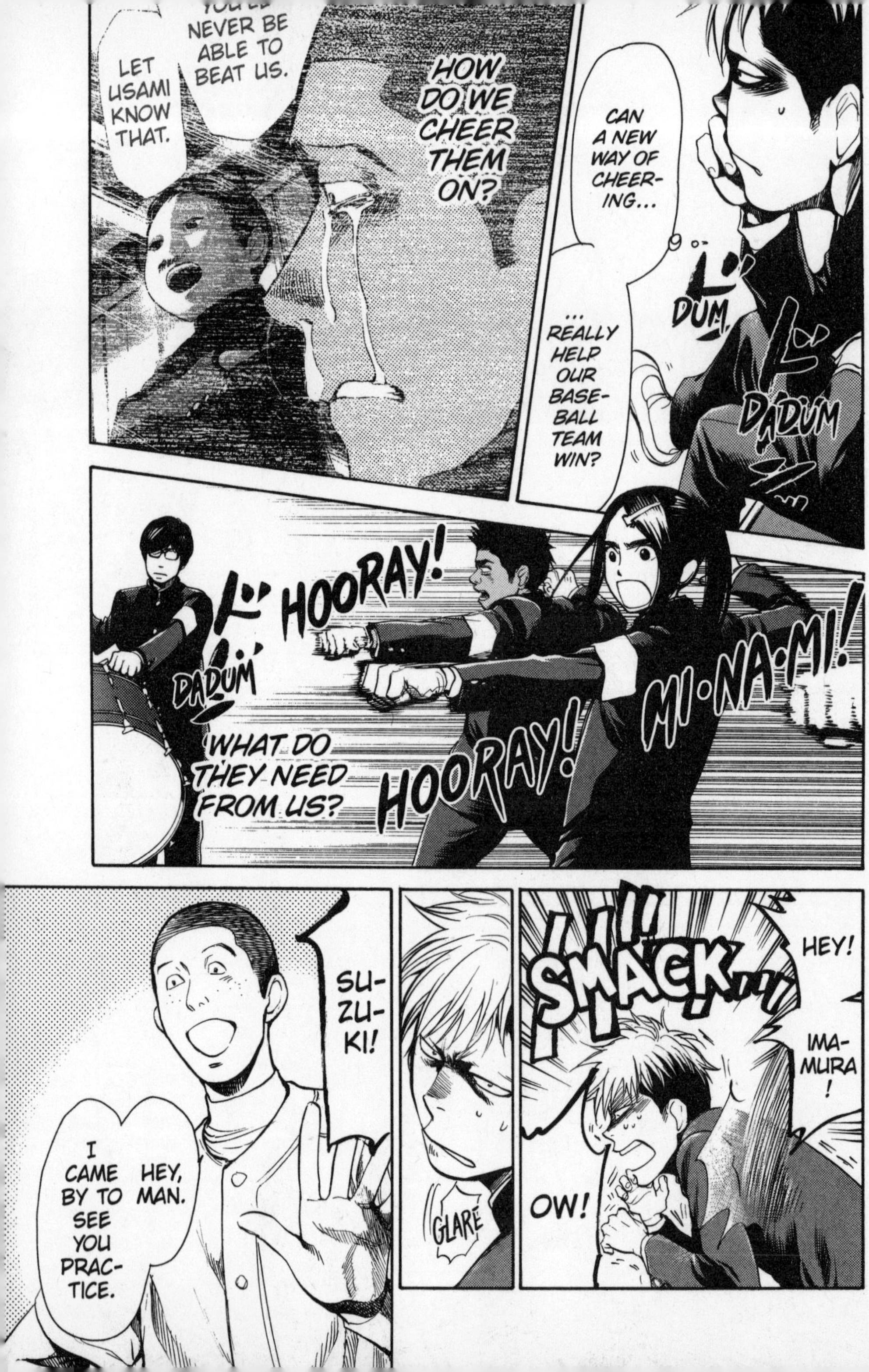
CAN A NEW WAY OF CHEER-ING...
DUM
DADUM
...REALLY HELP OUR BASE-BALL TEAM WIN?
HOW DO WE CHEER THEM ON?
NEVER BE ABLE TO BEAT US.
LET USAMI KNOW THAT.
HOORAY!
MI·NA·MI!
HOORAY!
DADUM
WHAT DO THEY NEED FROM US?
SMACK...
HEY!
IMA-MURA!
OW!
GLARE
SU-ZU-KI!
HEY, MAN.
I CAME BY TO SEE YOU PRAC-TICE.

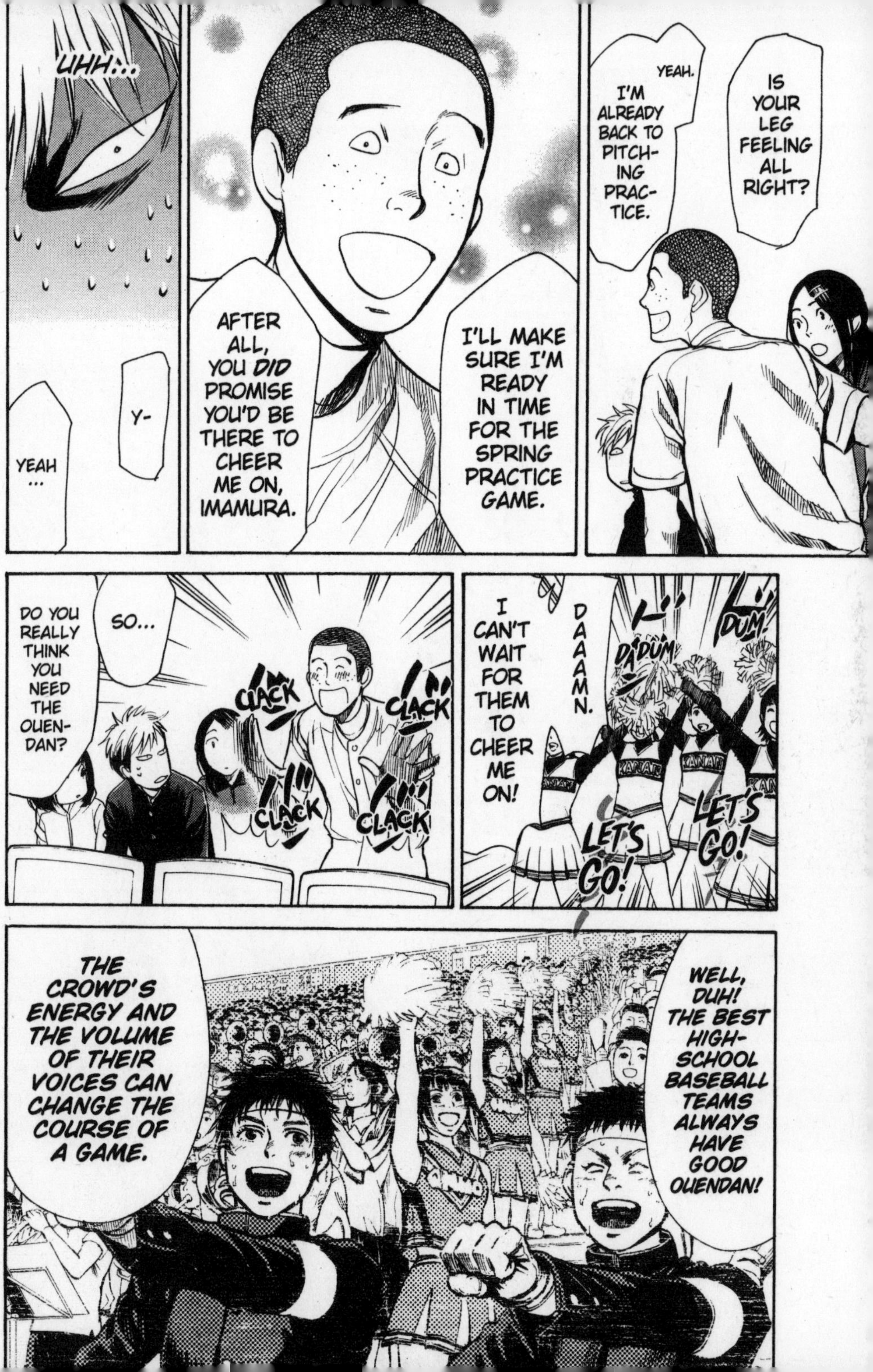
IS YOUR LEG FEELING ALL RIGHT?
YEAH.
I'M ALREADY BACK TO PITCH-ING PRAC-TICE.
I'LL MAKE SURE I'M READY IN TIME FOR THE SPRING PRACTICE GAME.
AFTER ALL, YOU *DID* PROMISE YOU'D BE THERE TO CHEER ME ON, IMAMURA.
UHH...
Y-
YEAH ...
DUM!
DA DUM
DAAAAMN.
I CAN'T WAIT FOR THEM TO CHEER ME ON!
LET'S GO!
LET'S GO!
SO...
DO YOU REALLY THINK YOU NEED THE OUEN-DAN?
CLACK
CLACK
CLACK
CLACK
WELL, DUH! THE BEST HIGH-SCHOOL BASEBALL TEAMS ALWAYS HAVE GOOD OUENDAN!
THE CROWD'S ENERGY AND THE VOLUME OF THEIR VOICES CAN CHANGE THE COURSE OF A GAME.

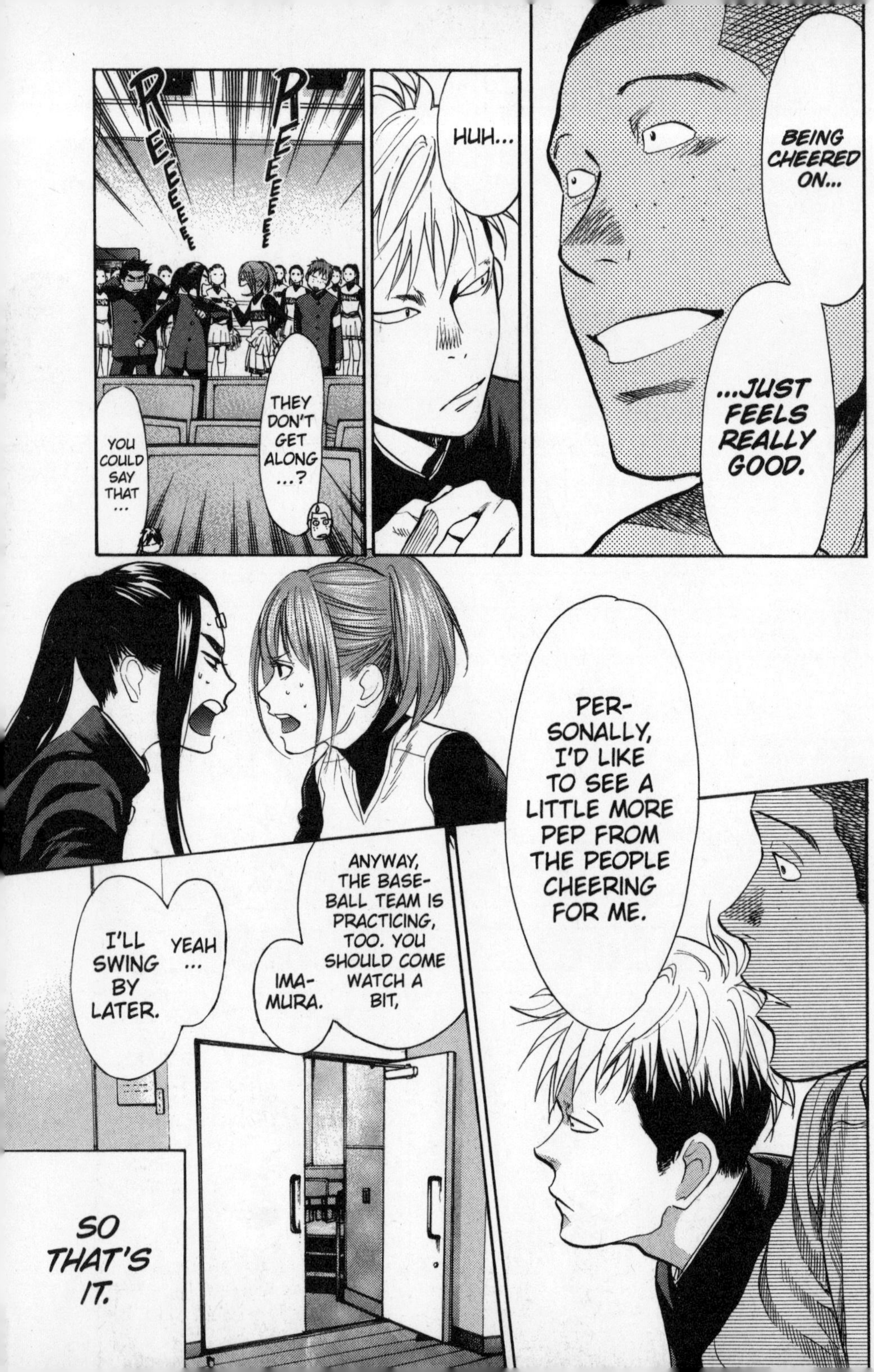
BEING CHEERED ON...
...JUST FEELS REALLY GOOD.
HUH...
R-EEEEEE
R-EEEEEEE
THEY DON'T GET ALONG ...?
YOU COULD SAY THAT ...
PER-SONALLY, I'D LIKE TO SEE A LITTLE MORE PEP FROM THE PEOPLE CHEERING FOR ME.
ANYWAY, THE BASE-BALL TEAM IS PRACTICING, TOO. YOU SHOULD COME WATCH A BIT,
IMA-MURA.
YEAH ...
I'LL SWING BY LATER.
SO THAT'S IT.

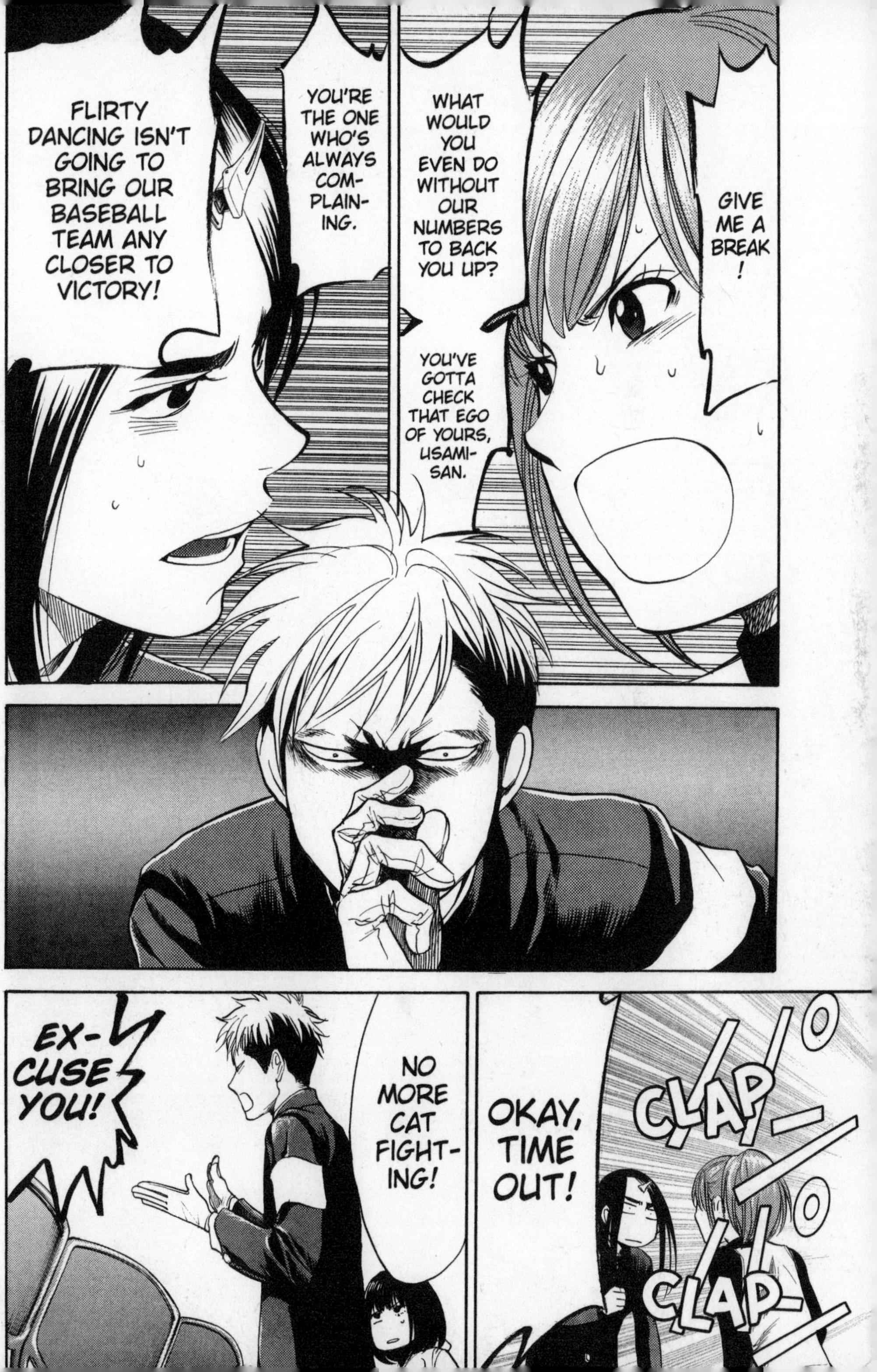

GIVE ME A BREAK!
WHAT WOULD YOU EVEN DO WITHOUT OUR NUMBERS TO BACK YOU UP?
YOU'VE GOTTA CHECK THAT EGO OF YOURS, USAMI-SAN.
YOU'RE THE ONE WHO'S ALWAYS COM-PLAIN-ING.
FLIRTY DANCING ISN'T GOING TO BRING OUR BASEBALL TEAM ANY CLOSER TO VICTORY!
CLAP- CLAP-
OKAY, TIME OUT!
NO MORE CAT FIGHT-ING!
EX-CUSE YOU!

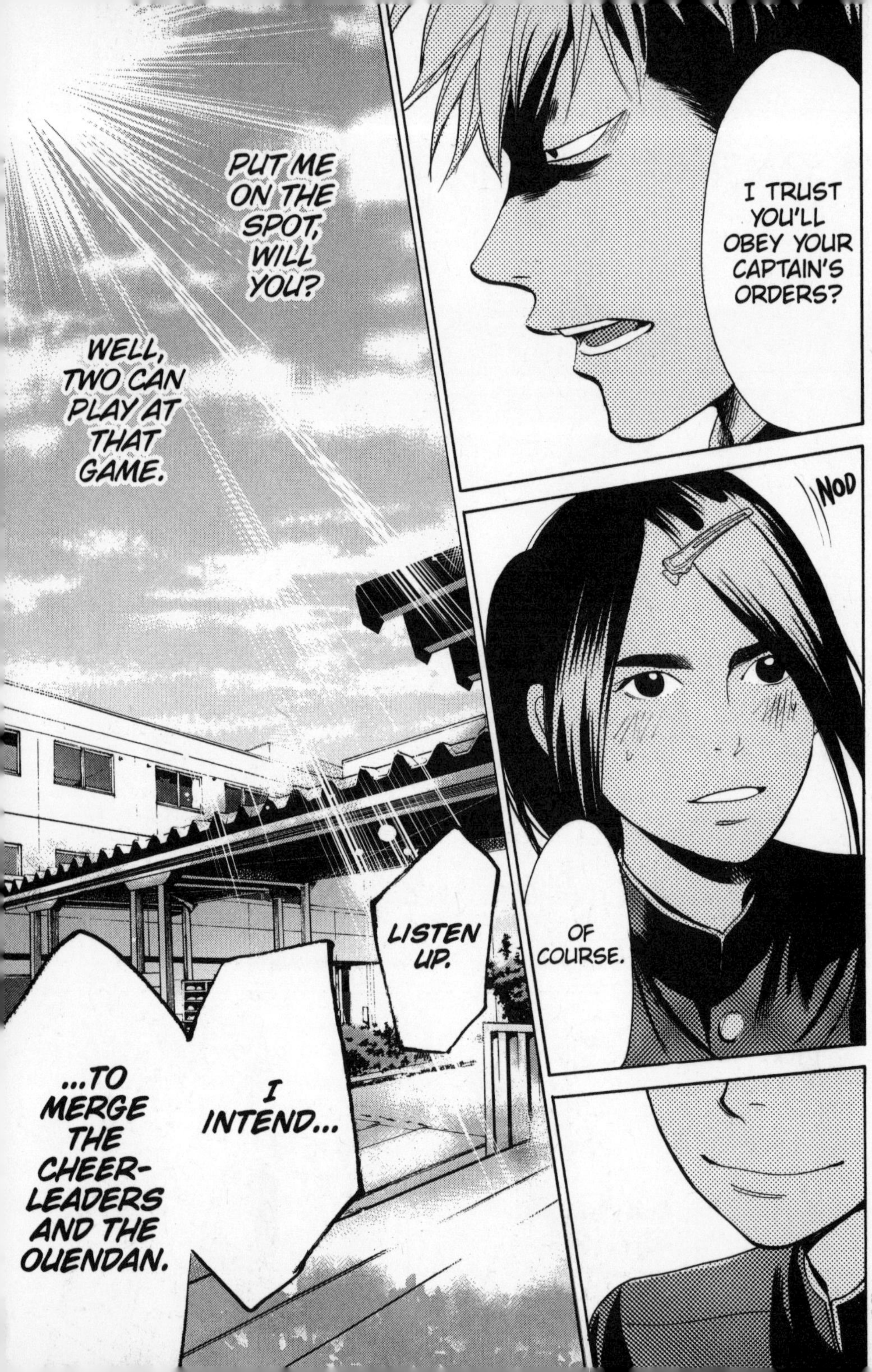
I TRUST YOU'LL OBEY YOUR CAPTAIN'S ORDERS?
NOD
OF COURSE.
PUT ME ON THE SPOT, WILL YOU?
WELL, TWO CAN PLAY AT THAT GAME.
LISTEN UP.
I INTEND...
...TO MERGE THE CHEER-LEADERS AND THE OUENDAN.

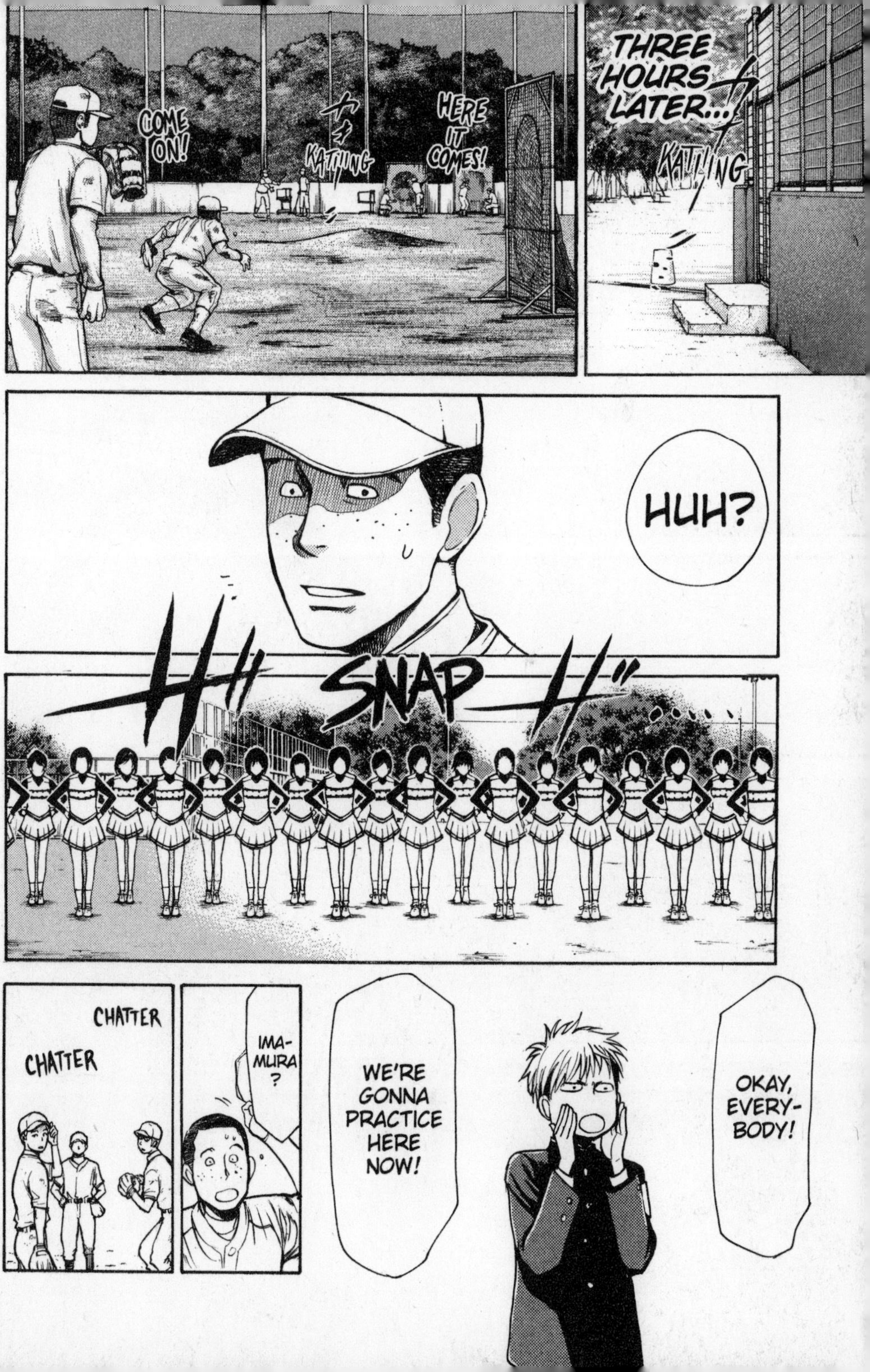
THREE HOURS LATER...
KATIIING
HERE IT COMES!
KATIIING
COME ON!
HUH?
SNAP
OKAY, EVERY-BODY!
WE'RE GONNA PRACTICE HERE NOW!
IMA-MURA?
CHATTER
CHATTER

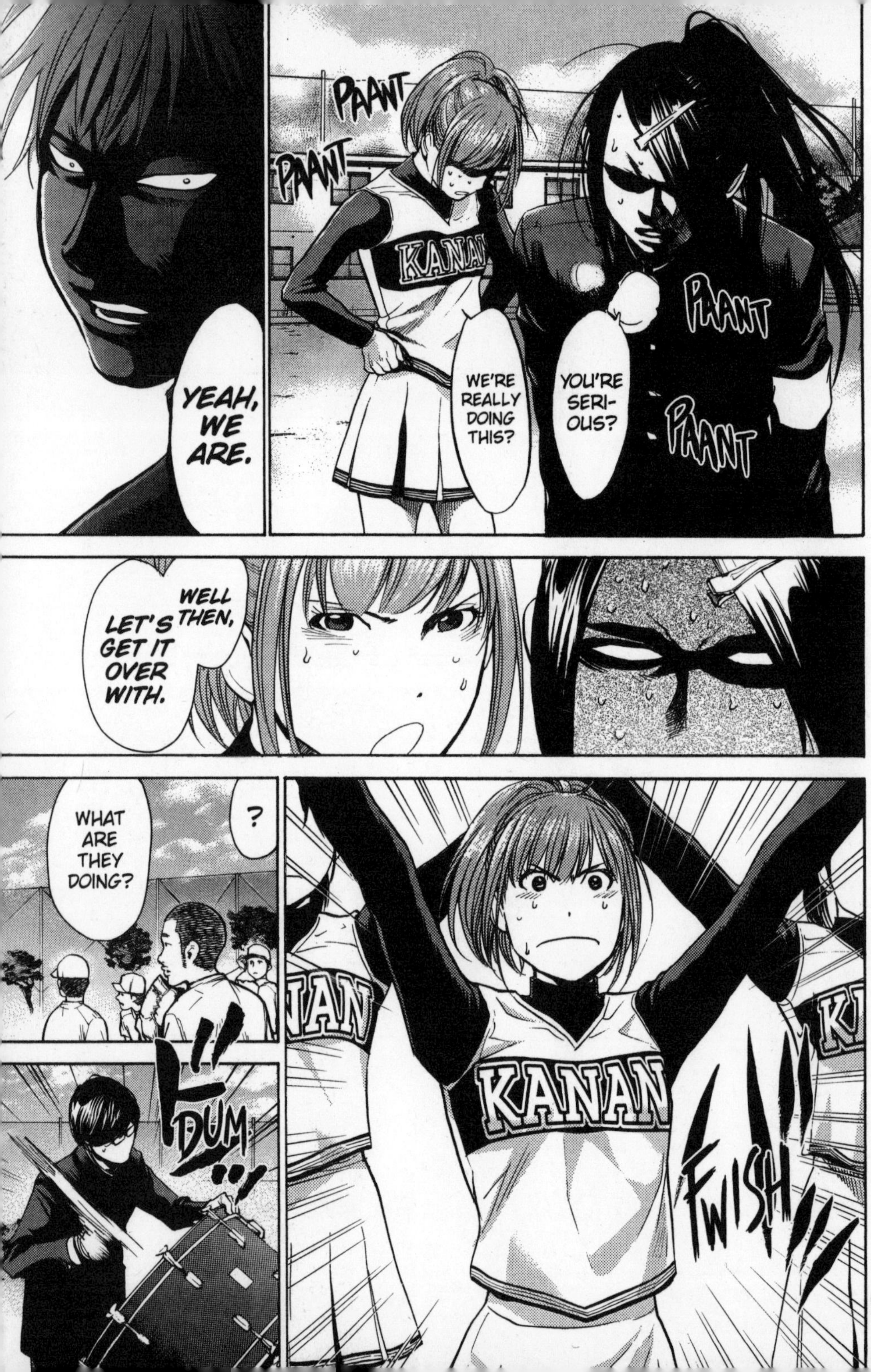
PAANT
YOU'RE SERI-OUS?
PAANT
PAANT
WE'RE REALLY DOING THIS?
PAANT
YEAH, WE ARE.
WELL THEN, LET'S GET IT OVER WITH.
FWISH
?
WHAT ARE THEY DOING?
DUM

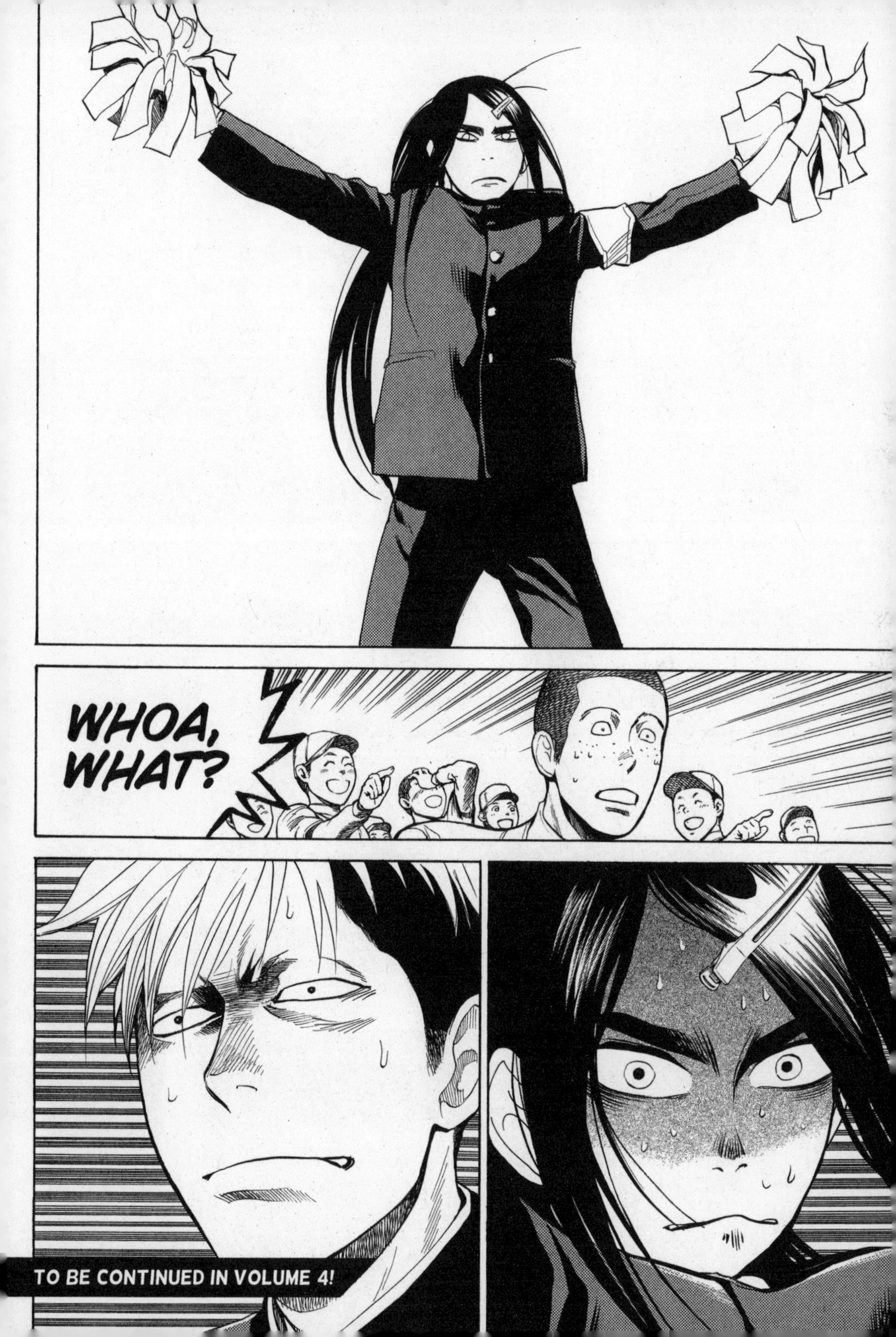
WHOA, WHAT?
TO BE CONTINUED IN VOLUME 4!

This is the AFTERWORD!

Since this manga's about going back in time from 2014 to 2011, I get anxious every time some big news event happens in the real world. I'm like, "I didn't put that in my manga!"

I don't think I'll ever forget 2011. It's been the opening of a new chapter in my life, what with Again!! beginning serialization and Moteki: Love Strikes! getting made into a movie and all.

It doesn't feel like we're too far off from catching up with Imamura in the year 2014. That sort of makes me nervous...

I think it will be pretty cool if I'm able to draw three special years of my own life at the same time as Again!!

2011. 12. 久保ミツロウ☆

Mitsurou Kubo, December 2011

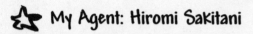 My Agent: Hiromi Sakitani

My Assistants: My Assistants: Shunsuke Ono, Hiromu Sugawara, Yousuke Takahashi, Yukinori Tateda, Shiori Mizoguchi, Youko Mikuni, and Four Hundred and Four Illnesses Tsunemine (a pseudonym)

IN VOLUME 4...

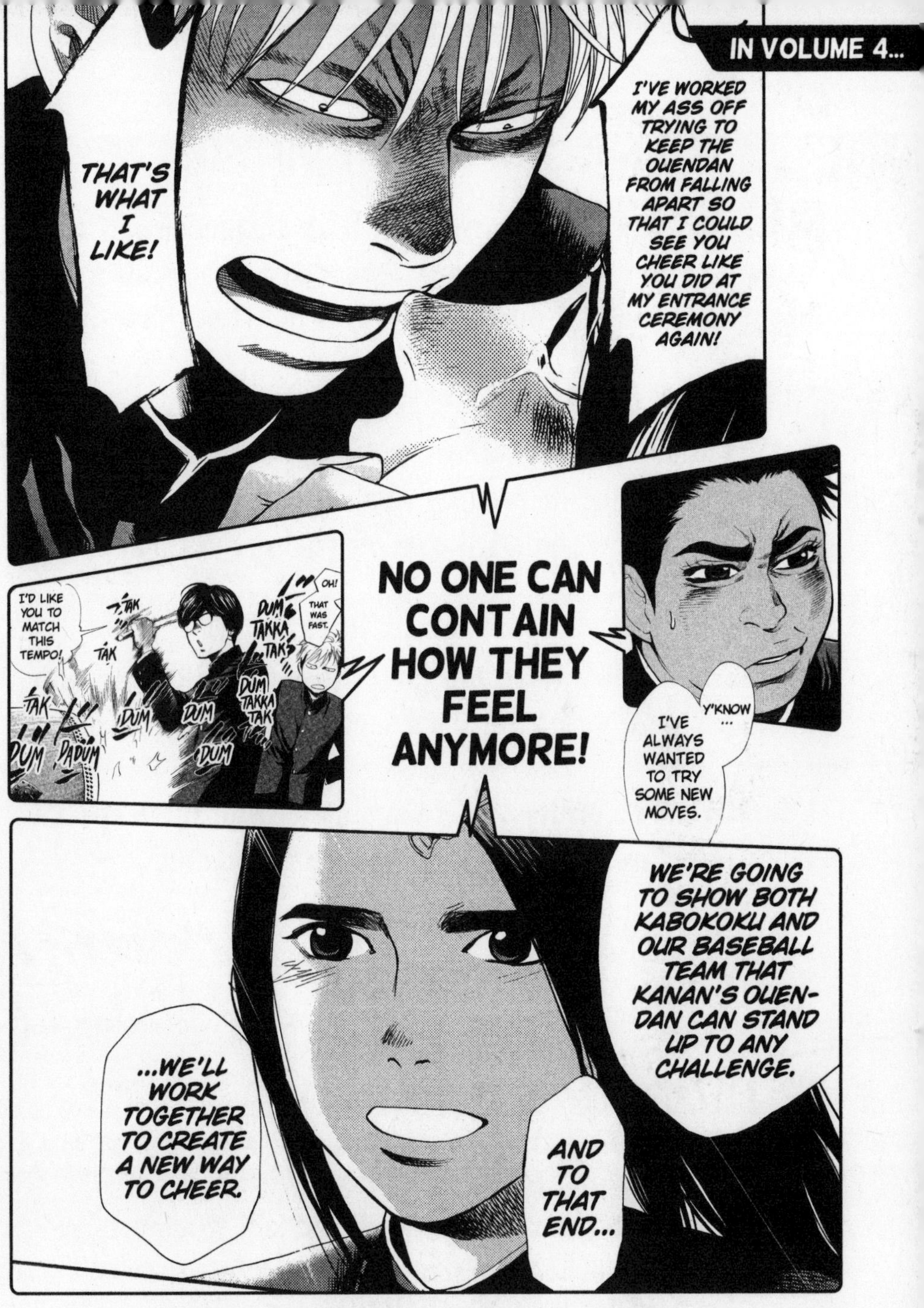
I'VE WORKED MY ASS OFF TRYING TO KEEP THE OUENDAN FROM FALLING APART SO THAT I COULD SEE YOU CHEER LIKE YOU DID AT MY ENTRANCE CEREMONY AGAIN!
THAT'S WHAT I LIKE!
Y'KNOW...
I'VE ALWAYS WANTED TO TRY SOME NEW MOVES.
NO ONE CAN CONTAIN HOW THEY FEEL ANYMORE!
OH!
THAT WAS FAST.
I'D LIKE YOU TO MATCH THIS TEMPO!
TAK
TAK
DUM TAKKA TAK
DUM TAKKA TAK
TAK
DUM
DUM
DADUM
DUM
DUM
WE'RE GOING TO SHOW BOTH KABOKOKU AND OUR BASEBALL TEAM THAT KANAN'S OUEN-DAN CAN STAND UP TO ANY CHALLENGE.
AND TO THAT END...
...WE'LL WORK TOGETHER TO CREATE A NEW WAY TO CHEER.

THE OUENDAN IS FINALLY STARTING TO COME TOGETHER...

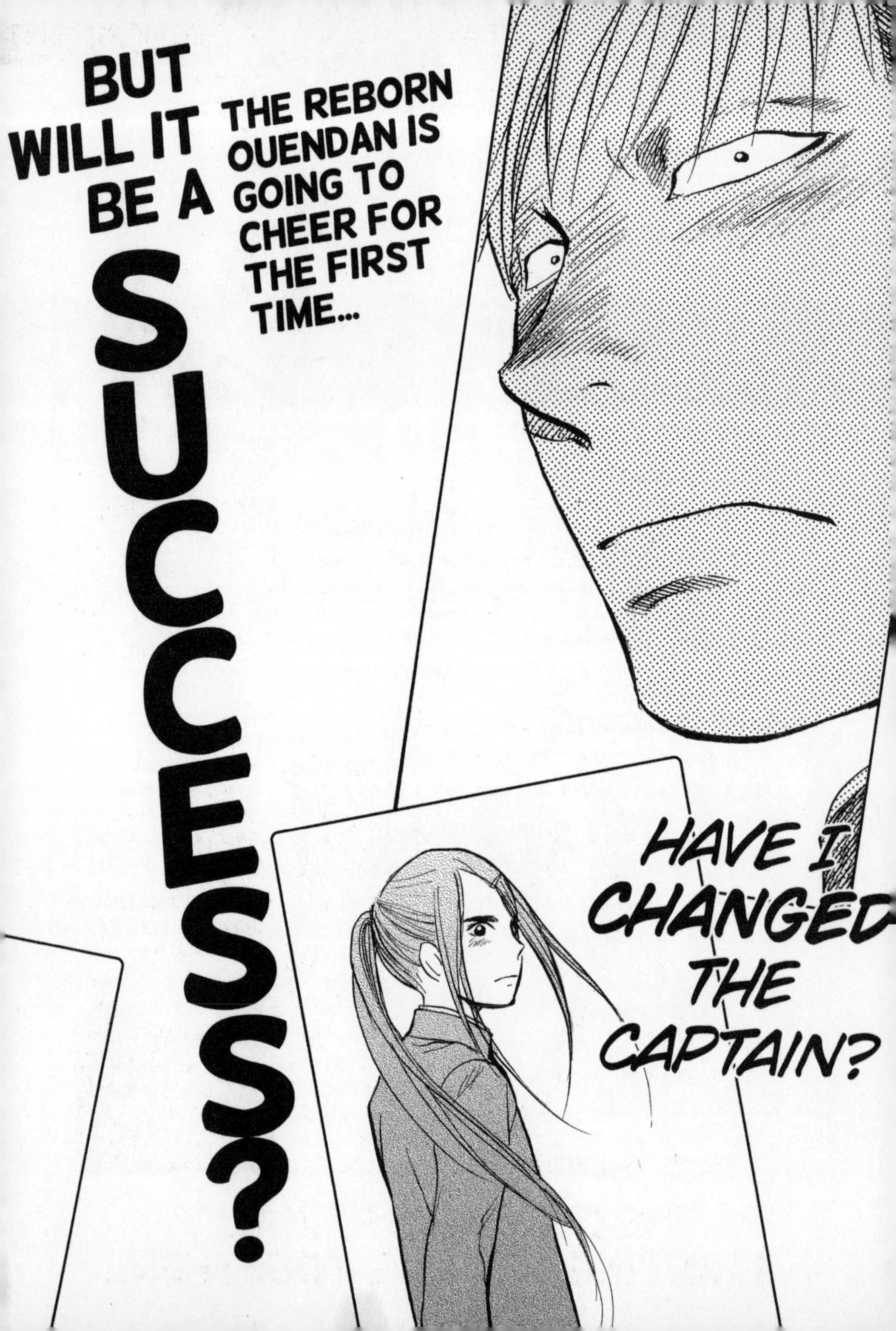
THE REBORN OUENDAN IS GOING TO CHEER FOR THE FIRST TIME...
BUT WILL IT BE A SUCCESS?
HAVE I CHANGED THE CAPTAIN?

Translation Notes

"They say he can throw any pitch!"
Page 7

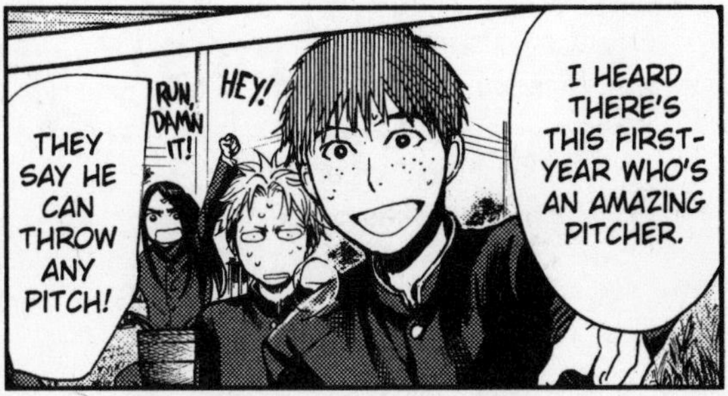
I HEARD THERE'S THIS FIRST-YEAR WHO'S AN AMAZING PITCHER.
HEY!
RUN, DAMN IT!
THEY SAY HE CAN THROW ANY PITCH!

The original Japanese line here uses the term "nanairo no henkakyu," or "seven colors of breaking ball." It was originally coined to describe the pitching of Tadashi Wakabayashi, a foundational player in the early history of professional baseball in Japan. Early in his career, Wakabayashi depended on the power of his fastball, but after injuring his arm he transitioned to a larger vocabulary of pitches. The seven pitches in question are: the fastball, the curveball, the *shuuto*, the slider, the sinker, the drop (or 12-6 curveball), and the knuckleball.

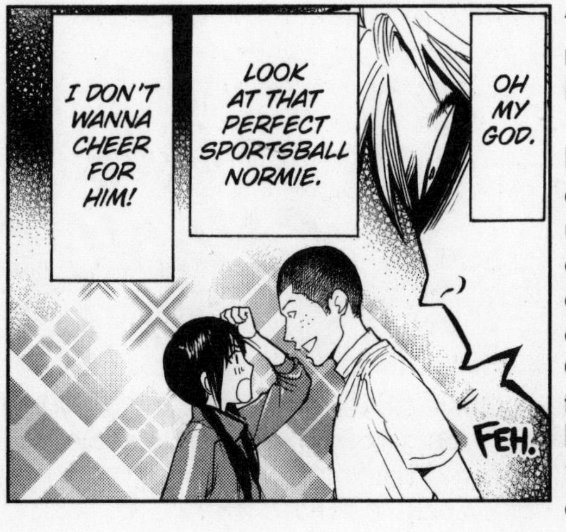
OH MY GOD.
LOOK AT THAT PERFECT SPORTSBALL NORMIE.
I DON'T WANNA CHEER FOR HIM!
FEH.

"That perfect sportsball normie"
Page 13

Imamura originally refers to Suzuki as an athletic *riajuu*. The term "riajuu" is ubiquitous in Japanese internet slang, and refers to someone who leads a fulfilling real-world life (i.e., the opposite of an otaku on the internet). Given Imamura's hatred of sports, the internet slang pejorative "sportsball" felt appropriate to substitute for "athletic," while "normie" is a fair approximation for *riajuu*.

The National Championship
Page 27

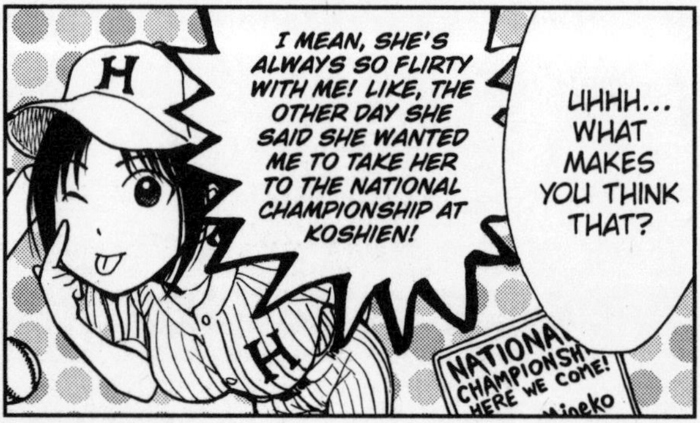
UHHH... WHAT MAKES YOU THINK THAT?
I MEAN, SHE'S ALWAYS SO FLIRTY WITH ME! LIKE, THE OTHER DAY SHE SAID SHE WANTED ME TO TAKE HER TO THE NATIONAL CHAMPIONSHIP AT KOSHIEN!
HERE WE COME!

Japan's National High School Baseball Championship is almost never referred to as such—rather, it is simply called "Koshien," after the venue in which it takes place: Hanshin Koshien Stadium. Teams representing every prefecture in Japan participate in the tournament, which is nationally televised. Koshien's history spans over a century, and is a foundational element of Japan's baseball mythology.

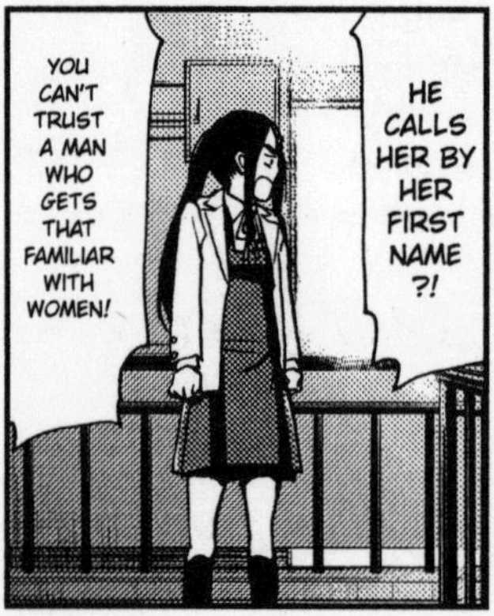
HE CALLS HER BY HER FIRST NAME ?!
YOU CAN'T TRUST A MAN WHO GETS THAT FAMILIAR WITH WOMEN!

"He calls her by her first name?!"
Page 30

Using someone's given name with no honorific is among the most intimate forms of address available in Japanese, and it's typically reserved for family members, lovers, or very close friends . Suzuki's use of "Mineko" in his ranting therefore comes across as somewhere between obstinately childish or creepily over-familiar, as he's implying a closeness between them that doesn't necessarily exist.

Heavy Rotation (chapter title)
Page 39

One of idol ensemble AKB48's biggest hits in 2010 was "Heavy Rotation," which topped karaoke charts for nearly a year following its release. "Heavy rotation" is a term from the radio broadcast industry, and refers to any track that makes frequent appearances on a DJ's playlist. The AKB48 song's lyrics, meanwhile, describe the singer's feelings for the listener being on "heavy rotation" in her heart.

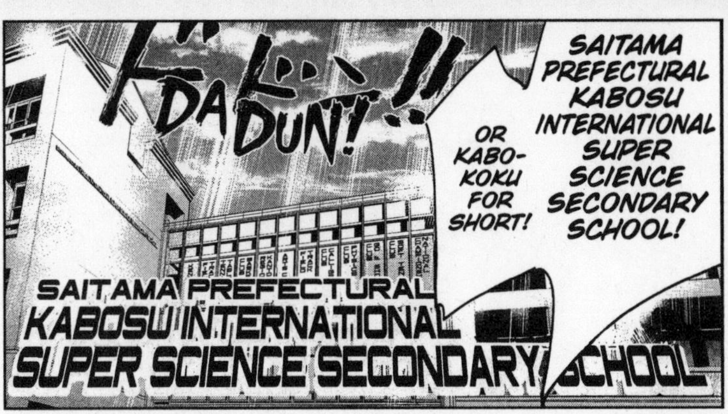
SAITAMA PREFECTURAL KABOSU INTERNATIONAL SUPER SCIENCE SECONDARY SCHOOL!
OR KABO-KOKU FOR SHORT!
DA DUN!!
SAITAMA PREFECTURAL KABOSU INTERNATIONAL SUPER SCIENCE SECONDARY SCHOOL

Saitama Prefectural Kabosu International Super Science Secondary School
Page 65

Our translation of this school's name is a fairly literal rendition of "Saitama Kenritsu Kabosu Kokusai Suupaa Saiensu Koutou Gakkou." It's unclear what's meant to be "international" about the school, but the words "Kabosu Kokusai" (Kabosu International) are where it gets its nickname of "Kabokoku."

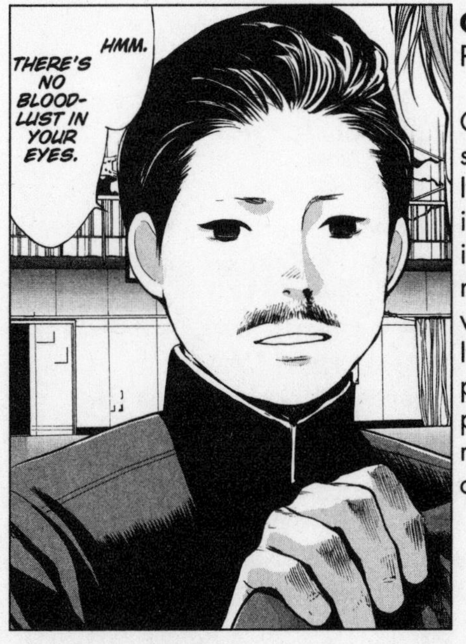
HMM.
THERE'S NO BLOODLUST IN YOUR EYES.

Chihiro Iwasaki
Page 79

One can't help but notice a certain visual similarity between the character Chihiro Iwasaki and the delicate watercolor illustrations of the real-world artist and illustrator of the same name—though notably, the *real* Chihiro Iwasaki was a woman. In the course of her long career, Iwasaki illustrated many famous children's picture books, and her art has a delicate, peaceful sensibility entirely unlike brusque machismo of the Kabokoku Ouendan's captain.

"Let Me Sleep in Your Arms" (chapter title)
Page 93

The Japanese title of this chapter is "Daite Kuretara Ii no ni," which in turn is a 1988 song by Shizuka Kudo. Kudo released the song early in her solo career, shortly after leaving the idol group Onyanko Club, which provided the template used by AKB48 to such success later. A decade later, Kudo released a collection of ballads which included an English version of the song, which was titled "Let Me Sleep in Your Arms," hence the title of this chapter. Perhaps coincidentally, the single she released immediately before this one was titled "Again."

Again!!
アゲイン!!

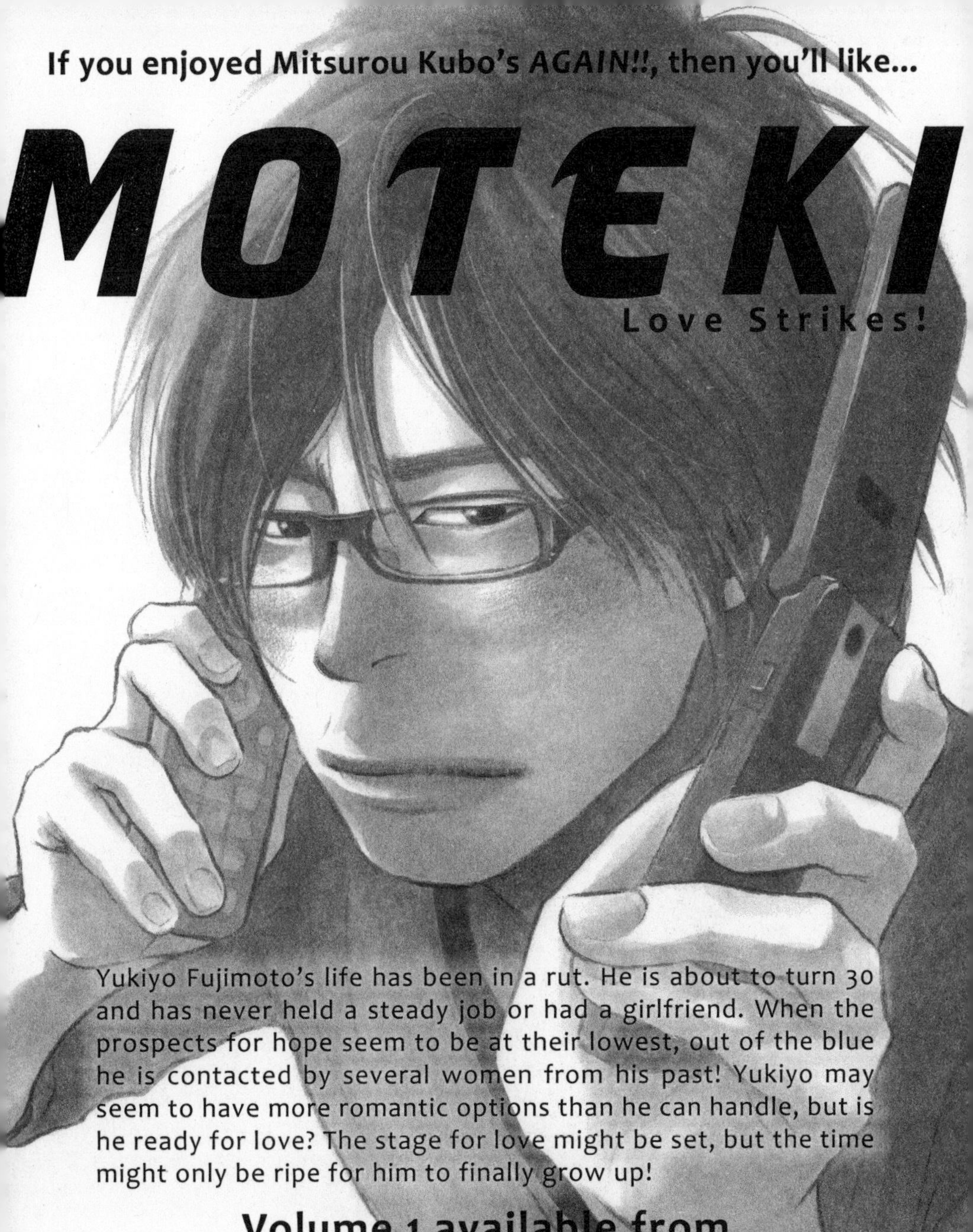

If you enjoyed Mitsurou Kubo's *AGAIN!!*, then you'll like...

MOTEKI

Love Strikes!

Yukiyo Fujimoto's life has been in a rut. He is about to turn 30 and has never held a steady job or had a girlfriend. When the prospects for hope seem to be at their lowest, out of the blue he is contacted by several women from his past! Yukiyo may seem to have more romantic options than he can handle, but is he ready for love? The stage for love might be set, but the time might only be ripe for him to finally grow up!

Volume 1 available from Vertical Comics in April 2018!

438 pages | $18.95 U.S./ 19.95 CAN | ISBN 9781945054808

www.vertical-comics.com

YURI!!! ON ICE!!!

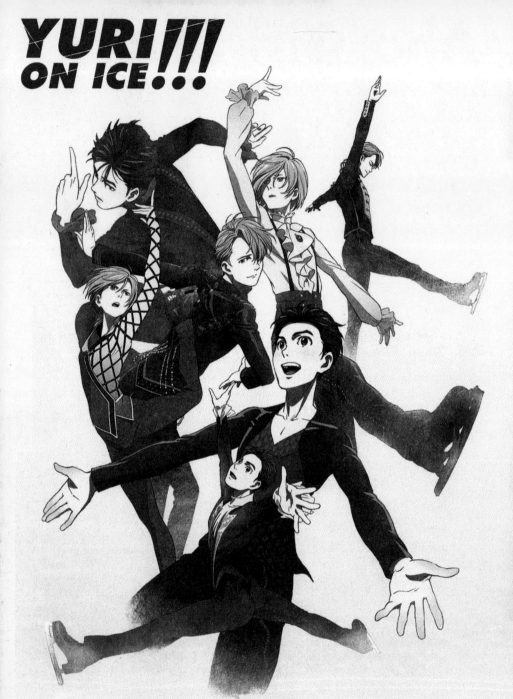

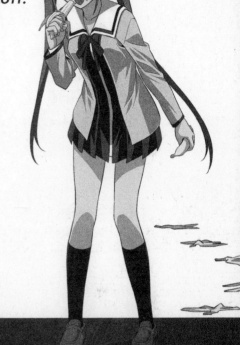

a Silent Voice

Now a feature-length animation from Kyoto Animation!

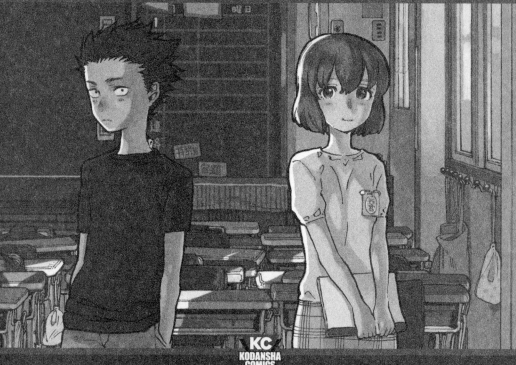

KC
KODANSHA
COMICS

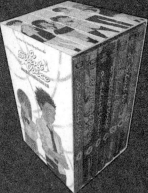

•Exclusive
2-sided poster
•Replica of
Shoko's notebook
•Preview of
Yoshitoki Oima's
new series, To
Your Eternity

Shoya is a bully. When Shoko, a girl who can't hear, enters his elementary school class, she becomes their favorite target, and Shoya and his friends goad each other into devising new tortures for her. But the children's cruelty goes too far. Shoko is forced to leave the school, and Shoya ends up shouldering all the blame. Six years later, the two meet again. Can Shoya make up for his past mistakes, or is it too late?

KC KODANSHA COMICS

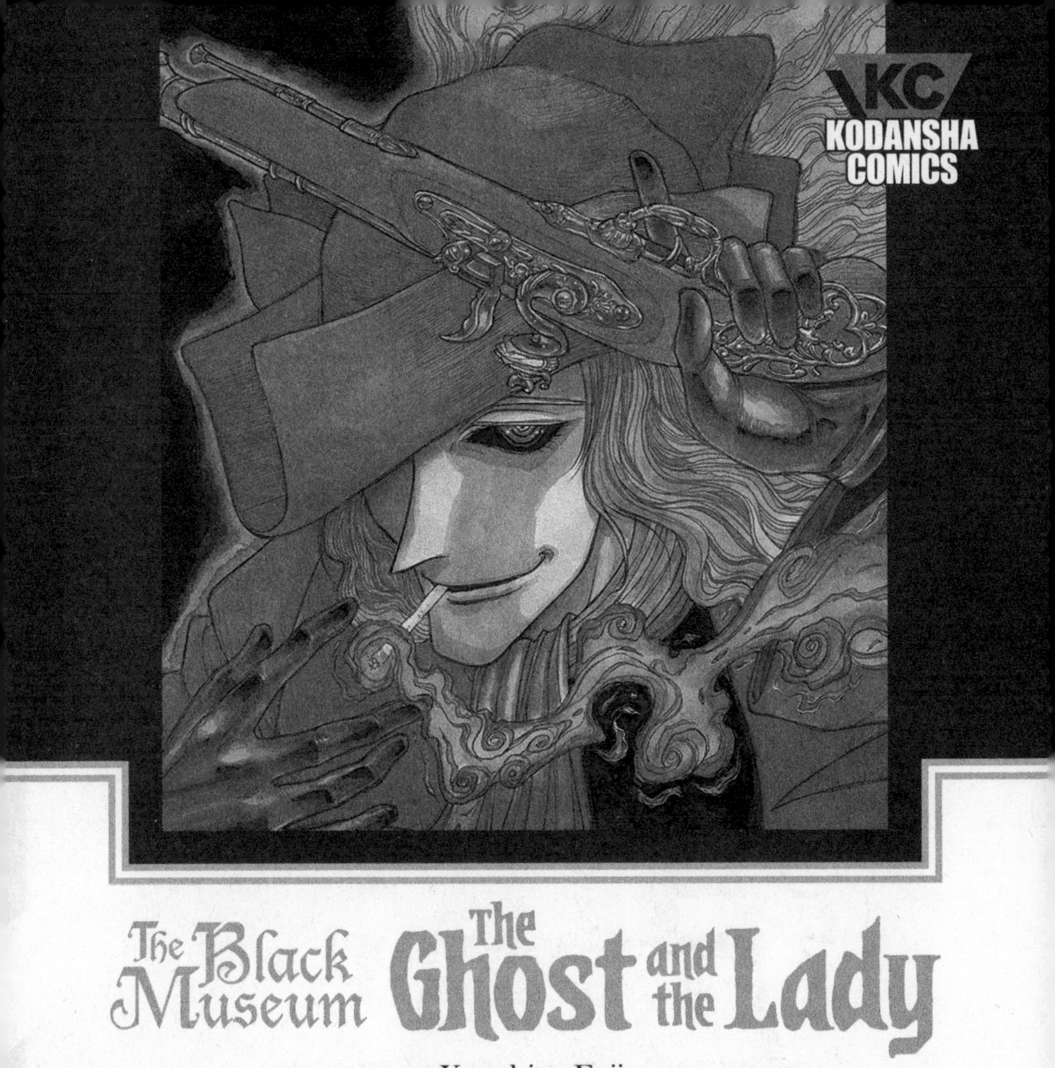

The Black Museum The Ghost and the Lady

By Kazuhiro Fujita

Deep in Scotland Yard in London sits an evidence room dedicated to the greatest mysteries of British history. In this “Black Museum” sits a misshapen hunk of lead–two bullets fused together–the key to a wartime encounter between Florence Nightingale, the mother of modern nursing, and a supernatural Man in Grey. This story is unknown to most scholars of history, but a special guest of the museum will tell the tale of The Ghost and the Lady...

Praise for Kazuhiro Fujita’s *Ushio and Tora*

“A charming revival that combines a classic look with modern depth and pacing... **Essential viewing both for curmudgeons and new fans alike.**” — Anime News Network

“**GREAT!** The first episode of Ushio and Tora captures the essence of '90s anime.” — IGN

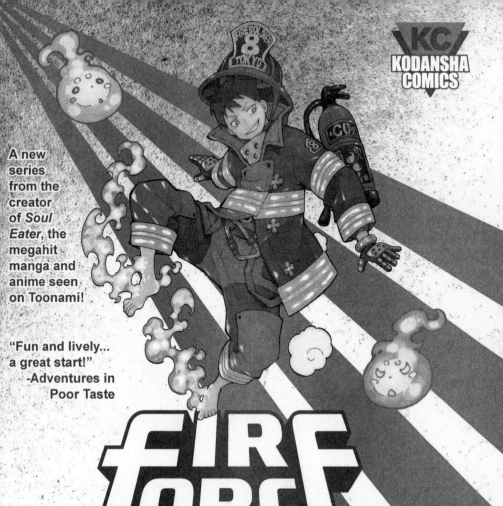

A new series from the creator of *Soul Eater*, the megahit manga and anime seen on Toonami!

"Fun and lively... a great start!"
-Adventures in Poor Taste

FIRE FORCE

By Atsushi Ohkubo

The city of Tokyo is plagued by a deadly phenomenon: spontaneous human combustion! Luckily, a special team is there to quench the inferno: The Fire Force! The fire soldiers at Special Fire Cathedral 8 are about to get a unique addition. Enter Shinra, a boy who possesses the power to run at the speed of a rocket, leaving behind the famous "devil's footprints" (and destroying his shoes in the process). Can Shinra and his colleagues discover the source of this strange epidemic before the city burns to ashes?

KC KODANSHA COMICS

Japan's most powerful spirit medium delves into the ghost world's greatest mysteries!

Story by Kyo Shirodaira, famed author of mystery fiction and creator of *Spiral*, *Blast of Tempest*, and *The Record of a Fallen Vampire*.

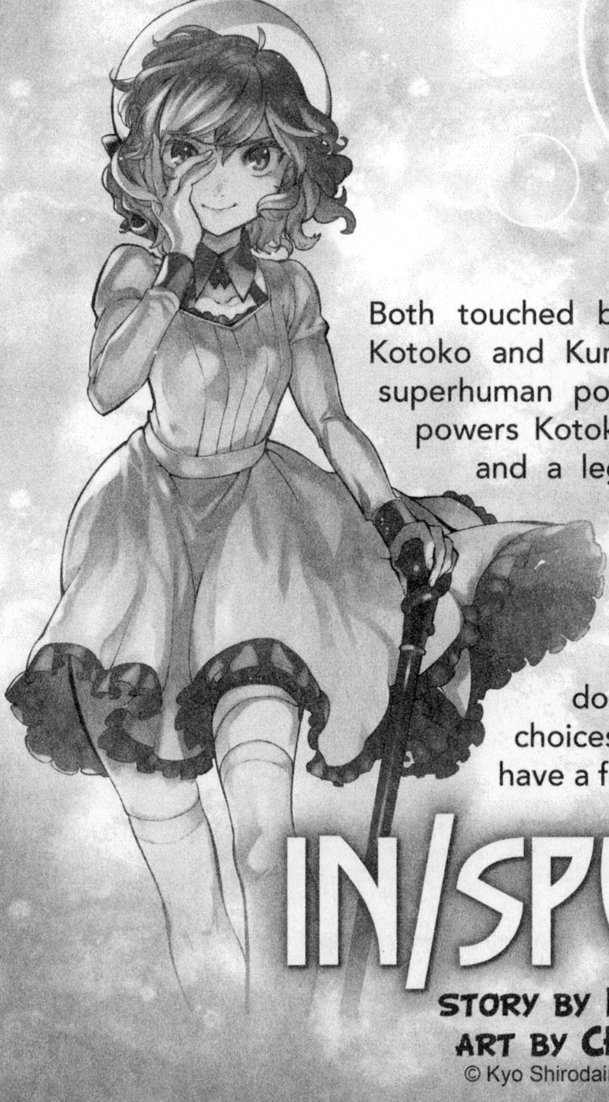

Both touched by spirits called yôkai, Kotoko and Kurô have gained unique superhuman powers. But to gain her powers Kotoko has given up an eye and a leg, and Kurô's personal life is in shambles. So when Kotoko suggests they team up to deal with renegades from the spirit world, Kurô doesn't have many other choices, but Kotoko might just have a few ulterior motives...

IN/SPECTRE

STORY BY KYO SHIRODAIRA
ART BY CHASHIBA KATASE

HAPPINESS

——ハピネス——

By Shuzo Oshimi

From the creator of *The Flowers of Evil*

Nothing interesting is happening in Makoto Ozaki's first year of high school. His life is a series of quiet humiliations: low-grade bullies, unreliable friends, and the constant frustration of his adolescent lust. But one night, a pale, thin girl knocks him to the ground in an alley and offers him a choice. Now everything is different. Daylight is searingly bright. Food tastes awful. And worse than anything is the terrible, consuming thirst...

Praise for Shuzo Oshimi's *The Flowers of Evil*

"A shockingly readable story that vividly—one might even say queasily—evokes the fear and confusion of discovering one's own sexuality. Recommended." —The Manga Critic

"A page-turning tale of sordid middle school blackmail." —Otaku USA Magazine

"A stunning new horror manga." —Third Eye Comics

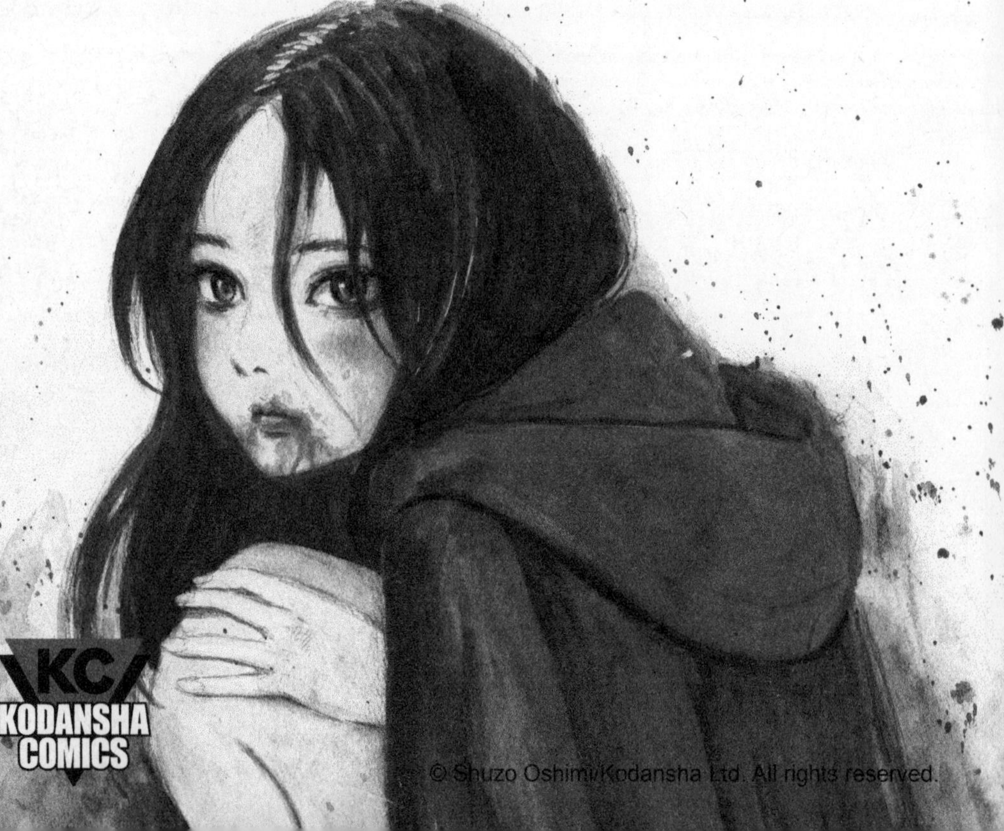

KC KODANSHA COMICS

Again!! volume 3 is a work of fiction. Names, characters, places, and incidents are the products of the author's imagination or are used fictitiously. Any resemblance to actual events, locales, or persons, living or dead, is entirely coincidental.

A Kodansha Comics Trade Paperback Original.

Published in the United States by Kodansha Comics, an imprint of Kodansha USA Publishing, LLC, New York.

Publication rights for this English edition arranged through Kodansha Ltd., Tokyo.

First published in Japan in 2012 by Kodansha Ltd., Tokyo, as *Agein!!* volume 3.

ISBN 978-1-63236-647-4

Printed in the United States of America.

www.kodanshacomics.com

9 8 7 6 5 4 3 2 1

Translator: Rose Padgett
Lettering: E. K. Weaver
Editing: Paul Starr
Editorial Assistance: Tiff Ferentini
Kodansha Comics edition cover design by Phil Balsman